Pseudoscience in Child and Adolescent Psychotherapy

Most infants, children, and adolescents facing mental health challenges – including autism, psychosis, mania, depression, anxiety, and substance use – do not receive evidence-based treatments. Instead, they commonly receive ineffective and even harmful treatments. In this book, leading experts from the fields of clinical psychology, school psychology, developmental psychology, pediatric neurology, applied behavior analysis, and social work identify the most problematic psychotherapy interventions used for each mental health issue. In addition to these primary authors, each chapter includes a sidebar from a specialist representing the disciplines of pediatrics, anthropology, neuroscience, and psychology. The contributors work in academia, hospitals, and private practice and include book authors, podcasters, and even a filmmaker. Not only does this book highlight the threats of potentially harmful pseudoscience, it also summarizes treatments that actually have a strong evidence base and deliver far more positive results.

Stephen Hupp is Professor of Psychology in the Clinical Child and School Psychology program at Southern Illinois University Edwardsville (SIUE), USA, and a licensed clinical psychologist. His other books include *Great Myths of Child Development* (2015), *Great Myths of Adolescence* (2019), and *Thinking Critically About Child Development, 4th edition* (forthcoming, 2020). In 2015, he won the Great Teacher Award from the SIUE Alumni Association. He is also an executive producer for the *Science Moms* documentary, and he holds the Guinness World Record for the "longest line of books." On Twitter he is @StephenHupp.

Pseudoscience in Child and Adolescent Psychotherapy

A Skeptical Field Guide

Edited by

Stephen Hupp
Southern Illinois University Edwardsville

Shaftesbury Road, Cambridge CB2 8EA, United Kingdom

One Liberty Plaza, 20th Floor, New York, NY 10006, USA

477 Williamstown Road, Port Melbourne, VIC 3207, Australia

314–321, 3rd Floor, Plot 3, Splendor Forum, Jasola District Centre, New Delhi – 110025, India

103 Penang Road, #05–06/07, Visioncrest Commercial, Singapore 238467

Cambridge University Press is part of Cambridge University Press & Assessment, a department of the University of Cambridge.

We share the University's mission to contribute to society through the pursuit of education, learning and research at the highest international levels of excellence.

www.cambridge.org
Information on this title: www.cambridge.org/9781316626955

DOI: 10.1017/9781316798096

First published 2019

A catalogue record for this publication is available from the British Library

Library of Congress Cataloging-in-Publication data
Names: Hupp, Stephen, editor.
Title: Pseudoscience in child and adolescent psychotherapy : a skeptical field guide /
edited by Stephen Hupp.
Description: New York : Cambridge University Press, 2019.
Identifiers: LCCN 2018042306I ISBN 9781107175310 (hardback) I
ISBN 9781316626955 (paperback)
Subjects: LCSH: Child psychotherapy. I Adolescent psychotherapy I
BISAC: PSYCHOLOGY / Clinical Psychology.
Classification: LCC RJ504 .P7325 2019 I DDC 618.92/8914–dc23
LC record available at https://lccn.loc.gov/2018042306

ISBN   978-1-107-17531-0   Hardback
ISBN   978-1-316-62695-5   Paperback

To my dad, Dennis Hupp, for being my best and biggest mentor

Contents

List of Sidebars   *page* ix
List of Contributors   xi
Foreword   xv
   Scott O. Lilienfeld
Preface   xix
Acknowledgments   xxii

1 Critical Thinking about Psychotherapy   1
Stephen Hupp, Jean Mercer, Bruce A. Thyer, and Monica Pignotti

2 Intellectual and Adaptive Functioning   14
Elizabeth M. Kryszak, Jessica F. Scherr, and James A. Mulick

3 Autism Spectrum   28
Jessica F. Scherr, Elizabeth M. Kryszak, and James A. Mulick

4 Inattention and Hyperactivity   50
Christine A. Lee and Richard Milich

5 Learning   66
Zachary LaBrot and Brad Dufrene

6 Tics   80
Michael B. Himle and Brianna Wellen

7 Psychosis   96
Rachel Waford and Carina A. Iati

8 Bipolar Spectrum   110
Guillermo Pérez Algorta and Eric Youngstrom

9 Depression   124
Thomas J. Huberty

10 Anxiety   140
Bruce A. Thyer and Monica Pignotti

11	**Obsessions and Compulsions**	159
	Monica Pignotti and Bruce A. Thyer	
12	**Trauma and Attachment**	172
	Jean Mercer	
13	**Feeding**	189
	Linda J. Cooper-Brown, Mary Louise E. Kerwin, and Keith E. Williams	
14	**Eating**	206
	Frances Bozsik, Brooke L. Bennett, Emily Stefano, Brooke L. Whisenhunt, and Danae L. Hudson	
15	**Toileting**	225
	Michael I. Axelrod and Joseph P. Deegan	
16	**Sleep**	243
	Stephanie Jackson and Sarah Morsbach Honaker	
17	**Disruptive Behavior and Conduct**	260
	Jeremy Jewell, Madison Schoen, Sydney Thompson, Emily Fischer, and Sarah Conoyer	
18	**Substance Use**	276
	Mariann Suarez	
19	**Skepticism and Psychotherapy**	291
	Stephen Hupp and Kathleen Dyer	
	Index	302

Sidebars

1   What is Guerrilla Skepticism on Wikipedia?   *page* 6
Susan Gerbic

2   Does craniosacral therapy improve cognitive functioning?   22
Jason Travers

3   Does Dolphin-Assisted Therapy have healing effects?   37
Lori Marino and Scott O. Lilienfeld

4   Does brain balancing improve attention?   57
Christian Jarrett

5   Should children be taught based on their preferred learning style?   68
Indre Viskontas

6   Can a dental device decrease tics?   89
Grant Ritchey and Clay Jones

7   Is homeopathy effective for schizophrenia?   105
Michael Marshall

8   Does naturopathic medicine help treat bipolar disorder?   115
Britt Hermes

9   Is psychoanalytic dream interpretation useful?   133
Caleb W. Lack

10   Should children be afraid of Bigfoot?   141
Carol E. Colaninno

11   Do superstitious rituals help cope with anxiety?   160
Stuart Vyse

12   Does attachment parenting promote attachment?   176
Amy Tuteur

13   Should parents avoid feeding their children GMOs?   196
Natalie Newell

14   Is it possible for breatharians to live without food or water?   211
Joe Nickell

15   Does self-acupressure work for constipation?   233
Harriet Hall

16   Do aliens abduct people while they are sleeping?   250
W. Blake Smith

17   Is lying always a sign of psychological problems?   261
Robert S. Feldman

18   Are specialized goggles effective at preventing impaired
     driving?   282
     Miranda Meeker and LeAnna Kehl
19a What is gay conversion therapy?   292
     Sheldon W. Helms
19b Should children be taught about pseudoscience?   299
     Henry Hupp

Contributors

Guillermo Pérez Algorta, PhD, Lecturer in Mental Health, Division of Health Research, Faculty of Health and Medicine, Lancaster University, United Kingdom.

Michael I. Axelrod, PhD, Professor, Psychology Department, University of Wisconsin – Eau Claire. Author of *Behavior Analysis for School Psychologists* (2017).

Brooke L. Bennett, MS, Doctoral candidate, Department of Psychology, University of Hawai'i at Mānoa.

Frances Bozsik, MS, Doctoral candidate, Department of Psychology, University of Missouri – Kansas City.

Sarah Conoyer, PhD, Assistant Professor, Department of Psychology, Southern Illinois University Edwardsville.

Linda J. Cooper-Brown, PhD, Clinical Associate Professor of Pediatrics, The University of Iowa, Iowa City. Director, Pediatric Psychology Feeding Disorders Service, University of Iowa Stead Family Children's Hospital.

Joseph P. Deegan, MSE, School psychology graduate student, University of Wisconsin – Eau Claire. District Assessment Coordinator for the School District of Marinette, Wisconsin.

Brad Dufrene, PhD, Professor, Department of Psychology, University of Southern Mississippi, Hattiesburg.

Kathleen Dyer, PhD, Associate Professor of Child and Family Science, California State University, Fresno. Author of *An Introduction to Effective Parenting Education* (2017).

Emily Fischer, BS, Graduate student, Department of Psychology, Southern Illinois University Edwardsville.

Michael B. Himle, PhD, Associate Professor, Department of Psychology, University of Utah. Co-director of the Tourette Association of America Designated Center of Excellence for Tourette and Tic Disorders.

Sarah Morsbach Honaker, PhD, CBSM, Assistant Professor of Pediatrics, Indiana University School of Medicine, Director of Behavioral Sleep Medicine at Riley Children's Hospital, Indianapolis.

Thomas J. Huberty, PhD, ABPP, Professor Emeritus, Counseling and Educational Psychology, Indiana University Bloomington. Author of *Anxiety and Depression in Children and Adolescents: Assessment, Intervention, and Prevention* (2012).

Danae L. Hudson, PhD, Professor, Department of Psychology, Missouri State University. Co-author of *Revel Psychology, 1st edition* (2019).

Stephen Hupp, PhD, Professor, Department of Psychology, Southern Illinois University Edwardsville. Co-author of *Great Myths of Child Development* (2015).

Carina A. Iati, PsyD, Clinical Psychologist, Tewksbury Hospital, Massachusetts. Co-author of *The Psychosis Response Guide: How to Help Young People in Psychiatric Crises* (2016).

Stephanie Jackson, MD, Assistant Professor of Clinical Pediatrics, Indiana University School of Medicine, Indianapolis.

Jeremy Jewell, PhD, Professor, Department of Psychology, Southern Illinois University Edwardsville. Co-author of *Great Myths of Adolescence* (2019).

Mary Louise E. Kerwin, PhD, BCBA-D, Department Head and Professor, Department of Psychology, Rowan University, Glassboro, New Jersey. Executive Director, Center for Behavior Analysis, Rowan University.

Elizabeth M. Kryszak, PhD, Psychologist, Child Development Center, Nationwide Children's Hospital.

Zachary LaBrot, PhD, Assistant Professor, Department of Psychology, University of Nebraska Medical Center, Munroe-Meyer Institute, Omaha, Nebraska.

Christine A. Lee, MS, Doctoral candidate, Psychology Department, University of Kentucky, Lexington.

Scott O. Lilienfeld, PhD, Professor, Department of Psychology, Emory University, Atlanta, Georgia. Co-editor of *Science and Pseudoscience in Clinical Psychology, 2nd edition* (2014).

Jean Mercer, PhD, Professor Emerita of Psychology, Stockton University, Galloway, New Jersey. Author of *Thinking Critically About Child Development, 3rd edition* (2016).

Richard Milich, PhD, Professor, Department of Psychology, University of Kentucky, Lexington.

James A. Mulick, PhD, Emeritus Professor of Pediatrics, The Ohio State University.

Monica Pignotti, PhD, Independent Scholar, Tallahassee, Florida and Austin, Texas. Co-author of *Science and Pseudoscience in Social Work Practice* (2015).

Jessica F. Scherr, PhD, Postdoctoral Psychology Fellow, Child Development Center, Nationwide Children's Hospital.

Madison Schoen, MS, Doctoral candidate, University of Missouri, Columbia.

Emily Stefano, MS, Doctoral candidate, Department of Psychology, University of Hawai'i at Mānoa.

Mariann Suarez, PhD, ABPP, Associate Professor, Psychiatry and Behavioral Neurosciences USF Health, Morsani College of Medicine, Tampa, Florida. Co-author of *Motivational Interviewing with Adolescents and Young Adults* (2011).

Sydney Thompson, MS, Doctoral candidate, Chicago School of Professional Psychology, Illinois.

Bruce A. Thyer, PhD, LCSW, BCBA-D, Distinguished Research Professor, College of Social Work, Florida State University, Tallahassee. Co-author of *Science and Pseudoscience in Social Work Practice* (2015).

Rachel Waford, PhD, Assistant Professor, Department of Psychiatry and Behavioral Sciences, Emory University, Atlanta, Georgia. Co-author of *The Psychosis Response Guide: How to Help Young People in Psychiatric Crises* (2016).

Brianna Wellen, BS, Graduate student, Department of Psychology, University of Utah.

Brooke L. Whisenhunt, PhD, Professor, Department of Psychology, Missouri State University. Co-author of *Revel Psychology, 1st edition* (2019).

Keith E. Williams, PhD, BCBA, Professor of Pediatrics, Penn State College of Medicine, Director, Feeding Program, Penn State Hershey Medical Center.

Eric Youngstrom, PhD, Professor, Department of Psychology and Neuroscience, University of North Carolina at Chapel Hill. Acting Director for the Center for Excellence in Research and Treatment of Bipolar Disorder.

Foreword

The Road to Hell Is Paved with Pseudoscientific Techniques

Scott O. Lilienfeld

When it comes to helping others with psychological problems, good intentions are essential. Still, as this immensely valuable volume edited by Stephen Hupp amply illustrates, good intentions are not sufficient. The history of medicine, including psychiatry, is a sobering reminder that even the best-meaning practitioners can do terrible harm. Most historians of medicine maintain that until about 1890, the substantial majority of physical procedures were useless or iatrogenic (Grove & Meehl, 1996). In the early twenty-first century, it is all too easy to forget that for decades or even centuries, such since-debunked interventions as bleeding, blistering, purging, leeching, bloodletting, spinning, and the like were widely accepted by many practitioners as effective for the treatment of mental disorders (Gambrill, 2012). Today, these "treatments" understandably strike most of us as barbaric and inhumane. Yet almost certainly, the health care providers who provided them were convinced that their nostrums were helpful. They meant well.

Yes, outright charlatans exist in mental health, and the sprawling discipline of child and adolescent psychological and psychiatric treatment is no exception. Nevertheless, deliberate snake oil salespersons are few and far between. Most of the practitioners of the dubious techniques surveyed in this remarkably comprehensive volume mean well, much as did past purveyors of bleeding, blistering, and the like. And most of these practitioners are almost surely convinced that their preferred ministrations work. Why?

The reason is that they rely largely on their clinical intuitions and informal clinical observations, both of which can often be helpful for generating fruitful hypotheses but which tend to be woefully ill suited to ascertaining whether treatments work. For this crucial task, we must turn to scientific methods, which are partial bulwarks against confirmation bias, the deeply entrenched tendency – to which we are all prone – to seek out, interpret, and recall evidence consistent with our hypotheses and to deny, dismiss, or distort evidence that is not (Nickerson, 1998;

Tavris & Aronson, 2008). In the domains of mental health treatment research, such methods encompass randomized controlled trials; systematic within-subject designs; and when these are not feasible, well-controlled case control designs (Lilienfeld, Ritschel, Lynn, Cautin, & Latzman, 2014). None of these designs is a panacea, but each affords a much-needed check against regression to the mean, placebo effects, multiple treatment interference, and a plethora of other sources of spurious therapeutic effectiveness (Lilienfeld, McKay, & Hollon, 2018). In this respect, these designs are also critical safeguards against our own propensity to dupe ourselves into believing that our favored interventions work when they do not. As the late Robert Pirsig (1974) wrote in his classic book, *Zen and the Art of Motorcycle Maintenance*, "the real purpose of the scientific method is to make sure nature hasn't misled you into thinking you know something you actually don't know" (p. 108).

Early in the course of their training, many clinicians may somehow find a scientific approach to clinical practice to be impersonal or heartless. "I don't want to learn about research; I just want to help people," they may think. Even some experienced practitioners may at times lapse into this fallacious reasoning. Nevertheless, one must be careful not to confuse *hard-headedness* with *hard-heartedness* (Meehl, 1973). Being a rigorous thinker is not incompatible with being a caring professional. To the contrary, a genuinely humane approach to practice *demands* the use of scientific methods, because these methods are ultimately our best hope for minimizing errors in our clinical inferences, including treatment decisions (McKay, 2017).

As soon as we believe ourselves to be immune to error in clinical settings, we are operating with intellectual hubris. In contrast, the adoption of a scientific approach embodies the attitude of intellectual humility, which mandates a willingness to acknowledge the possibility that we might be mistaken (see also Leary et al., 2017). As astrophysicist and science writer Carl Sagan (1995) noted, good scientists always hear a little voice in their heads that incessantly intones "you might be wrong." The same principle holds for clinical scientists, whether they are functioning in the therapy room, laboratory, or classroom.

In an influential but controversial recent book, Paul Bloom (2017) argued that empathy, which he defines as experiencing the same emotions as the person with whom one is identifying, is unhelpful and often harmful, as it tends to lead to a loss of perspective. Instead, Bloom maintained, we should strive to cultivate what he terms *rational compassion*, in which we combine caring with a dispassionate view of reality. All good surgeons understand this principle. They need to retain their concern for their patients, of course, but they also need to distance themselves appropriately from their emotions in the long-term service of helping. The merits or lack thereof of Bloom's specific arguments notwithstanding, the overarching point remains. Science is not the enemy of caring; it is its best friend.

As you read the chapters of this important volume, remember that virtually all advocates of the bewildering panoply of unsupported clinical techniques discussed within its pages sincerely want to help. Furthermore, almost all of them believe that they are helping. Yet in many or most cases, they are being fooled or more precisely, fooling themselves.

These practitioners are owed some of the blame, to be sure, but even more of the blame goes to the allied disciplines of mental health, such as psychology, psychiatry, psychiatric nursing, social work, and counseling, for not doing a better job of inculcating scientific thinking in their students. In this respect, this book is a crucial corrective: it is a wonderful resource for how to think clearly about childhood and adolescent mental health problems and their treatment. In addition, this book is a powerful antidote against the seductive temptations of pseudoscience. It reminds us that the impetus to help is by itself futile. It must be fused with an impetus to understand the human mind using the best available scientific methods.

References

Bloom, P. (2017). *Against empathy: The case for rational compassion*. New York: Random House.

Gambrill, E. (2012). *Social work practice: A critical thinker's guide*. New York: Oxford University Press.

Grove, W. M., & Meehl, P. E. (1996). Comparative efficiency of informal (subjective, impressionistic) and formal (mechanical, algorithmic) prediction procedures: The clinical–statistical controversy. *Psychology, Public Policy, and Law*, 2, 293–323.

Leary, M. R., Diebels, K. J., Davisson, E. K., Jongman-Sereno, K. P., Isherwood, J. C., Raimi, K. T. ... & Hoyle, R. H. (2017). Cognitive and interpersonal features of intellectual humility. *Personality and Social Psychology Bulletin*, 43, 793–813.

Lilienfeld, S. O., McKay, D., & Hollon, S. D. (2018). Why randomized controlled trials of psychological treatments are still essential. *Lancet Psychiatry*, 5, 536–538.

Lilienfeld, S. O., Ritschel, L. A., Lynn, S. J., Cautin, R. L., & Latzman, R. D. (2014). Why ineffective psychotherapies appear to work: A taxonomy of causes of spurious therapeutic effectiveness. *Perspectives on Psychological Science, 9*, 355–387.

McKay, D. (2017, December 16). Compassionate evidence-based treatment. *Psychology Today Blogs.* www.psychologytoday.com/blog/your-fears-and -anxieties

Meehl, P. E. (1973). Why I do not attend case conferences. In P. E. Meehl (ed.), *Psychodiagnosis: Selected papers* (pp. 225–302). Minneapolis: University of Minnesota Press.

Nickerson, R. S. (1998). Confirmation bias: A ubiquitous phenomenon in many guises. *Review of General Psychology, 2*, 175–220.

Pirsig, R. M. (1974). Zen and the art of motorcycle maintenance: An inquiry into values. New York: Random House.

Sagan, C. (1995). *The demon-haunted world: Science as a candle in the dark.* New York: Random House.

Tavris, C., & Aronson, E. (2008). *Mistakes were made (but not by me): Why we justify foolish beliefs, bad decisions, and hurtful acts.* Boston: Houghton Mifflin Harcourt.

Preface

Most other books about psychotherapy emphasize everything you need to learn. This is one of the rare books to focus on what you'd be better off to *avoid* learning. If fact, I'd be delighted if you never really learned anything described within. Unfortunately, I've come to realize that without knowing it, you and I have already learned much about great myths, fads, fallacies, frauds, and hoaxes. And so now we must take a moment to consider pseudoscience and other questionable ideas related to psychotherapy.

The goal is for this book to stand alone as a resource. That is, even though it was developed in tandem with a related book called *Child and Adolescent Psychotherapy* (Hupp, 2018), you can still hope to get plenty out of this book without also reading its companion. Reading both together has its advantages, but this book could actually serve as a companion book to any of the other excellent books about psychotherapy with youth.

This book has a few unique attributes. First, the coverage is broad. Second, the organization of topics mirrors the *Diagnostic and Statistical Manual.* Finally, in addition to chapters by many of the top scholars in the field of psychology, this book includes multidisciplinary contributions from the fields of science communication and skepticism.

Unique Attributes

This book is a skeptical field guide to be included in graduate and undergraduate courses related to child and adolescent psychology. Specifically, it supplements readings about evidence-based approaches in courses related to **Psychotherapy, Counseling, Behavior Therapy,** and even **Psychopathology**. Therapists who work with youth can also use this book as a starting point for learning more about pseudoscience. Parents may also benefit from reading about these topics.

Broad Coverage

This book was designed to have very broad coverage in a few different ways:

- ***Types of pseudoscience and questionable ideas.*** This book includes many treatment approaches that are problematic in different ways, and it also covers other areas that influence treatment. For their topic, the chapter authors were asked to consider the following issues:
    - implausible treatments
    - ineffective treatments
    - potentially harmful treatments
    - diagnostic controversies
    - questionable assessment practices
    - myths that influence treatment
    - undermining evidence-based approaches
- ***Topic selection and age range.*** This book covers a wide range of topics that mirror the same topics from *Child and Adolescent Psychotherapy*, which includes a broader coverage of topics than that found in most other similar books. This book also covers everything from infancy through adolescence.

Expert Contributors

Perhaps the greatest strength of this book is the lineup of contributors. If you don't recognize most of these names, now is the perfect time to start getting to know them!

Expert chapter authors. Our Foreword contributor really sets the stage for a star-studded lineup of psychological skepticism. All these authors regularly publish articles in top-tier academic journals, and several contributors have published influential books, some of which inspired the development of this book. Many chapter authors are in academia, while others work in hospitals or private practice. The represented fields of the chapter authors include clinical psychology, school psychology, developmental psychology, applied behavior analysis, pediatrics, and social work. A few students also chipped in and will likely continue the fight for evidence-based practices long into the future.

Sidebars from interdisciplinary science communicators. In addition to the experts who wrote each of the chapters, each chapter includes a sidebar written by a prominent science communicator. These sidebar authors come from fields including pediatrics, dentistry, obstetrics, anthropology, neuroscience, and psychology. Most of these authors are well known in the skeptical community, and many of them regularly contribute to skeptical magazines, blogs, and websites. Several of the

Sidebar contributors have written books or developed podcasts, and one even developed, directed, and produced a skeptical film!

Sidebar topics were selected to integrate well with the material in each chapter. It's important to note here, though, that in nearly all cases the chapter authors and the sidebar authors worked independently. That is, the views of the chapter authors do not necessarily reflect the views of the sidebars' authors (and vice versa).

Acknowledgments

In the first proposal of this project, there was only going to be one book that covered both evidence-based approaches and pseudoscientific ones. Fortunately, Matt Bennett saw the value in expanding to two books, and I am very thankful for his foresight. Other Cambridge staff who deserve credit for all they did during the development of this book include Brianda Reyes, Stephen Acerra, Emily Watton, Grace Morris, and David Repetto. Linda Benson from Integra also provided some heavy lifting toward moving the book to final publication. I can't give enough thanks to Scott O. Lilienfeld for helping to give me a big break and for continuing to support my work through his additions to this book. I've had a lot of academic mentors who taught me so much about critical thinking, and they include David Reitman, Kathleen Lemanek, William Pelham Jr., C. Daniel Batson, C. R. Snyder, John Northup, Mary Lou Kelley, Keith D. Allen, Mark Shriver, and Emily Krohn. Thanks also to the chapter authors and the sidebar authors who all provided amazing contributions.

I'm also very thankful for my family, especially Vyla, Evan, Henry, and my fiancée Farrah who works diligently to keep me from being too skeptical. The dedication for this book went to my father, Dennis Hupp, and for the companion book went to my mom, Deanna Hupp, who both have continued to always be there for me, our family, and each other.

Critical Thinking about Psychotherapy

Stephen Hupp, Jean Mercer, Bruce A. Thyer, and Monica Pignotti

We'll give you the good news first – multiple evidence-based treatments (EBTs) have been identified for most psychological challenges that children and adolescents face, and the Society of Clinical Child and Adolescent Psychology, also known as Division 53 of the American Psychological Association, has been at the forefront of identifying EBTs for youth (the term "youth" will be used throughout this book to represent both children and adolescents, and sometimes even infants). As you glance through the chapter titles of this book, you should know that authors writing on these same topics in the companion book, entitled *Child and Adolescent Psychotherapy* (Hupp, 2018), were able to find research-supported approaches to treating all of these topics. In some cases, the treatments are *well established*, meaning they have at least two well-designed studies by different research teams. In other cases, the research is not quite as strong, but there's enough to give any clinician a good starting point for conducting therapy. Admittedly, no treatment works for everyone. Moreover, even when a treatment does help a child improve psychological functioning, the child may still continue to experience some symptoms over time. That is to say, the science of clinical child and adolescent psychology is not perfect, is not complete, and is not finished moving forward.

Now for the bad news – the science of clinical child and adolescent psychology is not being utilized to its fullest. Not even close. Despite having access to information about which treatments have solid research support, many therapists are not using these treatments. Even worse, they are frequently using treatments that have already been shown to be ineffective (Lilienfeld, 2005; Lilienfeld, Ammirati, & David, 2012). In fact, one study identified 63 ineffective treatments for youth that have been discredited in a Delphi poll with experts (Koocher et al., 2015). Ineffective treatments are problematic because they (a) waste time, (b) cost money, (c) damage the credibility of therapists, and (d) may cause considerable harm to youth and their parents. The use of ineffective treatments is also disconcerting when considering the strong literature in support of several evidence-based approaches. With so many valuable treatments available, there is no good reason to use a treatment that has been shown to be ineffective, especially if it has been shown to be harmful.

1.1 Pseudoscience and Questionable Ideas

Some practitioners continue to argue that an ineffective treatment works, often relying on poorly designed studies to bolster their arguments, even after well-designed studies show the treatment is ineffective. Other times practitioners grossly misinterpret the results of other studies as a way to support their use of an ineffective treatment. Both cases are examples of engaging in pseudoscience. Although pseudoscience has been said to be a "fuzzy" term (McNally, 2003), a more formal definition was offered by the philosopher of science Mario Bunge as "a body of beliefs and practices whose practitioners wish, naively or maliciously, pass for science although it is alien to the approach, the techniques, and the fund of knowledge of science" (Bunge, 1998, p. 41). In essence, pseudoscientific practices give the superficial appearance of science, using scientific-sounding jargon borrowed from legitimate science, yet lacking the substance of having valid scientific research to back up their claims. Pseudoscience is distinguished from antiscience, another threat to the mental health profession (Olatunji, Parker, & Lohr, 2005) in that antiscience proponents denigrate science itself or maintain that there are different ways of knowing, all equally valid. Proponents of antiscience often unapologetically offer treatments that are utterly lacking in any kind of scientific support and often make no attempt to claim such support exists.

Pseudoscientific practices are insidious because unless the consumer is educated in how to evaluate claims of scientific evidence, they could be deceived into thinking that such practices, often widely promoted on the internet, have legitimate scientific evidence supporting their use. In recent years promotions have become increasingly sophisticated, with online newly established "peer-reviewed" journals where the peers doing the review are all proponents of the practice being published and stand to benefit financially. The unfortunate result is that increasingly, studies of inferior quality are being published in such journals and cited as scientific research, declaring that the practice is "evidence based" even though that concept is also widely misunderstood (Thyer & Pignotti, 2011).

To make matters even more confusing, some of these practices actually do meet the American Psychological Association's criteria for EBTs (Chambless et al., 1998; Southam-Gerow & Prinstein, 2014) in that some questionable practices, such as energy therapies, have managed to publish at least two group design experiments showing superiority to no treatment or even to a psychological placebo treatment (see Feinstein, 2008 for a review and Pignotti & Thyer, 2009 for a rebuttal). The American Psychological Association criteria have come under criticism for not being rigorous enough, since they do not take into account the mechanism of action, allowing for the possibility that these treatments may work better than placebo because they have other active elements, such as exposure therapy, in common with existing evidence-based practices, rather than anything unique to the novel treatment, such as energy meridians. Rosen and Davison (2003) have suggested using empirically supported principles of change as the key way to identify what works rather than using trademarked therapies or other treatment packages. Unless consumers are alert to what to look out for, they are at risk for being charged much larger fees for services than they would have paid for a well-researched practice that has undergone rigorous testing and has well-recognized empirically supported mechanisms of action.

A number of factors can give rise to a claim being made about the positive effects of a treatment being labeled pseudoscientific. Here are a few hallmarks of pseudoscience:

- Exploited expertise – a genuine expert in one field provides testimonials in an area outside the expert's area.
- Bogus expertise – a supposed expert claims to possess research or practice credentials that are simply false or originated from diploma mills or otherwise unaccredited institutions.
- No research support – patently unsupported claims are made by the treatment's promoters who usually have a vested financial interest in the treatment.
- Inflated research support – exaggerated claims are made on the basis of poorly designed or conducted research or research published in journals with very low scientific standards.
- Misleading research support – the findings from a well-done study are misinterpreted or misrepresented.
- False research support – a study is published in a scientific journal, but the actual study was never conducted. Sometimes even highly respected journals get hoaxed by unscrupulous authors.

- Purple hat component – a central mechanism of action of the touted treatment is extremely implausible based on existing scientific knowledge.
- Overly broad focus – the treatment is said to be highly effective for an amazing array of different conditions (presumably with different etiologies).

Not all pseudoscientific treatments will be associated with all of these features, and some scientific treatments will also share these features, but generally the more of these hallmarks are present, the greater the likelihood one has encountered a pseudoscientific practice.

With pseudoscience being the driving force behind this book, experts in each topical area were recruited to write each chapter. Authors were encouraged to write about treatments that were pseudoscientific in some way or at least seriously questionable. In particular, authors considered treatments that met these descriptions:

- Implausible treatments – when treatments have not yet been tested and do not have a plausible theory behind why they would be effective.
- Ineffective treatments – when treatments have been tested and shown not to work.
- Potentially harmful treatments – when research actually shows these treatments have made the problem worse or have a dangerous side effect.

Additionally, chapter authors were prompted to consider other misperceptions or practices that could influence treatments in a pseudoscientific way:

- Diagnostic controversies – when treatment providers invent their own diagnoses, and when experts have a hard time agreeing on diagnostic criteria.
- Questionable assessment practices – when assessment tools have poor reliability or validity.
- Myths that influence treatment – when misperceptions about etiology or the developmental course of a disorder affect treatment decision making.
- Undermining evidence-based approaches – when providers discourage treatments that have been shown to have strong research support.

Chapters vary in terms of how many of these areas they cover based on what was available in the literature, and authors chose which areas to cover based on which were the most alarming.

1.2 Introduction to Skepticism

If you haven't already noticed, psychology is rampant with pseudoscience. But our field is not alone in this regard. In his book, *Demon-Haunted World: Science as a Candle in the Dark* (Sagan, 1996), the great science communicator Carl Sagan pointed out that "Each field of science has its own complement of pseudoscience" (p. 43). Inspired by a list started by Sagan, here are some examples of different types of pseudoscience in their respective fields:

- Anthropology: Bigfoot
- Archaeology: ancient astronauts
- Architecture: Feng-shui
- Art: forgeries
- Astronomy: astrology
- Botany: emotionally passionate plants
- Business: pyramid schemes
- Chemistry: alchemy
- Economics: long-term economic forecasting
- Education: brain training
- Geophysics: flat Earth theory
- History: history denialism
- Journalism: fake news
- Law: pseudolaw (yes, this is a thing)
- Medicine: complementary and alternative medicine
- Meteorology: *Farmer's Almanac*
- Physics: perpetual motion machines
- Politics: conspiracy theories
- Psychology: parapsychology

When you see all of this pseudoscience in one list, it is really quite disturbing, isn't it? If you're not concerned about this list yet, maybe it's because you think nobody really believes in these examples, but a Gallup poll (Moore, 2005) will help to burst that bubble. For example, 24% of Americans reported believing "That extra-terrestrial beings have visited earth at some time in the past." Worse yet, 25% of Americans believe in "Astrology, or that the position of the stars and planets can affect people's lives." Even worse, 42% of Americans believe "That people on this earth are sometimes possessed by the devil."

And keep in mind that we only provided one example per field. This book focuses on only one small part of psychology – psychotherapy with youth. That said, this book contains well over 100 examples of pseudoscience and questionable ideas. Recent research shows that parents believe a lot myths related to psychotherapy with children (Hupp, Stary, & Jewell, 2017). For example, 64% of parents reported believing that "Programs like Scared Straight help prevent youth from breaking the law." Worse yet, 82% of parents believe that "Too much sugar causes hyperactivity." Even worse, 88% of parents believe that "The Attachment Parenting approach strengthens the mother-infant bond." In all of the examples, and many more, the results were replicated with a college student sample in a course about child psychology.

Fortunately, a new field has been developing to help combat all of the pseudoscience in all of these fields. The field of skepticism is unique in that it is one place where members of all of the other fields come together toward the goal of shining a light on pseudoscience. You don't have to look too hard these days to find skepticism conferences, magazines, podcasts, or even television shows. When skeptics communicate using any of these outlets, they spend a fair amount of time debunking pseudoscience in their respective areas. More than that, though, they spend a lot of time sharing with each other how to communicate with other professionals and the public about pseudoscience. That is, *science communication* is a large part of skepticism. One example of science communication is the Guerrilla Skepticism on Wikipedia (GSoW) project that aims to incorporate more critical thinking into entries on Wikipedia, a common place for people to find information (read the Sidebar to learn more about GSoW).

Sidebar Box: What is Guerrilla Skepticism on Wikipedia? by Susan Gerbic

There's so much nonsense everywhere. So where does one look for information disputing it all? If only there were a reliable, online resource containing well-written articles for the general public, backed up with notable secondary citations, and written in multiple languages. It should be a free resource, and it should be easy to find. Well, that material does exist. It's one of the most popular websites in the world, and It's managed by people who care about accurate, free information. It's called Wikipedia.

I run an editing team that focuses on scientific skepticism topics for that online encyclopedia, and we write articles in multiple languages. We train and mentor people who have never before edited Wikipedia; we are called Guerrilla Skepticism on Wikipedia (GSoW; Gerbic, 2013). Want to see some of our work? Check out

the Facilitated Communication article for one example of
a pseudoscientific treatment (Gerbic, 2017). We wrote this material
to educate Wikipedia's readers about this discredited technique
still in use today by schools and parents who are desperately
attempting to communicate with people who have severe
communication difficulties. These invalid practices have caused
emotional distress and great risk to families and caregivers, so we
believe making this known is important. We also contribute to
entries about influential members of the skeptical community such
as Ray Hyman, a professor of psychology, who along with James
Randi, Martin Gardner, and Paul Kurtz is a key founder of the
modern skeptical movement.

Susan Gerbic, BA, also known as the Wikapediatrician, is a skeptical
activist who educates others about pseudoscience, especially as it
relates to "clairvoyant mediums," or as she calls them, "Grief
Vampires." For more information about her project, and how to
get involved, you can visit https://abouttimeproject.wordpress
.com.

While you learn about all of the psychotherapy pseudoscience presented in
this book, you may get frustrated, you may get angry, and you may get
motivated to do something about it. GSoW is one example of something you
can start doing today. The final chapter of this book will also delve deeper
into the world of skepticism and will hopefully give you more ideas about
what you can do about pseudoscience.

1.3 The Concept of Plausibility

Skepticism is not the same as cynicism. Skeptics do not simply reject most
ideas on minor grounds because of a general wariness and suspicion
about motives and information. Skeptics do keep their minds open
about the evidence for and logic of claims – the *plausibility* of ideas
(Lilienfeld, 2011). When we think about psychotherapies, or educational
methods, or any proposed ways of changing human abilities and behavior, it's a good idea to put on our skeptics' hats and consider whether or
not a treatment is plausible. Pseudoscientific approaches are often
implausible, as will be seen throughout this book. When a treatment is

implausible, it may actually be harmful in minor or major ways – or conceivably, it may be a breakthrough that tells us how wrong we have been in much of our thinking about human beings.

What does it actually mean when we say that a treatment is plausible – or when we conclude that it is implausible? Plausible treatments have certain characteristics that are the mirror images of implausible treatments:

a. Plausible treatments have valid internal logic. Examining them, we do not see errors of critical thinking that characterize implausible therapies. For example, discussion of implausible treatments may assume that whatever outcome occurred was caused by the treatment, no matter how the research (if any) was designed. This is a particular problem for evaluation of psychotherapies for children and adolescents.

b. Plausible treatments are congruent with established psychological information about human beings and their development, whereas the rationales for implausible treatments may directly contradict much that is known. Although it might happen that an apparently implausible treatment would point to real errors in our psychological information, this has rarely, possibly never, occurred.

c. Plausible treatments can be evaluated in ways that make it possible to reject or disconfirm the assumptions behind a treatment – to falsify the basic hypotheses. Treatments based on the prediction of many possible outcomes from an event are implausible in that they are not testable; this has historically been a problem for psychoanalytic approaches.

d. Plausible treatments involve ideas about possible mechanisms by which a treatment could operate. If a claimed mechanism does not seem likely to work (for example, that viruses in the digestive tract cause autism spectrum disorder), the treatment may be regarded as implausible. Implausible treatments are sometimes associated with far-fetched suggestions for mechanisms that "sound scientific" because they are based on concepts in use in the biological or physical sciences (for example, details of brain anatomy or function) that are essentially thrown in for purposes of obfuscation and provide "a scientific veneer of legitimacy" (Grimes & Bishop, 2018, p. 141).

Are all plausible treatments necessarily good to use? No, because plausibility alone does not tell us whether a treatment is effective or whether any adverse effects are reported. Plausibility is a reasonable requirement before time and resources go into outcome research.

In times of limited resources, treatments that are implausible do not deserve the expenditures needed for systematic investigation.

1.4 Focusing on Children and Adolescents

In many ways, consideration of psychotherapies for adults and for youth should follow the same rules about plausibility and demonstrated effectiveness. However, there are some special issues about psychotherapies for minors. These issues include the potential harmfulness of treatments for youth, the role played by developmental change in the occurrence of (or recovery from) emotional disturbance, and the fact that treatment of children usually involves parents.

1.4.1 Potential Harmfulness

In recent years, there has been increasing discussion of the possibility that psychotherapies, like medical treatments, can be harmful as well as, or instead of, being beneficial (Dimidjian & Hollon, 2010; Lilienfeld, 2007; Linden, 2013). It is unlikely that any treatment will do major harm to most people treated – if it did, it would not be used again. Because of this, reference is made to potentially harmful treatments (PHTs; Lilienfeld, 2007). These range from demonstrably beneficial treatments with a small number of adverse events, to those whose use expends time and resources without being helpful, to those that are ineffective and have been associated with severe harm including death.

Potentially harmful treatments for children (PHTCs; Mercer, 2017) are included among those described in this book. They are of particular concern for several reasons. It is possible, though not clearly demonstrated, that adverse experiences of children do more lasting harm than similar experiences do for adults. Ongoing research is exploring the roles of adverse childhood experiences (ACEs), and some ACEs under study resemble experiences children may have in the course of PHTCs (e.g., forced holding in holding therapy). Children and adolescents are also more vulnerable than adults because of the problem of informed consent. Adults are able to understand the risks and possible benefits of a treatment and agree to undergo it, but this is not possible for young children and may be difficult even for older adolescents. In addition, refusal of consent by children or adolescents is sometimes interpreted as a symptom of emotional problems such as oppositional behavior, and this may lead to coerced use of a treatment that has clearly been rejected. Unlike most adults, children and adolescents in treatment are often in no position to seek help or report distressing and harmful events during the treatment, particularly if they are confined to residential treatment centers.

1.4.2 Developmental Change

From birth through adolescence, human beings go through dramatic developmental changes that occur no matter what their environments or experiences are like. These changes are most rapid and noticeable in infancy and early childhood and again become dramatic around the time of puberty. Ongoing developmental change means that for a therapy to be considered plausible, it must be evaluated in terms of known patterns of developmental change. For example, a treatment for autism spectrum disorder cannot be assessed simply by looking at child characteristics on two occasions a year apart, because the children will change and develop in some ways over that period even if no treatment is given.

Pseudoscientific therapies are often presented without consideration of developmental issues. For example, the pseudoscientific "orgone therapist" Wilhelm Reich claimed that he had "cured" his infant son of the Moro or startle reflex by physical treatment from birth to five months of age; in fact, babies normally lose this newborn reflex through maturation during about the same period.

Psychotherapists choosing treatments for children and adolescents need to realize that developmental changes mean that individuals respond to experiences differently at different times in their lives. A treatment suitable for an infant is not likely to be suitable for a school-age child or a teenager. But a number of pseudoscientific therapies are based on the idea of *recapitulation* of developmental events – that by repeating for an older child experiences that are part of the usual lives of infants, the child can be made to return to and renegotiate an earlier period of development. This pseudoscientific approach is evident in implausible treatments involving emotional attachment.

1.4.3 Parents

Because youth normally spend much more time with their families than in therapy sessions, most psychotherapies for children and adolescents include education and training for parents who are "in the trenches" of effort to treat emotional disturbance. This is a very different situation from what we most often see in treatment of adults, and it brings new factors into the picture. Although many parents welcome the chance to learn plausible and effective ways of helping their children, some are attracted to implausible, pseudoscientific approaches; because they have the legal responsibility for their children's care, they are in positions to choose implausible treatments that may even be harmful. These parents may deeply resent what they construe as blame for their parenting if it is suggested that they need to learn to handle their children in different ways. They may believe that good information can come only from people who have personally experienced similar issues (a position not infrequent among adoptive parents) and prefer to take their advice from relatable pseudoscientific practitioners rather than from science-based psychotherapists.

In most families, parents have the job of *buffering* a child's experiences with the environment, both physical and social. Parents would ordinarily have the job of protecting their child from harmful treatments and reporting such events to the authorities. Other than medical and school personnel, there is no one in our society who has similar powers and responsibilities toward children. This means that if parents are committed to implausible, potentially harmful treatments, and if children do not attend school or receive medical or dental treatment, there is no one to intervene until serious injury or even death has occurred.

1.5 Conclusion

Many therapists and parents believe that pseudoscience is a thing of the past. Unfortunately, it continues to thrive within most fields, and psychology is no exception. Even children and adolescents, along with their parents, frequently encounter ineffective, implausible, and sometimes harmful psychotherapy practices. But all hope is not lost. The science of psychotherapy with youth is also strong. It is our hope that this book will serve as a guide for both therapists and parents so that they can better identify and avoid pseudoscience in child and adolescent psychotherapy.

Works Cited in Sidebar

Gerbic, S. (2013). Wikapediatrician Susan Gerbic discusses her Guerrilla Skepticism on Wikipedia project. Retrieved from www.csicop.org

Gerbic, S. (2017). Facilitated communication on Wikipedia gets an update. Retrieved from www.csicop.org

References

Bunge, M. (1998). *Philosophy of science: From problem to theory*, Vol. 1 (rev. ed.). New Brunswick, NJ: Transaction Publishers.

Chambless, D. L., Baker, M. J., Baucom, D. H., Beutler, L. E., Calhoun, K. S., Crits-Christoph, P. ... & Woody, S. R. (1998). Update on empirically validated therapies, II. *The Clinical Psychologist, 51*(1), 3–16.

Dimidjian, S., & Hollon, S. (2010). How would we know if psychotherapy were harmful? *American Psychologist, 65,* 21–33.

Feinstein, D. (2008). Energy psychology: A review of the preliminary evidence. *Psychotherapy: Research, Practice, Training, 45,* 199–213.

Grimes, D. R., & Bishop, D. V. (2018). Distinguishing polemic from commentary in science: Some guidelines illustrated with the case of Sage and Burgio (2017). *Child Development, 89*(1), 141–147.

Hupp, S. (2018). *Child & adolescent psychotherapy: Components of evidence-based treatment for youth and their parents.* Cambridge: Cambridge University Press.

Hupp, S., Stary, A., & Jewell, J. (2017). Science vs. silliness for parents: Debunking the myths of child psychology. *Skeptical Inquirer, 41*(1), 44–47.

Koocher, G. P., McMann, M. R., Stout, A. O., & Norcross, J. C. (2015). Discredited assessment and treatment methods used with children and adolescents: A Delphi poll. *Journal of Clinical Child & Adolescent Psychology, 44*(5), 722–729.

Lilienfeld, S. O. (2005). Scientifically unsupported and supported interventions for childhood psychopathology: A summary. *Pediatrics, 115*(3), 761–764.

Lilienfeld, S. O. (2007). Psychological treatments that cause harm. *Perspectives on Psychological Science, 2*(1), 53–70.

Lilienfeld, S. O. (2011). Distinguishing scientific from pseudoscientific psychotherapies: Evaluating the role of theoretical plausibility, with a little help from Reverend Bayes. *Clinical Psychology: Science and Practice, 18*(2), 105–112.

Lilienfeld, S. O., Ammirati, R., & David, M. (2012). Distinguishing science from pseudoscience in school psychology: Science and scientific thinking as safeguards against human error. *Journal of School Psychology, 50*(1), 7–36.

Linden, M. (2013). How to define, find, and classify side effects in psychotherapy: From unwanted events to adverse treatment reactions. *Clinical Psychology and Psychotherapy, 20,* 286–296.

McNally, R. J. (2003). The demise of pseudoscience. *The Scientific Review of Mental Health Practice, 2,* 97–101.

Mercer, J. (2017). Evidence of potentially harmful treatments for children and adolescents. *Child and Adolescent Social Work, 34,* 107–125.

Moore, D. W. (2005). Three in four Americans believe in paranormal. Retrieved from http://news.gallup.com

Olatunji, B. O., Parker, L. M., & Lohr, J. M. (2005). Pseudoscience in contemporary psychology: Professional issues and implications. *The Scientific Review of Mental Health Practice, 4*(2), 19–36.

Pignotti, M. & Thyer, B. A. (2009). Some comments on "Energy psychology: A review of the evidence": Premature conclusions based on incomplete evidence? *Psychotherapy Theory, Research, Training, Practice, 46,* 257–261.

Rosen, G. M., & Davison, G. C. (2003). Psychology should list empirically supported principles of change (ESPs) and not credentialed trademarked therapies or other treatment packages. *Behavior Modification, 27,* 300–312.

Sagan, C. (1996). *The demon-haunted world: Science as a candle in the dark.* New York: Random House.

Southam-Gerow, M. A., & Prinstein, M. J. (2014). Evidence base updates: The evolution of the evaluation of psychological treatments for children and adolescents. *Journal of Clinical Child and Adolescent Psychology, 43* (1), 1–6. doi:10.1080/15374416.2013.855128

Thyer, B. A., & Pignotti, M. (2011). Evidence-based practices do not exist. *Clinical Social Work Journal, 39*(4), 328–333.

2

Intellectual and Adaptive Functioning

Elizabeth M. Kryszak, Jessica F. Scherr, and James A. Mulick

Intellectual functioning refers to a collection of abilities related to learning and processing information (e.g., reasoning, problem solving, planning, abstract thinking, judgment) used to understand the environment and perform roles and tasks needed to survive in the current environment. Adaptive functioning refers to one's ability to perform a set of skills across several domains (i.e., communication, daily living, socialization, work, motor) that allows functioning at an age-appropriate level in the current sociocultural environment (e.g., home, work, school). One's level of intellectual functioning will significantly impact one's level of adaptive functioning, although adaptive functioning is also affected by many other factors (e.g., mental illness, early learning environment, access to appropriate resources). Intellectual disability refers to significant deficits in both intellectual and adaptive functioning that impair a person's ability to function in their current society without significant supports (American Psychiatric Association, 2013). These deficits are often present at birth, although current diagnostic criteria stipulate that onset must occur during the "developmental period," and prevalence is currently estimated at 1% of the population (American Psychiatric Association, 2013; Schalock et al., 2007). Certain medical and genetic conditions are frequently associated with intellectual disability, including Down syndrome, fragile X syndrome, Rett syndrome, metabolic disorders, cerebral palsy, and many others, although the exact cause of an intellectual disability for many cases is unknown (Moeschler & Shevell, 2014). Impairment in functioning is typically life long, although the severity of the disability can vary greatly both between individuals and within individuals across their life spans. The focus of intervention is on improving functioning, maximizing strengths, decreasing maladaptive behavior, and providing effective supports to maximize an individual's potential.

The term "intellectual disability" is relatively new, replacing the term "mental retardation" in recent years, and several other terms to refer to this set of impairments have come and gone within the past century (e.g., moron, idiocy, feeblemindedness, mental deficiency, mental disability, mental handicap, and mental subnormality Schalock et al., 2007). These shifts in terms have accompanied shifts in how society has understood those with this disability, moving from an explanation based on "defective" personality traits to an understanding of how organic and/or social factors can limit development resulting in impaired functioning (Schalock et al., 2007). This shift in understanding intellectual disabilities has also accompanied a shift in the focus of interventions. Ideally, societal changes in attitudes, policies, and interventions are based on the compilation of empirical research providing better understanding of neurodevelopment, epigenetic causes of neurodevelopmental disorders, and effective learning principles. Unfortunately, as in any area humans try to understand, explanations of intellectual disability based on faulty or questionable scientific evidence have also developed and have continued to fester despite contrary evidence, leading to the creation and continued dissemination of attitudes, policies, and interventions that at the very least are unsupported by research and at the very worst are downright dangerous to one of society's most vulnerable populations.

2.1 Pseudoscience and Questionable Ideas

2.1.1 Myths That Influence Treatment

Overall, modern society has come a long way in our understanding and acceptance of those with intellectual disabilities. Nevertheless several harmful myths and beliefs continue to persist that stigmatize those with intellectual disabilities and/or promote interventions that are often ineffective if not harmful. It is human nature to seek and to find connections between events. Agency is our default. As a result, people are very good at finding explanations, even when they do not exist. Despite continued scientific advancement and understanding of heritability and epigenetic modification of gene expression, up to 50%–80% of intellectual disabilities have no current single identifiable cause (Rauch et al., 2006, 2012; van Karnebeek et al., 2005). This is understandably frustrating to families who seek to understand why their child is not developing like their peers. When scientific and medical explanations cannot be found, people turn elsewhere for explanations. The following are thinking patterns and myths that provide the supporting foundation for pseudoscience and poor practice in the area of intellectual disabilities. (See Foxx & Mulick, 2015, for a more in-depth consideration.)

Blind Faith. Blind faith is the strong belief that something is true even when evidence is lacking or evidence is present that actually contradicts the belief. Blind faith is problematic when it obscures good decision making. Continued belief that a treatment works despite the lack of scientific support or even in the face of multiple studies clearly debunking the practice is the lifeblood of all pseudoscience interventions. Bogus interventions often have an almost cult-like following, with followers banding together in their belief that the rest of the world is bent on destroying the only "cure" available for what ails their child. This blind faith can lead families to invest substantial time, effort, and monetary resources into treatments that simply do not work. Alternately, strong faith can also lead to inaction. This includes beliefs such as "he will grow out of it," "he's just like uncle so-and-so and he turned out fine," or a faith that improvement in skills and behavior can only come as a miracle from a higher power:

> In despair we and others sought God to remove the Down syndrome from him. We will pray for this all our remaining days, or until God or one of His disciples brings forth Jacob's healing, or until Jacob tells us to stop. We also sought out, through the internet, other parents of Down Syndrome (DS) to pray with us, but instead found a lot of Christians who believed God had put this on their children and that we needed to embrace DS as our friend. (Cardon Household, 2002)

Stigmatizing Religious and Cultural Beliefs. Many cultural and religious beliefs have their roots in attempts to explain how the world works. This includes myths to explain the presence of an intellectual disability. One of the most common origin beliefs that can be traced as far back as Ancient Greece is that the disability is a punishment from a higher power for sins either in a past life or perpetrated by the family of the person with the intellectual disability (Albrecht, Seelman, & Bury, 2001). A similar belief is that intellectual disability is the result of possession by spirits or devils, leading many to be burned at the stake or to other such punishments for witchcraft throughout the Middle Ages and later in Colonial America, as well as to traumatic exorcism practices meant to "heal" the person (Albrecht et al., 2001). Starting in the 1800s, the biological causes of intellectual disabilities started to be better understood, although even in modern culture harmful paranormal beliefs linger. For example, 41% of Americans still believe that people are sometimes possessed by the devil (Gallup Poll, 2005).

Not all cultural or religious beliefs about intellectual disability are negative. Many discuss these individuals as "God-touched" in that they have been specially chosen by a higher power or are able to have a deeper spiritual connection due to their "innocent" nature than those who are typically developing. Particular spiritual beliefs on the origin of intellectual disabilities can also serve as protective factors for families, including beliefs that "everything happens for a reason" or that "God would not give us something we cannot handle." Although this way of thinking can be helpful for a family, it also has the potential to decrease the likelihood that the family will seek effective interventions.

Miracle Cures. There is no "cure" for intellectual disabilities. Gains in skills and functioning are typically the result of numerous hours of educational and behavioral intervention teaching skills in small steps and then many hours of repetition and practice until skills are learned. Progress is often slow and, while the goal is maximizing independent functioning, the child is unlikely to ever function as well as their same-age peers. This process is understandably frustrating for families, leading them to turn to alternative treatment options, which often offer the promise of miraculous recovery or significant outcomes achieved with far less time and effort. There are, of course, multiple testimonies of instances where an individual's response to a particular intervention is uncharacteristically quick and substantial and, because prognosis is typically probabilistic in nature, there will always be some children who make better than expected gains. Medical science also recognizes the steady improvement of outcomes in cases that were once thought to have been hopeless, but the improvement in these cases is highly correlated with advancements in science and medical technology. For example, it used to be expected that babies born prematurely had little chance of survival, but now it is routine for these babies to have a much higher chance of surviving and even thriving (Saigal & Doyle, 2008). The belief that a quick fix or miracle cure is out there to be found, however, can lead families to waste valuable time and resources.

The Uneducable and Unfit. On the opposite end of the spectrum is the incorrect belief that children with intellectual disabilities cannot learn. This belief can result in families failing to seek any sort of treatment or services at all, or it can result in complacency with little to no progress from poor interventions. In the past, this belief led to discriminatory educational practices and unnecessary institutionalization of those with intellectual disabilities (Albrecht et al., 2001). While many institutions built in the 1700s and early 1800s were initially focused on attempting to educate those with disabilities, as these facilities became more and more overcrowded in the late 1800s, the focus turned away from education to confinement and management. Children with disabilities were often removed from families and placed in institutions at a young age or were segregated from the rest of society by being locked away in homes or barred from public education because they were "uneducable." Since the deinstitutionalization movement in the 1970s and creation of laws such as the Individuals with Disabilities Education Act (IDEA), attitudes toward those with intellectual disabilities have generally improved, leading to a significant percentage of people supporting more inclusionary educational practices and better rights for those with intellectual disabilities (Scior et al., 2013). It should be noted that past contact with a person with a disability was one of the best predictors of more positive attitudes toward those with disabilities (Scior et al., 2013), indicating that more integration of those with intellectual disabilities into society would have the outcome of creating better acceptance and understanding.

2.1.2 Questionable Assessment Practices

Intellectual disability is relatively straightforward to assess, although recent changes in the diagnostic practices (American Psychiatric Association, 2013) do allow for a broader assessment of impairment in functioning, rather than basing diagnosis on a hard IQ cutoff (IQ < 70). Difficulties come when providers misdiagnose intellectual disability as another mental health problem because cognitive functioning was not adequately assessed. This is a particular concern with more pediatricians and other providers diagnosing ADHD based on parent and, maybe, teacher report. Children with mild intellectual disability often have significant difficulty maintaining attention on cognitively demanding tasks, struggle with organization and completion of daily routines, often behave impulsively, and are often more active than peers, leading them to easily come out in the significant range on most parent-report measures of ADHD normed on typically developing children. While it is possible for ADHD and intellectual disability to occur comorbidly, current diagnostic guidelines stipulate, "A diagnosis of ADHD in intellectual disability requires that inattention or hyperactivity be excessive for mental age" (American Psychiatric Association, 2013, p. 64). Therefore, it is very important that children with these symptoms also complete an assessment of their cognitive and adaptive skills so an intellectual disability is not missed or misdiagnosed.

2.1.3 Implausible and/or Ineffective Treatments

Complementary and Alternative Medicine. Complementary and alternative medicine (CAM) describes a set of practices including diets, drugs, and various compounds made from "natural" and unregulated botanical and nutritional extracts. Most modern societies have set up a governing structure to protect the public by approving new medications and treatments through a rigorous process to demonstrate effectiveness (e.g., the US Food and Drug Administration). Unfortunately, similar rigorous standards of evidence are not required for substances designated and sold as nutritional extracts or dietary or nutritional advice, or for devices that are proffered as educational (unless the devices cause physical harm). Consumer protection in the area of CAM treatments is limited to protection from fraudulent claims of efficacy and injury, which account for the often vague claims of effectiveness seen on the labels and advertisements for these treatments as well as the fine print disclaimers often overlooked by consumers.

Diets and supplements are one example of a commonly used CAM. In a study looking at CAM use, 22% of families with a child with a developmental disability other than autism spectrum disorder were using supplements or vitamins (Valicenti-McDermott, 2014). Internet sites advertise that homeopathic therapies, including a range of various supplements, can be "definitely effective" for several disorders, including intellectual disabilities (Shah & Shah, 2002; see also Shah, 2014, and Ullman, 2002), although no sound research evidence supporting this claim is presented.

Another example of CAM is magnetic field therapy. *Alternatives for Healthy Living* (2002) states that intellectual disability and epilepsy are among 42 health-related conditions that may be treated by wearing magnets. The theory behind this treatment, called magnetic field deficiency syndrome, claims that the Earth's magnetic field has decreased as much as 50% in the past few centuries, which has then led to an increase in common diseases by effecting one's "bioelectric cellular equilibrium." People can address this deprivation of "natural" magnetic influences by using magnets in clothing or mattresses or worn about the person. Based on a review of the available research (Sabadell, 1998), any objective evidence of benefit from magnetic therapy remains limited, although no studies have been completed investigating the effectiveness of magnetic field therapies specifically for treating intellectual disability (Levy & Hyman, 2008).

Neural Organization Techniques. Psychomotor patterning, or "patterning" as it was generally known, involves a series of exercises through which children, and some adults, with mild to more severe mental retardation or cerebral palsy engaged in, or were passively guided through, movements of the head and limbs. It was claimed that these movements recapitulated the prenatal and postnatal movements of a young child and that these movements could improve the neurological organization (i.e., structure and functioning) of the central nervous system, thereby enhancing intellectual performance. More simply, engaging in these movements was said to alter the structure of the brain, so as to resemble more closely the brain structure of a typical child. No convincing evidence of these effects has ever been presented, but convincing evidence has been presented that it produces no appreciable benefits (Cummins, 1992; MacKay, Gollogly, & McDonald, 1986; Sparrow & Zigler, 1978). As with many pseudoscientific practices, there are periodic resurgences of patterning and belief in its utility (Bridgman et al., 1985); in response to this, the American Academy of Pediatrics issued statements on patterning and its lack of benefits in 1968, 1982, and 1999. Despite this overwhelming evidence, patterning, again like so many pseudoscience treatments, continues to exist. Patterning was long promoted by the Institute for Applied Human Potential, which today continues to operate as the Institutes for the Achievement of Human Potential (at www.iahp .org), which has offices or operations and offers training for therapists in Brazil, France, Italy, Japan, Mexico, and Spain. Training is limited to parents or immediate adult family members of children with brain injuries or intellectual disabilities, who are unlikely to have knowledge of disconfirming research and so may be culled into adopting these interventions for their children.

2.1.4 Potentially Harmful Treatments

The treatments and interventions discussed so far are not likely to cause direct harm to an individual with an intellectual disability. This can lead to a sense of complacency in the intervention community when faced with these interventions, summarized as "what's the harm in trying?" Instead of trying to dissuade families from these treatments, many providers may choose to ignore them or view them as "complementary" to more effective interventions. Yet all pseudoscience interventions can cause real harm due to their diversion of valuable resources. Wasting time, money, and effort on interventions that do not work reduces available resources that could be put into evidence-based treatments that have been shown to increase functioning level and reduce problematic behavior. That being said, a few current practices do hold the very real potential to cause direct and serious harm to those with intellectual disabilities.

Psychotropic Medication for Challenging Behavior. Challenging behaviors, including severe aggression, property destruction, and self-injury, are relatively common in people with intellectual disabilities (Matson & Neal, 2009). These behaviors are often difficult to treat and can cause significant distress for the individual, their family, and other caregivers. A range of psychotropic drugs are being prescribed to treat these behaviors. Antipsychotics, including both typical (i.e., first-generation drugs such as haloperidol and chlorpromazine) and atypical (i.e., second-generation drugs such as risperidone and olanzapine), are currently the most common class of medications prescribed to adults, with other types of drugs often prescribed, including mood stabilizers (e.g., lithium), antidepressants (e.g., paroxetine), anxiolytics (e.g., buspirone), and antiepileptic medication (e.g., topiramate; Matson & Neal, 2009). Reviews suggest anywhere from 25% to 85% of adults with an intellectual disability are prescribed psychotropic medications, with these medications often being prescribed off label (i.e., the individuals do not display the symptoms these drugs are currently approved by federal agencies to treat), and individuals are often prescribed multiple medications without clear rationale in treatment plans for polytrophic drug use (Deb, Unwin, & Deb, 2015; Scheifes et al., 2016a).

Despite widespread use of psychotropic medications, there is little evidence showing that these medications are actually effective in treating challenging behaviors in this population. Several flaws have been found in many of the studies that have been published, including lack of control groups or conditions; use of non-standardized, observational outcome measures; and lack of blinding to treatment conditions (Matson & Neal, 2009; Singh et al., 2010). Of those studies that are well controlled, a few showed some support for the atypical antipsychotic risperidone (Matson & Neal, 2009), although others showed no evidence of typical or atypical antipsychotics (including risperidone) being consistently more successful than a placebo at decreasing challenging behavior (Tyrer et al., 2008). Furthermore, psychotropic medications can have several serious common side effects, including impairment in memory and attention, sedation, significant weight gain, extrapyramidal symptoms, and tachycardia (Scheifes et al., 2016b; Singh et al., 2010). Data on psychotropic medication use in a pediatric population with intellectual disability is less available at this time. One study found that 20% of an adolescent outpatient population with intellectual disabilities was prescribed psychotropic medications for challenging behavior, with only a few participants taking more than one medication, and psychostimulant medications were the most common medication prescribed (Doan et al., 2014). A meta-analysis of antipsychotic use in a broader youth population found that 10% of the children prescribed medication had an autism spectrum and/or intellectual disability diagnosis (Park et al., 2016). It should be noted that no psychotropic medication is currently approved by the FDA to treat challenging behaviors in children or adolescents with intellectual disabilities, making all use of medication for this reason off label.

In conclusion, given the paucity of evidence showing that psychotropic medications are effective in treating behavior problems in a pediatric population with intellectual disabilities along with the high prevalence of several significant side effects, psychotropic medication should not be used in isolation with this population to treat challenging behaviors with this population at this time. When medications are used in conjunction with other evidence-based intervention, they should only be used with a clear rationale, treatment plan, and ongoing monitoring. Luckily, several behavioral treatments have been shown to be effective in treating behavior problems within this population.

> **Sidebar Box: Does craniosacral therapy improve cognitive functioning? by Jason Travers**
>
> Intellectual disabilities are very often the product of an individual's genetic endowment and/or injury to the brain, such as hypoxia during birth or toxic exposure to lead during childhood. Educational methods typically are the most effective means of improving functioning and quality of life. Craniosacral therapy (CST) has been claimed to be a useful alternative medical treatment for treating an array of health problems and disabling conditions, including intellectual disability.
>
> CST also is called craniopathy, cranial osteopathy, cranial therapy, sacro occipital technique, and bio-cranial therapy. The method typically is used by practitioners such as chiropractors,

physical therapists, massage therapists, osteopaths, and dentists. CST is based on the unsubstantiated notion that a craniosacral system is associated with the "primary respiratory mechanism" of cerebrospinal fluid that influences blood flow throughout the body. CST proponents claim they can detect a "craniosacral rhythm" in their clients and that applying pressure to the skull can influence the regulation of cerebrospinal fluid. They further claim that balancing cerebrospinal fluid is critical for good health and brain function, and this is an outcome of their treatment. CST practitioners believe they can use light touch to detect the flow of cerebrospinal fluid and therapeutically manipulate cranial bones. Manipulations are claimed to regulate cerebrospinal fluid, thereby improving cognitive functioning.

No underlying scientific justification or reliable scientific evidence exists for CST (Hartman & Norton, 2002). Several studies have found that CST practitioners are unable to reliably detect the craniosacral rhythm they claim informs their treatment (Hanteen et al., 1998; Rogers, Witt, Gross, Hacke, & Genova, 1998; Wirth-Pattullo & Hayes, 1994). At least two deaths associated with CST have been documented (Barret, 2012). CST is not a medical treatment and does not improve intellectual disability. CST has been described as wholly pseudoscientific, and its practice is often characterized as quackery

Jason Travers, PhD, is a board certified behavior analyst and associate professor of special education at the University of Kansas. He is author of the book *How to Provide Sexuality Education to Individuals with Autism* (forthcoming).

2.2 Research-Supported Approaches

It is the ethical responsibility of those working with vulnerable populations, such as children with intellectual disabilities and their families, to guide them through the difficult decision-making process that follows a diagnosis to help them overcome beliefs and biases that could lead to wasting precious resources on ineffective treatments. Instead, families should be taught how to evaluate the evidence available to identify interventions that hold true promise for behavior change. For intellectual disability, these are interventions grounded in learning theory that use effective behavior strategies to increase adaptive behavior and decrease problem behavior.

Effective interventions for teaching new skills include Systematic Instruction, Direct Instruction, and Massed Trial Training, which are grounded in the principles of Applied Behavior Analysis (ABA). These methods involve breaking skills down into small steps, teaching each step using effective reinforcement, repeated practice, and then skill generalization. Behavior interventions (also based on ABA) can be used to decrease maladaptive behavior through strategies including understanding the function of the maladaptive behavior, identifying alternative acceptable behaviors that could replace the maladaptive behavior, and then implementing behavior management strategies focused on increasing access to reinforcers for appropriate behavior (e.g., reinforcement of alternative behaviors) and decreasing access to reinforcers or using punishment for the maladaptive behavior. These interventions have several decades' worth of research evidence, making them a sound investment for a family's time, energy, and money (Lloyd & Kennedy, 2014; Spooner et al., 2011).

2.3 Conclusion

Children with intellectual disabilities are considered to be a vulnerable population, in need of particular supports, protections, and evidence-based services so that they are treated fairly and can achieve their fullest potential. It can be forgotten at times, however, that the families of these children are also often vulnerable. Their powerful love of their children, need to know why this is happening, and desire to help their children get better put them at great risk to be taken advantage of by those offering black-and-white answers, quick fixes, and results that are literally too good to be true. At times, these can be downright charlatans choosing to take advantage of families in need, but often they are well-meaning service providers and caretakers who want to help so much that they choose to ignore the need for careful research of promising interventions or evidence that is contrary to their current practices. Therefore, it must continue to be a priority of training programs and those who provide services to children to arm families and professionals with training on how to critically evaluate information and choose truly effective and safe interventions.

Works Cited in Sidebar

Barret, S. (2012, October 12). Why cranial therapy is silly. Retrieved from www .quackwatch.org/01QuackeryRelatedTopics/cranial.html

Hanten, W. P., Dawson, D. D., Iwata, M., Seiden, M., Whitten, F. G., & Zink, T. (1998). Craniosacral rhythm: Reliability and relationships with cardiac and respiratory rates. *Journal of Orthopaedic & Sports Physical Therapy, 27,* 213–218.

Hartman, S. E., & Norton, J. M. (2002). Craniosacral therapy is not medicine. *Physical Therapy, 82,* 1146–1147.

Rogers, J. S., Witt, P. L., Gross, M. T., Hacke, J. D., & Genova, P. A. (1998). Simultaneous palpation of the craniosacral rate at the head and feet: Intrarater and interrater reliability and rate comparisons. *Physical Therapy, 78,* 1175–1185.

Wirth-Pattullo, V., & Hayes, K. W. (1994). Interrater reliability of craniosacral rate measurements and their relationship with subjects' and examiners' heart and respiratory rate measurements. *Physical Therapy, 74,* 908–916.

References

Albrecht, G. L., Seelman, K. D., & Bury, M. (eds.). (2001). *Handbook of disability studies.* Thousand Oaks, CA: Sage Publications.

Alternatives for Healthy Living. (2002, October 19). Magnetic field therapy. Retrieved from www.alt-med-ed.com/practices/magnetic.htm

American Psychiatric Association. (2013). *Diagnostic and statistical manual of mental disorders.* 5th ed. Arlington, VA: American Psychiatric Publishing.

Bridgman, G. D., Cushen, W., Cooper, D. M., & Williams, R. J. (1985). The evaluation of sensorimotor-patterning and the persistence of belief. *British Journal of Mental Subnormality, 31,* 67–79.

Cardon Household. (2002, September 29). Down syndrome – preventing the mental retardation and improving the health. Retrieved from http:// home.austarnet.com.au/ caradonhouse/down.htm

Cummins, R. A. (1992). Coma arousal and sensory stimulation: An evaluation of the Doman-Delacato approach. *Australian Psychologist, 27,* 71–77.

Deb, S., Unwin, G., & Deb, T. (2015). Characteristics and the trajectory of psychotropic medication use in general and antipsychotics in particular among adults with an intellectual disability who exhibit aggressive behaviour. *Journal of Intellectual Disability Research, 59*(1), 11–25.

Doan, T., Ware, R., McPherson, L., Dooren, K., Bain, C., Carrington, S. ... & Lennox, N. (2014). Psychotropic medication use in adolescents with intellectual disability living in the community. *Pharmacoepidemiology and Drug Safety, 23*(1), 69–76.

Foxx, R. M., & Mulick, J. A. (eds.). (2015). *Controversial therapies for autism and intellectual disabilities: Fad, fashion, and science in professional practice.* New York: Routledge.

Gallup Poll. (2005). Retrieved from https://news.gallup.com/poll/16915/three-four-americans-believe-paranormal.aspx

Levy, S. E., & Hyman, S. L. (2008). Complementary and alternative medicine treatments for children with autism spectrum disorders. *Child and Adolescent Psychiatric Clinics of North America, 17*(4), 803–820.

Lloyd, B. P., & Kennedy, C. H. (2014). Assessment and treatment of challenging behaviour for individuals with intellectual disability: A research review. *Journal of Applied Research in Intellectual Disabilities, 27*(3), 187–199.

MacKay D. N., Gollogly, J., & McDonald, G. (1986). The Doman-Delacato methods, I: The principles of neurological organization. *British Journal of Mental Subnormality, 32*, 3–19.

Matson, J. L., & Neal, D. (2009). Psychotropic medication use for challenging behaviors in persons with intellectual disabilities: An overview. *Research in Developmental Disabilities, 30*(3), 572–586.

Moeschler, J. B., & Shevell, M. (2014). Comprehensive evaluation of the child with intellectual disability or global developmental delays. *Pediatrics, 134* (3), e903-e918.

Park, S. Y., Cervesi, C., Galling, B., Molteni, S., Walyzada, F., Ameis, S. H. . . . & Correll, C. U. (2016). Antipsychotic use trends in youth with autism spectrum disorder and/or intellectual disability: A meta-analysis. *Journal of the American Academy of Child & Adolescent Psychiatry, 55*(6), 456–468.

Rauch, A., Hoyer, J., Guth, S., Zweier, C., Kraus, C., Becker, C. . . . & Nürnberg, P. (2006). Diagnostic yield of various genetic approaches in patients with unexplained developmental delay or mental retardation. *American Journal of Medical Genetics Part A, 140*(19), 2063–2074.

Rauch, A., Wieczorek, D., Graf, E., Wieland, T., Endele, S., Schwarzmayr, T. . . . & Dufke, A. (2012). Range of genetic mutations associated with severe non-syndromic sporadic intellectual disability: An exome sequencing study. *The Lancet, 380*(9854), 1674–1682.

Sabadell, M. A. (1998). Biomagnetic pseudoscience and nonsense claims. *Skeptical Inquirer.* Retrieved from www.csicop.org/si/9807/magnet2.html, 927/02.

Saigal, S., & Doyle, L. W. (2008). An overview of mortality and sequelae of preterm birth from infancy to adulthood. *The Lancet, 371*(9608), 261–269.

Schalock, R. L., Luckasson, R. A., & Shogren, K. A. (2007). The renaming of mental retardation: Understanding the change to the term intellectual disability. *Intellectual and Developmental Disabilities, 45*(2), 116–124.

Scheifes, A., Egberts, T. C., Stolker, J. J., Nijman, H., & Heerdink, E. R. (2016). Structured medication review to improve pharmacotherapy in people with intellectual disability and behavioural problems. *Journal of Applied Research in Intellectual Disabilities, 29*(4), 346–355.

Scheifes, A., Walraven, S., Stolker, J. J., Nijman, H. L., Egberts, T. C., & Heerdink, E. R. (2016). Adverse events and the relation with quality of life in adults with intellectual disability and challenging behaviour using psychotropic drugs. *Research in Developmental Disabilities, 49*, 13–21.

Scior, K., Addai-Davis, J., Kenyon, M., & Sheridan, J. C. (2013). Stigma, public awareness about intellectual disability and attitudes to inclusion among different ethnic groups. *Journal of Intellectual Disability Research, 57*(11), 1014–1026.

Shah, M. (2014, January 22). Homepathic management of children with development disability & mental health dysfunctions. *Hpathy Ezine*. Retrieved from http://hpathy.com/homeopathy-papers/homeopathic-management-children-development-disability-mental-health-dysfunctions/

Shah, R., & Shah, R. (2002, September 28). Homeopathy for your child. Retrieved from www.indiaspace.com/homoeopathy/child.htm

Singh, A. N., Matson, J. L., Hill, B. D., Pella, R. D., Cooper, C. L., & Adkins, A. D. (2010). The use of clozapine among individuals with intellectual disability: A review. *Research in Developmental Disabilities, 31*(6), 1135–1141.

Sparrow, S., & Zigler, E. (1978). Evaluation of a patterning treatment for retarded children. *Pediatrics, 62*, 137–150.

Spooner, F., Knight, V., Browder, D., Jimenez, B., & DiBiase, W. (2011). Evaluating evidence-based practice in teaching science content to students with severe developmental disabilities. *Research and Practice for Persons with Severe Disabilities, 36*(1–2), 62–75.

Tyrer, P., Oliver-Africano, P. C., Ahmed, Z., Bouras, N., Cooray, S., Deb, S. . . . & Kramo, K. (2008). Risperidone, haloperidol, and placebo in the treatment of aggressive challenging behaviour in patients with intellectual disability: A randomised controlled trial. *The Lancet, 371*(9606), 57–63.

Ullman, D. (2002, October 1). Scientific evidence for homeopathic medicine. Retrieved from www.healthy.net/asp/templates/article.asp?PageType=Article&ID=942

Valicenti-McDermott, M., Burrows, B., Bernstein, L., Hottinger, K., Lawson, K., Seijo, R. . . . & Shinnar, S. (2014). Use of complementary and alternative medicine in children with autism and other developmental disabilities: Associations with ethnicity, child comorbid symptoms, and parental stress. *Journal of Child Neurology, 29*(3), 360–367.

Van Karnebeek, C. D., Scheper, F. Y., Abeling, N. G., Alders, M., Barth, P. G., Hoovers, J. M. . . . & Hennekam, R. C. (2005). Etiology of mental retardation in children referred to a tertiary care center: A prospective study. *American Journal on Mental Retardation, 110*(4), 253–267.

3

Autism Spectrum

Jessica F. Scherr, Elizabeth M. Kryszak, and James A. Mulick

Autism spectrum disorder (ASD) is a pervasive neurodevelopmental disorder characterized by impairment in two domains: social communication and restricted, repetitive behaviors (American Psychiatric Association [APA], 2013). Individuals with ASD have deficits in social-emotional reciprocity, nonverbal communicative behaviors, and difficulty maintaining and understanding social relationships. Symptoms associated with restricted and repetitive behaviors include stereotyped motor movements, restricted and repetitive interests, ritualized patterns of behavior, or reactivity to sensory input (APA, 2013). Prevalence rates for ASD have increased steadily over the years and about 1 in 68 children meets the diagnostic criteria for ASD, a 78% increase since the year 2002 (Baio, 2014). This increase is largely due to changing diagnostic criteria and greater awareness. Males are at an increased risk for ASD and are five times more likely than females to be diagnosed with ASD (Baio, 2014). Additionally, ASD is highly comorbid with anxiety (White et al., 2009), attention-deficit/hyperactivity disorder (ADHD; Mayes et al., 2012), intellectual disability (Matson & Shoemaker, 2009), and severe behavior problems (Lecavalier, 2006).

Behavioral characteristics of ASD emerge early in development, with the majority of individuals receiving a diagnosis by around 3 years of age (Mandell, Novak, & Zubritsky, 2005). Atypical gaze patterns have been identified as possible early indictors of ASD and have been reported to emerge in infants as young as 2 months of age (Jones & Klin, 2013). Research suggests certain genetic vulnerabilities that increase an individual's chance of receiving a diagnosis of ASD. For example, Ozonoff et al. (2011) found that younger siblings of a child previously diagnosed with ASD are about 20% more likely to develop ASD. Despite efforts to identify specific mechanisms that lead to the development of ASD, the precise cause of any given case of ASD is generally unknown. Further contributing to the challenge of identifying precise causal mechanisms of the development of ASD is the vast variability in symptom presentation.

In fact, Geschwind and Levitt (2007) highlighted that ASD may be better conceptualized as "the autisms" emphasizing the wide variability in etiology and presentation. This heterogeneity in how symptoms present suggests that ASD is complex and most likely influenced by a multitude of dynamic genetic and environmental factors. Unfortunately, interpreting the various uncertainties regarding the etiology of ASD has led to conceptualization and treatment efforts that are not empirically based, and in some circumstances not only harmful but scientifically absurd.

3.1 Pseudoscience and Questionable Ideas

3.1.1 Mistaken "Causes" of Autism

People have long attempted to find or explain the cause of autism, which has produced controversial and even harmful results. If you Google "What is the cause of autism?" the internet yields a large number of possibilities. Despite what the Google algorithm says, we do not have a clear picture regarding the cause of ASD. This uncertainty has led to mistaken theories, blame, and unfounded practice.

Cold Mothers. In early attempts to explain the cause of ASD, Kanner (1943) viewed the disorder as a result of problematic parenting styles, particularly involving "cold" mothering with a "genuine lack of maternal warmth," likely mistaking as causal parental sadness and depression that can be affected by caring for a child who is unresponsive in many ways. Bettelheim (1967) further promoted the theory of "refrigerator mothers" and described how lack of affection from the mother deprives the child of the ability to bond with others, thus causing autism. During this time, blame was placed on the parents for "causing" autism and oftentimes the child was encouraged to be removed from their parent's home to live in a residential setting (Cook & Willmerdinger, 2015). Unfortunately, the social and educational deprivation of children with autism and other developmental disabilities through institutionalization and other measures did little to help them and arguably made outcomes tragically worse (Scheerenberger, 1983).

Vaccines. One of the most harmful recent theories is that of vaccines as a cause. In 1998, Andrew Wakefield first proposed that the measles, mumps, and rubella (MMR) vaccine may be associated with autism and bowel disease. Eight of 12 children were reported by their parents to have developed "behavioral symptoms" and developmental regression within two weeks of the MMR vaccination. These results, ultimately disavowed by Wakefield's co-authors, led to speculation that vaccines may be an environmental trigger for ASD. As results from Wakefield's study gained public attention, significant limitations in the research design soon became apparent. The study was criticized for including a small sample size with no control group and the reliance of parent report and beliefs to retrospectively describe behaviors (Godlee et al., 2011). In 2004, 10 of Wakefield's 12 co-authors agreed to retract the paper's interpretation due to increased skepticism resulting from later studies failing to find any evidence of vaccines causing autism (Murch et al., 2004). Eventually, 12 years after publication, Wakefield's article was fully retracted in 2010 due to falsification of data and conflicts of financial interest (Eggertson, 2010; Rao & Andrade, 2011). To this day, Wakefield uses this debunked theory to earn speaking fees from its promotion to gullible audiences, despite his having lost his approval to practice medicine in the UK as a result of his inaccurate claims.

Numerous population-based studies have demonstrated no relationship between vaccines and ASD (Madsen et al., 2002; Taylor et al., 2002; Taylor, Swerdfeger, & Eslick, 2014). Despite the lack of scientific evidence linking vaccines to ASD, supporters and activist groups continue to believe vaccines cause ASD. This highly publicized viewpoint has had extremely detrimental and damaging effects nationwide. Parents are choosing to delay and/or refuse vaccination for their children, which has led to dramatic increases in vaccine-preventable diseases that can cause mortality and widespread epidemics (Omer et al., 2009). According to the Centers for Disease Control and Prevention (CDC), there has been a dramatic increase since measles elimination was documented in 2000 to a record-breaking 667 cases of measles, a potentially life-threatening disease, reported in the United States in 2014 (CDC, 2016). The vast majority of people who contracted measles were unvaccinated. This is one of many examples that highlight the danger of accepting pseudoscience that is not supported by scientific evidence as it relates to the conceptualization of what causes ASD.

3.1.2 Questionable Assessment Practices

Evidence-based assessment of children and adolescents with ASD includes assessment tools that have strong psychometric qualities and also provide relevance to service delivery (Mash & Hunsley, 2005; Ozonoff, Goodlin-Jones, & Solomon, 2005). Ozonoff and colleagues (2005) suggest that a core assessment battery should at minimum include measures of autism symptomology, intelligence, language, adaptive behavior, neuropsychological functions, comorbid psychiatric illnesses, and contextual or environmental factors. Two of the gold standards for measuring autism symptomology are the Autism Diagnostic Interview–Revised (ADI-R; Rutter, LeCouteur, & Lord, 2003) and the Autism Diagnostic Observation Schedule (ADOS; Lord, DiLavore, & Gotham, 2012). Additionally, when considering a diagnosis of ASD, it is important to maintain a developmental perspective, include information from multiple sources and contexts, and be multidisciplinary (Ozonoff et al., 2005).

Questionable assessment practices of ASD not only happen when clinicians fail to gather valid and enough clinical data but also when they let personal perceptions of the patient guide their diagnostic impressions. Klein (2005) also presents five examples of how *cognitive biases* can affect clinician's decisions about diagnosis and decision making. These pitfalls include the following:

a. Representativeness Heuristic: assuming that if something seems similar to other things in a category, it should be a member of that category
b. Availability Heuristic: placing weight on things that come to mind easily or that have been recently encountered
c. Overconfidence: overestimating both quantity and reliability of knowledge
d. Confirmatory Bias: tendency to look for, notice, and remember information that fits with preexisting expectations
e. Illusory Correlation: tendency to perceive co-occurring events as causally related, when in fact the connection between them is coincidental or even nonexistent

3.1.3 Implausible Treatments

The National Center for Complementary and Integrative Health (NCCIH) defines complementary medicine as "a non-mainstream used together with conventional medicine" and alternative medicine as "a non-mainstream practice used in place of conventional medicine" (https://nccih.nih.gov/health/integrative-health). Complementary and alternative medicine (CAM) is used frequently by families of children with ASD, with 74% reporting to use novel, unconventional, and off-label treatments (Rossignol, 2009). CAM treatments used for the treatment of ASD generally fall into either biological or nonbiological categories of treatment (Christon, Mackintosh, & Myers, 2010; Levy & Hyman, 2008). CAM treatments that are biologically based aim to alter physiology or biological mechanisms that contribute to ASD symptom presentation while nonbiological CAM treatments alter sensory experiences thought to influence symptoms of ASD. Christon et al. (2010) studied the perceptions of parents of children of ASD who were using CAM treatments and found that despite parents having high expectations at the start of treatment, there was considerable variability in whether these treatments helped their child. These results lend caution to the efficacy of CAM treatments such as those described next.

Dietary Supplements. The use of dietary interventions to improve mental health symptomology has had some historic success. For example, severe intellectual disability can be prevented by removing phenylalanine from the diets of individuals with phenylketonuria (Scriver & Clow, 1980). Therefore, it is not surprising that parents and medical providers have considered using dietary interventions to treat symptoms of ASD; however, there is no substantial evidence to support the manipulation of diet as an effective intervention to treat ASD (Metz, Mulick, & Butter, 2015). Popular dietary interventions include the use of added supplements or vitamins to an individual's diet to treat ASD symptoms, including the following: combination of magnesium and B6 (Mg-B6; Mousain-Bosc et al., 2006), dimethylglycine (DMG; Kern et al., 2001), amino acids (Zheng, Wang, & Li, 2017), and omega 3 fatty acids (Sliwinski et al., 2006). The efficacy of these types of dietary interventions have either not been studied or failed to demonstrate positive effects of reducing symptoms of ASD using randomized, double-blind studies (Gogou & Kolious, 2017; Levy & Hyman, 2008; Marti, 2014; Metz et al., 2015).

Gluten-Free/Casein-Free (GFCF) Diet. One of the most popular interventions involving dietary manipulation is the gluten-free/casein-free (GFCF) diet (Levy & Hyman, 2005; Williams & Foxx, 2015). The premise for the GFCF diet is that children with ASD have a "leaky gut" that causes them to be unable to breakdown foods completely that have the proteins gluten (e.g., barley, wheat, and rye products) and casein (e.g., milk product). Gluten and casein cross over a "leaky" membrane forming peptides that act as false opiate neuropeptides that cause or worsen symptoms of ASD. Therefore, the elimination of gluten and casein or a GFCF diet is thought to improve the behavior and symptom presentation of ASD. Yet, there are few findings related to the GFCF diet as a mode to improve symptoms of ASD that may be influenced by placebo effects and methodological flaws. For example, many case studies that include anecdotal reports from parents indicate subjective improvement of symptoms of ASD while using the GFCF diet;

however, randomized, double-blind studies have failed to replicate these effects (Elder et al., 2006; Hyman et al., 2016; Seung et al., 2007; Williams & Foxx, 2015). Williams and Foxx (2015) offer alternative explanations for why the GFCF diet may be beneficial for some families by improving behavior in children with ASD including (a) the child may have food allergies, (b) there is an improvement in overall diet quality, and (c) the GFCF diet may improve cooperation and compliance and more global improvements in the child's behavior. See Williams and Foxx (2015) for a more thorough review of the GFCF diet.

Oxytocin. Currently, no drugs or pharmaceutical interventions have been demonstrated to improve or treat the social impairment, a core diagnostic feature, associated with ASD. Recent and preliminary studies have sought to explore the use of oxytocin as a potential treatment modality for improving social functioning in ASD (Anagnostou et al., 2014; Peñagarikano et al., 2015). Oxytocin is a hormone that enhances social behavior, including social recognition, bonding, and regulating anxiety associated with social threat (Meyer-Lindenberg et al., 2011). Oxytocin also increases performance on tasks that require social cognition, including emotion recognition and social memory (Domes et al., 2007; Hollander et al., 2007). A pilot study with 19 adults with ASD found that acute intranasal oxytocin temporarily enhances empathy, social cognition, and social reciprocity (Anagnostou et al., 2014). However, larger clinical trials have yielded inconsistent and mixed results. A double-blind, placebo-controlled trial demonstrated no benefit or clinical efficacy following treatment in individuals with ASD who received oxytocin (Guastella et al., 2015). Currently, there is not enough evidence to support the use of oxytocin as viable treatment for ASD (Young & Barrett, 2015). The results of numerous ongoing clinical trials examining the efficacy of using oxytocin as a treatment for ASD will help provide more information on whether oxytocin can be used to help improve social functioning in ASD.

Sensory Integration Therapy. Many children with ASD have sensory sensitivities that are associated with their avoiding or seeking out auditory, visual, and tactile stimuli (Ben-Sasson et al., 2009). According to Ayres (1972), sensory integration problems result from neurological dysfunction that makes it difficult to process or interpret various sensory stimuli (e.g., movement, sight, sound, and touch) in the brain, thus causing behavioral, social-emotional, and learning problems. Sensory integration therapy, therefore, attempts to correct these dysfunctional sensory processes by providing exposure to specific types of sensory stimulation. Sensory integration therapy is typically delivered by occupational or physical therapists who use a sensory "diet" based on the child's sensory profile (Metz et al., 2015). Examples of therapy or a sensory diet include using weighted vests, brushing, squeezing between pillows, swinging, sitting on a bouncy ball, jumping on a trampoline, playing with textured toys, and joint compression (Lang et al., 2012; Smith, Mruzek, & Mozingo, 2015). Smith et al. (2015) describe three practitioner reported benefits of sensory integration therapy: (a) enhanced ability to focus on relevant materials in educational, therapeutic, and social environments; (b) reduction in the rate of disruptive behaviors such as self-injury: and (c) generalized improvements in nervous system functioning, reflected in high-level cognitive activity such as language and reading. However, research has failed to establish consistent findings related to the proposed theoretical and mechanistic functions involved with sensory integration therapy and improvements in behavioral, emotional, and cognitive outcomes (Baranek, 2002; Metz et al., 2015). In fact, a review of 25 studies involving the use of sensory integration therapy found that 14 studies reported no benefits, 8 studies found mixed results, and 3 studies suggested that sensory integration therapy was effective; however, it is important to note that those studies reporting positive results had significant methodological flaws (Lang et al., 2012; for a full review of sensory integration, please refer to Smith et al., 2015).

Auditory Integration Therapy. Similar to sensory integration therapy, auditory integration therapy is based on the premise that children with ASD have unique sensory needs that influence behavior and require remediation. Mudford and Cullen (2015) define auditory integration training as a "procedure in which acoustically modified music is played to a person for 10 hours" (p. 270). Music is delivered to an individual with ASD through a device that modulates the frequency of the audio clip and changes the volume. Research has shown inconsistent results on behavior of children or adults with autism using auditory integration therapy (Mudford et al., 2000; Mudford & Cullen, 2015; Zollweg et al., 1997).

Chiropractic Therapies and Massage. Other popular nonbiological CAM treatments include massage or chiropractic therapies (Hanson et al., 2007; Levy & Hyman, 2008). Chiropractic therapies often involve physical movement and manipulation of the spine and skull and are provided by chiropractors, occupational therapists, and osteopathic physicians (Levy & Hyman, 2008). Levy and Hyman (2008) caution for considering the risk for injury with spinal manipulation and missed medical diagnoses when using chiropractic therapy or craniosacral massage (Vohra, Johnston,

Cramer, & Humphreys, 2007). Massage therapy involves rubbing various parts of the body, sometimes with the use of oil, to reduce arousal and stress (Navidad et al., 2013). Message may have some benefit for reducing stress and anxiety; however, additional research is needed on the use of massage in treating actual symptoms of ASD (Klein & Kemper, 2016), although it is rather implausible.

3.1.4 Ineffective Treatments

Floortime and Relational Therapies. Relational-based interventions, including the Developmental, Individual Differences, Relationship-Based model (DIR/Floortime; Greenspan & Wieder, 1997), target improving social-communication functioning in ASD through an integrated developmental model that involves interaction with the child's caregivers and the environment. The child with ASD progresses through six developmental sequences that emphasize affect and interactions, as well as individual differences in motor, sensory, affective, cognitive, and language functioning (Greenspan & Wider, 2006). The stages include (a) staying calm and regulated, as well as demonstrating shared attention; (b) engagement and relatedness; (c) base intentional interaction and two-way communication; (d) problem-solving, mood regulation, and forming a sense of self; (e) creative symbols and meaningful use of ideas and words, and (f) emotional thinking, building logical bridges between ideas (Greenspan & Weider, 2006; Zane et al., 2015). Parents are encouraged to play with their child for 20- to 30-minute sessions 6 to 10 times per day to work and progress through these stages (Dionne & Martini, 2011; Greenspan & Wieder, 1998). The DIR/Floortime model also aims to increase generalizability and maintenance of skills through opportunities of incidental teaching in a naturalistic environment (Metz et al., 2015).

Unfortunately, research and reviews have continued to fail to document the efficacy of DIR/Floortime (Metz et al., 2015; Odom et al., 2010; Zane et al., 2015). Studies that have found positive outcomes are laden with methodical flaws, such as a lack of a comparison group, reliance on anecdotal data and other unreliable measures, that make it difficult to assume any causal relationships (Greenspan & Wieder, 1997; Gutstein et al., 2007; Liao et al., 2014; Solomon et al., 2007). This is important to consider because DIR/Floortime often appeals to parent, thereby competing with evidence-based interventions.

Hyperbaric Oxygen Therapy. Hyperbaric oxygen therapy (HBOT) involves delivering increased levels of oxygen in a pressurized chamber and is used for the treatment of carbon monoxide poisoning and pressure equalization or curing "the bends" after diving injuries (Levy & Hyman, 2008). HBOT is used with children with ASD in an attempt to help overcome cerebral hypoperfusion, as well as to reduce neuro inflammation and oxidative stress (Granpeesheh et al., 2010; James et al., 2004; Vargas et al., 2005). Treatment studies of HBOT use in ASD were retrospective and uncontrolled and included methodological flaws that make it difficult to accept HBOT as a viable treatment option for ASD (Rossignol & Rossignol, 2006). Granpeesheh and colleagues (2010) conducted a randomized double-blind placebo-controlled trial that did not detect any difference between HBOT and the placebo groups across any of the outcome measures. Therefore, no scientific evidence supports the clinical use of HBOT as a treatment modality for ASD.

3.1.5 Potentially Harmful Treatments

Facilitated Communication. One of the most clearly debunked treatments for ASD, with numerous scientific studies and reviews demonstrating its ineffectiveness, is facilitated communication (FC; Jacobson, Foxx, & Mulick, 2015; Jacobson, Mulick, & Schwartz, 1995; Metz et al., 2015; Mostert, 2001). The underlying premise behind FC is the perception that ASD is "a disorder of output," making it difficult for individuals to effectively express themselves or use language, independent of cognitive ability (Jacobson et al., 2015; Metz et al., 2015). Therefore, FC is said to provide an outlet to help give individuals with ASD a "voice" or communicate through "assisted" or "supported" typing aided by another person who guides their hand, wrist, or arm to type letters and words through a keyboard. Supporters of FC claim that the individual with ASD is able to demonstrate linguistic and cognitive abilities through the facilitator, oftentimes creating words, sentences, paragraphs, essays, speeches, poems, and/or books. These messages often are absent of grammatical errors and inconsistent with other adaptive or cognitive skills displayed by the individual. This inconsistency led to skepticism, and many research studies examining the validity of FC agreed that the facilitator unconsciously created the facilitated messages and *not* the individual with ASD. FC has harmfully contributed to inspiring false hope in families and has been used as a modality to accuse caregivers, teachers, and professional staff of abuse, most often sexual abuse, toward individuals with developmental disabilities (Margolin, 1994). Although the majority of these allegations were unsubstantiated and unfounded, the results created emotional and financial burdens on those accused due to stigmatization, loss of employment, and alienation (Jacobson et al., 2015; Levine, Shane, & Wharton, 1994).

Despite the overwhelming evidence demonstrating time and time again that FC is a bogus and unethical treatment, some families and providers still use or recommend FC as a treatment modality for ASD. Similar to FC, the Rapid Prompting Method (RPM) is a recent treatment for individuals with ASD to improve learning and communication that "involves the facilitator holding and moving the letter board while the individual with autism moves their own hand" (Tostanoski et al., 2014, p. 219). Empirical evidence does not support the efficacy of RPM in improving communication skills in ASD and suggests outcomes are related to prompt dependency (Hemsley, 2016; Lang et al., 2014). RPM is alarmingly similar to methods of FC, which warrants caution given the harmful and unethical effects of treatment associated with FC.

Chelation Therapy. In the 1960s, Bernard Rimland created the Autism Research Institute (ARI) and supported the Defeat Autism Now (DAN!) treatment approach for ASD (Graf, 2015; Rimland, 1964). Advocates for this approach believed that ASD was caused by biological factors, including weaknesses in the immune system, environmental pollutants, antibiotics, and vaccines, that led to harmful and ineffective treatments by doctors trained to perform them (Graf, 2015; Lofthouse et al., 2012). Chelation therapy was a popular intervention that targeted the removal of heavy metals from the body. This treatment involved administering DMPS (2,3-dimercaptopropane-1-sulfonate) or DMSA (2,3-dimercaptosuccinic acid) to bind to heavy metals, such as mercury or lead, and facilitate elimination (Levy & Hyman, 2008). Chelation therapy is an unethical treatment and has no scientific evidence with controlled studies to support the effectiveness of this intervention (Graf, 2015; Levy & Hyman, 2008). Additionally, deaths from hypocalcemia, or low calcium levels, have been reported, making this treatment equally harmful as it is invalid (Brown et al., 2006; Lofthouse et al., 2012).

> **Sidebar Box: Does Dolphin-Assisted Therapy have healing effects? by Lori Marino and Scott O. Lilienfeld**
>
> Dolphin-Assisted Therapy (DAT) is a popular treatment for a host of mental disorders and developmental disabilities. In particular, DAT is widely used around much of the world for autism spectrum disorder and other developmental disabilities in children, adolescents, and adults. DAT typically involves swimming or interacting with captive

dolphins with the expectation that contact with them generates powerful therapeutic effects. DAT was introduced in the 1970s and has become a highly lucrative business in several countries, including the United States. Most captive dolphin parks offer some version of a DAT experience for visitors, and many advance nonspecific and often expansive claims about its effectiveness. In doing so, they may appeal to a range of explanations, including increased concentration abilities, reward, changes in brain waves, and the purported "healing effects" of echolocation (the sonar that dolphins use to locate and identify living and nonliving objects). DAT facilities typically charge visitors exorbitant fees for "treatments" that can last anywhere from one session to several sessions over a week, and no professional accreditation is required.

DAT's popularity notwithstanding, several methodological reviews of published studies have revealed that there is no credible scientific evidence for its long-term effectiveness for autism spectrum disorder or any other condition (Humphries, 2003; Marino & Lilienfeld, 1998, 2007a, 2007b). Virtually all published studies alleging the effectiveness of DAT are seriously methodologically flawed and lack both internal validity (experimental rigor) and external validity (generalizability). For example, few if any studies adequately account for the nonspecific effects of hope and support from mental health professionals, so any apparent benefits of DAT may merely be due to what psychologists term a "placebo effect" – improvement resulting from the mere expectation of success. In addition, there is no compelling evidence that the seeming effects of DAT reflect anything more than the short-term boost in mood resulting from interacting with a highly charismatic and intelligent animal. In short, no credible peer-reviewed evidence shows that DAT is scientifically legitimate.

Most DAT facilities rely largely or entirely on testimonials from customers to tout their business. Nevertheless, testimonial evidence alone is insufficient to conclude that a treatment works. For example, customers who have something positive to say are often unrepresentative of all customers. Moreover, parents may notice naturally occurring improvements in their children's behavior and mistakenly attribute them to DAT.

> Aside from being scientifically unsupported, DAT is ethically problematic for several other reasons. First, DAT centers inform vulnerable and at times even desperate individuals that an unsupported technique is highly effective. Moreover, some children and adults have been injured, in a few cases seriously, while swimming with captive dolphins. Additionally, the dolphins used in DAT facilities are forced to participate in these activities in confined, often unhealthy, settings. Therefore, DAT is a physically risky, expensive, and ethically problematic intervention that is premised on unsubstantiated scientific assertions.
>
> **Lori Marino, PhD,** is a neuroscientist and the founder and executive director of the Kimmela Center for Animal Advocacy. For more information about this center, you can visit: www.kimmela.org.
>
> **Scott O. Lilienfeld, PhD,** is a professor of psychology at Emory University. He is co-editor of the book *Science and Pseudoscience in Clinical Psychology,* 2nd ed. (2014) and author of several other books about science and pseudoscience in psychology.

3.2 Research-Supported Approaches

It is unfortunate that numerous treatments and practices for ASD are implausible, ineffective, and potentially harmful when empirically supported treatments have been demonstrated to be effective through scientific study. Applied behavior analysis (ABA) has well-established success and has documented its effectiveness in treating individuals with ASD for more than 50 years (Eldevik et al., 2009; Ferster, 1964; Foxx, 2015). ABA delivers methods and practice that are founded on principles of behavior and learning and are used in a variety of populations, including individuals with autism and intellectual or developmental disabilities (Foxx, 2008, 2015; Grey & Hastings, 2005). There is an abundance of scientifically sound evidence in the research literature that ABA intervention leads to improvements in development, learning, and behavior in young children via early intensive behavioral intervention (EIBI; Eldevik et al., 2009; Harris & Delmolino, 2002; Peters-Scheffer et al., 2011; Reichow, 2012). Furthermore, the only interventions for ASD that produce prolonged results are those that use principles of ABA (Foxx, 2015; Metz et al., 2015). Foxx (2015) provides an excellent discussion and highlights how ABA differs from other fads and pseudoscientific treatments concluding with the statement that "ABA has no place in any discussion of fads or pseudoscientific, dubious, or controversial and politically correct treatments other than to epitomize what constitutes effective and ethical treatment of individuals with ASD" (p. 430).

3.3 Conclusion

The lack of a singular explanation for what causes ASD has led to many "quick fixes" or trendy fads that provide fast solutions. Parents of children with ASD are a vulnerable population and, unfortunately, targeted as consumers for a quick cure for their child's disability based on the premise that ASD is due to a simple cause. Smith (2005) lists characteristics of invalid treatments that include the reported outcomes of offering a cure, important-sounding but vague benefits (e.g., increased focus), and major gains that cannot be studied. The search for a quick fix has led to alternative treatments that are not effective and, in some cases, harmful. Therefore, it is critical that professionals in the field help educate families on how to be smart consumers of treatment and to identify evidence-based treatments from pseudoscientific ones using data-based decisions.

Works Cited in Sidebar

Humphries, T. L. (2003). Effectiveness of dolphin-assisted therapy as a behavioral intervention for young children with disabilities. *Bridges: Practice-Based Research Synthesis*, *1*, 1–19.

Marino, L., & Lilienfeld, S. O. (1998). Dolphin-assisted therapy: Flawed data, flawed conclusions. *Anthrozoos*, *11*, 194–199.

Marino L., & Lilienfeld, S. O. (2007a). Dolphin assisted therapy: More flawed data, more flawed conclusions. *Anthrozoos*, *20*, 239–269.

Marino L., & Lilienfeld, S. O. (2007b). Dolphin assisted therapy for autism and other developmental disorders: A dangerous fad. *Psychology in Intellectual and Developmental Disabilities (Division 33), American Psychological Association*, *33*(2), 2–3.

References

Allport, G. W. (1954). *The nature of prejudice*. New York: Harper & Row.

American Psychiatric Association. (2013). *Diagnostic and statistical manual of mental disorders*; 5th edn. Arlington, VA: American Psychiatric Association Publishing.

Anagnostou, E., Soorya, L., Brian, J., Dupuis, A., Mankad, D., Smile, S., & Jacob, S. (2014). Intranasal oxytocin in the treatment of autism spectrum disorders: A review of literature and early safety and efficacy data in youth. *Brain Research*, 1580, 188–198.

Ayres, A. J. (1972). *Sensory integration and learning disorders*. Los Angeles: Western Psychological Services.

Baio, J. (2014). Prevalence of autism spectrum disorder among children aged 8 years – Autism and developmental disabilities monitoring network, 11 sites, United States, 2010. *MMWR Surveillance Summaries*, *63*(2), 1–21.

Baranek, G. T. (2002). Efficacy of sensory and motor interventions for children with autism. *Journal of Autism and Developmental Disorders*, *32*(5), 397–422.

Ben-Sasson, A., Hen, L., Fluss, R., Cermak, S. A., Engel-Yeger, B., & Gal, E. (2009). A meta-analysis of sensory modulation symptoms in individuals with autism spectrum disorders. *Journal of Autism and Developmental Disorders*, *39*(1), 1–11.

Bettelheim, B. (1967). Empty fortress. New York: Simon and Schuster.

Bilu, Y., & Goodman, Y. C. (1997). What does the soul say?: Metaphysical uses of facilitated communication in the Jewish ultraorthodox community. *Ethos*, *25*(4), 375–407.

Brown, M. J., Willis, T., Omalu, B., & Leiker, R. (2006). Deaths resulting from hypocalcemia after administration of edetate disodium: 2003–2005. *Pediatrics*, *118*(2), e534–e536.

Carter, E. W., Boehm, T. L., Annandale, N. H., & Taylor, C. E. (2015). Supporting congregational inclusion for children and youth with disabilities and their families. Exceptional Children, 0014402915598773.

Centers for Disease Control and Prevention. (2016). Measles cases and outbreaks. Retrieved from www.cdc.gov/measles/cases outbreaks.html

Christon, L. M., Mackintosh, V. H., & Myers, B. J. (2010). Use of complementary and alternative medicine (CAM) treatments by parents of children with autism spectrum disorders. *Research in Autism Spectrum Disorders*, *4*(2), 249–259.

Cook, Kieran A., & Willmerdinger, Alissa N. (2015). "The History of Autism." Narrative Documents. Book 1. Retrieved from http://scholarexchange.fur man.edu/schopler-about/1

Dionne, M., & Martini, R. (2011). Floor time play with a child with autism: A single-subject study. *Canadian Journal of Occupational Therapy*, *78*(3), 196–203.

Domes, G., Heinrichs, M., Michel, A., Berger, C., & Herpertz, S. C. (2007). Oxytocin improves "mind-reading" in humans. *Biological Psychiatry*, *61*(6), 731–733.

Eggertson, L. (2010). Lancet retracts 12-year-old article linking autism to MMR vaccines. *Canadian Medical Association Journal*, *182*(4), E199–E200.

Elder, J. H., Shankar, M., Shuster, J., Theriaque, D., Burns, S., & Sherrill, L. (2006). The gluten- free, casein-free diet in autism: Results of a preliminary double blind clinical trial. *Journal of Autism and Developmental Disorders, 36*(3), 413–420.

Eldevik, S., Hastings, R. P., Hughes, J. C., Jahr, E., Eikeseth, S., & Cross, S. (2009). Meta-analysis of early intensive behavioral intervention for children with autism. *Journal of Clinical Child & Adolescent Psychology, 38* (3), 439–450.

Farrington, C. P., Miller, E., & Taylor, B. (2001). MMR and autism: Further evidence against a causal association. *Vaccine, 19*(27), 3632–3635.

Ferster, C. B. (1964). Positive reinforcement and behavioral deficits of autistic children. In C. M. Franks (ed.), *Conditioning Techniques in Clinical Practice and Research* (pp. 255–274). Heidelberg: Springer Berlin.

Foxx, R. M. (2008). Applied behavior analysis treatment of autism: The state of the art. *Child and Adolescent Psychiatric Clinics of North America, 17*(4), 821–834.

Foxx, R. M. (2015). Why ABA is not a fad, a pseudoscience, a dubious or controversial treatment, or politically correct. In R. M. Foxx & J. A. Mulick (eds.), *Controversial therapies for autism and intellectual disabilities: Fad, fashion, and science in professional practice* (pp. 422–432). New York: Routledge.

Geschwind, D. H., & Levitt, P. (2007). Autism spectrum disorders: Developmental disconnection syndromes. *Current Opinion in Neurobiology, 17*(1), 103–111.

Godlee, F., Smith, J., & Marcovitch, H. (2011). Wakefield's article linking MMR vaccine and autism was fraudulent. *BMJ,* 342, c7452.

Gogou, M., & Kolios, G. (2017). The effect of dietary supplements on clinical aspects of autism spectrum disorder: A systematic review of the literature. *Brain and Development, 39*(8), 656–664.

Graf, W. D. (2015). Communicating concern about early signs of autism to parents. *Virtual Mentor, 17*(4), 310.

Granpeesheh, D., Tarbox, J., Dixon, D. R., Wilke, A. E., Allen, M. S., & Bradstreet, J. J. (2010). Randomized trial of hyperbaric oxygen therapy for children with autism. *Research in Autism Spectrum Disorders, 4*(2), 268–275.

Gray, D. E. (2001). Accommodation, resistance and transcendence: Three narratives of autism. *Social Science & Medicine, 53*(9), 1247–1257.

Green, V. A., Pituch, K. A., Itchon, J., Choi, A., O'Reilly, M., & Sigafoos, J. (2006). Internet survey of treatments used by parents of children with autism. *Research in Developmental Disabilities, 27*(1), 70–84.

Greenspan, S. I., & Wieder, S. (1997). Developmental patterns and outcomes in infants and children with disorders in relating and communicating: A chart review of 200 cases of children with autistic spectrum diagnoses. *Journal of Developmental and Learning Disorders,* 1, 87–142.

Greenspan, S. I., & Wieder, S. (2006). *Engaging autism: Helping children relate, communicate and think with the DIR floortime approach.* Cambridge, MA: Da Capo Lifelong Books.

Greenspan, S. I., Wieder, S., & Simons, R. (1998). *The child with special needs: Encouraging intellectual and emotional growth.* Boston: Addison-Wesley/ Addison Wesley Longman.

Guastella, A. J., Gray, K. M., Rinehart, N. J., Alvares, G. A., Tonge, B. J., Hickie, I. B. . . . & Einfeld, S. L. (2015). The effects of a course of intranasal oxytocin on social behaviors in youth diagnosed with autism spectrum disorders: A randomized controlled trial. *Journal of Child Psychology and Psychiatry, 56*(4), 444–452.

Grey, I. M., & Hastings, R. P. (2005). Evidence-based practices in intellectual disability and behaviour disorders. *Current Opinion in Psychiatry, 18*(5), 469–475.

Gutstein, S. E., Burgess, A. F., & Montfort, K. (2007). Evaluation of the relationship development intervention program. *Autism, 11*(5), 397–411.

Hanson, E., Kalish, L. A., Bunce, E., Curtis, C., McDaniel, S., Ware, J., & Petry, J. (2007). Use of complementary and alternative medicine among children diagnosed with autism spectrum disorder. *Journal of Autism and Developmental Disorders, 37*(4), 628–636.

Harris, S. L., & Delmolino, L. (2002). Applied behavior analysis: Its application in the treatment of autism and related disorders in young children. *Infants & Young Children, 14*(3), 11–17.

Hemsley, B. (2016). Evidence does not support the use of Rapid Prompting Method (RPM) as an intervention for students with autism spectrum disorder and further primary research is not justified. *Evidence-Based Communication Assessment and Intervention, 10*(3–4), 122–130.

Hollander, E., Bartz, J., Chaplin, W., Phillips, A., Sumner, J., Soorya, L. . . . & Wasserman, S. (2007). Oxytocin increases retention of social cognition in autism. *Biological Psychiatry, 61*(4), 498–503.

Hyman, S. L., Stewart, P. A., Foley, J., Peck, R., Morris, D. D., Wang, H., & Smith, T. (2016). The gluten-free/casein-free diet: A double-blind challenge trial in children with autism. *Journal of Autism and Developmental Disorders, 46*(1), 205–220.

Jacobson, J. W., Foxx, R. M., & Mulick, J. A. (2015). Facilitated communication. In R. M. Foxx & J. A. Mulick (eds.), *Controversial therapies for autism and intellectual disabilities: Fad, fashion, and science in professional practice* (pp. 283–302). New York: Routledge.

Jacobson, J. W., Mulick, J. A., & Schwartz, A. A. (1995). A history of facilitated communication: Science, pseudoscience, and antiscience science working group on facilitated communication. *American Psychologist, 50*(9), 750.

James, S. J., Cutler, P., Melnyk, S., Jernigan, S., Janak, L., Gaylor, D. W., & Neubrander, J. A. (2004). Metabolic biomarkers of increased oxidative stress and impaired methylation capacity in children with autism. *The American Journal of Clinical Nutrition, 80*(6), 1611–1617.

Jones, W., & Klin, A. (2013). Attention to eyes is present but in decline in 2–6-month-old infants later diagnosed with autism. *Nature, 504*(7480), 427–431.

Kanner, L. (1943). Autistic disturbances of affective contact. *Nervous Child, 2*(3), 217–250.

Kern, J. K., Miller, V. S., Cauller, L., Kendall, R., Mehta, J., & Dodd, M. (2001). Effectiveness of N, N-dimethylglycine in autism and pervasive developmental disorder. *Journal of Child Neurology, 16*(3), 169–173.

Klein, J. G. (2005). Five pitfalls in decisions about diagnosis and prescribing. *BMJ, 330*(7494), 781–783.

Klein, N., & Kemper, K. J. (2016). Integrative approaches to caring for children with autism. *Current Problems in Pediatric and Adolescent Health Care, 46* (6), 195–201.

Koenig, H. G. (2009). Research on religion, spirituality, and mental health: A review. *The Canadian Journal of Psychiatry, 54*(5), 283–291.

Lang, R., Harbison Tostanoski, A., Travers, J., & Todd, J. (2014). The only study investigating the rapid prompting method has serious methodological flaws but data suggest the most likely outcome is prompt dependency. *Evidence-Based Communication Assessment and Intervention, 8*(1), 40–48.

Lang, R., O'Reilly, M., Healy, O., Rispoli, M., Lydon, H., Streusand, W. … & Didden, R. (2012). Sensory integration therapy for autism spectrum disorders: A systematic review. *Research in Autism Spectrum Disorders, 6*(3), 1004–1018.

Lecavalier, L. (2006). Behavioral and emotional problems in young people with pervasive developmental disorders: Relative prevalence, effects of subject characteristics, and empirical classification. *Journal of Autism and Developmental Disorders, 36,* 1101–1114.

Levine, K., Shane, H. C., & Wharton, R. H. (1994). What if: A plea to professionals to consider the risk-benefit ratio of facilitated communication. *Mental Retardation, 32*(4), 300.

Levy, S. E., & Hyman, S. L. (2008). Complementary and alternative medicine treatments for children with autism spectrum disorders. *Child and Adolescent Psychiatric Clinics of North America, 17*(4), 803–820.

Levy, S. E., & Hyman, S. L. (2005). Novel treatments for autistic spectrum disorders. *Developmental Disabilities Research Reviews, 11*(2), 131–142.

Liao, S. T., Hwang, Y. S., Chen, Y. J., Lee, P., Chen, S. J., & Lin, L. Y. (2014). Home-based DIR/Floortime™ intervention program for preschool children with autism spectrum disorders: Preliminary findings. *Physical & Occupational Therapy in Pediatrics*, *34*(4), 356–367.

Lofthouse, N., Hendren, R., Hurt, E., Arnold, L. E., & Butter, E. (2012). A review of complementary and alternative treatments for autism spectrum disorders. *Autism Research and Treatment*. doi:10.1155/ 2012/870391

Lord, C., DiLavore, P. C., & Gotham, K. (2012). *Autism diagnostic observation schedule*. Torrance, CA: Western Psychological Services.

Mackay, C. S., & Institoris, H. (2009). *The hammer of witches: A complete translation of the Malleus Maleficarum*. Cambridge: Cambridge University Press.

Madsen, K. M., Hviid, A., Vestergaard, M., Schendel, D., Wohlfahrt, J., Thorsen, P. . . . & Melbye, M. (2002). A population-based study of measles, mumps, and rubella vaccination and autism. *New England Journal of Medicine*, *347*(19), 1477–1482.

Mandell, D. S., Novak, M. M., & Zubritsky, C. D. (2005). Factors associated with age of diagnosis among children with autism spectrum disorders. *Pediatrics*, *116*(6), 1480–1486.

Margolin, K. N. (1994). How shall facilitated communication be judged? Facilitated communication and the legal system. In H. C. Shane (ed.), *Facilitated communication: The clinical and social phenomenon* (pp. 227–258). San Diego, CA: Singular Press.

Marti, L. F. (2014). Dietary interventions in children with autism spectrum disorder: An updated review of the research evidence. *Current Clinical Pharmacology*, 9(4), 335–349.

Mash, E. J., & Hunsley, J. (2005). Evidence-based assessment of child and adolescent disorders: Issues and challenges. *Journal of Clinical Child and Adolescent Psychology*, *34*(3), 362–379.

Matson, J. L., & Shoemaker, M. (2009). Intellectual disability and its relationship to autism spectrum disorders. *Research in Developmental Disabilities*, *30* (6), 1107–1114.

Mayes, S. D., Calhoun, S. L., Mayes, R. D., & Molitoris, S. (2012). Autism and ADHD: Overlapping and discriminating symptoms. *Research in Autism Spectrum Disorders*, *6*(1), 277–285.

Metz, B., Mulick, J. A., & Butter, E. M. (2015). A twenty-first century fad magnet. In R. M. Foxx & J. A. Mulick (eds.), *Controversial therapies for autism and intellectual disabilities: Fad, fashion, and science in professional practice* (pp. 169–195). New York: Routledge.

Meyer-Lindenberg, A., Domes, G., Kirsch, P., & Heinrichs, M. (2011). Oxytocin and vasopressin in the human brain: Social neuropeptides for translational medicine. Nature reviews. *Neuroscience*, *12*(9), 524.

Mostert, M. P. (2001). Facilitated communication since 1995: A review of published studies. *Journal of Autism and Developmental Disorders*, *31*(3), 287–313.

Mousain-Bosc, M., Roche, M., Polge, A., Pradal-Prat, D., Rapin, J., & Bali, J. P. (2006). Improvement of neurobehavioral disorders in children supplemented with magnesium-vitamin B6. *Magnesium Research*, *19*(1), 53–62.

Mudford, O. C., Cross, B. A., Breen, S., Cullen, C., Reeves, D., Gould, J., & Douglas, J. (2000). Auditory integration training for children with autism: No behavioral benefits detected. *American Journal on Mental Retardation*, *105*(2), 118–129.

Mudford, O. C., & Cullen, C. (2015). Auditory integration training. In R. M. Foxx & J. A. Mulick (eds.), *Controversial therapies for autism and intellectual disabilities: Fad, fashion, and science in professional practice* (pp. 270–282). New York: Routledge.

Murch, S. H., Anthony, A., Casson, D. H., Malik, M., Berelowitz, M., Dhillon, A. P. ... & Walker-Smith, J. A. (2004). Retraction of an interpretation. *Lancet* (London, England), *363*(9411), 750.

Navidad, F., Tan, H. V., Talledo, P. R., Tampos, G. J., & Tan, A. M. (2013). Touch therapy and therapeutic listening: An approach to improve attention span and behaviors of people with autism. *International Proceedings of Economics Development and Research*, 60, 9.

Odom, S. L., Boyd, B. A., Hall, L. J., & Hume, K. (2010). Evaluation of comprehensive treatment models for individuals with autism spectrum disorders. *Journal of Autism and Developmental Disorders*, *40*(4), 425–436.

Omer, S. B., Salmon, D. A., Orenstein, W. A., Dehart, M. P., & Halsey, N. (2009). Vaccine refusal, mandatory immunization, and the risks of vaccine-preventable diseases. *New England Journal of Medicine*, *360*(19), 1981–1988.

Ozonoff, S., Goodlin-Jones, B. L., & Solomon, M. (2005). Evidence-based assessment of autism spectrum disorders in children and adolescents. *Journal of Clinical Child and Adolescent Psychology*, *34*(3), 523–540.

Ozonoff, S., Young, G. S., Carter, A., Messinger, D., Yirmiya, N., Zwaigenbaum, L. ... & Hutman, T. (2011). Recurrence risk for autism spectrum disorders: A Baby Siblings Research Consortium study. *Pediatrics*, 128(3), 488–495.

Peñagarikano, O., Lázaro, M. T., Lu, X. H., Gordon, A., Dong, H., Lam, H. A. ... & Golshani, P. (2015). Exogenous and evoked oxytocin restores social behavior in the Cntnap2 mouse model of autism. *Science Translational Medicine*, 7(271), 271ra8. http://doi.org/10.1126/scitranslmed.3010257

Peters-Scheffer, N., Didden, R., Korzilius, H., & Sturmey, P. (2011). A meta-analytic study on the effectiveness of comprehensive ABA-based early intervention programs for children with autism spectrum disorders. *Research in Autism Spectrum Disorders, 5*(1), 60–69.

Rao, T. S., & Andrade, C. (2011). The MMR vaccine and autism: Sensation, refutation, retraction, and fraud. *Indian Journal of Psychiatry, 53*(2), 95.

Reichow, B. (2012). Overview of meta-analyses on early intensive behavioral intervention for young children with autism spectrum disorders. *Journal of Autism and Developmental Disorders, 42*(4), 512–520.

Rimland, B. (1964). *Infantile autism: The syndrome and its implications for a neural theory of behavior.* East Norwalk, CT: Appleton-Century-Croft.

Rossignol, D. A. (2009). Novel and emerging treatments for autism spectrum disorders: A systematic review. *Annals of Clinical Psychiatry, 21*(4), 213–236.

Rossignol, D. A., & Rossignol, L. W. (2006). Hyperbaric oxygen therapy may improve symptoms in autistic children. *Medical Hypotheses, 67*(2), 216–228.

Rutter, M., Le Couteur, A., & Lord, C. (2003). Autism diagnostic interview-revised. Los Angeles, CA: Western Psychological Services, 29, 30.

Scheerenberger, R. C. (1983). *A history of mental retardation.* Baltimore, MD: Paul H. Brookes.

Scriver, C. R., & Clow, C. L. (1980). Phenylketonuria: Epitome of human biochemical genetics. *New England Journal of Medicine, 303*(23), 1336–1342.

Seung, H., Rogalski, Y., Shankar, M., & Elder, J. (2007). The gluten- and casein-free diet and autism: Communication outcomes from a preliminary double-blind clinical trial. *Journal of Medical Speech Language Pathology, 15*(4), 337.

Sliwinski, S., Croonenberghs, J., Christophe, A., Deboutte, D., & Maes, M. (2006). Polyunsaturated fatty acids: Do they have a role in the pathophysiology of autism? *Neuro Endocrinology Letters, 27*(4), 465–471.

Smith, T. (2005). *The appeal of unvalidated treatments.* In R. M. Foxx & J. A. Mulick (eds.), *Controversial therapies for autism and intellectual disabilities: Fad, fashion, and science in professional practice* (pp. 29–42). New York: Routledge.

Smith, T., Mruzck, D. W., & Mozingo, D. (2015). *Sensory integration therapy.* In R. M. Foxx & J. A. Mulick (eds.), *Controversial therapies for autism and intellectual disabilities: Fad, fashion, and science in professional practice* (pp. 247–269). New York: Routledge.

Solomon, A. H., & Chung, B. (2012). Understanding autism: How family therapists can support parents of children with autism spectrum disorders. *Family Process, 51*(2), 250–264.

Solomon, R., Necheles, J., Ferch, C., & Bruckman, D. (2007). Pilot study of a parent training program for young children with autism: The PLAY Project Home Consultation program. *Autism, 11*(3), 205–224.

Taylor, B., Miller, E., Lingam, R., Andrews, N., Simmons, A., & Stowe, J. (2002). Measles, mumps, and rubella vaccination and bowel problems or developmental regression in children with autism: Population study. *BMJ, 324* (7334), 393–396.

Taylor, L. E., Swerdfeger, A. L., & Eslick, G. D. (2014). Vaccines are not associated with autism: An evidence-based meta-analysis of case-control and cohort studies. *Vaccine, 32*(29), 3623–3629.

Tostanoski, A., Lang, R., Raulston, T., Carnett, A., & Davis, T. (2014). Voices from the past: Comparing the rapid prompting method and facilitated communication. *Developmental Neurorehabilitation, 17*(4), 219–223.

Travers, J. C., Tincani, M. J., & Lang, R. (2014). Facilitated communication denies people with disabilities their voice. *Research and Practice for Persons with Severe Disabilities, 39*(3), 195–202.

Travers, J. C., Tincani, M., Thompson, J. L., & Simpson, R. L. (2016). Picture exchange communication system and facilitated communication: Contrasting an evidence-based practice with a discredited method. In *Instructional practices with and without empirical validity* (pp. 85–110). Bingley, UK: Emerald Group Publishing Limited.

Vargas, D. L., Nascimbene, C., Krishnan, C., Zimmerman, A. W., & Pardo, C. A. (2005). Neuroglial activation and neuroinflammation in the brain of patients with autism. *Annals of Neurology, 57*(1), 67–81.

Vohra, S., Johnston, B. C., Cramer, K., & Humphreys, K. (2007). Adverse events associated with pediatric spinal manipulation: A systematic review. *Pediatrics, 119*(1), e275–e283.

Wesselmann, E. D., & Graziano, W. G. (2010) Sinful and/or possessed? Religious beliefs and mental illness stigma. *Journal of Social and Clinical Psychology, 29*(4), 402–437.

White, S. W., Oswald, D., Ollendick, T., & Scahill, L. (2009). Anxiety in children and adolescents with autism spectrum disorders. *Clinical Psychology Review, 29*(3), 216–229.

Williams, G. (1993). Chronic illness and the pursuit of virtue in everyday life. In A. Radley (ed.), *Worlds of illness: Biographical and cultural perspectives on health and disease* (pp. 92–108). London: Routledge.

Williams, K. E., & Foxx, R. M. (2015). *The gluten-free, casein-free diet.* In R. M. Foxx & J. A. Mulick (eds.), *Controversial therapies for autism and intellectual disabilities: Fad, fashion, and science in professional practice* (pp. 410–421). New York: Routledge.

Young, L. J., & Barrett, C. E. (2015). Can oxytocin treat autism? *Science, 347* (6224), 825–826.

Zane, T., Weiss, M. J., Dunlop, K., & Southwick, J. (2015). Relationship-based therapies for autism spectrum disorders. In R. M. Foxx & J. A. Mulick (eds.), *Controversial therapies for autism and intellectual disabilities: Fad, fashion, and science in professional practice* (pp. 357–371). New York: Routledge.

Zheng, H. F., Wang, W. Q., Li, X. M., Rauw, G., & Baker, G. B. (2017). Body fluid levels of neuroactive amino acids in autism spectrum disorders: A review of the literature. *Amino Acids, 49*(1), 57–65.

Zollweg, W., Palm, D., & Vance, V. (1997). The efficacy of auditory integration traininga double blind study. *American Journal of Audiology, 6*(3), 39–47.

4

Inattention and Hyperactivity

Christine A. Lee and Richard Milich

Attention-deficit/hyperactivity disorder (ADHD) is defined by age-inappropriate levels of inattention, such as difficulty focusing or remaining organized; hyperactivity, such as excessive fidgeting or leaving one's seat; and impulsivity, such as interrupting or blurting out answers (American Psychiatric Association [APA], 2013). Often thought of as a childhood disorder, age of onset must occur before age 12, though 36%–50% of children with ADHD in childhood continue to display symptoms in adulthood (Kessler et al., 2005; Lara et al., 2009). ADHD is associated with severe deficits in both social and academic domains and is frequently comorbid with other disorders, such as oppositional defiant disorder, substance use, and anxiety (Barkley, 2015). With a prevalence rate of 5% in childhood and 2.5% in adulthood (APA, 2013), ADHD is a clear public health concern.

In reviewing the treatment literature on ADHD, however, an interesting paradox is evident. On the one hand, evidence-based treatments have strong roots in the field of child psychopathology, including ADHD. Since the 1960s and 1970s, behavioral approaches, which place a strong emphasis on empirical validation, have been the dominant strategy for treating child behavior problems (Nietzel et al., 2003). Based on this work, there are now several well-validated and effective treatments for ADHD, including both psychosocial approaches and medication (Evans, Owens, & Bunford, 2014). Nevertheless, the field remains plagued by controversies and pseudoscience, where treatments are frequently proposed and implemented based on possible face validity but no empirical validation. These "scientifically questionable treatments" can be seductive, giving a façade of efficacy (Lilienfeld, 2005, p. 761). Further, the very existence of ADHD remains in dispute (Barkley et al., 2002). This chapter aims to correct myths and misconceptions concerning the treatment of ADHD. To do so, the chapter first addresses the issue of whether ADHD is actually a valid disorder.

4.1 Pseudoscience and Questionable Ideas

4.1.1 Criticism of ADHD as an Invalid Disorder

ADHD is arguably one of the most widely investigated disorders over the past 100 years (Barkley, 2015). Yet, despite such ubiquity, there is still ongoing debate about the diagnosis, assessment, and treatment of ADHD. Surprisingly, given the work in this area, many clinicians still question the legitimacy of ADHD. The belief that ADHD may not be a real disorder is so pervasive that Dr. Russell Barkley, one of the leading experts in the field, wrote a consensus statement, cosigned by more than 80 other respected investigators, arguing for the validity of the disorder (Barkley et al., 2002). So how is it that such a prevalent, widely investigated, and treated disorder could be judged as nonexistent? Several factors may account for this misunderstanding. One reason may be the many name and criteria changes for ADHD over the years. Changes in the *Diagnostic and Statistical Manual* (DSM) criteria have occurred every 10–15 years, with the focus switching from hyperkinesis (DSM-II; APA, 1968) to attention problems (DSM-III; APA, 1980) to hyperactivity/impulsivity (DSM-IV; APA, 1994). Similarly, the name of the disorder has changed from minimal brain dysfunction to hyperkinesis to attention-deficit disorder to the present ADHD. More recently, subtypes of the disorder (i.e., inattentive, hyperactive/impulsive, combined) have been added, further confusing the diagnosis (Milich, Balentine, & Lynam, 2001). With such frequent name and criteria changes, it is understandable that people may feel like the disorder is haphazard or fleeting. However, the core symptoms of the disorder have remained the same, regardless of surface name changes.

Another potential cause for criticism regarding ADHD is the belief that the purported increase in ADHD diagnoses over the past 20 years (Akinbami et al., 2011) is influenced by pharmaceutical companies "hawking" drugs or clinicians receiving kickbacks from these companies (Diller, 1998; Rosemond & Ravenel, 2008). However, a better explanation is that the general rise in knowledge about ADHD and an increasing public awareness over time have led to increased diagnoses. In addition, the fact that ADHD is now included as a handicapping condition for which the child is entitled to special school services probably contributes to increases in prevalence because parents often need a formal diagnosis to obtain these services (Hinshaw & Scheffler, 2014).

Further controversy may be due to the inclusion of the inattentive subtype under the ADHD umbrella, which by definition led to higher rates of diagnoses. Differentiating between these subtypes is important, since the inattentive subtype may not only have a completely separate presentation but results in different outcomes as well (Milich et al., 2001). However, a thorough meta-analysis found that such increases in ADHD prevalence were mainly attributable to methodological differences in studies rather than actual changes in prevalence (Polanczyk et al., 2014). Thus, despite changes in name and subtype differentiation, ADHD has been a stable disorder over time with increased diagnostic rates partially attributed to the public's growing awareness of the disorder.

Several clinicians have criticized the diagnosis of ADHD on the ground that it is pathologizing normal everyday behavior, especially among boys (Diller, 1998; Rosemond & Ravenel, 2008). Although at times the behavior of children may appear to be situationally normative and developmentally appropriate (e.g., on the playground), these children are often unable to modulate their behavior as the environmental demands change (e.g., in the classroom; Landau & Milich, 1988). Thus, though children with ADHD may display behavior common to all children at one time point, these behaviors may no longer be appropriate or acceptable for their current age group or in the current setting (e.g., recess vs. the classroom).

Finally, critics frequently point out how ADHD diagnoses rely on subjective measurements, such as parent and teacher rating scales or clinical interviews. Unlike many physical disorders, there is no objective measure, such as a blood test, to determine ADHD status. However, most psychological disorders lack such objective measures as well. Indeed, other disorders, such as depression and autism spectrum diagnoses, are also diagnosed largely through parent and/or teacher reports on rating scales. Yet, depression and autism spectrum disorders are more generally accepted psychological disorders than ADHD and do not seem to be subject to the same level of criticism.

Most importantly, what supports ADHD as a real disorder is the associated impairments these children experience in the major life domains. Children with ADHD commonly struggle socially, academically, and in their home life. They are rejected more often by peers than comparison children, even after an initial five-minute interaction (Diener & Milich, 1997), with such peer rejection persisting over time. Those with ADHD are more likely to have a lower GPA, fail more courses, be suspended more often from school, drop out of school, and not attend college. There is increased family conflict for those who have ADHD, and these patterns of conflict continue in romantic relationships as well

(Barkley, 2015). While previously it was thought that children would grow out of ADHD, it is now known that ADHD may persist into adulthood and that those with ADHD in adulthood continue to struggle in many of the same domains that they had difficulties with in childhood. For example, they are more likely to engage in substance use and develop other comorbid psychological disorders (Murphy & Barkley, 1996). Similarly, the driving of adults with ADHD is indistinguishable from that of adults without ADHD who are at a .08 blood alcohol content (BAC), which is considered the legal definition of drunk driving (Weafer et al., 2008). This clear, persisting pattern of impairment over multiple domains and across different developmental stages solidifies the legitimacy of ADHD as a disorder.

4.1.2 Dietary Interventions

One of the most prevalent, but least empirically supported, beliefs about ADHD is the idea that sugar and other dietary supplements can affect children's behavior and even cause their ADHD symptoms. In the 1970s, there was widespread concern that certain red dyes or lack of vitamins might contribute to ADHD difficulties (Feingold, 1975). Although a very small number of children may respond adversely to food dyes (Lilienfeld, 2005; Nigg et al., 2012), for the vast majority of children with ADHD, these concerns have never been substantiated (Barkley, 2015). However, similar concerns about sugar re-emerged in the 1990s and 2000s. There was, and continues to be, a widespread belief that sugar causes increased symptoms of hyperactivity. In fact, many parents of children without ADHD also believe and perpetuate this myth. Yet, multiple investigations (Hoover & Milich, 1994; Milich, Wolraich, & Lindgren, 1986; Wolraich et al., 1994) and a meta-analysis (Wolraich, Wilson, & White, 1995) have found that there is no impact of sugar on behavior and that a sugar-reduced diet will not improve the behavior of children with ADHD.

Why does this myth persist? There are alternative explanations for why children appear to be more excitable in the presence of sugar. For example, sugar is often ingested during special events, such as birthday parties, that can themselves be exciting due to their novelty and stimulation (Milich et al., 1986). Moreover, these types of events can have multiple transitions, which can be triggers to disinhibit for children with ADHD. Parents of those with ADHD may have expectations that their children will become more hyperactive, leading to a self-fulfilling prophecy. Mothers who believed that sugar affected their children's behavior were asked to rate their children's behavior after being told their children ingested sugar (Hoover & Milich, 1994). Despite the fact that their children had not actually ingested any sugar, mothers still rated their children as more hyperactive and disruptive. Further, when diet replacement studies focusing on the effects of aspartame or a placebo compared to sugar were run, no differences in behavior were found among substances (Wolraich et al., 1994). Therefore, it may be the expectation of hyperactive behavior that reinforces this myth rather than actual behavior change. Confounding factors, such as environmental change and expectancies, may lead to incorrect causal interpretations of the effects of sugar on hyperactivity.

4.1.3 Brain Training

There has been a long history in ADHD of trying to repair the brain deficits found for the disorder through intensive training. As of late, several, theory-driven interventions have attempted to directly address the potential brain deficits among those with ADHD (e.g., underdeveloped brain structures, smaller brains, smaller frontal lobes; Cubillo et al., 2012; Seidman, Valera, & Makris, 2005). These interventions focus on "brain training," or having children perform repeated cognitive tasks with the idea that such repetition will improve their purported brain functioning in areas that are underdeveloped. Children complete exercises focused on specific skills, such as working memory, over and over and receive positive feedback for good performance. Exercises include focusing on a specific target item despite similar distractor items to improve processing speed, determining if a word's meaning and color match to focus on flexibility, and recreating a pattern after viewing it for a short period of time to advance memory. These types of interventions are argued to be effective due to the brain's plasticity, or ability to change throughout one's lifetime. By intensely focusing on areas of deficits, brain training is proposed to maximize the brain's plasticity and strengthen performance (Rapport et al., 2013; Simons et al., 2016).

Brain training is already being aggressively marketed. Promises of lower health costs, better memory, and improved ADHD symptoms are plastered over many of these companies' websites. Such campaigns appear to be successful; it is estimated that $3.38 billion will be spent by 2020 on brain training, with $715 million spent in 2013 alone (Yong, 2016). In fact, the producers of one such program have already been fined $2 million by the Federal Trade Commission for making claims that were not scientifically supported (Federal Trade Commission, 2016). It's easy to understand why brain training may be so popular. The reasoning underlying the intervention has face validity and intuitively makes sense. The adage "practice makes perfect" is applicable in many other domains, such as sports, and children do improve on the specific computer tasks they complete during this training. The activities are fun and engaging and, unlike medication, there are no side effects. Moreover, neuroscientists often endorse brain-training companies, lending an air of authority to this work. In fact, two competing "consensus" statements by scientists have been generated, one legitimizing the effects of brain training and one arguing against the validity of this training (Cognitive training data response letter, 2014; Max Planck Institute for Human Development & Stanford Center on Longevity, 2014). However, a deeper investigation into the empirical support for this type of treatment uncovers large gaps in its potential validity.

Four major reviews about brain training have been published, three of which deal directly with children (Evans et al., 2014; Rapport et al., 2013; Shipstead, Redick, & Engle, 2012; Simons et al., 2016). All of these studies focus on the major problems with this type of research as it is currently implemented. The biggest gap in the research is the lack of double-blind randomized control trials (RCTs), which are the gold standard for treatment research. In such trials, both the subjects and experimenters are unaware of which condition each subject is in so as to avoid expectancy effects. Moreover, subjects are assigned to groups randomly to ensure that no other confounds account for treatment effects (e.g., if those who call first are placed in the treatment group, effects may be due to conscientiousness rather than treatment mechanisms). Since RCTs have such rigorous standards and control for so many variables, treatments that are found to be effective under these conditions have a more solid base of efficacy. However, not only have there been no RCTs evaluating the validity of brain training for children with ADHD, but also very few of the studies overall met criteria for a rigorous, unbiased study. In fact, the only study that was suggested to meet standards for appropriate research did not even focus on children with ADHD but rather on older adults (Ball et al., 2002). This extensive study cost millions of dollars and took ten years to run among six sites, clearly not easily replicable or even feasible to run with children with ADHD. Even with such extensive resources, the results did not find meaningful improvement in real-world outcomes. Furthermore, the mechanisms between preventing skill loss in older adults and facilitating skill gain in children may be quite different, thus making generalization of results from one population to the other difficult. The lack of appropriate and valid research on brain training, particularly for children with ADHD, precludes drawing conclusions about its effectiveness.

One major flaw of previous brain training research is the lack of an appropriate comparison group. Without comparison to an active control group, it cannot be concluded that brain training is superior to other treatments, or even more than a placebo effect. Most research on brain training used a waitlist, or passive, control group. By using a waitlist control group, raters of outcomes (i.e., parents, teachers) are not blinded to the study. Thus, expectancy effects regarding treatment may lead to confounding results. Indeed, since training is usually completed at home, parents, who were aware of which condition their children were in, more often reported improvement after treatment compared to teachers, who were more likely to be blind to treatment conditions (Rapport et al., 2015). A general finding in this field is that the more blinded the raters were, the less likely is the reporting of significant effects. Lack of teacher-reported improvement is especially concerning, given that academic improvement is arguably the most relevant outcome for these types of training. Without adhering to basic research practices, conclusions about brain training are severely limited.

Moreover, and perhaps most importantly, the improvements from brain training do not generalize to real-world applications (Rapport et al., 2013). Those who complete brain training may demonstrate "near transfer" of abilities, or improvement in tasks that are very similar to what they have been trained on, but not "far transfer," or improvement on unrelated tasks. Thus, they may become quicker at the specific working memory task on the computer but not remember to bring completed homework to class each day. This lack of generalization is a major limitation since ideally these abilities would apply to the classroom, such as staying on task and acting less impulsively. This lack of effects is especially salient given the lack of teacher-reported effects and, in addition, that better constructed studies are less likely to find effects. Perhaps this is due to the stark differences between brain-training tasks and real-world situations. Whereas brain training is done in isolation and is focused on one specific area, real-world tasks are present with many different stimuli and people and often require a composite of abilities. For example, improving visual tracking does not automatically equal better accuracy in hitting baseballs. It would make more sense to practice hitting baseballs if that is the area one wishes to improve. Therefore, though children may improve in the specific brain-training tasks, such as repeating back numbers, these skills have not been found to generalize to everyday classroom performance, where improvement is actually needed.

Some treatment providers for ADHD claim the root cause of ADHD is diminished right-hemisphere brain function, which is fixed by their "sensory-motor" exercises. Unfortunately, this account of ADHD is a gross oversimplification. No honest expert knows what the correct or equal balance between the brain hemispheres ought to be, especially since the relative involvement of each hemisphere will vary according to task demands. While it is true that many studies point to abnormal lateralization of function in ADHD – that is, unusual activation of one hemisphere or the other, compared with controls – findings in this area are incredibly messy, and there is certainly no consensus that these activation patterns represent the root cause of the condition.

For instance, while there is some evidence for reduced right-hemisphere function in people with ADHD compared to controls, other studies have actually documented enhanced right-hemisphere function (Hale et al., 2005). Another study found enhanced transfer of information across the hemispheres in teens with ADHD, contradicting the central "brain balancing" idea that ADHD is caused by disconnection between the hemispheres (Brown & Vickers, 2004).

Despite claims of groundbreaking research to support the brain balancing approach, only one published pilot study (Leisman, Mualem, & Machado, 2013) supports the use of brain balancing exercises for the treatment of ADHD, and it lacked any control group (Leisman et al., 2010). Curiously, what appear to be the exact same participants and data return in a second paper presented as new research three years later, now with a control group bolted on. There was obviously no randomization to this control group and they engaged in no comparison treatment. What's more, the children who completed the brain balancing exercises and the controls were all taking stimulant medication during the study. In short, there are no well-done studies to show that brain balancing improves attention.

Christian Jarrett, PhD, is the editor of the Research Digest blog and author of several books about psychology including *Great Myths of the Brain* (2015).

4.1.4 Medication Used Alone

Many believe that medication alone is sufficient for treating the symptoms and related impairment of those with ADHD (MTA Cooperative Group, 1999). Though medication has clear benefits for treating ADHD, it is limited because it does not teach skills. Medication's primary benefit is reducing the severity of symptoms, which then reduces the frequency of disruptive behavior (e.g., can stay on task longer, fewer interruptions; Smith & Shapiro, 2015). However, medication is not effective for everyone. Rather, medication is effective for 66%–82% of children treated, leaving 18%–34% of children unreached (Smith, Barkley, & Shapiro, 2006; Smith & Shapiro, 2015). Moreover, stimulant medication can be associated with side effects, such as reduced appetite and stunted growth (Swanson et al., 2008). Parents are also hesitant to medicate their children, especially younger children. Lastly, medication is only effective for as long as the children are taking it; there are no long-term effects of medication over time in the various realms of impairment (Smith & Shapiro, 2015). Though many general practitioners and pediatricians are satisfied with prescribing medication only, this may be because there are limited options that medical doctors can provide. However, parents show greater satisfaction with more hands-on behavioral treatments than medication alone (MTA Cooperative Group, 1999).

A major drawback of medication, even when it improves symptomatic behavior, is that it does not substitute for skill training (Smith & Shapiro, 2015). Though a child with ADHD may be able to focus better with stimulant medication, the child will not suddenly obtain social or academic skills. For example, when children were medicated and then participated in a baseball game, their attention to the game did improve over placebo (26% vs. 61%), but they did not improve in their game skills (Pelham et al., 1990). Similarly, when asked to recall a story narrative, children with ADHD on medication increased the length of their recalls relative to their performance on placebo, but the quality (e.g., including important events or causal relationships) of recalls did not differ between conditions (Bailey et al., 2011; Derefinko et al., 2009). Finally, recent work suggests that medication alone was less effective compared to behavior therapy or the combination of both (Pelham et al., 2016). In particular, the sequencing of treatment was important: implementing medication before behavior therapy led to fewer gains than implementing behavior therapy first.

4.2 Research-Supported Approaches

Although medication can improve the behavior of children with ADHD, other interventions targeting skill building are still needed. This is why a combined treatment of medication and behavioral therapy often is the most effective treatment for children with ADHD (Majewicz-Hefley & Carlson, 2007). First, not only does the combined treatment produce the best outcome (Conners et al., 2001), but it is also the one with which parents are most satisfied (MTA Cooperative Group, 1999). Second, medication and skills training can complement each other, in that medication is relatively fast acting and may be needed to first attenuate symptom severity so that children can then focus and persist enough to learn new skills. Third, evidence indicates that when a behavior system is in place, a lower dose of medication may be sufficient (Fabiano et al., 2007). Thus, though medication can still be considered a frontline treatment for ADHD, it is only a part of an effective treatment strategy that must also be supplemented by behavior therapy and skills training.

Many children with ADHD experience significance improvement from behavior therapy without even needing medication (Pelham et al., 2016). Behavior therapy primarily focuses on parent management training, or teaching parents how to set up a contingency system of rewards and punishments. Parents also learn how to implement effective, consistent discipline so children know what to expect. Teachers may use a similar system at school, tracking children's target behaviors with a Daily Report Card with children earning home rewards based on their behavior during the school day (Evans et al., 2014).

4.3 Conclusion

Several well-known and widely marketed treatments claim to have empirical support. However, several significant methodological problems characterize these studies that preclude allowing them to be identified as efficacious. One of the most important aspects of treatment research is an active comparison group (Rapport et al., 2013). With treatment, a placebo effect exists, whereby merely the act of being in treatment may produce a beneficial effect (Foroughi et al., 2016). For example, parents may feel more confident that they are ostensibly taking action toward helping their child, which could translate into more effective parenting. Therefore, the use of an active control group, or one where children in the control group receive some form of attention and believable treatment (i.e., attention placebo), is necessary to show that a specific treatment is more helpful than simply allowing time to pass (e.g., a waitlist control group). By keeping the only differences between groups the targeted treatment itself, if improvements are found, these effects can be more confidently attributed to the studied treatment, since all other conditions will have been kept constant.

Another key aspect of treatment research is blinded raters, or raters who do not know who is receiving treatment or which type of treatment is being given. Because many of the outcomes of child treatment studies involve parent or teacher rating scales, it is crucial that raters are blind to avoid expectancy effects; those who know which children are receiving treatment may, consciously or unconsciously, rate the child as improved since that is what people assume would occur after treatment. One way around this potential problem is to employ dependent variables that may not be so subject to demand characteristics or expectancy effects. Such measures could include schoolwork samples, behavioral observations, or ratings from individuals not involved in the treatment.

Moreover, replication of results is important to show that results of a single study were not due to statistical error or chance. Rather, if effects can be shown repeatedly, a better foundation is built for treatment efficacy.

In conclusion, even though medication and behavior therapy have a strong and comprehensive research base, it must still be acknowledged that no one treatment is effective for all children. Second, it is also true that the more a treatment approximates the real world, the greater chance the treatment will generalize. Third, therapies that are not evidence based may not only be ineffective but can also cause harm as well (Lilienfeld, 2007).

Works Cited in Sidebar

Brown, L. N., & Vickers, J. N. (2004). Temporal judgments, hemispheric equivalence, and interhemispheric transfer in adolescents with attention deficit hyperactivity disorder. *Experimental Brain Research, 154*(1), 76–84.

Hale, T. S., McCracken, J. T., McGough, J. J., Smalley, S. L., Phillips, J. M., & Zaidel, E. (2005). Impaired linguistic processing and atypical brain laterality in adults with ADHD. *Clinical Neuroscience Research, 5*(5–6), 255–263.

Leisman, G., Melillo, R., Thum, S., Ransom, M. A., Orlando, M., Tice, C., & Carrick, F. R. (2010). The effect of hemisphere specific remediation strategies on the academic performance outcome of children with ADD/ADHD. *International Journal of Adolescent Medicine and Health, 22*(2), 275–284.

Leisman, G., Mualem, R. Z., & Machado, C. (2013). The integration of the neurosciences, child public health, and education practice: Hemisphere-specific remediation strategies as a discipline partnered rehabilitation tool in ADD/ADHD. *Frontiers in Public Health*, *1*, 22.

References

Akinbami, L. J., Liu, X., Pastor, P. N., & Reuben, C. (2011). Attention deficit hyperactivity disorder among children aged 5–17 years in the United States, 1998–2009 (NCHS Data Brief No. 70). Retrieved from http://files.eric.ed.gov/fulltext/ED524624.pdf

American Psychiatric Association (APA). (1968). *Diagnostic and statistical manual of mental disorders*. 2nd ed. Washington, DC: Author.

American Psychiatric Association. (1980). *Diagnostic and statistical manual of mental disorders*. 3rd ed. Washington, DC: Author.

American Psychiatric Association. (1994). *Diagnostic and statistical manual of mental disorders*, 4th ed. Washington, DC: Author.

American Psychiatric Association. (2013). *Diagnostic and statistical manual of mental disorders*. 5th ed. Washington, DC: Author.

American Psychological Association (2002). Criteria for evaluating treatment guidelines. *American Psychologist*, *57*, 1052–1059.

Bailey, U. L., Derefinko, K. J., Milich, R., Lorch, E. P., & Metze, A. (2011). The effects of stimulant medication on free recall of story events among children with ADHD. *Journal of Psychopathology and Behavioral Assessment*, *33*, 409–419.

Ball, K., Berch, D. B., Helmers, K. F., Jobe, J. B., Leveck, M. D., Marsiske, M. . . . & Willis, S. L. (2002). Effects of cognitive training interventions with older adults: A randomized controlled trial. *Journal of the American Medical Association*, *288*, 2271–2281.

Barkley, R. A., Cook, E. H., Jr., Diamond, A., Zametkin, A., Thapar, A., Teeter, A. . . . & Pelham, W., Jr. (2002). International consensus statement on ADHD. *Clinical Child and Family Psychology Review*, *5*, 89–111.

Barkley, R. A. (ed.). (2015). *Attention-deficit hyperactivity disorder: A handbook for diagnosis and treatment*. 4th edn. New York: Guilford.

Cognitive training data response letter. (2014). Retrieved from www.cognitivetrainingdata.org/the-controversy-does-brain-training-work/response-letter/

Conners, C. K., Epstein, J. N., March, J. S., Angold, A., Wells, K. C., Klaric, J. . . . Wigal, T. (2001). Multimodal treatment of ADHD in the MTA: An alternative outcome analysis. *Journal of the American Academy of Child & Adolescent Psychiatry*, *40*, 159–167.

Cubillo, A., Halari, R., Smith, A., Taylor, E., & Rubia, K. (2012). A review of the fronto-striatal and fronto-cortical brain abnormalities in children and adults with attention deficit hyperactivity disorder (ADHD) and new evidence for dysfunction in adults with ADHD during motivation and attention. *Cortex, 48,* 194–215.

Derefinko, K. J., Bailey, U. L., Milich, R., Lorch, E. P., & Riley, E. (2009). The effects of stimulant medication on the online story narrations of children with ADHD. *School Mental Health, 1,* 171–182.

Diener, M. B. & Milich, R. (1997). Effects of positive feedback on the social interactions of boys with attention deficit hyperactivity disorder: A test of the self-protective hypothesis. *Journal of Clinical Child Psychology, 26,* 256–265.

Diller, L. H. (1998). *Running on Ritalin: A physician reflects on children, society, and performance in a pill.* New York: Bantam Books.

Evans, S. W., Owens, J. S., & Bunford, N. (2014). Evidence-based psychosocial treatments for children and adolescents with attention-deficit/hyperactivity disorder. *Journal of Clinical Child & Adolescent Psychology, 43,* 527–551.

Fabiano, G. A., Pelham, W. E., Jr., Gnagy, E. M., Burrows-MacLean, L., Coles, E. K., Chacko, A. … & Robb, J. A. (2007). The single and combined effects of multiple intensities of behavior modification and methylphenidate for children with attention deficit hyperactivity disorder in a classroom setting. *School Psychology Review, 36,* 195–216.

Federal Trade Commission. (2016). Lumosity to pay $2 million to settle FTC deceptive advertising charges for its "brain training" program [Press Release]. Retrieved from www.ftc.gov/news-events/press-releases/2016/01/lumosity-pay-2-million-settle-ftc-deceptive-advertising-charges

Feingold, B. F. (1975). Hyperkinesis and learning disabilities linked to artificial food flavors and colors. *American Journal of Nursing, 75,* 797–803.

Foroughi, C. K., Monfort, S. S., Paczynski, M., McKnight, P. E., & Greenwood, P. M. (2016). Placebo effects in cognitive training. *Proceedings of the National Academy of Sciences, 113,* 7470–7474.

Hinshaw, S. P., & Scheffler, R. M. (2014). *The ADHD explosion.* New York: Oxford University Press.

Hoover, D. W., & Milich, R. (1994). Effects of sugar ingestion expectancies on mother-child interactions. *Journal of Abnormal Child Psychology, 22,* 501–515.

Kessler, R. C., Adler, L. A., Barkley, R., Biederman, J., Conners, C. K., Faraone, S. V. … & Zaslavsky, A. M. (2005). Patterns and predictors of ADHD persistence into adulthood: Results from the National Comorbidity Survey Replication. *Biological Psychiatry, 57,* 1442–1451.

Landau, S., & Milich, R. (1988). Social communication patterns of attention-deficit-disordered boys. *Journal of Abnormal Child Psychology, 16,* 69–81.

Lara, C., Fayyad, J., de Graaf, R., Kessler, R. C., Aguilar-Gaxiola, S., Angermeyer, M. ... & Sampson, N. (2009). Childhood predictors of adult ADHD: Results from the WHO World Mental Health (WMH) survey initiative. *Biological Psychiatry*, *65*, 46–54.

Lilienfeld, S. O. (2005). Scientifically unsupported and supported interventions for childhood psychopathology: A summary. *Pediatrics*, *115*, 761–764.

Lilienfeld, S. O. (2007). Psychological treatments that cause harm. *Perspectives on Psychological Science*, *2*, 53–70.

Majewicz-Hefley, A., & Carlson, J. S. (2007). A meta-analysis of combined treatments for children diagnosed with ADHD. *Journal of Attention Disorders*, *10*, 239–250.

Max Planck Institute for Human Development & Stanford Center on Longevity. (2014). A consensus on the brain training industry from the scientific community [Press Release]. Retrieved from http://longevity3.stanford.edu/blog/2014/10/15/the- consensus-on-the-brain-training-industry-from-the-scientific-community-2/

Milich, R., Balentine, A. C., & Lynam, D. R. (2001). ADHD combined type and ADHD predominantly inattentive type are distinct and unrelated disorders. *Clinical Psychology: Science and Practice*, *8*, 463–488.

Milich, R., Wolraich, M., & Lindgren, S. (1986). Sugar and hyperactivity: A critical review of empirical findings. *Clinical Psychology Review*, *6*, 493–513.

MTA Cooperative Group (1999). A 14-month randomized clinical trial of treatment strategies for attention-deficit/hyperactivity disorder. *Archives of General Psychiatry*, *56*, 1073–1086.

Murphy, K., & Barkley, R. A. (1996). Attention deficit hyperactivity disorder adults: Comorbidities and adaptive impairments. *Comprehensive Psychiatry*, *37*, 393–401.

Nietzel, M. T., Bernstein, D. A., Kramer, G. P., & Milich, R. (2003). *Introduction to clinical psychology*. 6th ed. Upper Saddle River, NJ: Prentice-Hall.

Nigg, J. T., Lewis, K., Edinger, T., & Falk, M. (2012). Meta-analysis of attention-deficit/hyperactivity disorder or attention-deficit/hyperactivity disorder symptoms, restriction diet, and synthetic food color additives. *Journal of the American Academy of Child & Adolescent Psychiatry*, *51*, 86–97.

Pelham, W. E., Jr., Fabiano, G. A., Waxmonsky, J. G., Greiner, A. R., Gnagy, E. M., Pelham, W. E., III ... & Murphy, S. A. (2016). Treatment sequencing for childhood ADHD: A multiple-randomization study of adaptive medication and behavioral interventions. *Journal of Clinical Child & Adolescent Psychology*, *45*, 396–415.

Pelham, W. E., Jr., McBurnett, K., Harper, G. W., Milich, R. M., Murphy, D. A., Clinton, J., & Thiele, C. (1990). Methylphenidate and baseball playing in

ADHD children: Who's on first? *Journal of Consulting and Clinical Psychology*, *58*, 130–133.

Polanczyk, G. V., Willcutt, E. G., Salum, G. A., Kieling, C., Rohde, L. A. (2014). ADHD prevalence estimates across three decades: An updated systematic review and meta-regression analysis. *International Journal of Epidemiology*, *43*, 434–442.

Rapport, M. D., Orban, S. A., Kofler, M. J., & Friedman, L. M. (2013). Do programs designed to train working memory, other executive functions, and attention benefit children with ADHD? A meta-analytic review of cognitive, academic, and behavioral outcomes. *Clinical Psychology Review*, *33*, 1237–1252.

Rapport, M. D., Orban, S. A., Kofler, M. J., Friedman, L. M., & Bolden, J. (2015). Executive function training for children with ADHD. In R. A. Barkley (ed.), *Attention-deficit hyperactivity disorder: A handbook for diagnosis and treatment*. 4th edn, pp. 641–665. New York: Guilford.

Rosemond, J., & Ravenel, B. (2008). *The diseasing of America's children: Exposing the ADHD fiasco and empowering parents to take back control.* Nashville, TN: Thomas Nelson.

Seidman, L. J., Valera, E. M., & Makris, N. (2005). Structural brain imaging of attention- deficit/hyperactivity disorder. *Biological Psychiatry*, *57*, 1263–1272.

Shipstead, Z., Redick, T. S., & Engle, R. W. (2012). Is working memory training effective? *Psychological Bulletin*, *138*, 628–654.

Simons, D. J., Boot, W. R., Charness, N., Gathercole, S. E., Chabris, C. F., Hambrick, D. Z., & Stine-Morrow, E. A. (2016). Do "brain-training" programs work? *Psychological Science in the Public Interest*, *17*, 103–186.

Smith, B. H., Barkley, R. A., & Shapiro, C. J. (2006). Attention-deficit/hyperactivity disorder. In E. J. Mash & R. A. Barkley (eds.), *Treatment of childhood disorders*. 3rd edn, pp. 65–136. New York: Guilford.

Smith, B. H., & Shapiro, C. J. (2015). Combined treatments for ADHD. In R. A. Barkley (ed.), *Attention-deficit hyperactivity disorder: A handbook for diagnosis and treatment*. 4th edn, pp. 686–704. New York: Guilford.

Swanson, J., Arnold, L. E., Kraemer, H., Hechtman, L., Molina, B., Hinshaw, S. … & MTA Cooperative Group (2008). Evidence, interpretation, and qualification from multiple reports of long-term outcomes in the Multimodal Treatment Study of Children with ADHD (MTA): Part I: Executive summary. *Journal of Attention Disorders*, *12*, 4–14.

Waschbusch, D. A., & Hill, G. P. (2004). Empirically supported, promising, and unsupported treatments for children with attention-deficit/hyperactivity disorder. In S. O. Lilienfeld, S. J. Lynn, & J. M. Lohr (eds.), *Science and pseudoscience in clinical psychology*. 1st edn, pp. 333–362. New York: Guilford.

Weafer, J., Camarillo, D., Fillmore, M. T., Milich, R., & Marczinski, C. A. (2008). Simulated driving performance of adults with ADHD: Comparison with alcohol intoxication. *Experimental and Clinical Psychopharmacology, 16,* 251–263.

Wolraich, M. L., Lindgren, S. D., Stumbo, P. J., Stegink, L. D., Appelbaum, M. I., & Kiritsy, M. C. (1994). Effects of diet high in sucrose or aspartame on the behavior and cognitive performance of children. *The New England Journal of Medicine, 330,* 301–306.

Wolraich, M. L., Wilson, D. B., & White, J. W. (1995). The effect of sugar on behavior or cognition in children: A meta-analysis. *Journal of the American Medical Association, 274,* 1617–1621.

Yong, E. (2016, October). The weak evidence behind brain-training games. *The Atlantic.* Retrieved from www.theatlantic.com/science/archive/2016/10/the-weak- evidence-behind-brain-training-games/502559/

5

Learning

Zachary LaBrot and Brad Dufrene

Learning is the process of changing cognitions and behaviors due to exposure to various experiences (Chance, 2009). A student learns to read by exposure to reading instruction; a musician learns to play an instrument through instruction and repeated practice; and a toddler learns to avoid touching a hot stove after touching the stove. Unfortunately, in spite of exposure to experiences that generally promote learning (e.g., opportunities to read, write, and complete math problems), some individuals have difficulties learning particular skills. The American Psychiatric Association (2013) describes specific learning disorder (SLD) as a neurodevelopmental disorder that causes cognitive deficits for learning and significantly impairs academic or occupational performance. Individuals with SLD have specific impairment in reading (accuracy, fluency, or comprehension), written expression (spelling, grammar, or organization), or mathematics (number sense, arithmetic, calculation, or math reasoning). SLD manifests during school-age years and is not attributable to intellectual disabilities, insufficient vision, poor academic or educational instruction, neurological disorders, or other underlying psychopathologies (American Psychiatric Association, 2013). Although empirically supported approaches have been developed for improving academic outcomes in individuals with learning difficulties (e.g., Fuchs et al., 2008; Roberts et al., 2008), some theories and strategies that have little to no empirical support have been widely disseminated and adopted by education professionals.

The field of neuroscience has advanced tremendously and enhanced the medical and psychological understandings of how the brain develops and functions. Naturally, researchers have attempted to utilize neurological findings and apply them to improve outcomes for struggling learners. While the use of neurological findings to enhance learning makes intuitive sense, limited empirical evidence demonstrates that promoting behaviors that purportedly alter neurological functioning leads to improved learning outcomes (Goswami, 2006). In spite of this, a number of neurologically based strategies to improve learning have been developed, disseminated, and marketed using findings from neuroscience as the theoretical underpinnings of their alleged effectiveness. These leaps of faith from the basic neuroscience literature to the applied instruction literature have been termed "neuromythologies" (Geake, 2008) and are appealing because they offer brief, simple, and inexpensive strategies for improving learning outcomes. The remainder of this chapter discusses four prominent neuromythologies and their derivatives as they pertain to learning and concludes with a brief discussion of evidence-based approaches to improving academic outcomes for struggling learners.

5.1 Pseudoscience and Questionable Ideas

5.1.1 Left-brain vs. Right-brain Learners

For decades, a pervasive misinterpretation of neuroscientific research regarding roles and functions of the left and right hemispheres of the brain has led to the belief that some learners are "left-brained" while others are "right-brained." Proponents of this belief postulate that left-brain learners are analytical while right-brain learners are creative and holistic (Mercer, 2016). The roots of this belief derive from surgeries conducted in the 1940s in which patients' corpus callosum (i.e., the tract between the two brain hemispheres) was cut to prevent severe cases of epilepsy. After the corpus callosum had been severed, doctors and researchers noticed the unconnected hemispheres of the brain could process different types of information separately (Geake, 2008). For example, information from one eye usually is processed in both sides of the brain; but after split-brain surgery, only one side of the brain processed the visual input (Mercer, 2016). This brain hemisphere isolation allowed researchers to observe specialties and tasks the left and right hemispheres could perform.

However, brain imaging studies examining the roles of the left and right hemispheres of the brain consistently demonstrate both hemispheres work in coordination, as opposed to working in isolation (Geake, 2008; Mercer, 2016). In fact, researchers in music cognition assert music is not exclusively processed in the right hemisphere. Both left and right hemispheres cooperatively process music, and both develop with continued exposure to musical experience (Geake, 2008). As such, the conceptualization of brain functioning should be based on coordination, as opposed to modularization, between the left and right hemispheres. While individuals may have personal preferences for certain tasks and types of learning, there is limited evidence to suggest this is the result of dominance of specialized abilities that are attributable to the left or right hemisphere of the brain.

> **Sidebar Box: Should children be taught based on their preferred learning style? by Indre Viskontas**
>
> Every first-time parent is surprised at how quickly their child's character appears: whether they're spirited or compliant, shy or outgoing, every child is unique. And the emphasis on developmental milestones online and in the pediatrician's office has parents and teachers mentally checking boxes every month and comparing their children's behavior and abilities with those of peers. Well-meaning parents and teachers often reinforce activities in which the child shows precociousness while limiting time in tasks that expose weaknesses – exactly the opposite of what is needed. Research has shown that conditions that make learning seem more difficult are actually more effective for long-term retention (Bjork, 1994). For example, spending an hour a day over the course of several weeks reviewing material for an exam is a better way of ensuring that you'll remember it a year later than waiting until the night before and cramming for eight hours. Distributing practice (instead of massing practice) is just one "desirable difficulty" that slows down the rate of learning in the short term but provides long-term benefits. Even though it *feels* harder, distributive practice ultimately leads to better learning outcomes, if the goal is to retain information for the long term. What's more, when tasks feel easy, we intuitively believe that we are learning. But while we make large gains in learning a new skill at first, with repeated practice, we experience diminishing returns (Heathcote, Brown, & Mewhort, 2000). Once it feels easy, we've stopped learning. By the same token, teaching students using a variety of styles is much more effective than sticking to one mode of instruction. Students might differ in their preferences, or in what feels easy to them, but the evidence shows that teaching students only in their preferred learning style is not effective (Pashler et al., 2008). Different material might benefit from different modalities, but

students should be exposed to a diverse array of teaching styles, and those that feel most difficult might end up yielding the best results.

Indre Viskontas, PhD, is a cognitive neuroscientist and co-host of the Inquiring Minds podcast. She also co-hosted the *Miracle Detectives* television show.

5.1.2 Educational Kinesiology

Educational kinesiology (also termed perceptual motor programs) is the practice of enhancing learning by having individuals engage in a series of various fine and gross motor movements to integrate visual, auditory, and kinesthetic sensory input to facilitate whole-brain learning (Hyatt, Stephenson, & Carter, 2009; Spaulding, Mostert, & Beam, 2010). Educational kinesiology is based on the assertion that neurological-processing deficits interfere with perceptual and motor functioning and consequently inhibit academic learning. Essentially, educational kinesiology posits simple motor exercises can alter the brain's neural structure and promote learning. Programs such as the Domain-Delacato Patterning Program; the Dore Achievement Center's Individualized Dyslexia, Dyspraxia, and Attention Treatment (DDAT); and the Primary Movement Programme have based their approaches on this premise so as to ameliorate neurological-processing deficits and improve learning (Hyatt et al., 2009).

Notably, Brain Gym® International (BGI; Dennison & Dennison, 1994) is an educational kinesiology program that has been heavily marketed and has gained a great deal of acceptance among educators and education consultants. Anecdotes of its effectiveness, the promise of learning anything quickly and simply, and its theoretical foundations originating from neuroscience are persuasive and make BGI an appealing approach to resolving learning difficulties. However, BGI's mechanism of action and its relative effectiveness become questionable when the three main theoretical foundations that comprise BGI are more closely examined.

BGI is based on the theories of neurological re-patterning, mixed cerebral dominance, and perceptual-motor training (Hyatt, 2007). Neurological re-patterning posits that an individual must acquire specific motor skills throughout development to achieve proper neurological functioning, and a series of various motor movements can form undeveloped neural pathways from early stages of neurological development. Mixed cerebral dominance assumes reading difficulties are attributable to one hemisphere of the brain being more dominant than the other, and left- and right-brain functions can be assimilated through a combination of tactile learning strategies that include visual and auditory components (e.g., saying sounds of letters while tracing the letters in the air). Finally, perceptual-motor training involves engaging in activities (e.g., crawling, walking on a balance beam) that are designed to remedy inefficient integration of perceptual-motor skills that inhibit learning (Hyatt, 2007; Spaulding et al., 2010). While an exhaustive discussion of each of the theoretical foundations of BGI is beyond the scope of this chapter, it should be noted that each of these theories has little to no empirical support that validates its effectiveness for remediating learning difficulties (Hyatt, 2007; Spaulding et al., 2010). Regardless of its questionable theoretical underpinnings, some researchers have reported BGI is an effective approach for improving learning (e.g., Camissa, 1994; de los Santos, Hume, & Cortes, 2002; Khalsa, Morris, & Sifft, 1988; Sifft & Khalsa, 1991).

To date, only five studies published in peer-reviewed journals have evaluated BGI's purported effectiveness (Hyatt, 2007). One study included the author as the participant (Wolfsont, 2002) and is therefore not credible due to such a small sample size and the great likelihood of bias that may be involved when a researcher is the sole participant in a study. In a comprehensive review of the literature, Hyatt (2007) found the remaining four studies (Camissa, 1994; de los Santos et al., 2002; Khalsa et al., 1988; Sifft & Khalsa, 1991) contained serious methodological limitations that included (a) limited description of BGI procedures, (b) lack of controls for treatment fidelity (i.e., demonstration of the extent to which the intervention was implemented as planned), and (c) the use of subjective and unreliable outcome measures. Consequently, the existing literature indicates BGI is not likely to be an effective procedure for improving learning outcomes.

More broadly, there is a lack of empirical work supporting the effectiveness of educational kinesiology as a whole. For example, Kavale and Mattson (1983) conducted a comprehensive meta-analysis of 180 studies evaluating the effects of educational kinesiology for improving reading, achievement and perceptual and motor skills and found an overall small effect size. Moreover, although some studies do report positive effects of educational kinesiology for improving learning outcomes, these studies contain serious methodological flaws that diminish confidence in the extent to which learning gains may be attributed to educational kinesiology procedures (Hyatt et al., 2009). Given the overall small effect of interventions, lack of rigorous methodological studies, and questionable theoretical underpinnings, educational kinesiology does not likely promote learning and should be regarded with a great deal of skepticism.

5.1.3 Vision Therapies

Behavioral optometry (or vision therapy) is an extension of traditional optometry in which practitioners employ a holistic approach to the treatment of visual disorders. That is, these behavioral optometrists (or vision therapists) believe they can influence visual processes such as perception and visual problem-solving. The origins of vision therapy have generally been based on a series of clinical observations as opposed to rigorous experimental investigations (Barrett, 2009). Nevertheless, children with dyslexia, dyspraxia, attention-deficit/hyperactivity disorder (ADHD), and behavior problems experiencing difficulties with academics and poor coordination are referred to vision therapists.

The underlying theory of vision therapy is deficits in visual processing and perception may result in reading and writing difficulties. That is, some individuals struggle with reading because they have difficulties visually processing written letters and words. Vision therapy involves engaging in various eye movements and eye-hand coordination exercises to develop visual-spatial orientation skills, visual closure and memory, and visual-motor integration and subsequently improve visual processing and perception. Vision therapists suggest these exercises improve visual processes and therefore make an individual more responsive to educational instruction (Handler & Fierson, 2011).

Unfortunately, there is currently inadequate empirical support to suggest vision therapy is effective for improving reading and writing skills (Barrett, 2009; Handler & Fierson, 2011). Literature reviews indicate studies examining vision therapy are generally methodologically flawed or characterized by professional opinion as opposed to rigorous empirical investigations. Moreover, assertions of the effectiveness of vision therapy are often found in newsletters, brochures, books that do not present empirical support, and poorly reviewed journals, as opposed to peer-reviewed scientific journals (Handler & Fierson, 2011). Although difficulties with vision can certainly impact an individual's ability to read written letters and words, there is little evidence vision therapy can improve outcomes for struggling readers and writers.

Similar to vision therapy, tinted lenses have been utilized to treat a variety of reading difficulties attributable to scotopic sensitivity syndrome (SSS), also termed Irlen syndrome and Meares-Irlen syndrome. SSS ostensibly causes visual discomfort and reading difficulties due to light sensitivity and visual distortion, stress, and fragmentation from sensitivities to specific wavelengths of light. Alleged reading difficulties include poor reading fluency and comprehension, misreading words, and skipping words and lines (Handler & Fierson, 2011). Proponents for the treatment of SSS posit that wearing tinted lenses filters offending wavelengths of light, thereby ameliorating reading difficulties.

As with vision therapy, use of tinted lenses has limited empirical evidence to support its effectiveness for the treatment of reading problems in individuals with SSS. In fact, most medical and education professionals maintain that SSS is not a recognized medical syndrome, and there are currently no established criteria for diagnosing SSS (Handler & Fierson, 2011; Hyatt et al., 2009). Additionally, there is a lack of documented evidence supporting selection criteria for which particular tint of the lenses works best for specific individuals. Regarding its evidence base, the *Journal of Learning Disabilities* published a special issue in 1990 on tinted lenses in which the editor-in-chief cautioned that each of the published studies had serious theoretical and methodological flaws (Wiederhold, 1990). Furthermore, studies that have since examined tinted lenses contain methodological inadequacies such as subjective reports of outcomes, lack of control for placebo effects, no control groups, no equivalence determination at pretest, multiple treatment interferences, lack of control for threats to internal validity, experimenter bias, and use of inappropriate outcome measures (Hyatt et al., 2009).

5.1.4 Working Memory Training

Working memory refers to the cognitive system of temporarily storing and manipulating information to complete tasks (Melby-Lervåg & Hulme, 2013). Research in working memory as it pertains to education and development has become progressively more prominent as studies consistently demonstrate working memory functioning is correlated with academic outcomes (e.g., Alloway & Alloway, 2010). Moreover, research suggests children who struggle with reading and mathematics as well as children with ADHD have been observed to have deficits in working memory (Redick et al., 2015). Given this information, it seems reasonable that interventions targeting working memory deficits could improve academic performance.

Working memory training programs include a range of procedures involving (a) training strategies to improve scores on working memory tests, as opposed to improving the remembering of information; (b) procedures specifically focused on working memory functioning (e.g., reproducing presented patterns of spatial stimuli); and (c) rigorous training programs that gradually become more difficult as individuals improve on working memory tasks (Shipstead, Redick, & Engle, 2012). Working memory tasks such as listening span and rotation span (i.e., recalling a series of symbols' orientation as presented verbally and visually; Matzen et al., 2016), verbal span (recalling presented digits in a correct order; McKendrick et al., 2014), and backward digit span (i.e., recalling presented digits correctly in backward order; Klingberg, Forssberg, & Westerberg, 2002), to name a few, involve repeated practice with these tasks so as to attain mastery. The goal of practicing working memory tasks is to achieve far transfer, which is transferring improved performance on practice tasks (e.g., digit span) to relevant real-world tasks (e.g., reading fluency and comprehension). The arrival of training programs accessible from computers and mobile devices makes working memory training enticing due to its easy availability and cost effectiveness (Redick et al., 2013). Consequently, researchers have tested working memory training programs to evaluate their effects on improvements for practiced tasks as well as far transfer tasks.

Findings from the working memory training programs literature are not promising. Many studies have indicated working memory training reliably produces improvements in working memory for the tasks participants repeatedly practice; however, participants did not always maintain improvements in performance for these tasks. Most importantly, Melby-Lervåg and Hulmes' (2013) meta-analysis of 23 group comparison studies indicated there was no convincing evidence participants transferred training gains to meaningful reading and math tasks. Nevertheless, memory training programs such as CogMed, BrainTwister, and Lumosity that purportedly improve working memory and academic outcomes are still marketed heavily.

More recently, Melby-Lervåg, Redick, and Hulmes (2016) conducted a meta-analysis of 87 studies that tested working memory programs and evaluated effects on far transfer tasks such as nonverbal ability, verbal ability, word decoding, reading comprehension, and math. Similar to their previous meta-analysis, results indicated working memory training programs produced negligible short- and long-term effects for far transfer tasks. Additionally, the authors reported serious methodological flaws in studies that touted the effectiveness of working memory training programs (e.g., untreated control groups, small sample sizes).

In short, research consistently demonstrates working memory training programs typically produce short-term improvements for working memory tasks that have been repeatedly practiced (e.g., Melby-Lervåg & Hulme, 2013; Melby-Lervåg et al., 2016; Redick et al., 2013). However, literature on working memory training demonstrates that it does not produce long-term improvement with working memory tasks and does not transfer to meaningful tasks (e.g., reading comprehension, arithmetic), which should really be the primary goal of treatment for SLDs.

5.2 Research-Supported Approaches

Although myriad pseudoscientific practices are touted as effective for improving academic performance, there are fortunately a range of empirically supported practices for improving academic outcomes for struggling learners. School-based response to intervention (RtI) systems (Jimerson, Burns, & VanDerHeyden, 2016), for example, include early identification of students at risk for specific learning disorders and a series of increasingly intensifying interventions for remediating students' academic deficits. RtI systems typically include three tiers of service of delivery with increasingly intensifying assessment and instructional procedures at each tier (Fuchs & Fuchs, 2006). Tier 1 consists of universal screening two to three times per year (e.g., fall, winter, and spring) in core academic areas (e.g., reading, math, written expression) as well as empirically supported curricula in core instructional areas (e.g., reading/language arts, math). The goal of Tier 1 is to reduce the number of students who qualify for special education with SLDs through early identification of at-risk students and provision of evidence-based core instruction. Students who fail to respond to Tier 1 may receive Tier 2 supplemental supports, which consist of targeted academic interventions in small-group settings three to five times per week. Additionally, students in Tier 2 receive regular progress monitoring (e.g., biweekly) for their deficit area so their response to intervention may be gauged and future instruction is informed by progress-monitoring data. Tier 2 supplemental supports are designed to reduce the number of students who are referred for more costly, intensive interventions. Finally, students who do not respond to Tier 2 supports may receive intensive, individualized intervention in the area noted as deficient. Moreover, students receiving Tier 3 intensive interventions receive frequent progress monitoring (e.g., once per week) to evaluate their response to intervention.

Students who do not respond favorably to a Tier 3 intensive intervention may then be referred for a comprehensive evaluation to determine whether or not the student meets eligibility criteria for an SLD and needs to receive special education services. Research indicates that RtI systems are effective for improving students' academic outcomes (Burns, Appleton, & Stehouwer, 2005).

RtI intervention systems are designed to be flexible in terms of the specific assessment and intervention procedures that are used at each tier. One widespread method of screening students and progress monitoring their responses to an intervention is curriculum-based measurement (CBM; Deno, 1987). CBM includes brief, timed trials for basic academic skills that include fluency as the metric across all skill areas assessed. CBM is a general outcome measurement model designed to predict students' performance in more widely scoped areas. For example, oral reading fluency is a commonly used CBM procedure in reading and adequately predicts students' reading comprehension and performance in reading on end-of-year state-wide tests (Reschly et al., 2009). CBM procedures for reading, math, and written expression have demonstrated reliability and validity across a range of student populations (Gansle et al., 2006; Reschly et al., 2009; Thurber, Shinn, & Smolkowski, 2002).

With regard to core instruction in RtI systems, Tier 1 instruction should include (a) differentiated instruction to account for variability in learners in the classroom, (b) high-quality curricula that are supported by scientific evidence for effectiveness, and (c) monitoring for teachers' implementation of instructional quality. Moreover, Tier 2 and Tier 3 supports and interventions should include (a) explicit instruction for the targeted skill, (b) routine progress monitoring to determine students' response to intervention, and (c) regular evaluation of the fidelity of intervention implementation (Fuchs et al., 2005; Fuchs & Fuchs, 2006; Graham & Perin, 2007; Lembke, Hampton, & Beyers, 2012).

5.3 Conclusion

Approximately 5%–15% of school-age children experience an SLD that impairs their ability to succeed academically and occupationally (American Psychiatric Association, 2013). Numerous procedures have been developed to address learning difficulties associated with SLD and subsequently promote academic outcomes. Several of these procedures (e.g., educational kinesiology, vision therapies, and working memory training) have little to no empirical support for improving academic outcomes for struggling learners. Unfortunately, these approaches have been widely disseminated and marketed to parents and educators as quick, simple, and cost-effective procedures for improving learning. For these reasons, it is critical that professionals in the education field (e.g., school psychologists, educators) be diligent consumers of the scientific literature so as to disseminate to parents and educators procedures that have an evidence base for improving academic outcomes. This involves being skeptical of new procedures, yet keeping an open mind to the possibility that a given procedure could be effective for improving academic outcomes. In addition, researchers in the field of education are tasked with subjecting new procedures for improving learning to rigorous experimental evaluations. Without these efforts, questionable procedures to improve learning may flourish, and struggling learners may continue to struggle.

Works Cited in Sidebar

Bjork, R. A. (1994). Memory and metamemory considerations in the training of human beings. In J. Metcalfe & A. Shimamura (eds.), *Metacognition: Knowing about Knowing* (pp. 185–205). Cambridge, MA: MIT Press.
Heathcote, A., Brown, S., & Mewhort, D. J. K. (2000). The power law repealed: The case for an exponential law of practice. *Psychonomic Bulletin & Review*, 7(2), 185–207.
Pashler, H., McDaniel, M., Rohrer, D., & Bjork, R. (2008). Learning styles: Concepts and evidence. *Psychological Science in the Public Interest*, 9(3), 105–119.

References

Alloway, T. P., & Alloway, R. G. (2010). Investigating the predictive roles of working memory and IQ in academic attainment. *Journal of Experimental Child Psychology, 106,* 20–29.
American Psychiatric Association. (2013). *Diagnostic and statistical manual of mental disorders.* 5th edn. Arlington, VA: American Psychiatric Publishing.
Barrett, B. T. (2009). A critical evaluation of the evidence supporting the practice of behavioral vision therapy. *Ophthalmic and Physiological Optics, 29* (1), 4–25.
Burns, M. K., Appleton, J. J., & Stehouwer, J. D. (2005). Meta-analytic review of responsiveness-to-intervention research: Examining field-based and research-implemented models. *Journal of Psychoeducational Assessment, 23,* 381–394.

Cammisa, K. M. (1994). Educational kinesiology with learning disabled children: An efficacy study. *Perceptual and Motor Skills*, *78*, 105–106.

Chance, P. (2009). *Learning and behavior: Active learning edition*. 6th edn. Belmont, CA: Wadsworth.

de los Santos, G., Hume, E. C., & Cortes, A. (2002). Improving the faculty's effectiveness in increasing the success of Hispanic students in higher education – Pronto! *Journal of Hispanic Higher Education*, *1*(3), 225–237.

Dennison, P.E., & Dennison, G. E. (1994). *Brain Gym® teacher's edition – Revised*. Ventura, CA: Edu-Kinesthetics.

Deno, S. L. (1987). Curriculum-based measurement. *Teaching Exceptional Children*, *20*, 40–42.

Fuchs, L. S., Compton, D. L., Fuchs, D., Paulsen, K., Bryant, J. D., & Hamlett, C. L. (2005). The prevention, identification, and cognitive determinants of math difficulty. *Journal of Educational Psychology*, *97*, 493.

Fuchs, D. & Fuchs, L. S. (2006). Introduction to response to intervention: What, why, and how valid is it? *Reading Research Quarterly*, *41*, 93–99.

Fuchs, L. S., Fuchs, D., Powell, S. R., Seethaler, P. M., Cirino, P. T., & Fletcher, J. M. (2008). Intensive intervention for students with mathematics disabilities: Seven principles of effective practice. *Learning Disabilities Quarterly*, *31*(2), 79–92.

Gansle, K. A., VanDerHeyden, A. M., Noell, G. H., Resetar, J. L., & Williams, K. L. (2006). The technical adequacy of curriculum-based and rating-based measures of written expression for elementary school students. *School Psychology Review*, *35*(3), 435–450.

Geake, J. (2008). Neuromythologies in education. *Educational Research*, *50*(2), 123–133.

Goswami, U. (2006). Neuroscience and education: From research to practice? *Nature Reviews Neuroscience*, *7*(5), 406–413.

Graham, S., & Perin, D. (2007). A meta-analysis of writing instruction for adolescent students. *Journal of Educational Psychology*, *99*, 445.

Handler, S. M., & Fierson, W. M. (2011). Joint technical report – learning disabilities, dyslexia, and vision. *Pediatrics*, *127*(3), e818–e856.

Hyatt, K. J. (2007). Brain Gym®: Building stronger brains or wishful thinking? *Remedial and Special Education*, *28*(2), 117–124.

Hyatt, K. J., Stephenson, J., & Carter, M. (2009). A review of three controversial educational practices: Perceptual motor programs, sensory integration, and tinted lenses. *Education and Treatment of Children*, *32*(2), 313–342.

Jimerson, S. R., Burns, M. K., & VanDerHeyden, A. M. (2016). From response to intervention to multi tiered systems of support: Advances in the science and practice of assessment and intervention. In S. R. Jimerson, M. K. Burns, & A. M. VanDerHeyden (eds.), *Handbook of Response to Intervention*. 2nd edn, pp. 1–6. New York: Springer.

Kavale, K. A., & Mattson, P. D. (1983). "One jumped off the balance beam": Meta-analysis of perceptual-motor training. *Journal of Learning Disabilities*, *16*, 165–173.

Khalsa, G. K., Morris, G. S. D., & Sifft, J. M. (1988). Effect of educational kinesiology on static balance of learning disabled students. *Perceptual and Motor Skills*, *67*, 51–54.

Klingberg, T., Forssberg, H., & Westerberg, H. (2002). Training of working memory in children with ADHD. *Journal of Clinical and Experimental Neuropsychology*, 24(6), 781–791.

Lembke, E. S., Hampton, D., & Beyers, S. J. (2012). Response to intervention in mathematics: Critical elements. *Psychology in the Schools*, *49*, 257–272.

Matzen, L. E., Trumbo, M. C., Haass, M. J., Hunter, M. A., Silva, A., Stevens-Adams, S. M. ... & O'Rourke, P. O. (2016). Practice makes imperfect: Working memory training can harm recognition memory performance. *Memory & Cognition*, *44*, 1168–1182.

McKendrick, R., Ayaz, H., Olmstead, R., & Parasuraman, R. (2014). Enhancing dual-task performance with verbal and spatial working memory training: Continuous monitoring of cerebral hemodynamics with NIRS. *Neuroimaging*, *85*, 1014–1026.

Melby-Lervåg, M., & Hulme, C. (2013). Is working memory training effective? A meta-analytic review. *Developmental Psychology*, *49*(2), 270–291.

Melby-Lervåg, M., Redick, T. S., & Hulme, C. (2016). Working memory training does not improve performance on measures of intelligence or other measures of "far transfer": Evidence from a meta-analytic review. *Perspectives on Psychological Science*, *11*(4), 512–534.

Mercer, J. (2016). *Thinking critically about child development: Examining myths and misunderstandings*. 3rd edn. Los Angeles, CA: SAGE Publications, Inc.

Rathvon, N. (2008). *Effective school interventions: Evidence-based strategies for improving student outcomes*. 2nd edn. New York: Guilford Press.

Redick, T. S., Shipstead, Z., Harrison, T. L., Hicks, K. L., Fried, D. E., Hambrick, D. Z. ... & Engle, R. W. (2013). No evidence of intelligence improvement after working memory training: A randomized, placebo-controlled study. *Journal of Experimental Psychology: General.* *142*(2), 359–379.

Redick, T. S., Shipstead, Z., Wiemers, E. A., Melby-Lervåg, M., & Hulme, C. (2015). What's working in working memory training? An educational perspective. *Educational Psychology Review*, *27*(4), 617–633.

Reschly, A. L., Busch, T. W., Betts, J., Deno, S. L., & Long, J. D. (2009). Curriculum-based measurement oral reading as an indicator of reading achievement: A meta-analysis of the correlational evidence. *Journal of School Psychology*, *47*(6), 427–469.

Roberts, G., Torgesen, J. K., Boardman, A., & Scammacca, N. (2008). Evidence-based strategies for reading instruction of older students with learning disabilities. *Learning Disabilities Research & Practice*, *23*(2), 63–69.

Shapiro, E. S. (2011). *Academic skills problems: Direct assessment and intervention*. 4th edn. New York: The Guilford Press.

Shipstead, Z., Redick, T. S., & Engle, R. W. (2012). Is working memory training effective? *Psychological Bulletin*, *138*(4), 628–654.

Sifft, J. M., & Khalsa, G. C. K. (1991). Effect of educational kinesiology upon simple response times and choice response times. *Perceptual and Motor Skills*, *73*, 1011–1015.

Spaulding, L. C., Mostert, M. P., & Beam, A. P. (2010). Is Brain Gym® an effective educational intervention? *Exceptionality*, *18*, 18–30.

Therrien, W. J. (2004). Fluency and comprehension gains as a result of repeated reading: A meta-analysis. *Remedial and Special Education*, *25*(4), 252–261.

Thurber, R. S., Shinn, M. R., & Smolkowski, K. (2002). What is measured in mathematics tests? Construct validity of curriculum-based mathematics measures. *School Psychology Review*, *31*, 498.

Wiederholt, J. L. (1990). A preface to the special series. *Journal of Learning Disabilities 23*(10), 588–598.

Wolfsont, C. (2002). Increasing behavioral skills and level of understanding in adults: A brief method integrating Dennison's Brain Gym® balance with Piaget's reflective processing. *Journal of Adult Development*, *9*(3), 187–203.

6

Tics

Michael B. Himle and Brianna Wellen

Tic disorders are a class of childhood-onset, neurodevelopmental disorders that includes Tourette's disorder (aka Tourette syndrome), persistent motor/vocal tic disorder, and provisional tic disorder (American Psychiatric Association [APA], 2013). The defining symptoms of tic disorders are involuntary, spontaneous, recurrent, nonrhythmic motor movements and vocalizations (i.e., motor and phonic tics). A diagnosis of Tourette's disorder requires the presence of both multiple motor *and* at least one vocal tic that persist, in some form, for at least one year. Persistent motor/vocal tic disorder involves motor *or* vocal tics, but not both, that persist for at least one year (APA, 2013). Finally, provisional tic disorder is defined by motor and/or vocal tics that have been present for less than one year and was included in the fifth edition of the *Diagnostic and Statistical Manual of Mental Disorders* (DSM-5) to reflect the fact that up to 25% of children will exhibit one or more motor and/or vocal tics at some point during childhood, but for many of these children the tics will not persist (Snider et al., 2002). While tic disorders are highly heterogeneous in their presentation and course, symptoms typically emerge in early childhood, wax and wane in severity, and change in topography and appearance over time (Bloch & Leckman, 2009). Early in the course of the disorder, tics typically involve subtle and brief movements or sounds that are relatively easy to distinguish from purposeful behavior. For some individuals, tics evolve over time to include more complex and orchestrated movements or sounds that mimic volitional behaviors and are elicited by contextual stimuli, giving them a more purposeful appearance. Most individuals also report that their tics are preceded by unpleasant somatic sensations, referred to as "premonitory urges" (PUs) that are typically localized to the area of the body involving the tic (Leckman, Walker, & Cohen, 1993). Although the exact cause of tic disorders remains unclear, there is convincing evidence that tics are the direct result of dysfunction within basal ganglia and associated brain circuitry (Shprecher, Schrock, & Himle, 2014). It is also well documented that the severity and course of tics are influenced by psychosocial factors (Himle et al., 2014). Unfortunately, this has been historically misunderstood to imply causation. The fact that tics can be temporarily controlled with active effort, fluctuate in response to contextual cues and during certain activities (e.g., stress worsens tics and concentration decreases tics for most individuals), and the fact that many individuals experience an urge to tic have all been used to justify pseudoscientific conceptual models that posit that tics have a psychological cause. Unfortunately, such beliefs have led to several enduring myths, misunderstandings, and unsupported treatments.

6.1 Pseudoscience and Questionable Ideas

6.1.1 Conceptual Controversies

To understand the origins of pseudoscientific and questionable ideas related to tic disorders, it is necessary to provide a brief historical context of how tic disorders have been conceptualized and treated over the past two centuries. French neurologist Georges Gilles de la Tourette published in 1885 what are widely recognized as the first systematic case descriptions of motor and vocal tics (Lajonchere, Nortz, & Finger, 1996). In his original case series, Tourette described nine patients who exhibited strange, "convulsive" movements that were inconsistent with known neurological insults or disorders at the time but nevertheless appeared to be involuntary and outside of the individual's control. In addition to the motor manifestations, several of the patients also displayed dramatic, involuntary vocalizations, such as swearing and echolalia, which Tourette considered to be a defining feature of the syndrome. Although he suspected that tics had an organic etiology, Tourette offered few insights into their underlying cause. By the middle of the twentieth century, in the absence of a known cause, psychoanalytic explanations gained popularity (Kushner, 1999). Psychoanalysts argued that tics, like other psychiatric problems, were manifestations of unresolved psychic conflict, repressed sexual impulses, or character flaws (e.g., lack of willpower, attention seeking) that could be traced to early life experiences and parenting practices (Ascher, 1948; Ferenczi, 1921). Despite a lack of empirical support, the psychoanalytic view remained largely unchallenged until the 1960s when researchers began to draw parallels between tic disorders and other movement disorders with known biological causes. Among the most influential studies in this period were those demonstrating the efficacy of dopamine antagonists for suppressing tics (Kushner, 1999; Shapiro & Shapiro, 1968). These findings, along with advancements in understanding the role of various brain structures and processes in motor control, led to a rapid increase in empirical investigations examining biological correlates of tics as well as experimentation with new medical therapies.

At the same time that biological models of tic disorders began to gain acceptance, several behavioral models were also proposed as alternatives to the psychoanalytic view. The most influential of these models was the habit model proposed by Azrin and Nunn (1973). Based on this model, they developed and tested a behavioral treatment, known as habit reversal training (HRT), that was designed to teach and reinforce behaviors that were incompatible with tics. Despite early studies showing HRT to be effective (see Himle et al., 2006), biological models and medical therapies gained favor while nonmedical treatments, including HRT, were largely rejected or ignored (Kushner, 1999). However, those who advocated the neurological view of tic disorders were faced with the reality that existing medical therapies were often limited by intolerable side effects and rarely resulted in complete symptom relief. In addition, the number and quality of studies demonstrating HRT to be effective for reducing tics increased considerably through the turn of the century (Himle et al., 2006). In an attempt to bridge the biological-behavioral gap, the Tourette Association of America (www.tourette .org) brought together a group of leading behavioral and medical experts to better understand the biopsychosocial aspects of tic disorders. The resulting product was an integrative biobehavioral model that conceptualized tics as neurologically based symptoms that are influenced by environmental factors (Woods et al., 2008). Based on this model, an expanded version of HRT, called Comprehensive Behavioral Intervention for Tics (CBIT), was developed and tested in two large randomized controlled trials. In these trials, CBIT was shown to be more effective than psychosocial support for reducing tics in both children and adults (Piacentini et al., 2010; Wilhelm et al., 2012). Based on this evidence, the integrated biobehavioral model and CBIT have been gaining widespread acceptance among interdisciplinary professionals (Murphy et al., 2013). Nevertheless, the contentious history of how to best conceptualize and treat tic disorders has left in its wake several pseudoscientific and questionable ideas that persist today.

6.1.2 Diagnostic Controversies, Myths, and Misunderstandings

Controversies Surrounding the Classification of Tic Disorders as Mental Disorders.   How and where to classify tic disorders in various versions of the DSM has been a source of controversy across each iteration of the manual. Much of the controversy stems from the argument that where they are placed, and which disorders they are grouped with, will influence how they are conceptualized, treated, and studied. In fact, their inclusion in a manual of "mental disorders" at all could be viewed as controversial given their known neurobiological underpinnings. The concern about where to place tic disorders in the DSM is understandable given the contentious history of how tic disorders have been conceptualized by the psychiatric profession. For example, tics were included in the first version of the DSM as "neurotic traits" and were viewed as symptoms of neurosis (Woods & Thomsen, 2014), which is a reflection of the psycho-analytic conceptualization of tics in the 1950s. It could be argued that such classifications perpetuated stigma and misunderstanding, promoted mistreatment, and hindered research efforts. As recently as the DSM-IV, tic disorders were included as disorders of infancy, childhood, and ado-lescence and were included alongside disruptive behavior disorder, learning disorders, and mental retardation (APA, 2000). The tic disorder community has long fought to dispel myths that individuals with tic disorders are being purposefully disruptive, have learning disabilities (though some do have specific comorbid learning problems), or are less intelligent than their peers (see www.tourcttc.org/myths). So the inclu-sion of tic disorders alongside these other disorders is questionable. In the DSM-5, tic disorders were placed under the grouping of neurode-velopmental disorders (APA, 2013). Although this label more ade-quately captures the current conceptualization of tic disorders, this section also includes intellectual disabilities, ADHD, autism spectrum disorders, and communication disorders – disorders that share little overlap with tic disorders other than that tics typically onset at a young age and tic disorders are often comorbid with ADHD. While some have promoted their inclusion in the section on obsessive-compulsive spec-trum disorders (Roessner, Hoekstra, & Rothenberger, 2011) based on the high comorbidity of tic disorders with OCD, the similarity between compulsions and complex tics (which are sometimes performed to achieve a "just right" feeling) and a purported genetic link. However, such a grouping will remain controversial until there is a better understanding of the etiological overlap (or lack thereof) between tic disorders and OCD.

Swearing as a Hallmark Symptom. Although Tourette proposed that inappropriate vocal tics (i.e., coprolalia) were a hallmark symptom of tic disorders, subsequent research has shown that such tics occur in a relatively small subset of individuals with a tic disorder (Freeman et al., 2009). Unfortunately, coprolalia has continued to be portrayed in the media as a defining symptom of tic disorders, and Tourette's disorder in particular. Such portrayals have contributed to misunderstandings among the lay public and have been a source of stigma for individuals with tics. It is not uncommon to hear the uninformed argument that if a person with a tic disorder has a tic in which they shout an insult, such as a racial slur, they must "mean it on some level," a way of thinking that harkens back to the invalid psychoanalytic view. In fact, for individuals with coprolalia, the content of the tic is typically the very thing that the individual least wants to say (and thus tries, but fails, to inhibit).

Tics vs. Comorbid Symptoms. In addition to tics, most individuals with tic disorders exhibit comorbid internalizing and/or externalizing symptoms. A common misunderstanding among many patients, as well as some professionals, is that comorbidity is required for a diagnosis of Tourette's disorder. Although some research has suggested that tics and comorbid symptoms might be etiologically related and have argued that tics and comorbidity are part of a clinical continuum (Kurlan, 1994), motor and vocal tics are the only symptoms required for a diagnosis of Tourette's disorder.

The Significance of Motor versus Vocal Tics. Although the types of tics that are present (motor, vocal, or both) are the determining factor for whether an individual meets criteria for Tourette's disorder versus per-sistent motor/vocal tic disorder, the distinction between motor and vocal tics has not yet been shown to be of any particular significance in under-standing or treating tic disorders. In fact, vocal tics can be conceptualized as motor tics involving the various muscles that are involved in producing speech and other sounds (stomach, diaphragm, mouth, etc.). The fact that both motor and vocal tics are required for a diagnosis of Tourette's disorder is primarily an homage to the historical works of Gilles de la Tourette and is not necessarily indicative of a more severe or compli-cated form of tic disorder.

6.2 Myths and Misunderstandings That Influence Treatment

Myths That Influence Medical Treatments. One common misbelief in tic disorder treatment is that medication should be categorically avoided due to the potential for serious and irreversible side effects. This myth has been promoted to justify the use of a variety of unsupported alternative treatments. While it is true that some of the most effective tic suppressing medications (e.g., typical and atypical antipsychotics) carry the risk of serious side effects, safer (albeit somewhat less effective) medications are available and have been shown to be beneficial for reducing tics and associated impairment (Shprecher et al., 2014). Historical concerns that stimulant medication will cause or exacerbate tics have also resulted in limited treatment options for children with tics and comorbid ADHD despite the fact that ADHD has been shown to be more strongly associated with functional impairment than tics and can interfere with behavioral tic management (Sukhodolsky et al., 2003). Recent studies have shown that stimulants can be safely used to manage ADHD in individuals with tics (Bloch et al., 2009).

Myths That Influence Behavioral Treatments. Although behavior therapy is gaining recognition and acceptance as an effective alternative or adjunct to medication for treating tics, it remains underutilized (Woods et al., 2010). While there are several practical reasons that patients might not seek behavior therapy (e.g., ease of administration of medication, lack of behavioral treatment providers), surveys have shown that many patients resist behavioral interventions due to several enduring misbeliefs about potential side effects (Woods et al., 2010). Among the most common myths are that drawing attention to tics will make them worse and/or damage self-esteem, that behavioral therapy will suppress tics in the short term but worsen them in the long term (symptom rebound), and that suppressing tics will cause new tics or other behavior problems to emerge (i.e., symptom substitution). While the origin of these myths is unclear, they appear to be a historical hangover stemming from invalid assumptions of early psychoanalytic models and the unfortunate lumping and rejection of all psychosocial treatment approaches during the biological movement of the 1960s and 1970s. In fact, some early reports issued strong cautionary statements that behavioral therapies were not only ineffective but also carried the potential for harm (e.g., Burd & Kerbeshian, 1987). These myths have resisted correction despite strong empirical evidence showing each of the aforementioned concerns to be unfounded (Woods, Conelea, & Walther, 2007).

6.2.1 Questionable and Implausible Treatments

Nutritional and Dietary Supplements. Patients might turn to supplements to manage symptoms for numerous reasons, including misunderstandings about the etiology of the problem, misunderstandings regarding how supplements are metabolized and their effect (or lack thereof) on brain and body functions, beliefs that "natural" treatments are safer than traditional medications, lack of effective symptom management resulting from other interventions, and inability to take traditional medications due to intolerable side effects (Kompoliti, Fan, & Leurgans, 2009). Given that the exact cause of tic disorders remains unclear, along with the fact that the most effective medications for reducing tics (i.e., neuroleptics) are known to have adverse side effect profiles and rarely result in complete symptom remission (Scahill et al., 2006), it should not come as a surprise that up to 89% of patients with a tic disorder report having used nutritional and dietary supplements in an attempt to control tics (Mantel et al., 2005). While one study found that the majority of supplement users reported tic reduction while taking supplements (Mantel et al., 2005), such subjective accounts should be viewed cautiously in the absence of empirical studies demonstrating their benefit. In addition, one study reported that 80% of patients who acknowledged using complementary and alternative treatments for tics (including supplements) did not ask their doctor prior to beginning the treatment or inform their doctor after treatment initiation (Kompoliti et al., 2009). This is particularly concerning given that 60% of respondents were taking concomitant psychotropic medication and the effect of most nutritional supplements on the metabolism of common psychotropic medications is unclear (Izzo & Ernst, 2009).

Special Diets. The notion that dietary factors (specific foods, additives, gluten, etc.) can cause or exacerbate behavioral disorders in children has been the source of ongoing controversy for decades. Despite a lack of research-supported causal models or data supporting their efficacy, numerous "special diets" have been developed and marketed as treatments for a host of psychiatric, developmental, and behavioral problems, including motor and vocal tics (Kompoliti et al., 2009). While some individuals report subjective improvement in tic symptoms while on such diets (Kompoliti et al., 2009), no studies have examined their efficacy or outlined a plausible mechanism of action, aside from the fact that most people generally feel better when they eat a nutritious and balanced diet. Several studies have shown, however, that some (but not all) patients report that central nervous system stimulants (e.g., caffeine) and depressants (e.g., alcohol) cause a transient increase or decrease in tics (Muller-Vahl et al., 2008). The known involvement of dopamine in the etiology of tics, along with the fact that both caffeine and alcohol are known to influence dopaminergic activity, provides a tentatively plausible model by which the consumption of specific compounds could influence tics in the short term. As such, it is plausible that reducing or eliminating the consumption of *specific* tic-exacerbating beverages or foods from one's diet could have a beneficial effect. Indeed, some evidence-based behavioral interventions include therapeutic strategies for identifying and modifying tic-exacerbating factors, including foods and drinks, as part of a comprehensive behavioral treatment package (Woods et al., 2008). However, within this treatment model, dietary modifications are not conceptualized as a standalone treatment, but rather as a practical strategy for decreasing problematic tic exacerbations that are associated with the consumption of particular food, drinks, or other substances.

Chiropractic Treatments. Chiropractic interventions involve locating and correcting putative lesions or misalignments of the spinal column (i.e., vertebral subluxation) through a variety of physical "adjustment" techniques. The rationale for this approach is that spinal misalignments, such as loss of juxtaposition of vertebra, can interfere with the transmission of nerve impulses throughout the body thereby causing a variety of adverse health outcomes, including tics (DeMaria et al., 2013). Several published case reports have claimed to have identified and corrected subluxations in individuals with tics resulting in significant, or even complete, remission of symptoms in as few as two (and as many as 108) treatment sessions (see DeMaria et al., 2013, for a review). To date, no controlled studies have examined the efficacy of chiropractic interventions in the treatment of tic disorders, and there is no empirical support for a causal link between spinal misalignment and tics.

Hypnosis and Relaxation Training. The origins of the idea that hypnosis can be used to treat tics is rooted in early psychoanalytic conceptualizations that viewed hypnosis as an effective therapeutic tool for circumventing defense mechanisms so that the therapist could help the patient uncover and correct unconscious psychic conflicts that were believed to be responsible for tics. More recently, proponents of hypnosis have shifted away from the psychodynamic view favoring a model that views hypnosis, usually in the form of self-hypnosis, as a clinical tool to teach self-regulation and relaxation. The rationale for the use of such strategies is based on research showing that many individuals report that their tics increase during periods of stress and decrease during periods of concentration (Silva et al., 1995). Several uncontrolled studies have examined self-hypnosis, relaxation training, or their combination and found a short-term benefit for some individuals (Bergen et al., 1998; Flamand-Roze et al. 2016). However, well-controlled studies have found relaxation to be inferior to other therapeutic approaches, and treatment gains are usually temporary and limited to the treatment setting (Bergen et al., 1998). These results suggest that while such strategies might be a useful tool for decreasing the severity and impact of tics in the short term, their status as a monotherapy capable of sustained and generalized symptom improvement is questionable.

Biofeedback Training. Biofeedback training (including neurofeedback) involves measuring and presenting to the patient in real time covert physiological responses (e.g., heart rate, galvanic skin response, or specific brain wave patterns) that are hypothesized to underlie a set of symptoms and/or symptom-control networks. The rationale is that by viewing these physiological processes, the patient can learn to actively modify the processes for clinical benefit. Plausible and compelling research-based models outlining the potential clinical utility of neurofeedback as a monotherapy or as an adjunctive technique to enhance other therapies for tic disorders (e.g., HRT) have been proposed (Farkas et al., 2015), and several early case studies have reported the successful use of biofeedback to reduce tics (Benvenuti et al., 2011). However, a small, randomized controlled trial compared electrodermal biofeedback training to a sham biofeedback condition and found that while tics reduced in both conditions, the experimental treatment group did not differ from the control (sham) group (Nagai et al., 2014). Based on the current state of the literature, additional studies on the efficacy and proposed mechanism of biofeedback as a treatment for tics seem warranted. However, as noted earlier, other interventions that are intended to regulate autonomic activity (e.g., relaxation training) have been shown to reduce tics in only a minority of cases and the benefits have been shown to be largely constrained to the treatment setting (Bergen et al., 1998), so it will be important that future studies on biofeedback carefully examine the durability and generalization of treatment gains.

Other Complementary and Alternative Medicine (CAM) Approaches.
Several studies have shown that many patients with tics report having
tried a host of CAM treatments for tics, including massage therapy,
spiritual healing, meditation, acupuncture, and sensory integration, to
name just a few (Kompoliti et al., 2009). To date, none of these
approaches has been subjected to sufficient empirical investigation to
draw definitive conclusions regarding efficacy. More importantly, evidence-based theoretical models capable of explaining a plausible
mechanism by which these treatments would be effective for reducing
tics are lacking or are inconsistent with neurobiological models of tic
etiology. It should also be noted that existing studies examining the use
of CAM have not adequately assessed the reasons for their use. For
example, it seems plausible that some patients might seek massage
therapy to decrease muscle soreness resulting from motor tics or meditation to reduce stress, which for many individuals exacerbates tics.
In such cases, these alternative approaches could plausibly result in
a modest temporary reduction in tic severity and/or have secondary
benefit unrelated to tic reduction.

Sidebar Box: Can a dental device decrease tics? by Grant Ritchey and Clay Jones

Whenever gaps in the scientific understanding of a challenging
medical condition exist, you can be confident that a long line of
people will be attempting to fill those gaps with unscientific
diagnostic and treatment recommendations. Tic disorders, in
particular Tourette's, are no exception to this rule. In fact, because
of its unique and fascinating clinical presentation, patients with
Tourette's disorder are especially vulnerable to all manner of
blatant snake-oil peddlars and well-meaning believers in
implausible and unsupported remedies.

One mode of unconventional therapy being marketed is the
fabrication of a dental appliance to manage tics. The hypothesis
behind this approach is that many of the habitual movements of
people with Tourette's are due to reflexive tics of muscles
innervated by the trigeminal nerve, or the fifth cranial nerve
(which also innervates the mandible, or lower jaw). This
observation is then extrapolated to infer that the symptoms of
Tourette's disorder and other movement disorders are a function
of an "overstimulation" of the neural impulses carried by the
trigeminal nerve to the brain due to dysfunction within the

temporomandibular (jaw) joint. Realigning the mandible therefore will ostensibly reduce this "neural noise," resulting in a reduction or elimination of tics.

While this might have a small amount of biological plausibility, very little good research supports this approach. A handful of case reports can be found in the literature, but they demonstrate little evidence. Tics are found in all muscle groups, not just those innervated by the trigeminal nerve. Moreover, it cannot explain the other features of Tourette's disorder not correlated with jaw position (e.g., brain chemistry changes, familial and genetic patterns).

More studies are needed, but as of now, this treatment cannot be recommended or endorsed. We go into greater detail on dental appliances and tics on the Science-Based Medicine blog (Ritchey & Jones, 2016; Ritchey & Jones, 2018).

Grant Ritchey, DDS, practices general dentistry in Kansas. He is co-host of the Prism Podcast.

Clay Jones, MD, is a pediatrician at Newton-Wellesley Hospital in Massachusetts. He is the other co-host of the Prism Podcast.

6.3 Research-Supported Approaches

Several evidence-based treatments are available for treating tic disorders. The most commonly used are medication and behavior therapy (or their combination). The most effective tic-suppressing medications (e.g., neuroleptics) are limited by the potential for intolerable side effects and are typically only used in severe cases (Scahill et al., 2006). Safer medication options are available but are somewhat less effective (e.g., alpha-2 agonists; Shprecher et al., 2014) and/or require additional research. The behavior therapies with the most research support are HRT and the expanded CBIT treatment package that includes HRT as a primary component (Himle et al., 2006; Piacentini et al., 2010). Deep brain stimulation (DBS), which involves surgically implanting neurostimulator electrodes in subcortical motor control structures, has shown to substantially reduce tics in some individuals but is only appropriate for severe, treatment refractory, and life-threatening cases (Schrock et al., 2014).

6.4 Conclusion

Despite recent advancement in understanding and treating tic disorders, conceptual, diagnostic, and treatment controversies and misunderstandings persist. The exact genetic and biological cause of tics remains elusive, and empirically based treatments are not effective for every individual. As a result, pseudoscientific ideas and treatments have flourished, often justified by implausible conceptual models and uncontrolled case reports or clinical observations. The need for well-controlled research is highlighted by the facts that tics can be temporarily suppressed, subjective self-ratings of tic severity have been shown to be unreliable (Muller-Vahl, Riemann, & Bokemeyer, 2014), the well-documented tendency for tics to wax and wane in severity over time and high rates of remission during early and late developmental periods (Bloch & Leckman, 2009), and the possibility of placebo effects and other biases. In tic disorders, like other complex neurodevelopmental conditions, it seems to be the case that nothing works for everyone but everything works for somebody. While there is little reason to believe that unsupported treatments will make tics worse, some can be expensive and time consuming. Research has shown that the burden of care coordination is a major source of stress for patients with tic disorders (Bitsko et al., 2012) and one of the main reasons patients do not seek empirically based treatments (Woods, Conelea, & Himle, 2010). In addition, we have learned from history that acceptance of implausible models and treatments can result in misunderstandings and stubborn myths that decrease treatment utilization, stigmatize patients, and hinder scientific progress.

Works Cited in Sidebar

Ritchey, G., & Jones, C. (2016). Use of dental appliances in the management of Tourette syndrome. Retrieved from https://sciencebasedmedicine.org

Ritchey, G., & Jones, C. (2018). Tic'd off. Retrieved from https://sciencebased medicine.org

Reference

American Psychiatric Association.(2000). *Diagnostic and statistical manual of mental disorders*. 4th edn, text revision. Washington, DC: American Psychiatric Association.

American Psychiatric Association. (2013). *Diagnostic and statistical manual of mental disorders*. 5th edn. Washington, DC: American Psychiatric Association.

Ascher, E. (1948). Psychodynamic considerations in Gilles de la Tourette's disease. *The American Journal of Psychiatry, 105*, 267–276.

Azrin, N. H., & Nunn, R. G. (1973). Habit-reversal: A method of eliminating nervous habits and tics. *Behaviour Research and Therapy, 11*, 619–628.

Benvenuti, S. M., Buodo, G., Leone, V., & Palomba, D. (2011). Neurofeedback training for Tourette syndrome: An uncontrolled single case study. *Applied Psychophysiology and Biofeedback, 26*, 281–288.

Bergen, A., Waranch, H. R., Brown, J., Carson, K., & Singer, H. S. (1998). Relaxation therapy in Tourette syndrome: A pilot study. *Pediatric Neurology, 18*, 136–142.

Bitsko, R. H., Danielson, M., King, M., Visser, S. N., Scahill, L., & Perou, R. (2012). Health care needs of children with Tourette syndrome. *Journal of Child Neurology, 28*, 1626–1636.

Bloch, M. H., & Leckman, J. F. (2009). Clinical course of Tourette syndrome. *Journal of Psychosomatic Research, 6*, 497–501.

Bloch, M. H., Panza, K. E., Landeros-Weisenberger, A., & Leckman, J. F. (2009). Meta-analysis: Treatment of attention-deficit/hyperactivity disorder in children with comorbid tic disorders. *Journal of the American Academy of Child and Adolescent Psychiatry, 48*, 884–893.

Burd, L., & Kerbeshian, J. (1987). Treatment-generated problems associated with behavior modification in Tourette disorder. *Developmental Medicine & Child Neruology, 29*, 831–833.

DeMaria, A., DeMaria, C., DeMaria, R., & Alcantara, J. (2013). The chiropractic care of an adolescent with Tourette's syndrome using the Pierce Results System. *Journal of Pediatric, Maternal, & Family Health Chiropractic, 2*, 34–38.

Farkas, A., Bluschke, A., Roessner, V., & Beste, C. (2015). Neurofeedback and its possible relevance for the treatment of Tourette syndrome. *Neuroscience & Biobehavioral Reviews, 51*, 87–99.

Ferenczi, S. (1921). Psycho-analytical observations on tic. *International Journal of Psychoanalysis, 2*, 1–30.

Flamand-Roze, C., Celestin-Lhopiteau, I., & Roze, E. (2016). Hypnosis and movement disorders: State of the art and perspectives. *Revue Neurologique, 172*, 530–536.

Freeman, R. D., Zinner, S. H., Muller-Vahl, K. R., Fast, D. K., Burd, L. J., Kano, Y. ... Berlin C. M. (2009). Coprophenomena in Tourette syndrome. *Developmental Medicine & Child Neruology, 51*, 218–227.

Himle, M. B., Capriotti, M. R., Hayes, L. P., Ramanujam, K., Scahill, L., Sukhodolsky, D. G. ... & Piacentini, J. (2014). Variables associated with tic exacerbation in children with tic disorders. *Behavior Modification, 38*, 163–183.

Himle, M. B., Woods, D. W., Piacentini, J., & Walkup, J. (2006). A brief review of habit reversal training for Tourette syndrome. *Journal of Child Neurology, 21*, 719–725.

Izzo, A. A., & Ernst, E. (2009). Interactions between herbal medicines and prescribed drugs: An updated systematic review. *Drugs, 69*, 1777–1798.

Kompoliti, M. D., Fan, W., & Leurgans, S. (2009). Complementary and alternative medicine use in Gilles de la Tourette syndrome. *Movement Disorders, 24*, 1998–2019.

Kurlan, R. (1994). Hypothesis II: Tourette's syndrome is part of a clinical spectrum that includes normal brain development. *Archives of Neurology, 51*, 1145–1150.

Kushner, H. I. (1999). *A curing brain? The histories of Tourette syndrome.* Cambridge, MA: Harvard University Press.

Lajonchere, C., Nortz, M., & Finger, S. (1996). Gilles de la Tourette and the discovery of Tourette syndrome. *Archives of Neurology, 53*, 567–574.

Leckman, J. F., Walker, D. E., & Cohen, D. J. (1993). Premonitory urges in Tourette's syndrome. *American Journal of Psychiatry, 150*, 98–102.

Mantel, B. J., Meyers, A., Tran, Q., Rogers, S., & Jacobson, J. S. (2005). Nutritional supplements and complementary/alternative medicine in Tourette syndrome. *Journal of Child & Adolescent Psychopharmacology, 14*, 582–589.

Muller-Vahl, K. R., Buddensiek, N., Gomelas, M., & Emrich, H. (2008). The influence of different food and drinks on tics in Tourette syndrome. *Acta Pediatrica, 97*, 442–446.

Muller-Vahl, K. R., Riemann, L., & Bokemeyer, S. (2014). Tourette patients' misbelief of a tic rebound is due to overall difficulties in reliable tic rating. *Journal of Psychosomatic Research, 76*, 472–476.

Murphy, T. K., Lewin, A. B., Storch, E. A., Stock, S., & American Academy of Child and Adolescent Psychiatry. (2013). Practice parameters for the assessment and treatment of children and adolescents with tic disorders. *Journal of the American Academy of Child & Adolescent Psychiatry, 52*, 1341–1359.

Nagai, Y., Cavanna, A. E., Critchley, H. D., Stern, J. J., Robertson, M. M., & Joyce, E. M. (2014). Biofeedback treatment for Tourette syndrome: A preliminary randomized controlled trial. *Cognitive & Behavioral Neurology, 27*, 17–24.

Piacentini, J. C., Woods, D. W., Scahill, L. D., Wilhelm, S., Peterson, A., Chang, S. . . . & Walkup, J. T. (2010). Behavior therapy for children with Tourette syndrome: A randomized controlled trial. *Journal of the American Medical Association, 303*, 1929–1937.

Rossner, V., Hoekstra, P. J., & Rothenberger, A. (2011). Tourette's disorder and other tics disorders in DSM-5: A comment. *European Child & Adolescent Psychiatry, 20*, 71–74.

Scahill, L., Erenberg, G., Berlin, C.M., Budman, C., Coffey, B.J., Jankovic, J. … & Walkup, J. (2006). Contemporary assessment and pharmacotherapy of Tourette syndrome. *NeruoRX, 3*, 192–206.

Schrock, L. E., Mink, J. W., Woods, D. W., Porta, M., Servello, D., Visser-Vandewalle, V. … & Okun, M. S. (2014). Tourette syndrome deep brain stimulation: A review and updated recommendations. *Movement Disorders, 30*, 448–471.

Shapiro, A. K., & Shapiro, E. (1968). Treatment of Gilles de la Tourette's syndrome with Haloperidol. *The British Journal of Psychiatry, 114*, 345–350.

Shprecher, D. R., Schrock, L., & Himle, M. B. (2014). Neurobehavioral aspects, pathophysiology, and management of Tourette syndrome. *Current Opinion in Neurology, 4*, 484–492.

Silva, R. R., Munoz, D. M., Barickman, J., & Friedhoff, A. J. (1995). Environmental factors and related fluctuation of symptoms in children and adolescents with Tourette's disorder. *Journal of Child Psychology and Psychiatry, 36*, 305–312.

Snider, L. A., Seligman, L. D., Ketchen, B. R., Levitt, S. J., Bates, L. R., Garvey, M. A., & Swedo, S. E. (2002). Tics and problem behaviors in schoolchildren: Prevalence, characterization, and associations. *Pediatrics, 110*, 331–336.

Sukhodolsky, D. G., Scahill, L., Zahng, H., Peterson, B. S., King, R. A., Lombroso, P. J. … & Leckman, J. F. (2003). Disruptive behavior in children with Tourette's syndrome: Association with ADHD comorbidity, tic severity, and functional impairment. *Journal of the American Academy of Child & Adolescent Psychiatry, 41*, 98–105.

Wilhelm, S., Peterson, A. L., Piacentini, J., Woods, D. W., Deckersbach, T., Sukhodolsky, D. G. … & Scahill, L. (2012). Randomized trial of behavior therapy for adults with Tourette syndrome. *Archives of General Psychiatry, 69*, 795–803.

Woods, D. W., Conelea, C. A., & Himle, M. B. (2010). Behavior therapy for Tourette's disorder: Utilization in a community sample and an emerging area of practice. *Professional Psychology: Research & Practice, 41*, 518–525.

Woods, D. W., Conelea, C. A., & Walther, M. R. (2007). Barriers to dissemination: Exploring the criticisms of behavior therapy for tics. *Clinical Psychology: Science & Practice, 14*, 279–282.

Woods, D. W., Piacentini, J. C., Chang, S. W., Deckersbach, T., Ginsburg, G. S., Peterson, A. L. ... & Wilhelm, S. (2008). *Managing Tourette syndrome: A behavioral intervention for children and adults: Therapist guide.* New York: Oxford University Press.

Woods, D. W., & Thomson, P. H. (2014). Tourette and tic disorders in ICD-11: Standing at the diagnostic crossroads. *Revista Brasileira de Psiquiatria, 36,* S51-S58.

7

Psychosis

Rachel Waford and Carina A. Iati

Psychosis refers to a set of symptoms that impair a person's ability to interact with reality. Individuals who experience psychosis may have some or all of the possible symptoms. Symptoms of psychosis are divided into roughly four categories: positive symptoms, negative symptoms, symptoms of disorganization, and cognitive symptoms. Positive symptoms refer to experiences that were not present before the illness and are *in addition to* typical experience. Positive symptoms include hallucinations (false sensory experiences) and delusions (firmly held false beliefs). Negative symptoms refer to qualities that are typically present before the onset of the illness but are now decreased or absent. Loss of motivation, decreased ability to display emotion in facial expression, and social isolation are examples of possible negative symptoms. Symptoms of disorganization generally present as a confused way of speaking or behaving. An individual who is disorganized may speak or behave in ways that do not make sense to the people around them. Cognitive symptoms may present as a newly emerging difficulty with attention, concentration, impulse control, or memory.

Psychosis can occur as part of a number of mental health conditions. Up to 3% of the general population may experience psychosis in their lifetime (Perälä et al., 2007). Each condition differs from the others in a meaningful way and is defined by a set of criteria that describe the particular set of symptoms comprising the illness. The *Diagnostic and Statistical Manual of Mental Disorders* (5th ed) (DSM-5; American Psychiatric Association, 2013) classifies these illnesses under Schizophrenia Spectrum and Other Psychotic Disorders section and identifies illnesses that *always* include a component of psychosis. These illnesses include schizophreniform disorder, schizophrenia, brief psychotic disorder, delusional disorder, and schizoaffective disorder. Some other mental health conditions may *sometimes* include psychosis, but not in every case. Examples of such conditions are major depressive disorder and bipolar disorder. Though each of these conditions varies in most ways, when the symptoms of psychosis are present, they share a common experience of a difficulty accessing reality.

Illnesses such as schizophrenia may have one of the longest histories, and stories of "insanity" and "madness" have shown up in virtually every culture in recorded history. Different stages of history had their own ideas about psychotic illness, leading to varying approaches to treatment over time. This chapter outlines the history and myths associated with the various treatment approaches used throughout the story of psychotic illness. While it was established in the early nineteenth century that psychotic illness often included an adolescent onset, the account of the antiquated treatments of psychotic illness in children is limited. Thus, primarily adult accounts are provided.

The complex nature and relative rarity of psychotic illnesses have made them a target for stigma and misunderstanding. This chapter discusses and corrects some of the common myths and pseudoscience related to psychosis. The chapter also discusses treatments for psychosis: those based in pseudoscience that have been proven unhelpful and those that are supported by research.

7.1 Pseudoscience and Questionable Ideas

7.1.1 Psychotic Disorders Have Inconsistent Diagnostic Criteria

Diagnosing mental illness, including psychosis, is determined based on criteria in the DSM-5 (APA, 2013). Each diagnosis is described in detail with symptoms outlined, and the requirements for diagnosis specified. For example, to meet criteria for schizophrenia, an individual must have two or more from a list of five symptoms and meet a number of requirements including duration and frequency of symptoms (APA, 2013). This means that each person who receives a particular diagnosis meets these requirements. However, this is not to say that every person with a particular illness will present in the same way. Various combinations of symptoms exist, as well as presentations where one symptom is more prominent than others. The heterogeneity of schizophrenia and other psychotic illness is what often leads to concern about inconsistencies. Perceived inconsistencies may then call the validity of the diagnosis into question, leading to confusion about the appropriate treatment approach. The hallmark of psychotic disorders may be the heterogeneous presentation, which has historically caused much difficulty for those who research and treat these disorders (Carpenter & Kirkpatrick, 1988; Keller, Fisher & Carpenter, 2011). Nonetheless, there is indeed a standardized set of criteria used to identify persons with these particular illnesses, each of which is outlined in detail in the DSM-5 (APA, 2013) and remains the standard for diagnosis in the United States.

7.1.2 Children Cannot Be Diagnosed

The age of onset for most psychotic illnesses is late teens and early adulthood, generally between the ages of 16 and 30. However, occasionally individuals experience an onset of psychosis during childhood, or later in adulthood. While these occurrences are not the norm, they are possible. None of the psychotic illnesses outlined in the DSM have stated age restrictions on diagnosis and can thus be diagnosed at any age at which symptoms present (APA, 2013). However, it is important to follow diagnostic criteria and consider the context and rule outs for differential diagnoses, as it is not unusual for children to exhibit apparent symptoms of psychosis when the condition is not psychotic in nature. For instance, it is not uncommon for children who have experienced trauma to exhibit symptoms that may outwardly appear psychotic, such as talking to oneself, stating beliefs not based in reality, confusion and disorganization, or social isolation. Moreover, some childhood behaviors are perfectly developmentally appropriate but can be easily misconstrued as psychosis, such as having and communicating with imaginary friends.

7.1.3 Youth with Psychosis Are Dangerous

A myth that seems to drive much of the stigma and fear about psychosis is that individuals who experience these symptoms are dangerous and often violent. The relationship between psychosis and violence risk is a complicated one, with research on both sides of the argument. While some research supports a relationship between the experience of psychosis and physical aggression (Fazel et al., 2009; Hodgins, 2008), the interacting variables are notable and help to provide context. First, the relationship between psychosis and violence is strongly moderated by the presence of substance use (Fazel et al., 2009; Mulvey et al., 2006). That is, the risk of violence for an individual who has a psychotic illness and a substance abuse problem is the same as if that individual had only a substance abuse issue. It appears that the presence of substances in the context of psychosis, rather than psychotic symptoms themselves, results in an increased risk of physically aggressive behavior. Alternately, a separate body of literature supports that serious mental illnesses, including psychosis, do not independently increase violence risk (Elbogen & Johnson, 2009).

Moreover, even if psychosis has a statistical relationship to violence risk, individuals with psychosis account for a small minority of violent offenders (Taylor, 2008). This means that individuals without psychotic illness are responsible for the vast majority of violent offending. To view mental illness in general or psychosis as a common cause of violence is to overly simplify issues of violence (Elbogen & Johnson, 2009).

In contrast, the portrayal of individuals with psychosis in popular media hyperbolizes this association in order to enhance the fear associated with the unfamiliar (Moran, 2012). To this point, Owen (2012) reports that in an analysis of media depictions of psychosis, a vast majority (83%) were portrayed as dangerous or violent, and nearly one-third (31%) exhibited specifically homicidal behavior. This greatly exaggerates any minute association that may exist, as research unwaveringly supports that most individuals with a psychotic illness will not perpetrate violence (Elbogen & Johnson, 2009; Fazel et al., 2009; Moran, 2012; Mulvey et al., 2006). These media depictions cause the public to greatly overemphasize the likelihood of becoming victim to someone with a psychotic illness. In fact, much literature suggests that individuals with psychotic illnesses are more likely to become victims of violence than perpetrators (Appleby et al., 2001; Hiday, 2006).

7.1.4 Psychosis Involves Split Personalities

One of the most common misconceptions about psychosis, and specifically schizophrenia, is that it involves having "split" or "multiple" personalities. While people with psychosis may interact with the world differently than they did previously, the development of "alters" or independent personality structures is not a component of psychosis. Rather, this is a defining feature of dissociative identity disorder (formerly multiple personality disorder). Several sources appear to largely contribute to the confusion between these two conditions. First is the term schizophrenia itself, coined by Eugen Bleuler (1911/1950), which translates to "split-mind"; Bleuler intended it to describe the disconnection between psychic functions in people with psychosis. In the case of schizophrenia, the "split" being described is within the same personality, not between them. Nevertheless, it is easy to see how the two concepts became confused.

Furthermore, in popular media and movies, it is not unusual for these concepts to be mislabeled or confused. For example, both of the films *Donnie Darko* and *Me, Myself and Irene* include main characters who are purported to have a psychotic disorder, but whose symptoms as characterized in the film appear to be more analogous to dissociative identity disorder (Owen, 2012). These inaccurate portrayals of psychosis further a misunderstanding of these illnesses. It is important to clarify this distinction to validate the experiences of individuals living with each of these illnesses and to reduce misinformation. Accurate information is critical to the destigmatization and increased support (political, social, and financial) that is necessary for successful advancements and treatment.

7.1.5 Psychosis Is Caused by Poor Parenting

A number of mischaracterizations of psychosis have developed over time. These etiological myths led to treatments that were misguided and largely ineffective, thereby prolonging our understanding and treatment of these illnesses. One of the first explanations for psychosis, and one that has proven to have some longevity, is the notion that psychotic illness is caused by poor parenting, particularly, poor mothering. This idea originated as a concept called "the schizophrenigenic mother," referring to a mother with an oscillating pattern of overprotection and rejection that was popularized from the 1940s into the early 1970s. However, as research methodology became more sophisticated in regard to analyzing family systems, the research support for the schizophrenigenic mother as an etiology crumbled (Neill, 1990).

7.1.6 Psychosis Is Caused by Drug Use

An alternative proposal that has gained popularity is that psychosis is caused by substance use. While existing literature does support a relationship between psychosis and cannabis and stimulants like cocaine or prescription drugs like Ritalin or Adderall, it does not appear to be a causal link (Gururajan et al., 2012; Moon, 2011). That is, everyone who uses these substances does not develop psychosis, and everyone who develops psychosis has not necessarily used these substances. However, it is important to note that individuals who are vulnerable to developing psychotic illness may experience exacerbations in symptoms when using cannabis and hallucinogens, and drug use may be the catalyst to the development of a first psychotic experience.

Current research supports a diathesis-stress model of psychotic disorders that considers a complex interaction of genetics, biological factors, and life experience (Lenzenweger, 2010; Tsuang et al., 2002). An individual must have the underlying biological predisposition for the condition to occur, but that alone is not sufficient to result in the manifestation of an illness state. Rather, it is the interaction of the biological predisposition with environmental influences that increases the likelihood that the illness will be expressed. Such environmental influences could certainly consist of substantial difficulties in the family of origin, as well as substance use. However, present research does not support that either of these conditions alone, without the biological underpinnings, could result in a psychotic disorder like schizophrenia.

7.1.7 Adults with Psychosis Are Very Likely to Have Children with Psychosis

While it has been well documented that genes contribute to the presence of psychotic illness, the diathesis-stress model implies that it is not the determining factor of whether psychosis ultimately develops. Nonetheless, individuals who have a genetic relative with a psychotic illness are more likely to develop psychosis than someone who does not. Let's consider the prevalence rates of schizophrenia as an example. Approximately 1% of the general population will experience schizophrenia (APA, 2013). Alternatively, if an individual has a parent with schizophrenia, the prevalence rate increases to 6%. This relative risk increases and decreases with the genetic similarity of the relative in question (Gottesman, 1991). However, nearly 80% of individuals considered genetically "at risk" due to having any biological relative with schizophrenia never develop any symptoms of the illness (Lenzenweger, 2010). This suggests that like many other conditions, having a parent or family member with a psychotic illness may increase risk of developing such an illness, but it is in no way deterministic. The vast majority of children born to individuals with psychotic illness will not develop psychosis themselves.

Nevertheless, this misconception has perpetuated stigma and prejudice against individuals with psychosis. In the early twentieth century, this prejudice led to drastic and fear-based measures. Negative eugenics is the sterilization or reduced sexual reproduction of those demonstrating undesirable traits. While sterilization was not widely used, it was one method in an attempt to reduce the prevalence of psychotic illnesses and was later implemented as an extreme measure during World War II (History Cooperative, 2015).

7.1.8 Youth with Psychosis Do Not Have Feelings

This myth appears to be an extrapolation of negative symptoms, which result in a loss of ability or function in particular areas. One domain that is commonly impacted is "affect" or the ability to display emotion using facial expression. Some individuals with psychosis will display what is known as "flat affect," meaning that their facial expression remains more or less the same regardless of the situation. That is, they may have an identical expression when talking about a death in the family as they do when speaking about an upcoming birthday. This diminished affect may make it difficult for people to interpret the person's emotional experience, as it may outwardly look as if they are indifferent. However, research has supported that despite outward appearances, individuals with psychosis report similar experiences of emotion as individuals without psychosis (Kring et al., 1993). Moreover, the presence of disorganized symptoms may cause an emotional response that is incongruent with a particular situation, such as laughing when discussing a death in the family. Again, this is related to an underlying process associated with the illness and does not reflect an individual's emotional capacity.

7.1.9 Spiritual Etiology and Treatment

Descriptions of psychotic-like symptoms are found as far back as 2000 B.C. and across a variety of cultural contexts (History Cooperative, 2015). Ancient cultures characterized illnesses marked by bizarre behavior, lack of self-control, insanity, and seizures as supernatural and demonic, and efforts were largely designed to expel spirits or demons in some fashion. Religious examples included exorcism, where a priest or spiritual leader was brought in to facilitate the release of a demonic spirit that had taken over the individual (History Cooperative, 2015). A physical treatment often used in the ancient Greek and Roman cultures was trepanning. Trepanning refers to drilling holes in the skull to "release" spirits or allow them to exit the individual they were occupying (History Cooperative, 2015). At times, ancient Roman societies viewed psychotic-like experiences as evidence of angering the Gods, which was met with flogging or other punitive methods of punishment (History Cooperative, 2015).

7.1.10 Imbalance of Bodily Fluids

Ancient Greek societies may have demonstrated one of the first documented biological approaches to psychosis. Their theory of humoral pathology postulated that an imbalance of bodily fluids (black bile, yellow bile, phlegm, and blood) could induce "madness," contemporarily characterized as psychotic illness. The imbalance was thought to be caused by too much blood, and the preferred "treatment" approach included correcting this imbalance through methods such as bloodletting, whereby blood was released from the body through cutting or leeches.

7.1.11 History of Ineffective Treatments

The nineteenth century began a shift toward characterizing psychosis as a disease that starts in adolescence and has a chronic, deteriorating trajectory. This shift contributed to trials and research focused on treatment of psychotic illness. The twentieth century introduced a number of approaches focused on addressing a severe brain disorder, and physical interventions were designed to shock, change, or calm the system.

Insulin Coma Therapy. Insulin coma therapy (ICT) was introduced in the 1930s, following notable improvements in psychotic symptoms when giving insulin to individuals with psychotic illness (Jones, 2000). Patients were administered large doses of insulin to reduce blood sugar levels and produce a comatose state. Common effects were confusion, weakness, slurred speech, unsteady gait, increased breathing rate, and sweating (Fink & Karliner, 2002; Jones, 2000). Symptom remission was documented and ICT remained in use for two decades. Evidence of ICT use in children with psychosis also demonstrated positive improvements with no serious complications (Annell, 1955).

Unfortunately, the aftercare for ICT was quite demanding. The therapy was continued over the course of several days, and patients required round-the-clock care (Fink & Karliner, 2002; Jones, 2000). Moreover, a paper published in 1953 on the "insulin myth" called into question many of ICT findings and outcomes (Jones, 2000), and a 1957 randomized control trial demonstrated no significant differences in an ICT group compared with a non-insulin group receiving another compound. The authors concluded that insulin was "not a specific therapeutic agent" (Jones, 2000). This, along with the introduction of effective pharmacological treatments (Thorazine) led to the fall of ICT and the closure of these units in psychiatric hospitals (Fink & Karliner, 2002).

Convulsive Therapies. It has been reported that Hippocrates first noted a reduction in psychotic-like symptoms caused by (malaria-induced) convulsions. Over time, physicians also noted a very low prevalence of co-morbid epilepsy and psychotic symptoms (Fink & Karliner, 2002; Sabbatini, 1997). This led to the development of treatments that induced convulsions beginning in the 1930s. Chemically induced convulsions showed promise and were cheaper, easier, and more reliably induced than coma states with ICT (Sabbatini, 1997). However, this method was harder to control and incurred more side effects such as bone fractures from violent shaking. Moreover, while a coma state in ICT could be reversed quickly and predictably by administering glucose, there was no such mechanism for chemical convulsions.

In 1937, shock therapy was used to induce convulsive experiences, with remission rates of 30%–88% (Fink & Karliner, 2002). While positive outcomes were demonstrated for affective psychosis in particular, ECT began to be used as a method to subdue or punish patients, rather than a treatment-informed approach for psychosis. Thus, its benefits were overshadowed, and the practice garnered negative support and a reputation as a torturous treatment method. Moreover, ECT became particularly unpopular after its depictions in *One Flew Over the Cuckoo's Nest* in 1975 (Sabbatini, 1997). Concurrent introduction of medications also greatly contributed to reduced use of this method for some time.

Lobotomy. The 1930s also introduced lobotomies. Lobotomies were used to disconnect or sever the connections between the frontal and the anterior portions of the brain. The earliest methods included boring holes in the skull, while later methods inserted instruments into the eye socket to create cuts or lesions in the brain. The goal was to disrupt connections or circuitry thought to be related to psychotic experience. While this method was often accompanied by a reduction in symptoms, severe and devastating side effects also presented, such as impairments in executive and social functioning. Unfortunately, these effects were expected and were often viewed as consequences that were more preferable than the devastating effects of psychosis (History Cooperative, 2015). Like ICT and ECT before it, lobotomies also became less popular with the advent of pharmacological treatments in the 1950s.

Sidebar Box: Is homeopathy effective for schizophrenia? by Michael Marshall

Homeopathy is promoted for all manner of ailments, including physical conditions ranging from hay fever to cancer. Its promotion for psychological issues is equally broad ranging – with homeopaths promoting their treatment for most mental health issues, including schizophrenia (Fountainhead Clinic, n.d.).

The breadth of therapeutic indications claimed by homeopaths runs contrary to the strength of its evidence base: while it's hard to find a single condition not treated by one homeopath or another, it's equally hard to find any credible and replicable evidence that the treatment is effective. In fact, based on a review of the research, the National Health and Medical Research Council (NHMRC) in Australia concluded that "there are no health conditions for which there is reliable evidence that homeopathy is effective" (NHMRC, 2015, p. 1).

The reason for this inefficacy lies in a central tenet of homeopathy, "the law of infinitesimals." Homeopathy is based on the misguided principle that solutions get stronger the more they are diluted, with the strongest remedies diluted far past the point where any trace of the original active ingredient can still be found, even with the most accurate measuring equipment. As such, the vast majority of homeopathic remedies contain nothing but water (The 10:23 Campaign, n.d.) and the sugar that makes up the blank pill. It is therefore no surprise when a chemically inert pill fails to be effective for any condition.

Michael Marshall, BA, is Project Director of the Good Thinking Society. He is also one of the organizers of the QED: Question, Explore, Discover conference in Manchester, United Kingdom.

7.2 Research-Supported Approaches

The robust effects of contemporary treatments for psychosis are well documented. The birth of typical and then atypical medications for psychotic disorders offered relief from distressing symptoms, and medication side effects. This also afforded opportunities for reengagement and reconnection in a number of important areas of life.

A number of psychotherapeutic interventions for psychosis have also demonstrated substantial positive effects. Cognitive-behavior therapy (CBT; Kingdon & Turkington, 2008), third-wave therapies such as mindfulness-based therapy and acceptance and commitment therapy (ACT; Abba, Chadwick, & Stevenson, 2008; Bach et al., 2012; Morris, Johns, & Oliver, 2013), and family therapy (McFarlane, 2004) have been quite effective. Despite misrepresentations suggesting that psychotic symptoms are not amenable to therapy, and individuals with psychotic disorders cannot engage in therapy, findings show tremendous gains that include increased subjective quality of life, decreased symptoms, and greater functioning, overall (Lysaker et al., 2010). An exciting new area of research over the past decade is early intervention for psychotic disorders. A number of randomized control trials have demonstrated significant, durable effects for recovery-oriented, coordinated specialty care programs that include medication management, psychotherapy, supported employment and/or academic support, and family support and education (Kane et al., 2015). This shift from "maintenance" to recovery has proved fruitful in our understanding of psychotic illnesses and effective treatment approaches and has broadened expectations for potential outcomes and prognosis.

7.3 Conclusion

As our knowledge of mental health has expanded, so has our understanding of effective treatment approaches. Fortunately, all of the aforementioned pseudoscience treatments are no longer used in their historical form, as the introduction of Thorazine and other pharmacological treatments challenged their effectiveness and necessity. Moreover, these approaches became less popular as harmful side effects, poor treatment outcomes, and misuse came to light. Only ECT has been modified to be an acceptable and safe treatment used today, and ECT now demonstrates positive findings for psychotic illness, particularly in conjunction with medication (Grover, Hazari, & Kate, 2015; Pawełczyk et al., 2014; Zervas, Theleritis, & Soldatos, 2012).

The treatment of psychotic disorders has come quite a long way in our understanding and treatment of psychotic disorders. While we still have a long way to go, important lessons have been learned along the way that inform the journey. Youth living with psychotic disorders can and do recover in meaningful ways. Thus, we should challenge our notions of what is possible, and what can be achieved when the sky is the limit, and health and happiness are the priority and goal.

Works Cited in Sidebar

Fountainhead Clinic. (n.d.). Naturopathic treatment of schizophrenia. Retrieved from http://fountainheadclinic.com/schizophrenia/

National Health and Medical Research Council. (2015). Statement on homeopathy. Retrieved from www.nhmrc.gov.au

The 10:23 Campaign. (n.d.). What is homeopathy? Retrieved from www.1023 .org.uk

References

Abba, N., Chadwick, P., & Stevenson, C. (2008). Responding mindfully to distressing psychosis: A grounded theory analysis. *Psychotherapy Research*, *18*(1), 77–87.

American Psychiatric Association. (2013). *Diagnostic and statistical manual of mental disorders*. 5th edn. Arlington, VA: American Psychiatric Publishing.

Annell, A. (1955). Insulin shock treatment in children with psychotic disturbances. *Acta Psychotherapeutics*, *3*, 193–205.

Appleby, L., Mortensen, P. B., Dunn, G., & Hiroeh, U. (2001). Death by homicide, suicide, and other unnatural causes in people with mental illness: A population-based study. *The Lancet*, *358*, 2110–2112.

Bach, P., Hayes, S. C., & Gallop, R. (2012). Long-term effects of brief acceptance and commitment therapy for psychosis. *Behavior Modification*, *36*(2), 165–181.

Bleuler, E. (1911/1950). *Dementia praecox or the group of schizophrenias* (J. Zinkin, trans.). New York: International Universities Press.

Carpenter, W. J., & Kirkpatrick, B. (1988). The heterogeneity of the long-term course of schizophrenia. *Schizophrenia Bulletin*, *14*(4), 645–652.

Elbogen, E. B., & Johnson, S. C. (2009). The intricate link between violence and mental disorder: Results from the national epidemiologic survey on alcohol and related conditions. *Archives of General Psychiatry*, *66*, 152–161.

Fazel, S., Gulati, G., Linsell, L., Geddes, J. R., & Grann, M. (2009). Schizophrenia and violence: Systematic review and meta-analysis. *Plos Medicine*, *6(8)*, 1–15. doi:10.1371/journal.pmed.1000120

Fink, M., & Karliner, W. (2002). A brilliant madness. Primary sources: Insulin coma therapy. Retrieved from www.pbs.org/wgbh/amex/nash/filmmore/ ps_ict.html

Gottesman, I. I., 1991. *Schizophrenia genesis: The origins of madness*. New York: W. H. Freeman & Co.

Grover, S., Hazari, N., & Kate, N. (2015). Combined use of clozapine and ECT: A review. *Acta Neuropsychiatrica, 27*(3), 131–142. doi:10.1017/neu.2015.8

Gururajan, A., Manning, E., Klug, M., & van den Buuse, M. (2012). Drugs of abuse and increased risk of psychosis development. *Australian and New Zealand Journal of Psychiatry, 46*(12), 1120–1135. doi:10.1177/0004867412455232

Hiday, V. A. (2006). Putting community risk in perspective: A look at correlations, causes and controls. *International Journal of Law and Psychiatry, 29*, 316–331.

History Cooperative. (2015). Divine madness: A history of schizophrenia. Retrieved from http://historycooperative.org/divine-madness-a-history-of-schizophrenia/

Hodgins, S. (2008). Violent behavior among people with schizophrenia: A framework for investigation of causes, and effective treatment, and prevention. *Philosophical Transactions of the Royal Society of London. Series B: Biological Sciences, 363*(1503), 2505–2518.

Institute of Medicine. (2006). *Improving the quality of health care for mental and substance-use conditions*. Washington, DC: Institute of Medicine.

Jones, K. (2000). Insulin coma therapy in schizophrenia. *Journal of the Royal Society of Medicine, 93*, 147–149.

Kane, J. M., Robinson, D. G., Schooler, N. R., Mueser, K. T., Penn, D. L., Rosenheck, R. A. ... & Marcy, P. (2015). Comprehensive versus usual community care for first-episode psychosis: 2-year outcomes from the NIMH RAISE Early Treatment Program. *American Journal of Psychiatry, 173*(4), 362–372.

Keller, W. R., Fischer, B. A., & Carpenter, J. T. (2011). Revisiting the diagnosis of schizophrenia: Where have we been and where are we going? *CNS Neuroscience & Therapeutics, 17*(2), 83–88. doi:10.1111/j.1755-5949.2010.00229.x

Kingdon, D. G., & Turkington, D. (2008). *Cognitive therapy of schizophrenia*. New York: Guilford Press

Kring, A. M., Kerr, S. L., Smith, D. A., & Neale, J. M. (1993). Flat affect in schizophrenia does not reflect diminished subjective experience of emotion. *Journal of Abnormal Psychology*, 102(4), 507–517. doi:10.1037/0021-843X.102.4.507

Lenzenweger, M. F. (2010). *Schizotypy and schizophrenia: The view from experimental psychopathology*. New York: Guilford.

Lysaker, P. H., Glynn, S. M., Wilkniss, S. M., & Silverstein, S. M. (2010). Psychotherapy and recovery from schizophrenia: A review of potential applications and need for future study. *Psychological Services, 7*(2), 75–91.

Martin, J. K., Pescosolido, B. A., & Tuch, S. A. (2000). Of fear and loathing: The role of "disturbing behavior," labels, and causal attributions in shaping public attitudes toward people with mental illness. *Journal of Health and Social Behavior*, *41*(2), 208–223.

McFarlane, W. R. (2004). *Multifamily groups in the treatment of severe psychiatric disorders*. New York: Guildford Press.

Moon, M. A. (2011). Marijuana use linked to earlier psychosis onset. *Clinical Psychiatry News*, *39*(3), 4.

Moran, M. (2012). Schizophrenia and violence risk: Media distort the picture. *Psychiatric News*, *47*, 13.

Morris, E., Johns, L, & Oliver, J. (eds.). (2013). *Acceptance and commitment therapy and mindfulness for psychosis*. West Sussex, UK: John Wiley & Sons.

Mulvey, E. P., Odgers, C., Skeem, J., Gardner, W., Schubert, C., & Lidz, C. (2006). Substance use and community violence: A test of the relation at the daily level. *Journal of Consulting and Clinical Psychology*, *74*(4), 743–754. doi:10.1037/0022-006X.74.4.743

Neill, J. (1990). Whatever became of the schizophrenogenic mother? *American Journal of Psychotherapy*, *44*(4), 499.

Owen, P. R. (2012). Portrayals of schizophrenia by entertainment media: A content analysis of contemporary movies. *Psychiatric Services*, *63*(7), 655–659.

Pawełczyk, T., Kołodziej–Kowalska, E., Pawełczyk, A., & Rabe-Jabłońska, J. (2014). Effectiveness and clinical predictors of response to combined ECT and antipsychotic therapy in patients with treatment-resistant schizophrenia and dominant negative symptoms. *Psychiatry Research*, *220*(1–2), 175–180. doi:10.1016/j.psychres.2014.07.071

Perälä, J., Suvisaari, J., Saarni, S. I., Kuoppasalmi, K., Isometsä, E., Pirkola, S. . . . & Härkänen, T. (2007). Lifetime prevalence of psychotic and bipolar I disorders in a general population. *Archives of General Psychiatry*, *64*(1), 19–28.

Sabbatini, R. (1997). The history of shock therapy in psychiatry. Retrieved from www.cerebromente.org.br/n04/historia/shock_i.htm

Taylor, P. J. (2008). Psychosis and violence: Stories, fears, and reality. *The Canadian Journal of Psychiatry*, *53*(10), 647–659.

Tsuang, M. T., Stone, W. S., Tarbox, S. I., & Faraone, S. V. (2002). An integration of schizophrenia with schizotypy: Identification of schizotaxia and implications for research on treatment and prevention. *Schizophrenia Research*, *54*(1–2), 169–175.

Zervas, I. M., Theleritis, C., & Soldatos, C. R. (2012). Using ECT in schizophrenia: A review from a clinical perspective. *The World Journal of Biological Psychiatry*, *13*(2), 69–105. doi:10.3109/15622975.2011.564653

8

Bipolar Spectrum

Guillermo Pérez Algorta and Eric Youngstrom

In the space of a decade, pediatric bipolar disorder (PBD) went from being virtually unheard of to being all the rage in many parts of the United States. From the occasional case report published every decade or so, PBD suddenly became a national headline, with books explaining how to recognize it selling hundreds of thousands of copies (Papolos & Papolos, 1999). There was a 40-fold increase in billing diagnoses (Moreno et al., 2007), and a third to half of psychiatrically hospitalized youths getting assigned bipolar diagnoses in some regions (Blader & Carlson, 2007). Where had all this bipolar been hiding? How had clinicians missed such an obviously impairing condition for years? Or was there actually a sudden increase in how many children had it – a pandemic increase in bipolar disorder?

A countervailing view was that the new trend was a mistake – people were getting swept up in a trend not backed by scientific data. Research has surged in the more than two decades from the mid-1990s to now as the field tries to sort among fact, fad, and fiction. The data is nudging the scientific community toward the middle – bipolar is not lurking behind every rock and tree, but it is also possible to be too skeptical about it occurring in youth, which can lead to delayed treatment, longer periods of illness, and worse prognoses.

Most research uses the operational definitions from the *Diagnostic and Statistical Manual* (DSM) (American Psychiatric Association, 2000, 2013). The term bipolar spectrum disorder (BPSD) refers to different diagnostic categories defined in the DSM-5 that include bipolar I and II disorder, cyclothymic disorder, and other specified/unspecified bipolar and related disorders (American Psychiatric Association, 2013). The clinical determinants of these categories are three mood episodes (manic, hypomanic, and depressive episodes) that vary in terms of symptom composition, severity, and duration. The components of these mood episodes can manifest in dynamic ways (sequential or overlapping), leading to potentially complex and personalized patterns of clinical presentations. The only formal developmental difference in terms of diagnostic criteria in the DSM-5 for bipolar disorder in children and adolescents as compared to adults, is based on criteria A for cyclothymic disorder, where instead of requiring two years with numerous periods with hypomanic and depressive symptoms (that do not meet criteria for a full episode), the rule is shortened to one year.

At the symptom level, bipolar spectrum disorders are characterized by irritability and/or euphoria with somatic (e.g., increased energy, decreased need for sleep), cognitive (e.g., distractibility, grandiosity), and behavioral disturbances (e.g., increase in goal-directed activity, excessive involvement in pleasurable activities with high potential for painful consequences). Anhedonia and/or sadness/irritability with associated features (e.g., insomnia/ hypersomnia, feelings of worthlessness/ guilt, thoughts of death/suicide) characterize depressive symptoms.

8.1 Pseudoscience and Questionable Ideas

8.1.1 Diagnostic Controversies

When attention to the diagnosis exploded, almost no rigorous studies had looked for bipolar disorder in youth. Because the field assumed that it only occurred in adults, there was no point in even asking about it. A meta-analysis looked at more than 1,500 abstracts and papers to find just 12 epidemiological studies that reported results for hypomania or mania in youth. Those studies still encompassed a lot of data, based on more than 13,000 youth from seven countries, but it is still remarkable that 99% of the research had not even addressed the question. Based on the global data, the estimated prevalence of BPSD when formal diagnoses are considered in children and adolescents is approximately 1%–2% (Van Meter, Moreira, & Youngstrom, 2011). The community rate is not different in the United States versus the rest of the world, and it increases following puberty, though cases that meet strict diagnostic symptom and duration criteria occur in childhood as well. Another meta-analysis shows that the most prevalent symptoms (> 70%) of mania and hypomania in children and adolescents diagnosed with bipolar disorder are increased energy (79%), irritability (77%), mood lability (76%), distractibility (74%), goal-directed activity (72%; Van Meter et al., 2016).

The burden of disease data shows that PBD is not a good diagnosis to ignore. Symptoms, episodes, and full diagnoses are all associated with significant functional impairment and decrements in quality of life, affecting all domains of life including family functioning and social and academic life (Axelson et al., 2006; Freeman et al., 2009; Goldstein et al., 2009; Keenan-Miller et al., 2012). Not surprisingly, suicide-related behaviors are common among these youth (Algorta et al., 2011; Hauser, Galling, & Correll, 2013).

Despite substantive advances in knowledge about BPSD in children and adolescents, with at least nine prospective longitudinal studies covering periods from 2 to 22 years (Youngstrom & Algorta, 2014) that show developmental continuity and associated features consistent with adult samples of cases with bipolar disorder, still there is a perception of controversy about the validity of this condition in young populations, in particular, when bipolar I criteria are not fulfilled.

The concept of a "bipolar spectrum" has been strongly criticized as an example of "disease mongering" (Healy, 2006) (see details in Youngstrom, Van Meter, & Algorta, 2010). Overly skeptical arguments mainly focus on the marked increase in diagnoses and prescriptions for mood-stabilizing medications for youth (Olfman, 2015). Some talk arose about the "imperialism of bipolar disorder" when the pendulum of practice swung from "there is no such diagnosis in children" to "every rage is a sign of bipolarity" (see Fristad & Algorta, 2013).

But the discussion about the validity of BPSD is a good teaching example of our tendency to ignore the true prevalence of a disease, driven by a cognitive disposition called "base-rate neglect" (Croskerry, 2003). This bias occurs when our brain uses a shortcut to anchor its estimates of probability based on past beliefs or current trendiness rather than focusing on an objective benchmark. The bias contributes to overdiagnosis of issues that are "in vogue" and on the minds of both clinicians and families, and it also can lead to discounting of quiet but common issues.

Using the cognitive distortion hypothesis, we expose paradoxes associated with the overdiagnosis and overmedication scenarios mentioned earlier. Thus, the figure often portrayed as evidence of overdiagnosis in clinical settings (approximating 1 diagnosis per 200 billing visits) (Moreno et al., 2007) is actually smaller than the number of people expected to experience the condition based on epidemiological data (e.g., 2 to 4 cases per 200 youths; Van Meter, Moreira, & Youngstrom, 2011).

One of the main causes for concern about the increase in bipolar diagnoses is the rate of prescription of psychotropic medication. The current practice parameters recommend medication as a first-line treatment for mania and for depression (McClellan, Kowatch, & Findling, 2007). The fear is that increasing rates of diagnosis will drive the increase in prescription of medication for youth, with incomplete knowledge about the long-term effects of these drugs on the developing brain and body. If the diagnosis is incorrect, the youth are less likely to benefit from a medication chosen to treat a mood disorder, but they still are exposed to all of the side effects.

There are several flaws to the over-prescription argument. One is that, empirically, psychiatrists and pediatricians are prescribing more medication to youth with attention-deficit/hyperactivity disorder (ADHD) and disruptive behavior disorders than with bipolar disorders – including the second-generation atypical antipsychotics and anticonvulsants that some worry about being overused for bipolar disorder (Kowatch et al., 2013; Olfson et al., 2012). Medications are used more commonly than psychotherapy for treatment of anxiety, depression, ADHD, autism spectrum disorder, and other common conditions. Psychotherapy is difficult to scale: it takes more time to deliver therapy to each family, and it is harder to teach the practice community about breakthroughs and advances in treatment.

Professionals need more of an array of titrated treatment options; when people stay fixed on debating whether bipolar disorders even exist, it is hard to get psychotherapy trials designed and funded. Worrying only about overmedication ignores the risks and costs that are associated with delayed or inappropriate treatment. As is the case with most mental health issues, most children who actually meet the criteria for bipolar disorder may not have access to treatment (Goldstein, Sassi, & Diler, 2012; Merikangas et al., 2010; Merikangas et al., 2011).

8.1.2 Questionable and Ineffective Treatments

Malinowski (1948) wrote that on the open sea, where catches were uncertain and there was considerable danger, the Trobriand islanders used a variety of magical practices. On the other hand, when fishing within the safety and plenty of the inner lagoon, they used none. Unfortunately, a lot of families are sailing on fickle and dangerous seas, trying to navigate the best course for dealing with their child's unpredictable mood swings and serious behavior problems. Many mental health practitioners are also sailing on the open sea, without a clear strategy to respond to these families. When they are dealing with potential bipolar spectrum disorders, there is not yet an evidence-based inner lagoon with well-established guidelines and practices. Families and clinicians can use the science to make educated estimates of safer courses of action that are more likely to help, but it also would be crucial to have some methods for sorting the best evidence from pseudoscience and magical thinking. Here we will use "magic" to refer to options that come with hope of benefit that is not yet supported (or even tested and unsupported) by scientific study.

Several magical options are considered complementary and/or alternative treatments. Gene Arnold and colleagues offered a commonsense guideline, saying that "a treatment that is safe, easy, cheap, and sensible (SECS) in light of the other knowledge, does not need as much evidence to justify trying it as does a treatment that is risky, unrealistic, difficult, or expensive (RUDE)" (Arnold, Hurt, & Lofthouse, 2013, p. 382). However, they called attention to this caveat: "passing the SECS criterion does not necessarily mean a treatment is evidence-based in the usual sense. The criterion is merely an interim guide awaiting further research" (p. 382).

Today, several alternative or complementary treatments are offered as over-the-counter SECS options, without regulations. These include dietary supplements and lifestyle and healing practices. How would we decide whether one of these options is currently more SECS or RUDE? The evolutionary need for dietary nutrients is well established, but there is not yet clear evidence for an evolutionary need for herbs (Arnold et al., 2016). For example, when it comes to herbs, raising our security threshold becomes important, because natural does not mean harmless. The expense also can be considerable, and the potency and quality control highly variable. A warning supported by results coming from a systematic review on the efficacy, safety, and types of herbal medicine for depression showed that more than 90% of randomized controlled trials had poor methodological quality (Yeung et al., 2014). Thus, popular herbal remedies associated with antidepressant effects to target bipolar symptoms such as St. John's wort (*Hypericum perforatum*) need careful consideration (for more details, see Waltz, 2000). Herbal remedies thus often entail more risk and expense – two of the RUDE criteria.

Things turn mistier when decisions about SECS and RUDE are related to practices residing in the intersection between dietary supplements and lifestyle, such as ketogenic diets, for which there are no studies to date with pediatric bipolar samples and only a few case studies with adults (Phelps, Siemers, & El-Mallakh, 2013; Yaroslavsky, Stahl, & Belmaker, 2002). And the list of diets extends to other variants, such as Feingold diet, based on the principle of avoiding synthetic flavoring and food colors, not to mention casein-free (free milk protein) and gluten-free (protein found in wheat and other grains) diets. Moreover, in orthomolecular therapy the use of vitamin mega-doses needs careful monitoring to prevent serious side effects.

In terms of healing practices, there is a broad range of alternatives from meditation and relaxation techniques to acupuncture. There are studies for depression with heterogeneous quality levels in terms of design rigor. There are no studies with youth with bipolar disorders, but there is consensus that the level of acceptance, availability, tolerability, cost, and durability of effect are factors that deserve further consideration, entailing elements of the SECS criteria (Gracious et al., 2014). But the list can go on endlessly, including practices such as massage, Reiki, yoga, and Tai-Chi. Qureshi and Al-Bedah (2013) offer a list of around 120 variants of complementary and alternative treatments for mood disorders. To our knowledge, none of them has been formally tested in terms of safety, efficacy, and effectiveness for BPSD in children and adolescents.

> **Sidebar Box: Does naturopathic medicine help treat bipolar disorder? by Britt Hermes**
>
> Naturopathic doctors (NDs) are complementary and alternative Medicine (CAM) practitioners who claim they are trained similarly to physicians. It is critical to understand the education and philosophy behind naturopathy, as all patients are likely to encounter NDs.
>
> NDs believe the body has a mystical energy force called the *vis* that can be harnessed to heal through magical options. NDs passionately advertise that their therapies work, but no naturopathic treatment has been clinically proven to be safe and effective for bipolar disorder or any other condition. NDs attend four-year programs in which students take abbreviated versions of medical courses and study a plethora of CAM practices that include homeopathy, acupuncture, high-dose vitamins, and "functional medicine," the pseudoscientific use of excessive laboratory tests to prescribe supplements. The ND curriculum relies on the trappings of science and is accredited by a naturopathic council.
>
> NDs can become licensed to practice in 20 US states and Washington DC and are regulated by naturopathic boards. NDs have lobbied aggressively for these markers of legitimacy and have been successful by exploiting the public's scientific illiteracy and

proclivity for natural solutions. Lay naturopaths, on the other hand, do not attend accredited programs and are not regulated. The two professions, however, share the same health philosophy and use the same methods. Since NDs attach "doctor" to their name, patients perceive them as medically competent practitioners capable of diagnosing and treating disease. This misperception makes NDs uniquely dangerous (for more information, see Hermes, 2015a, 2015b).

Britt Hermes, MSc, doctoral student, writes about her former life as a naturopathic doctor and the risks of CAM at Naturopathic-Diaries.com.

8.2 Research-Supported Approaches

The first step to effective treatment is knowing with an acceptable level of accuracy whether a youth meets the criteria for a bipolar disorder or one of the more common issues that can look similar (Kim & Miklowitz, 2002). Getting the assessment right has been a major research focus, and there are established risk factors and rating scales (Youngstrom et al., 2015) as well as test sequences and algorithms (Youngstrom, Freeman, & Jenkins, 2009) and cognitive debiasing strategies (Jenkins & Youngstrom, 2016) that are free of charge and fast and produce large gains in the accuracy of diagnosis and clinical decision making about treatment (Jenkins et al., 2011; Jenkins et al., 2012).

The second step is collaborating with the client to review and decide among different treatment strategies. Depending on symptom severity, impairment, and family preferences, these options could be organized into a gradient that ranges from psychological to pharmacotherapeutic interventions (Straus et al., 2011; Youngstrom et al., 2009). Fristad and MacPherson (2014) reviewed 13 psychological intervention trials for the treatment of BPSD. Only three interventions (one with children, one with adolescents, and one with both age groups) were considered *probably efficacious treatments* (family psychoeducation plus skill building) and none was considered a *well-established* treatment intervention. The remaining interventions were evaluated as *possibly efficacious* (CBT interventions) or *experimental treatments* (dialectical behavior therapy [DBT] and interpersonal and social rhythm therapy for adolescents [IPSRT-A]).

Thus, there are some potentially effective approaches containing some common elements. However, effectiveness and generalizability are still limited by the small number of studies, sample characteristics, and settings where these studies were conducted. More trials have been carried out about pharmacological intervention for BPSD. These studies have been summarized in different reviews (Hamrin & Iennaco, 2010; Liu et al., 2011; Thomas, Stansifer, & Findling, 2011) or organized in the format of clinical guidelines (Dawson et al., 2007; McClellan, Kowatch, & Findling, 2007). The big picture includes consensus that second-generation antipsychotics (SGA) are highly efficacious for the treatment of acute manic/mixed episodes, but tolerability of these compounds is still a major challenge (Correll, Sheridan, & DelBello, 2010). There is only one study regarding lithium for the treatment of Bipolar I manic/mixed episodes (Findling et al., 2015), but no studies for bipolar depression in pediatric samples; and there is lack of evidence supporting Divalproex as an anti-manic among youth. Also, the reviews show the lack of evidence in terms of the best approach for bipolar depression in this age group, in particular because depression is the most burdensome mood polarity. They call for the need for long-term studies for recovery maintenance and additional research to increase our knowledge to prevent recurrence. Emphasis is also placed on the need for studies about tolerability considering the cost-benefit in terms of metabolic side effects versus anti-manic effect during the treatment of acute mania or cost-benefit of maintenance treatments. Finally, the reviews highlight the lack of evidence about interventions to target comorbid conditions such as anxiety (a major source of burden and functional impairment) and call for the need for studies about family history of treatment responsiveness (Goldstein et al., 2012; Kowatch et al., 2013).

8.3 Conclusion

Research is making significant progress in contributing to the understanding of BPSD in children and adolescents. Despite current difficulties, there is room for optimism regarding the navigation of challenging waters soon. Unfortunately, many professionals have been forced to consider some magical thinking until more research is conducted. New discoveries about pathophysiologic mechanisms involving oxidative stress, mitochondrial dysfunction, and inflammation in BPSD (Data-Franco et al., 2016; Nierenberg et al., 2013) are repositioning some old magical strategies as potentially hopeful ones (Sylvia et al., 2013).

Clearly, more work is needed. It is premature to extract firm conclusions about some of these alternative or complementary interventions for BPSD, but it is worth recognizing that sometimes they are more accepted by families than evidence-based treatments. Therefore, professionals need to accompany families during this decision-making process, especially while the levels of evidence are still so varied. Professionals also need to recognize our lack of understanding about the reasons explaining favorable changes when they are happening and make clear to clients that we do not yet know the final answers about dosing, efficacy, and safety. Professionals need to be firm when alternative practitioners encourage families to abandon prescription medications or encourage caution about reducing current dosages to eliminate side effects and complementing with some alternative treatment. The reason is simple: it is most likely that this combination never has been systematically tested. Professionals and our clients should "think smart" in terms of attributing therapeutic effect when adding additional options to previous prescribed treatments. It is important to encourage transparency with prescribing doctors to avoid surprises because of parallel treatments. Absent an emphasis on communication, parents may decide to add alternative options without telling doctors. Professionals need to facilitate a mature dialog in a climate where distrust in pharmaceutical companies is often the core belief supporting alternative treatment options. Professionals need to engage consumer advocacy groups in our request for more funding support to test approved medications and other treatments.

These are a few examples of how clinicians and families can work together to make high-stakes decisions based on the limited evidence available now, combined with principles and clear communication as we metaphorically try to rely on the sky to guide us to safety while sailing perilous seas. Professionals also need to continue working on dissemination strategies to overturn both practical and ideological barriers to incorporate established evidence-based practices to our toolbox to provide more satisfactory answers to families experiencing the consequences of BPSD in children and adolescents.

Works Cited in Sidebar

Hermes, B. (2015a). ND Confession, Part I: Clinical training inside and out. Retrieved from https://sciencebasedmedicine.org/

Hermes, B. (2015b). ND Confession, Part II: The accreditation of naturopathic "medical" education. Retrieved from https://sciencebasedmedicine.org/

Reference

Algorta, G. P., Youngstrom, E. A., Frazier, T. W., Freeman, A. J., Youngstrom, J. K., & Findling, R. L. (2011). Suicidality in pediatric bipolar disorder: Predictor or outcome of family processes and mixed mood presentation? *Bipolar Disorders*, *13*, 76–86. doi:10.1111/j.1399-5618.2010.00886.x

American Psychiatric Association. (2000). *Diagnostic and statistical manual of mental disorders*. 4th edn – Text Revision edn. Washington, DC: Author.

American Psychiatric Association. (2013). *Diagnostic and statistical manual of mental disorders*. 5th edn. Washington, DC: Author.

Arnold, L. E., Fristad, M. A., Gracious, B. L., Johnstone, J. M., Kaplan, B. J., Popper, C. W., & Rucklidge, J. J. (2016). Psychosis resulting from herbs rather than nutrients. *Primary Care Companion for CNS Disorders*, 18(2). doi:10.4088/PCC.16l01940

Arnold, L. E., Hurt, E., & Lofthouse, N. (2013). Attention-deficit/hyperactivity disorder: Dietary and nutritional treatments. *Child and Adolescent Psychiatric Clinics of North America*, *22*, 381–402.

Axelson, D., Birmaher, B., Strober, M., Gill, M. K., Valeri, S., Chiappetta, L. ... & Iyengar, S. (2006). Phenomenology of children and adolescents with bipolar spectrum disorders. *Archives of General Psychiatry*, *63*, 1139–1148.

Blader, J. C., & Carlson, G. A. (2007). Increased rates of bipolar disorder diagnoses among U.S. child, adolescent, and adult inpatients, 1996–2004. *Biological Psychiatry*, *62*, 107–114. doi:10.1016/j.biopsych.2006.11.006

Correll, C. U., Sheridan, E. M., & DelBello, M. P. (2010). Antipsychotic and mood stabilizer efficacy and tolerability in pediatric and adult patients with bipolar I mania: A comparative analysis of acute, randomized, placebo-controlled trials. *Bipolar Disorders*, *12*, 116–141. doi:10.1111/j.1399-5618.2010.00798.x

Croskerry, P. (2003). The importance of cognitive errors in diagnosis and strategies to minimize them. *Academic Medicine*, *78*, 775–780.

Data-Franco, J., Singh, A., Popovic, D., Ashton, M., Berk, M., Vieta, E. ... & Dean, O. M. (2016). Beyond the therapeutic shackles of the monoamines: New mechanisms in bipolar disorder biology. *Progress in Neuro-Psychopharmacology & Biological Psychiatry*. doi:10.1016/j.pnpbp.2016.09.004

Dawson, R., Lavori, P. W., Luby, J. L., Ryan, N. D., & Geller, B. (2007). Adaptive strategies for treating childhood mania. *Biological Psychiatry*, *61*, 758–764.

Findling, R. L., Robb, A., McNamara, N. K., Pavuluri, M. N., Kafantaris, V., Scheffer, R. ... & Taylor-Zapata, P. (2015). Lithium in the acute treatment of bipolar I disorder: A double-blind, placebo-controlled study. *Pediatrics*, *136*, 885–894. doi:10.1542/peds.2015-0743

Freeman, A. J., Youngstrom, E. A., Michalak, E., Siegel, R., Meyers, O. I., & Findling, R. L. (2009). Quality of life in pediatric bipolar disorder. *Pediatrics, 123,* e446–e452. doi:10.1542/peds.2008-0841

Fristad, M. A., & Algorta, G. P. (2013). Future directions for research on youth with bipolar spectrum disorders. *Journal of Clinical Child and Adolesentc Psychology, 42,* 734–747. doi:10.1080/15374416.2013.817312

Fristad, M. A., & Macpherson, H. A. (2014). Evidence-based psychosocial treatments for child and adolescent bipolar spectrum disorders. *Journal of Clinical Child and Adolescent Psychology, 43,* 339–355. doi:10.1080/15374416.2013.822309

Goldstein, B. I., Sassi, R., & Diler, R. S. (2012). Pharmacologic treatment of bipolar disorder in children and adolescents. *Child and Adolesentc Psychiatic Clinics of North America, 21,* 911–939. doi:10.1016/j.chc.2012.07.004

Goldstein, T. R., Birmaher, B., Axelson, D., Goldstein, B. I., Gill, M. K., Esposito-Smythers, C. ... & Keller, M. (2009). Psychosocial functioning among bipolar youth. *Journal of Affective Disorders, 114,* 174–183.

Gracious, B. L., Gurumurthy, S., Cottle, A., & McCabe, T. M. (2014). Complementary and alternative medicine in child and adolescent bipolar disorder. In S. M. Strakowski, M. P. DelBello, & C. M. Adler (eds.), *Bipolar disorder in youth: Presentation, treatment and neurobiology.* Oxford: Oxford University Press.

Hamrin, V., & Iennaco, J. D. (2010). Psychopharmacology of pediatric bipolar disorder. *Expert Review of Neurotherapeutics, 10,* 1053–1088.

Hauser, M., Galling, B., & Correll, C. U. (2013). Suicidal ideation and suicide attempts in children and adolescents with bipolar disorder: A systematic review of prevalence and incidence rates, correlates, and targeted interventions. *Bipolar Disordors, 15,* 507–523.

Healy, D. (2006). The latest mania: Selling bipolar disorder. *PLoS Medicine, 3,* e185.

Jenkins, M. M., & Youngstrom, E. A. (2016). A randomized controlled trial of cognitive debiasing improves assessment and treatment selection for pediatric bipolar disorder. *Journal of Consulting & Clinical Psychology, 84,* 323–333. doi:10.1037/ccp0000070

Jenkins, M. M., Youngstrom, E. A., Washburn, J. J., & Youngstrom, J. K. (2011). Evidence-based strategies improve assessment of pediatric bipolar disorder by community practitioners. *Professional Psychology: Research and Practice, 42,* 121–129. doi:10.1037/a0022506

Jenkins, M. M., Youngstrom, E. A., Youngstrom, J. K., Feeny, N. C., & Findling, R. L. (2012). Generalizability of evidence-based assessment recommendations for pediatric bipolar disorder. *Psychological Assessment, 24,* 269–281. doi:10.1037/a0025775

Keenan-Miller, D., Peris, T., Axelson, D., Kowatch, R. A., & Miklowitz, D. J. (2012). Family functioning, social impairment, and symptoms among adolescents with bipolar disorder. *Journal of the American Academy of Child & Adolescent Psychiatry*, *51*, 1085–1094.

Kim, E. Y., & Miklowitz, D. J. (2002). Childhood mania, attention deficit hyperactivity disorder and conduct disorder: A critical review of diagnostic dilemmas. *Bipolar Disorders*, *4*, 215–225.

Kowatch, R. A., Youngstrom, E. A., Horwitz, S., Demeter, C., Fristad, M. A., Birmaher, B. … & Findling, R. L. (2013). Prescription of psychiatric medications and polypharmacy in the LAMS cohort. *Psychiatric Services*, *64*, 1026–1034. doi:10.1176/appi.ps.201200507

Liu, H. Y., Potter, M. P., Woodworth, K. Y., Yorks, D. M., Petty, C. R., Wozniak, J. R. … & Biederman, J. (2011). Pharmacologic treatments for pediatric bipolar disorder: A review and meta-analysis. *Journal of the American Academy of Child & Adolescent Psychiatry*, *50*, 749–762. e739.

Malinowski, B., & Redfield, R. (1948). *Magic, science and religion, and other essays*. Boston: Beacon Press.

McClellan, J., Kowatch, R., & Findling, R. L. (2007). Practice parameter for the assessment and treatment of children and adolescents with bipolar disorder. *Journal of the American Academy of Child & Adolescent Psychiatry*, *46*, 107–125. doi:10.1097/01.chi.0000242240.69678.c4

Merikangas, K. R., He, J.-P., Burstein, M., Swanson, S. A., Avenevoli, S., Cui, L. … & Swendsen, J. (2010). Lifetime prevalence of mental disorders in US adolescents: Results from the National Comorbidity Survey Replication–Adolescent Supplement (NCS-A). *Journal of the American Academy of Child & Adolescent Psychiatry*, *49*, 980–989.

Merikangas, K. R., He, J.-P., Burstein, M., Swendsen, J., Avenevoli, S., Case, B. … & Olfson, M. (2011). Service utilization for lifetime mental disorders in US adolescents: Results of the National Comorbidity Survey–Adolescent Supplement (NCS-A). *Journal of the American Academy of Child & Adolescent Psychiatry*, *50*, 32–45.

Moreno, C., Laje, G., Blanco, C., Jiang, H., Schmidt, A. B., & Olfson, M. (2007). National trends in the outpatient diagnosis and treatment of bipolar disorder in youth. *Archives of General Psychiatry*, *64*, 1032–1039. doi:10.1001/archpsyc.64.9.1032

Nierenberg, A. A., Kansky, C., Brennan, B. P., Shelton, R. C., Perlis, R., & Iosifescu, D. V. (2013). Mitochondrial modulators for bipolar disorder: A pathophysiologically informed paradigm for new drug development. *Australian and New Zealand Journal of Psychiatry*, *47*, 26–42. doi:10.1177/0004867412449303

Olfman, S. (2015). *The science and pseudoscience of children's mental health: Cutting edge research and treatment.* Santa Barbara, CA: Praeger an imprint of ABC-CIO, LLC.

Olfson, M., Blanco, C., Liu, S. M., Wang, S., & Correll, C. U. (2012). National trends in the office-based treatment of children, adolescents, and adults with antipsychotics. *Archives of General Psychiatry*, 1–10. doi:10.1001/archgenpsychiatry.2012.647

Papolos, D. F., & Papolos, J. (1999). *The bipolar child: The definitive and reassuring guide to childhood's most misunderstood disorder.* New York: Broadway Books.

Phelps, J. R., Siemers, S. V., & El-Mallakh, R. S. (2013). The ketogenic diet for type II bipolar disorder. *Neurocase, 19,* 423–426.

Qureshi, N. A., & Al-Bedah, A. M. (2013). Mood disorders and complementary and alternative medicine: A literature review. *Neuropsychiatric Disease and Treatment, 9,* 639–658.

Straus, S. E., Glasziou, P., Richardson, W. S., & Haynes, R. B. (2011). *Evidence-based medicine: How to practice and teach EBM.* 4th edn. New York: Churchill Livingstone.

Sylvia, L. G., Peters, A. T., Deckersbach, T., & Nierenberg, A. A. (2013). Nutrient-based therapies for bipolar disorder: A systematic review. *Psychotherapy and Psychosomatics, 82,* 10–19. doi:10.1159/000341309

Thomas, T., Stansifer, L., & Findling, R. L. (2011). Psychopharmacology of pediatric bipolar disorders in children and adolescents. *Pediatric Clinics of North America, 58,* 173–187.

Van Meter, A., Moreira, A. L., & Youngstrom, E. A. (2011). Meta-analysis of epidemiological studies of pediatric bipolar disorder. *Journal of Clinical Psychiatry, 72,* 1250–1256. doi:10.4088/JCP.10m06290

Van Meter, A. R., Burke, C., Kowatch, R. A., Findling, R. L., & Youngstrom, E. A. (2016). Ten-year updated meta-analysis of the clinical characteristics of pediatric mania and hypomania. *Bipolar Disorders, 18,* 19–32. doi:10.1111/bdi.12358

Waltz, M. (2000). *Bipolar disorders: A guide to helping children & adolescents.* Sebastopol, CA: O'Reilly & Associates.

Yaroslavsky, Y., Stahl, Z., & Belmaker, R. (2002). Ketogenic diet in bipolar illness. *Bipolar Disorders, 4,* 75.

Yeung, W.-F., Chung, K.-F., Ng, K.-Y., Yu, Y.-M., Ziea, E. T.-C., & Ng, B. F.-L. (2014). A systematic review on the efficacy, safety and types of Chinese herbal medicine for depression. *Journal of Psychiatric Research, 57,* 165–175.

Youngstrom, E. A., & Algorta, G. P. (2014). Pediatric bipolar disorder. In E. J. Mash & R. A. Barkley (eds.), *Child psychopathology.* 3rd edn, pp. 264–316. New York: The Guilford Press.

Youngstrom, E. A., Freeman, A. J., & Jenkins, M. M. (2009). The assessment of children and adolescents with bipolar disorder. *Child and Adolescent Psychiatric Clinics of North America*, *18*, 353–390. doi:10.1016/j.chc.2008.12.002

Youngstrom, E. A., Genzlinger, J. E., Egerton, G. A., & Van Meter, A. R. (2015). Multivariate meta-analysis of the discriminative validity of caregiver, youth, and teacher rating scales for pediatric bipolar disorder: Mother knows best about mania. *Archives of Scientific Psychology*, *3*, 112–137. doi:10.1037/arc0000024

Youngstrom, E., Van Meter, A., & Algorta, G. P. (2010). The bipolar spectrum: Myth or reality? *Current Psychiatry Reports*, *12*, 479–489. doi:10.1007/s11920-010-0153-3

9

Depression

Thomas J. Huberty

Interest in child and adolescent depression has increased significantly, partially due to unfounded perspectives based on unsupported theory and lack of relevant research and the need to address clinical problems that affect social, personal, and educational functioning. This chapter will address several topics, including historical perspectives, diagnostic issues, unsupported assessment and intervention techniques, and implications for practice that are based on research evidence.

Depressive disorders are some of the most common disorders ranging from 2.5% in children age 8 to 11 and 4.8% in adolescents age 12 to 15 at a 12-month prevalence rate for major depressive disorder (MDD) and dysthymia (Merikangas, He, Brody et al., 2010). The typical age of onset for MDD and dysthymia in children increases as children get older, with rates in middle to late adolescence approximating adult rates (Rudolph, 2009). The typical age of onset for mood disorders has been reported as about 13 (Merikangas, He, Burstein et al., 2010); symptoms appear in cognitive, affective, behavioral, and physiological manifestations in varying degrees, but not all are shown in each person. In the *Diagnostic and Statistical Manual of Mental Disorders* 5th ed (DSM-5; American Psychiatric Association, 2013), three primary depressive disorders that can affect children and adolescents are described. The following list summarizes the primary symptoms of major depressive disorder, persistent depressive disorder (dysthymia), and disruptive mood dysregulation disorder, all of which can occur in children and adolescents. The primary symptoms of each of these disorders are as follows:

- **Major depressive disorder** – Depressed mood and markedly diminished interest in all, or almost all, activities
- **Persistent depressive disorder (dysthymia)** – Depressed mood most of the day for most days for at least two years that can be shown as irritability and must be shown for at least two years in children and adolescents

- **Disruptive mood dysregulation disorder** – Severe recurrent temper outbursts (verbal or physical) that are out of proportion in duration or intensity for the situation and are inconsistent with developmental level

Although bipolar disorders and cyclothymia have depressive features, the DSM-5 categorizes them separately from depressive disorders. Other disorders may have depressive features (e.g., anxiety disorders or trauma and stressor-related disorders), but they are separate classes of disorders in the DSM-5. Therefore, only the DSM-5 depressive disorders will be addressed in this chapter.

9.1 Pseudoscience and Questionable Ideas

9.1.1 Diagnostic Issues and Controversies

Although depression and mood disorders in adults have been a research and clinical focus for many decades, they have received increased attention in children and adolescents over the past two to three decades. Perspectives on childhood depression have ranged from the view that it could not exist in children to seeing it as comparable to adult depression. Kaslow and Rehm (1991) discussed four perspectives on the nature of childhood depression that had been proposed by various authors over many years: (a) it could not exist in children; (b) there is a "depressive equivalent" that depression is "masked" in children; (c) if it is present, it is transitory; and (d) it parallels adult depression. Kaslow and Rehm (1991) then discuss the viability and support for each of the positions, which are discussed next. Additionally, other controversies exist regarding depression as a general construct with adults, and there are additional issues regarding children and adolescents. Klein et al. (2013) discuss five controversies in the diagnosis and classification of depression in general and in children and adolescents more specifically. Taken together, there are at least nine notable diagnostic controversies.

Depression Cannot Exist in Children. In the first perspective, depression was not seen as possible because of the influence of psychoanalytic thought that depression was anger turned inward due to a harsh, guilt-arousing superego. Because children were presumed to not develop a superego and self-awareness until adolescence when they could experience guilt, they could not develop depression (e.g., Finch, 1960; Rie, 1966). This perspective contributed to not viewing depression as a form of child psychopathology, leading to a lack of treatment and research.

Depressive Equivalent. The second perspective focused on "depressive equivalent" or that depression could be "masked" in children when they experienced internal distress but expressed it as aggression, delinquency, or other externalizing behavior (e.g., Toolan, 1962). Kaslow and Rehm (1991) contended that this position could not be supported, because depression could not be distinguished from other child behavior problems. Further, such behaviors could be manifestations of typical developmental levels, cultural factors, parenting practices, or attempts to deal with stress. There is little empirical support for this perspective, but it is related to the notion of comorbidity of childhood disorders, which is a common occurrence (Fonagy et al., 2015) and should be a consideration in practice and research.

Depression in Childhood Is Transitory. The third perspective proposed that depression in childhood is transitory and therefore does not correspond with typical notions of disorder. Kaslow and Rehm (1991) presented the ideas of Lefkowitz and Burton (1978), who posited that (a) if depressive behaviors were to occur in all children, they are not pathological; (b) symptoms that are commonly associated with depression are transitory developmental manifestations that would occur in all children; and (c) if the symptoms subside spontaneously, there would be no need for treatment. Kaslow and Rehm (1991) address each of these points. With regard to the first point, although isolated behaviors may occur, depression is a combination of several symptoms that comprise a syndrome. Further, just because symptoms might occur in a large number of people, they are not any less problematic. On the second point, developmental stages are transitory by nature, but a child may still be trying to cope with stress and the fact that the behavior may dissipate does not mean that there has not been a negative impact. Thus, even if depressive behaviors might be "normal," they may still require intervention. It should not be assumed that a child will "grow out" of a behavior and attention may be warranted if it is indicative of impairment. From a developmental psychopathology perspective, many problem behaviors that are not treated may worsen over time or evolve into one or more other disorders (Huberty, 2012). Thus, the notion that childhood depression is transitory is not supported by research or developmental theory and is not a viable perspective.

Childhood Depression Parallels Adult Depression. The final perspective discussed by Kaslow and Rehm (1991) is that childhood depression parallels adult depression. Aaron Beck (1967), in one of the seminal works on understanding and treating depression, proposed that depression has four core components: (a) affective problems (e.g., dysphoria, mood problems), (b) cognitive problems (e.g., low self-esteem, pessimism), (c) motivational problems (e.g., avoidance, passivity, low energy), and (d) vegetative and psychomotor problems (e.g., sleep problems, appetite disturbances, somatic complaints). Youth with depression may show these disturbances, as well as others that may be developmentally typical, such as temper tantrums, withdrawal, or avoidance. Alternatively, they could be experiencing depression along with another disorder, such as conduct disorder. In children, however, irritability may be a common characteristic of depression, which might not be as readily seen as a depressive symptom in adults. This fourth perspective is considered to be the current view of childhood depression, and particular attention must be given to developmental differences and comorbid conditions by clinicians working with individual cases (Kaslow & Rehm, 1991).

Continuity among Child, Adolescent, and Adult Depression. Klein et al. (2013) discuss the similarity between adult and adolescent depression, which has been shown in many studies, but there is less evidence for this pattern in younger children. This continuity is consistent with Kaslow and Rehm's (1991) fourth perspective that, in general, depression in children parallels adult depression, in that depressive symptoms are manifested similarly across the age span. Studies have shown some mixed results, however, when comorbidity is considered and controlled. Copeland et al. (2009) found that the association of depression between adolescents and young adults disappeared when comorbid anxiety and externalizing behaviors in the adolescents were controlled. They found that most adults with psychiatric disorders met diagnostic criteria as adolescents, but that specific homotypic and heterotypic patterns are yet to be established. It is meaningful from a clinical perspective in that comorbidity in children and adolescents is common, creating challenges for treatment by mental health professionals.

Discreteness and Boundaries. This controversy focuses on whether there are specific mood disorders or whether they fall on a continuum, which has implications for definitions of disorders and possible subtypes, as well as determining etiology and selecting assessment approaches and statistical models (Klein et al., 2013). It can be particularly difficult to distinguish psychopathological symptoms from normal developmental variations, particularly in younger children. Thus, this perspective suggests that boundaries may not be sufficiently well-defined on the basis of consideration of symptoms. On the other hand, Klein et al. (2013)

suggest that current boundaries for depressive disorders are too strict, given that many youth and adults have sub-threshold levels of symptoms that do not meet diagnostic criteria but are nevertheless associated with significant impairment.

Subtypes. Although much effort has been placed on identifying homogeneous subtypes of depressive disorders in addition to the unipolar-bipolar distinction, relatively little effort has been directed toward this delineation in children and adolescents (Klein et al., 2013). An exception to this pattern was introduced in the DSM-5 (APA, 2013), with its inclusion of disruptive mood dysregulation disorder, which is discussed later. Thus, the question of whether MDD and dysthymia vary as a function of developmental level remains unanswered, but the clinician will nevertheless have to consider the possible impact of developmental differences on the diagnosis and treatment of mood disorders in children and adolescents.

Age-specific Manifestations of Symptoms. As with questions regarding subtypes, the matter of whether there are age-specific manifestations of symptoms remains unanswered (Klein et al., 2013). Although the primary symptomatology is similar across school-aged children, adolescents, and adults, some symptoms such as vegetative states, sleep and appetite disturbances, and motivation (e.g., loss of interest or pleasure) may be more common in adolescents (Weiss & Garber, 2003). Children's cognitive and developmental levels may have an impact on how well children can express symptoms, such as being sad, but have difficulty reporting their moods (Weiss & Garber, 2003). As with subtypes, clinicians will need to consider children's developmental status in cognitive, social, and cultural domains when addressing mood problems in clinical work. For example, if parents report child depression on a behavior rating scale, corresponding self-ratings or verbal reports by the child may be discrepant.

Depression in Very Young Children. Research into mood disorders historically has focused on school-age children and adolescents, and relatively little has been conducted on preschool and very young children (Klein et al., 2013). The reasons for this lack of research include the inherent difficulties with young children having the language and experience to relate their moods and feelings to others. The primary source of diagnostic information on preschoolers' symptoms of depression has been adult informants, usually parents. Luby et al. (2007) developed an interview for preschoolers using puppets and found that the children could provide useful reports of core and basic depressive and anxiety symptoms, based on correlations with parent reports. However, the authors did not find significant correlations with more complex and abstract symptoms. Thus, getting accurate diagnostic information directly from young children remains challenging and should be approached with caution. A common method to obtain diagnostic information from children is through the use and interpretation of figure drawings, but these methods have been found to lack adequate psychometric properties and should not be used to make diagnoses (Sattler, 2014).

Another issue has been whether the diagnostic criteria for children and adults can be applied to such young children and even infants. Luby and colleagues (2002, 2003) conducted studies on preschool children using modified DSM-IV (APA, 2000) criteria that required a shorter duration of time for symptoms to occur. They asserted that these children have impairments and neurobiological abnormalities that are similar to adolescents and adults who demonstrate melancholic MDD. Using these modified criteria, Luby et al. (2009) found an 11-fold greater risk of preschoolers showing signs of MDD in the following 12 to 24 months, as compared to typical children.

The diagnosis of depression in very young children is problematic, and there is limited research to confirm whether it exists and is, in fact, the same syndrome. If the criteria are different, then the question is raised as to whether the construct is the same across the age span. Therefore, more research is needed and caution should be exercised in formulating diagnoses of depression and mood disorders in very young children.

A final controversy that has emerged in recent years is the addition of the diagnosis of disruptive mood dysregulation disorder (DMDD) in the DSM-5, which applies only to children between the ages of 6 and 18. Many of the symptoms are indicative of behaviors (e.g., temper outbursts) that are beyond typical developmental expectations in frequency, severity, or duration. DMDD was added to the DSM-5 as a means to address the concerns about possible overdiagnosis of bipolar disorder in children (APA, 2013). For example, Moreno et al. (2007) reported that the diagnosis of pediatric bipolar disorder increased by as much as 4000% between 1995 and 2003 in the United States. DMDD was based on research on severe mood dysregulation (SMD), which refers to impairment in the ability to control emotions and moods that can interfere with the ability to cope with typical life stressors. It has also been termed temper dysregulation disorder with dysphoria (Copeland et al. 2013). DMDD has some of the same symptoms as SMD, such as temper outbursts and chronic irritability, but it does not include hyperarousal features, such as flight of ideas, pressured speech, agitation, distractibility, racing thoughts, and insomnia that may occur in SMD (Dougherty et al., 2014). Copeland et al. (2013) suggest a prevalence rate of SMD in about 2% to 5% of the general population of children and adolescents. Fristad et al. (2016) estimate a higher frequency in boys and school-aged children than in females and adolescents. Both SMD and DMDD address the presence of disruptive behavior and depressed mood that have been considered as diagnostic criteria for pediatric bipolar disorder.

The removal of the hyperarousal criteria is intended to reduce the overlap between attention-deficit/hyperactivity disorder (ADHD) and pediatric bipolar disorder and to make DMDD a disorder unique to childhood. The DSM-5 does not rule out the possibility that a child age 6 to 18 could be diagnosed with bipolar disorder but suggests that DMDD be considered in the process of differential diagnosis. The DSM-5 also suggests caution in that ADHD can be misdiagnosed as bipolar disorder. Given the overlap of symptoms of DMDD, bipolar disorder, and ADHD, caution is needed in conducting differential diagnosis (APA, 2013).

The inclusion of DMDD in the DSM-5 remains controversial, as it was not based on a large body of research available at the time. At present, little systematic research exists on the nature and course of DMDD, comorbidities with other disorders, and life course path into adulthood. Thus, the issue of DMDD and its relationship to other disorders, especially bipolar disorder, remains controversial and more research is needed. The clinician is advised to approach this challenging disorder and its differential diagnosis with caution.

9.1.2 Projective Measures for Assessment

The assessment of child and adolescent depression typically involves observations, clinical interviews, completion of behavior rating scales and self-report measures, and developmental histories. Multidimensional measures include commonly used behavior rating scales, such as the *Behavior Assessment System for Children*–3rd edn (BASC-3; Reynolds & Kamphaus, 2015) and the *Conners Comprehensive Behavior Rating System* (Conners, 2008). Examples of narrow band scales include the *Children's Depression Inventory*–2nd edn (CDI-2; Kovacs, 2010) and the *Reynolds Adolescent Depression Scale*–2nd edn (RADS-2; Reynolds, 2002). With the exception of clinical interviews that are not typically subjected to external validation or measurement, the other measures listed generally have good empirical support. Although clinical interviews typically are not empirically validated, they are an essential component of the assessment process. Interviews with parents and teachers are particularly important, as younger children often are not reliable reporters of their symptoms. Published measures such as behavior rating scales, self-report measures, and multidimensional scales generally have good psychometric properties, and observations typically use data such as frequency counts and interval recording.

Assessment measures that are questionable include the majority of projective techniques, such as figure drawings, thematic apperception methods, and incomplete sentences exercises. Proponents of projective measures assert that they provide information about suppressed and repressed content, less faking is likely due to their subjective nature, and the unstructured nature helps to build rapport with children (Sattler, 2014). Critics of projective techniques assert that because they are not standardized, clinicians may make different interpretations across situations. Also, interrater reliability, internal consistency, test-retest reliability, and validity tend to be inadequate for most of the projective measures, rendering their recommended use to creating sources of hypotheses and that important decisions are not based on a child's performance (Sattler, 2014).

The Rorschach Inkblot Test is a projective measure that has a long and controversial history in psychological assessment, dating back to its development by Herman Rorschach (Rorschach, 1921/1964). Several systems have been developed for administration and interpretation, but the Comprehensive System by John Exner (1974) is the most widely used approach that was revised and developed over several years. It has been subjected to psychometric development with reliability and validity data, standardization procedures, and norms. Despite these developments, the research on the Rorschach has revealed serious flaws in the psychometric qualities and administration procedures that suggest it should be used with caution (for a thorough review of the questionable utility of the Rorschach, see Hunsley et al. (2015). There is much more research on adults than on children, which makes its use with children even more questionable.

Some projective measures, such as figure drawings, could be used by non-psychologists who may have little to no background in personality assessment and psychometric theory and research, increasing the potential for misuse or misinterpretation of the collected information. Generally, figure drawings lack adequate psychometric properties and are often used as indicators of sexual abuse in children, which has not been substantiated in research (Hunsley et al., 2015). Therefore, mental health professionals from all backgrounds should be cautious in using these kinds of measures.

Koocher et al. (2015) conducted a Delphi poll of clinicians regarding discredited assessment and treatment methods that might be used with children and youth. They asked 139 psychologists to rank 36 assessment measures ranging from "1 – not at all discredited" to "3 – possibly discredited" to "5 – certainly discredited." The measures included neuropsychological measures, intellectual measures, behavior checklists, adaptive behavior scales, and projective measures. All of the 24 projective assessment measures had mean ratings greater than 3 ("possibly discredited") with half of them exceeding "4" ("probably discredited" to "certainly discredited"). Because many of these projective measures could be used to assess depressive mood states in children, their use for this purpose is questionable for formulating diagnoses, based on the ratings of the psychologists. The measures may be useful for clinical hypothesis generation (Sattler, 2014) but should be used with caution.

9.1.3 Alternative or Questionable Treatments

Several treatments for psychological problems of children and adolescents have been attempted over the past several decades, including treatment for depressive and mood disorders. Some of these treatments have been shown to be effective for depression, such as cognitive-behavioral therapy (CBT; Weersing et al., 2016). However, some treatments for a range of child disorders have been discredited by practitioners. In the study conducted by Koocher et al. (2015) regarding discredited assessment and treatment methods for children and adolescents, the authors found that of 67 treatments, the vast majority received mean ratings between of "3 – possibly discredited" to "5 – certainly discredited" with many receiving mean ratings of "4" or higher. None of those treatments specifically addressed depression in children and youth, but many of them were related to the general area of child psychopathology, which would presumably include depression.

Psychodynamic or Psychoanalytic Treatment. These treatments have the longest history in psychology and psychiatry; but until relatively recently, these theories denied that depression could occur in children and adolescents. Outcomes of psychodynamic treatments have been narrative in nature and have not been subjected to rigorous investigation. There is little objective evidence that psychodynamic treatment is effective for treating depression (Fonagy et al., 2015). Therefore, psychodynamic or psychoanalytic treatments for depression in children and adolescents are not well established and should be used with caution.

People have attempted to make sense of dreams for the entirety of recorded history, from the Sumerian *Epic of Gilgamesh* to Freud's *Die Traumdeutung*. But is there anything to dream analysis? Most modern dream analysis flows from the psychoanalytic ideas of Freud, which posit that the content of dreams, if properly understood, can allow us to understand the true roots of our mental health problems. This insight would then lead us to become more mentally healthy. In particular, Freud believed that dreams were wish fulfillments, and that what happened in them was the true expression of (often repressed) desires. However, modern research has poked huge holes into Freud's assumptions and the overall idea of the usefulness of dream interpretation.

First, most of our dreams do not have hidden, secret meanings but instead are about our daily lives. While oddities certainly occur in REM dreams in particular, even those can often be traced back to what we were talking about, seeing, reading, or playing on a given day. Second, most emotionally charged dreams are negative, rather than being positive or enjoyable. For instance, less than 10% of our dreams involve sexual activity, which Freud considered to be the most common type of desire that would manifest in dreams. Third, given well-understood problems with human memory and recall, it is quite likely that most of the dreams we can remember have only a passing resemblance to the actual dream we experienced. How accurate could such an interpretation even be?

Finally, and of the most relevance to most readers of this book, there is no evidence at all that understanding or interpreting dreams has a positive impact on mental health. Assessing sleep length and quality is crucial for the child clinician, but dwelling on dream content or searching for hidden meanings only wastes everyone's time. For an in-depth critique, see Domhoff (2000).

Caleb W. Lack, PhD, is a professor of psychology at the University of Central Oklahoma. Among other works, he is co-author of the book *Critical Thinking, Science, and Pseudoscience: Why We Can't Trust Our Brains* (2016).

Herbal Treatments. Herbal treatments (phytotherapeutics) to treat psychological disorders have been used for many years, with mixed results. Perhaps the most well-known herbal treatment that has been studied is *Hypericum* (St. John's Wort). *Hypericum* has been used since the Middle Ages as a treatment for depression and is a regulated substance in Germany with standards for its preparation. In the United States, it is treated as a food supplement with no regulations as to its content and preparation. Although some studies have shown positive effects for mild to moderate depression and that it is well tolerated with few side effects (Walach & Kirsch, 2015), the majority of studies suggests inconsistent results for mild depression and that there is some risk for negative interactions with prescribed medications (Rey, Bella-Awusah, & Liu, 2015). For example, hypericum may reduce the effectiveness of anticonvulsant drugs, as well as increasing the side effects of other prescription drugs. It may also reduce the effectiveness of contraceptive medications, which may be an added risk factor for sexually active adolescents (Fonagy et al., 2015).

A comprehensive review of herbal treatments (DeSmet, 2004) found little support for their therapeutic benefits and indicated negative effects, including adverse side effects (e.g., gastrointestinal problems), indirect health effects due to not receiving supported treatments, and inadequate control of access to products, such as via the internet. In summary, DeSmet (2004) concluded that most herbal remedies fall into the category of inadequately proven treatments.

9.2 Research-Supported Approaches

In general, studies of psychotherapeutic treatments for child and adolescent depression have found that cognitive-behavioral therapy and interpersonal psychotherapy have strong evidence as effective techniques for mild to moderate depression in youth (Fonagy et al., 2015; Rey et al., 2015). Meta-analyses of CBT studies with clinically referred populations of youth have found about 60% favorable responses, compared to 40% for placebo conditions. There is also evidence that using components of CBT compared to full manualized treatment yields comparable results (Fonagy et al., 2015).

Interpersonal psychotherapy (IPT) focuses on treatment of depression at three levels: symptom formation, social functioning, and personality, but its adaptation for depressed adolescents focuses on the first two (Mufson et al., 2004). Overall, IPT adapted for adolescents has received good support for effectiveness with depressed adolescents (Fonagy et al., 2015).

An important consideration is whether medication alone, psychotherapy alone, or a combination of the two approaches produces the best therapeutic outcomes. Fonagy et al. (2015) report that there is no evidence for or against the value of pharmacological treatments to treat adolescent depression. The Treatment for Adolescent Depression Study (TADS; Treatment for Adolescents with Depression Study Team, 2005) is the most comprehensive study of its type to date. It was composed of four treatment conditions: (a) fluoxetine only, (b) CBT only, (c) combination of fluoxetine and CBT, and (d) placebo pill. Some limited evidence from the TADS study and meta-analyses indicates that medication plus CBT is more effective than either treatment alone (Fonagy et al., 2015). Therefore, the existing literature suggests that medication or CBT alone may not be as effective as a combination of treatments. Thus, if medication is used, it should be combined with CBT to enhance treatment outcomes.

9.3 Conclusion

Depression is one of the most common and impairing mental disorders that affect youth with possible long-term negative effects into adulthood, affecting personal, social, and educational functioning. A number of diagnostic controversies include whether childhood depression exists as a separate entity, whether there is continuity across the age span, and whether it exists or is manifested in the same way with very young children. These diagnostic controversies may have significant implications for evidence-based assessment and treatment. A developmental perspective to understanding and treating youth depression should be combined with supported assessment and treatment practices. Avoidance or minimization of unsupported assessment practices, such as projective measures, will help to obtain accurate diagnostic information that will inform practice. Adherence to evidence-based treatment practices for depression such as CBT, interpersonal psychotherapy, and other supported interventions are recommended to enhance the likelihood for positive outcomes.

Work Cited in Sidebar

Domhoff, G. W. (2000, September 23). *Moving Dream Theory beyond Freud and Jung*. Paper presented to the symposium "Beyond Freud and Jung?," Graduate Theological Union, Berkeley, CA.

References

American Psychiatric Association. (2000). *Diagnostic and statistical manual of mental disorders*. 4th edn, text revision. Washington, DC: Author.

American Psychiatric Association. (2013). *Diagnostic and statistical manual of mental disorders*. 5th edn. Washington, DC: Author.

Beck, A. T. (1967). *Depression: Clinical, experimental, and theoretical aspects*. New York: Hoeber.

Conners, C. K. (2008). *Conners Comprehensive Behavior Rating System*. North Tonawanda, NY: Multi Health Systems.

Copeland, W. E., Angold, A., Costello, E. J., & Egger, H. (2013). Prevalence, comorbidity, and correlates of DSM-5 of proposed disruptive mood dysregulation disorder. *American Journal of Psychiatry*, *170*, 173–179. doi: http://dx.doi.org/10.1176/appi.ajp.2012.12010132

Copeland, W. E., Shanahan, L., Miller. S., Costello, E. J., & Angold, A. (2009). Child and adolescent psychiatric disorders as predictors of young adult disorders. *Archives of General Psychiatry*, *66*, 764–772. doi: 10.1001/archgenpsychiatry.2009.85

DeSmet, P. A. G. M. (2004). Health risks of herbal remedies: An update. *Clinical Pharmacology and Therapeutics*, *76*, 1–17.

Dougherty, L. R., Smith, V. C., Bufferd, S. J., Carlson, G. A., Stringaris, A., Leibenluft, E., & Klein, D. N. (2014). DSM-5 disruptive mood dysregulation disorder: Correlates and predictors in young children. *Psychological Medicine*, *44*, 2339–2350. doi:https://doi.org/10.1017/S0033291713003115

Exner, J. (1974). *The Rorschach: A comprehensive system*. Vol. 1. New York: Wiley.

Finch, S. M. (1960). *Fundamentals of child psychiatry*. New York: Norton.

Fonagy, P., Cottrell, D., Phillips, J., Bevington, D., Glaser, D., & Allison, E. (2015). *What works for whom? A critical review of treatments for children and adolescents*. 2nd edn. New York: Guilford.

Fristad, M. A., Wolfson, H., Algotta, G. P., Youngstrom, E. A., Arnold, L. E., Birmaher, B. . . . & LAMS Group. (2016). Disruptive mood dysregulation disorder and bipolar disorder not otherwise specified: Fraternal or identical twins? *Journal of Child and Adolescent Psychopharmacology*, *26*, 138–146. doi: 10.1089/cap.2015.0062

Huberty, T. J. (2012). *Anxiety and depression in children and adolescents: Assessment, intervention, and prevention*. New York: Springer.

Hunsley, J., Lee, C. M., Wood, J. M., & Taylor, W. (2015). Controversial and questionable assessment techniques. In S. O. Lilienfeld, S. J. Lynn, & J. M. Lohr (eds.), *Science and pseudoscience in clinical psychology* (pp. 42–82). New York: Guilford.

Kaslow, N. J., & Rehm, L. P. (1991). Childhood depression. In T. J. Kratochwill & R. J. Morris (eds.), *The practice of child therapy*. 2nd edn (pp. 43–75). New York: Pergamon.

Klein, D. N., Kujawa, A. J., Black, S. R., & Pennock, A. T. (2013). Depressive disorders. In T. P. Beauchaine & S. P. Shaw (eds.), *Child and adolescent psychopathology*. 2nd edn (pp. 543–575). New York: Wiley.

Koocher, G. P., McMann, M. R., Stout, A. O., & Norcorss, J. C. (2015). Discredited assessment and treatment methods used with children and adolescents: A Delphi poll. *Journal of Clinical Child and Adolescent Psychology*, *44*, 722–729. doi:http://dx.doi.org/10.1080/15374416.2014.895941

Kovacs, M. (2010). *Children's Depression Inventory–Second Edition*. Manual. North Tonawanda, NY: Multi Health Systems.

Lefkowitz, M. M., & Burton, N. (1978). Childhood depression: A critique of the concept. *Psychological Bulletin*, *85*, 716–726. doi:http://dx.doi.org/10.1037/0033-2909.85.4.716

Luby, J. L., Belden, A., Sullivan, J., & Spitznagel, E. (2007). Preschoolers' contribution to their diagnosis of depression and anxiety: Uses and limitations of young child self-report of symptoms. *Child Psychiatry and Human Development*, *38*, 321–338. doi: 10.1007/s10578-007-0063-8

Luby, J. L., Heffelfinger, A., Mrakotsky, C., Brown, K., Hessler, M., & Spitznagel, E. (2003). Alterations in stress cortisol reactivity in depressed preschoolers relative to psychiatric and no-disorder comparison groups. *Archives of General Psychiatry*, *60*, 1248–1255. doi: 10.1001/archpsyc.60.12.1248

Luby, J. L., Heffelfinger, A., Mrakotsky, C., Hessler, M., Brown, K., & Hildebrand, T. (2002). Preschool major depressive disorder: Preliminary validation for developmentally modified DSM-IV criteria. *Journal of the American Academy of Child and Adolescent Psychiatry*, *41*, 923–937. doi: http://dx.doi.org/10.1097/00004583-200208000-00011

Luby, J. L., Si, X., Belden, A. C., Tandon, M., & Spitznagel, E. (2009). Preschool depression: Homotypic continuity and course over 24 months. *Archives of General Psychiatry*, *66*, 897–205. doi: 10.1001/archgenpsychiatry.2009.97

Merikangas, K. R., He, J.-P., Brody, D., Fisher, P. W., Bourdain, K., & Koretz, D. S. (2010). Prevalence and treatment of mental disorders among U. S. children in the 2001–2004 NHANES. *Pediatrics*, *125*, 75–81. doi: 10.1542/peds.2008-2598

Merikangas, K. R., He, J.-P., Burstein, M., Swanson, S. A., Avenevoli, S., Cui, L. . . . & Swendsen, J. (2010). Lifetime prevalence of mental disorders in U.S. adolescents: Results from the National Comorbidity Survey Replication–Adolescent Supplement (NCS-A). *Journal of the American*

Academy of Child & Adolescent Psychiatry, 49, 980–989. doi:http://dx.doi.org/10.1016/j.jaac.2010.05.017

Moreno, C., Laje, C., Blanco, C., Jiang, H., Schmidt, A. B., & Olfson, M. (2007). National trends in the outpatient diagnosis and treatment of bipolar disorder in youth. *Archives of General Psychiatry, 64*, 1032–1039. doi:10.1001/archpsyc.64.9.1032

Mufson, L., Dorta, K. P., Wickramaratne, P., Nomura, Y., Olfson, M., & Weissman, M. M. (2004). A randomized effectiveness trial of interpersonal psychotherapy for depressed adolescents. *Archives of General Psychiatry, 61*, 577–584.

Rey, J. M., Bella-Awusah, T. T., & Liu, J. (2015). Depression in children and adolescents. In J. M. Rey (ed.), *IACAPAP e-Textbook of child and adolescent mental health* (pp. 1–36). Geneva, Switzerland: International Association for Child and Adolescent Psychiatry and Allied Professions.

Reynolds, C. R., & Kamphaus, R. W. (2015). *Behavior Assessment System for Children–Third Edition*. Manual. Bloomington, MN: Pearson Assessments.

Reynolds, W. M. (2002). *Reynolds Adolescent Depression Scale–Second Edition*. Manual. Lutz, FL: Professional Assessment Resources.

Rie, H. E. (1966). Depression in childhood: A survey of some pertinent contributions. *Journal of the American Academy of Child Psychiatry, 5*, 753–685.

Rorschach, H. (1921/1964). *Psychodiagnostics*. New York: Grune & Stratton. (Original work published in German in 1921 and in English in 1942)

Rudolph, K. D. (2009). Adolescent depression. In I. H. Gotlib & C. L. Hammen (eds.), *Handbook of depression*. 2nd edn (pp. 444–466). New York: Guilford.

Sattler, J. M. (2014). *Foundations of behavioral, social, and clinical assessment of children*. 6th edn. San Diego, CA: Jerome M. Sattler.

Toolan, J. M. (1962). Depression in children and adolescents. *American Journal of Orthopsychiatry, 32*, 404–414.

Treatment for Adolescents with Depression Study Team. (2005). Treatment for Adolescents with Depression Study (TADS): Rationale, design, and methods. *Journal of the American Academy of Child and Adolescent Psychiatry, 42*, 531–542.

Walach, H., & Kirsch, I. (2015). Herbal treatment and antidepressant medication: Similar data, divergent conclusions. In S. O. Lilienfeld, S. J. Lynn, & J. M. Lohr (eds.), *Science and pseudoscience in clinical psychology*. 2nd edn (pp. 364–390). New York: Guilford.

Weersing, V. R., Jeffreys, M., Do, M. T., Schwartz, K. T. G., & Bolano, C. (2016). Evidence base update of psychosocial treatments for child and adolescent depression. *Journal of Clinical Child and Adolescent Psychology*, *46*(1), 11–43. doi: 10.1080/15374416.2016.1220310

Weiss, B., & Garber, G. (2003). Developmental differences in the phenomenology of depression. *Development and Psychopathology*, *15*, 403–430.

10

Anxiety

Bruce A. Thyer and Monica Pignotti

The approach to defining anxiety disorders in the United States and much of the Western world is found in the *Diagnostic and Statistical Manual of Mental Disorders* (DSM; American Psychiatric Association, 2013). It is postulated that "Anxiety disorders include disorders that share features of excessive fear and anxiety and related behavioral disturbances. *Fear* is the emotional response to real or perceived imminent threat, whereas *anxiety* is anticipation of future threat" (APA, 2013, p. 189). It is important to note that the DSM is primarily a descriptive book, recognizing that the etiologies for many of the several hundred conditions found therein are not well established. Nor does it recommend treatments.

The DSM chapter on the anxiety disorders contains seven primary diagnoses, all of which may be applied to youth (APA, 2013). Briefly stated, these are

- Separation anxiety disorder – "Developmentally inappropriate and excessive fear of anxiety concerning separation from those to whom the individual is attached" (p. 190).
- Selective mutism – "Consistent failure to speak in specific social situations in which there is an expectation for speaking (e.g., at school) despite speaking in other situations" (p. 195).
- Specific phobia – "Marked fear or anxiety about a specific object or situation (e.g., flying, heights, animals, receiving an injection, seeing blood" (p. 197).
- Social anxiety disorder – "Marked fear or anxiety about one or more social situations in which the individual is exposed to possible scrutiny by others. Examples include social interactions (e.g., having a conversation, meeting unfamiliar people), being observed (e.g., eating or drinking), and performing in front of others (e.g., giving a speech)" (p. 202).

- Panic disorder – "Recurrent unexpected panic attacks. A panic attack is an abrupt surge of intense fear or intense discomfort that reaches a peak within minutes" (p. 208).
- Agoraphobia – "Marked fear or anxiety about two (or more) of the following five situations: using public transportation, being in open spaces, being in enclosed places, standing in line or being in a crowd, being outside of the home alone" (p. 217).
- Generalized anxiety disorder – "Excessive anxiety and worry (apprehensive expectation) occurring more days than not for at least six months, about a number of events or activities (such as work or school performance)" (p. 222).

Each of these criteria is accompanied by some other criteria pertaining to duration of the condition, distress the condition causes, and possible differential diagnoses, all needing to be taken into account before deciding if a client meets or does not meet the criteria for a given DSM diagnosis.

There are some other conditions listed in the anxiety disorders chapter (substance/medication-induced anxiety disorder, anxiety disorder due to another medical condition, other specified anxiety disorder, unspecified anxiety disorder), but they will not be considered here, neither will some related conditions that are covered elsewhere (e.g., disorders related to obsessions, compulsions, trauma, attachment, and/or sleep).

Sidebar Box: Should children be afraid of Bigfoot? by Carol E. Colaninno

Throughout history, children have feared many types of monsters. Often hiding under the bed; in the deep, dark forest; or in murky, muddy waters, the fear of monsters can have profound impacts on children and even adults. One "monster" receiving modern day publicity and causing both children and their parents to fear the forest is Bigfoot. The pursuit of documenting the existence of this hairy, humanlike giant with big feet is the subject of headlines, blogs, and even television series and documentaries. But does the scientific community have evidence for children to be weary? The short answer is: well, not really. There is little empirical evidence to support claims that Bigfoot exists. The evidence we do have suggests our imaginations have morphed creatures of the past and present into a mythical monster.

In the very distant past before human civilization, creatures that resembled Bigfoot existed. Known as *Gigantopithecus*, this now extinct genus of apes, most closely related to present-day orangutans, is estimated to have stood 9 feet tall and weighed more than 1,000 pounds (Ciochon, 1991). This giant primate roamed the forests of present-day China, India, and Vietnam. *Gigantopithecus* did co-occur with our humanlike ancestors, *Homo erectus* (Ciochon et al., 1996), but even then, our ancestors had little reason to fear them. Scientists studying the fossilized teeth of *Gigantopithecus* have concluded that members of this genus ate fibrous vegetation, mostly bamboo with some seeds and fruit (Ciochon, 1991): not children! It is also safe to say that *Gigantopithecus* went extinct during the last ice age (Pleistocene) when many very large mammals suffered mass extinction due to global climate change.

So, millions and thousands of years ago, there was an animal that was Bigfoot-like, but how does that explain recent sightings? Ecologists have pulled together data on Bigfoot sightings and the ecological habitats where these sightings were reported to construct an ecological niche model: a method used to predict the distribution of a species within a geographic space (Lozier, Aniell, & Hickerson, 2009). These scientists concluded that those geographic regions and niches where people report Bigfoot sightings overlap with those of another large, hairy mammal, the American black bear (*Ursus americanus*; Lozier et al., 2009).

Under the framework of the scientific method, we are able to disprove those explanations not consistent with evidence. As great as this method is, we cannot disprove the existence of something we have no evidence for, in this case, Bigfoot. We can merely say that there is no evidence to support its existence. Although many have used this limitation of the scientific method to profit from the search for this mythical monster, the scientific community can safely say there is no evidence to support fears of Bigfoot.

Carol E. Colaninno, PhD, is an anthropologist specializing in archeology and assistant research professor for the STEM Center at Southern Illinois University Edwardsville.

10.1 Pseudoscience and Questionable Ideas

10.1.1 Diagnostic Controversies

The DSM anxiety disorders have not been subject to the same level of controversy in terms of the numbers, types, and labels of the conditions contained therein and some other mental illnesses. However, the anxiety disorders do remain subject to more fundamental flaws pertaining to the basic assumptions of the DSM. For example, the DSM definition (abbreviated) of a mental disorder is given as follows: "A mental disorder is a syndrome characterized by clinically significant disturbance in ... processes underlying mental functioning" (APA, 2013, p. 20). Simply repeating the same thing in different words is mere sophistry, as well as being philosophically tautological. The assertion that mental disorders have their origins in mental functioning is itself an etiological assumption, not well supported in many of the conditions found in the DSM. For example, the DSM contains sleep apnea, which is caused by obstructed airways, and neurocognitive disorder, which can result from Alzheimer's, an organic condition. While these biological conditions have mental sequelae, it would not be correct to assert that they are mental disorders in and of themselves. Rather, the mental disturbances should be seen as effects, not causes. Including biological conditions such as these is an example of diagnostic overreach by the discipline of psychiatry to claim more and more instances of abnormal behavior as their "turf," even if the conditions are not caused by disordered mentation.

Many specific phobias have their origins in the child experiencing a frightening event, and later displaying physiological arousal and avoidance and expressing statements of fear when they encounter that event, object, or situation again. Clearly the origins of the phobia reside in the person's learning history, which changed their mental functioning, arousal patterns, and behavior. By asserting that the origins of so-called mental disorders have their causes in mental functioning, treatment efforts may be incorrectly focused on changing the person's thoughts via verbal or insight-oriented therapies (which have little effect on alleviating phobias), as opposed to a behavioral therapy such as graduated real-life desensitization to phobic stimuli, which helps change behavior, arousal, and thinking. There is no good evidence that the anxiety disorders have their causes in a child's mental functioning. Rather, disorders in mental functioning seen in many of the anxiety disorders are more likely effects, not causes, of more central etiological agents, such as traumatic events. Regardless, unlike infections, the anxiety disorders do not necessarily share a common etiology; hence, it makes no sense to assert, a priori, that they are the result of a disturbance in mental functioning. Merely labeling something with a diagnostic term does not necessarily explain its origin. Rabies was a recognized disease and its mechanism of transmission (bites from infected animals) was known before Pasteur discovered the causative virus.

Using a diagnostic label such as "specific phobia" to describe someone's condition, and then using that term to attempt to explain that condition involves two separate errors in reasoning – reification and circular reasoning. We reify when we use a descriptive term as if it reflects a real entity, absent good independent evidence for the existence of that entity. If a child has a fever, fatigue, and very swollen salivary glands, we can label that state as the disease called the mumps. The objective reality of the mumps can be independently verified by a laboratory test showing positive for the mumps virus. In this case, we can use the diagnostic label "mumps" with confidence, knowing we are dealing with a real disease. But if a child screams and runs away when seeing a dog, and we say "this child has a phobia," there is no independent evidence for the existence of an entity called a phobia, apart from the child's behavior. This action, saying someone suffers from a particular diagnosis absent the evidence of the behavior from which we infer the existence of the diagnosis, is reification. The evidence-based clinician may use the DSM terms as a shorthand way to communicate but is also aware that the label is not necessarily a real thing, in the same sense that the mumps are real.

When a clinician succumbs to using a reified term as an explanation for behavior, the further logical error known as circular reasoning has occurred. Picture the following dialog:

- Clinician – Sally has a phobia.
- Parent – How do you know that?
- Clinician – She screams and runs away when she sees dogs.
- Parent – I see. I wonder why she runs away when she sees dogs.
- Clinician – Oh, that's easy to explain. She has a phobia.

When behavior is used to explain itself, we have circular reasoning, and in truth nothing is explained. And because an "apparent" explanation has been arrived at, further useful etiological explorations may be missed.

A more legitimate dialog could look as follows:

- Clinician – The term we use for Sally's running away when she sees dogs is "specific phobia." This is just a shorthand way of expressing her behavior.

- Parent – I wonder why she runs away when she sees dogs.
- Clinician – Well from what you told me, this problem did not occur until she saw a scary dog movie. I suspect the movie scared her so much she developed a generalized fear of dogs. This is a common way that children develop new fears.

Unfortunately for the DSM, most conditions contained therein do not have some consistent etiological factors underlying the onset of these problems; hence, many of the diagnostic labels are used in a reified manner, as well as in a form of circular reasoning.

Psychotherapists may choose to employ the diagnostic labels found in the DSM. This is acceptable providing there are no assumptions being made that these terms reflect a true underlying organic disease state, and that the terms are not used to explain a child's fear, avoidance, and anxious thoughts. Alternatively, they may choose not to use the DSM language and restrict themselves to more parsimonious descriptions of what children do (overt actions), and what they say, and perhaps physiological assessments of arousal, like heart rate when being exposed to an anxiety-evoking situation. A sizeable proportion of mental health therapists do not use the DSM terminology, and several viable and more scientifically grounded alternatives exist, such as behavioral assessment (Thyer, 2015).

10.1.2 Implausible Treatments

The numbers of pseudoscientific therapies being promoted to treat children and adolescents with anxiety disorders are immense. A few of these will be reviewed, and later, interventions that are better supported by empirical research will be presented.

Homeopathy. Homeopathic medicines are advertised as being effective for a wide array of conditions. These medicines actually contain no active ingredients and any positive effects following their use can be attributed to placebo influences. One such product, advertised as a treatment for anxiousness, nervousness, fearfulness, social fear, and panic is called *Anxetin* and is advertised as safe for adults and children who are 2 years of age and older. It has also been claimed that the adolescent diagnosed as agoraphobic may benefit from *AgoraFear Relief* (Native Remedies, n.d.). The website claims it reduces the fear and stress of leaving home; eases anxiety induced by wide open spaces or crowds; and reduces shortness of breath, sweating, palpitations, and trembling. Other selling points include the following:

AgoraFear Relief is taken internally and works by helping the mind and body to restore balance at a cellular level. Presented in small dissolvable tablets, AgoraFear Relief is easy to ingest and hassle-free with **no artificial colors or preservatives**. Due to its unique homeopathic formula, it is also **safe for all ages**. (Emphasis in original; Native Remedies, n.d.a)

The same website sells a homeopathic product called SocialFear Relief to youth with social anxiety disorder, claiming that the product "Alleviates symptoms of anxiety related to social fear" and "Reduces the mental fear of stage fright and embarrassment" (Native Remedies, n.d.b).

All these products sell for $30–$40 a bottle (said to last 30 days). Websites selling these products look similar to those advertising real medicines, and the consumer is soothed by assurances that the products have no bad taste, side effects, or addictive potential. Homeopathic medicines possess a number of pseudoscientific features – overstated claims, disproven mechanisms of action, and no well-done research.

The mechanism of action of homeopathic products is based upon the pseudoscientific principle that in healing "like cures like." If a person has a fever, a homeopathic medicine is prepared by taking a small amount of a substance that *causes* a fever and dissolving it in a liter of distilled water, and then taking a drop of this highly dilute water and placing it into another liter of water. And then this process is repeated 10–20 times, to the extent that it is mathematically nearly impossible for a single mole-cule of the original substance to remain in the final dilutation. This final bottle of water is used to place water drop on inert pills, and it is these pills that constitute homeopathic medicine. Homeopaths claim that the final liter of water possesses a vibrational memory of the original sub-stance, another unproven claim.

Recently the National Health and Medical Research Council (NHMRC) of Australia conducted a thorough review of the scientific evidence on the usefulness of homeopathic cures, concluding as follows:

Based on the assessment of the evidence of effectiveness of homeop-athy, NHMRC concludes that there are no health conditions for which there is reliable evidence that homeopathy is effective. Homeopathy should not be used to treat health conditions that are chronic, serious, or could become serious. People who choose homeopathy may put their health at risk if they reject or delay treatments for which there is good evidence for safety and effective-ness. (NHMRC, 2015)

Healing with Crystals. Crystals are a widely used form of alternative treatment said to be effective in preventing and treating an array of mental and physical disorders. Healing crystals and books describing their use with children (e.g., Tingle, 2013) are sold at health food stores, online, and in shops specializing in complementary medicines. The pseudoscientific theory is that certain stones emit vibrations of a certain frequency that then produce specific effects, and that some crystals worn as jewelry, held, or placed near a child can have antianxiety effects. For example:

> [O]ur bodies and quartz crystals are both made up of mineral silicon-dioxide on a cellular level. Because of this we are naturally receptive to the vibrations of crystals as they transmit, reflect, store light and receive energy. When crystals are placed directly on your body, they have a powerful vibratory effect that surges from the crystal to you. According the laws of physics, thoughts direct energy and energy follows thought. (Natureal Mom, 2015)

Among the claims made are blue lace agate for stress relief, jade for children who are emotionally sensitive, moonstone to help prevent nightmares, and orange calcite to dissolve fears.

It is also said,

> Children can respond very quickly to the healing energy of crystals ... Each quartz crystal has its own energy signature and healing mission. When a child makes contact with the right crystal, the energy is discharged either very slowly, or quite suddenly so it feels like a very mild electric shock. This natural energy can be just enough to transform a disharmonious thought pattern, burn off some negative emotional state ... Rose quartz soothes erratic emotional states, anxiety, fear, compulsions and many other mental disorder. (Ryan, 1996)

None of these healing claims has been subjected to scientific evaluation, and science has yet to detect the special vibrations each crystal is said to emit. Both the crystals themselves and the books describing their use can be expensive. Unfortunately, a quick web search unveiled several licensed therapists using crystal healing as part of their services. Sadly, such practitioners are not difficult to locate. Parents seeking help for their child with an anxiety disorder may be easily persuaded by the fact that a psychotherapist has been licensed by their state, which means that all the services such practitioners provide are somehow evidence based or otherwise legitimate. Such is definitely not the case.

Energy Therapies. Energy therapies postulate that the human body creates and is permeated and surrounded by an invisible energy field, an energy force that has been given various labels, such as a thought field or quantum energy (not to be confused with the quantum phenomena studies by physicists). Disturbances in the thought field are claimed to be caused by trauma or exposure to supposed allergens that in turn cause symptoms of a very wide variety of mental disorders and psychical conditions. It is claimed that these disturbances in the energy force can be healed by a psychotherapist engaging in various practices that are quite diverse. In versions of energy therapies called Reiki, polarity therapy, or therapeutic touch, the psychotherapists hold their hands over areas of the body where they intuitively feel the energy is blocked. Sometimes these centers are synonymous with the meridians of acupuncture (nodes or supposed energy centers). Hands may be held over parts of the body, or gestures can be made to represent removing or adding "energy." The body is not touched. Variations include the therapist or client tapping specified parts of the body in particular places or patterns (patterns called algorithms in thought field therapy; Callahan & Callahan, 2000), with precise algorithms prescribed for particular disorders. Acupuncture, the insertion of small needles under the skin, can also be called an energy therapy since the point is to realign the body's energy. Here is a description on how acupuncture is said to work:

> Ancient Chinese medicine describes an energy force called Qi that regulates the body's overall health ... Like blood in the circulatory system, Qi moves throughout the body via pathways called meridians. When factors like injury, stress, poor nutrition, or a change in environment disrupt the flow of Qi, health issues follow ... By inserting needles at specific points in the body, acupuncturists restore the balance of Qi and the body's overall health. (Hohman, 2014, para. 3)

All of the so-called energy therapies postulate similar mechanisms of action, the realignment of energies unknown to science, which the sensitive therapist can feel with their hands.

The claims of the proponents of energy therapies are not modest. On a website page titled "Thought Field Therapy for Babies, Children and Teenagers," the following is claimed:

> TFT for Babies, Children and Teenagers is a highly effective treatment for children of all ages ... This process has the capability of

disabling and quite often completly **eliminating** troublesome emotional and physical responses … The simplicity and safety of TFT makes it especially suitable for nervous children who might find conventional and talking approaches intimidating … It is believed that Thought Field Therapy *is the most effective psychotherapy ever discovered or devised.* Time and after time it has proven to be extremely successful in treating children for: *fears and phobias … stress and anxiety, Trauma (PTSD), Exam nerves, Panic attacks.* (Bold in original, emphasis added; Mead, n.d.)

Another therapy called moxibustion involves holding a bundle of smoldering herbs near parts of the body, and this is also an energy therapy since the mechanism of action is said to be the same. Another variant, increasingly incredible, is a form of tapping therapy called tong ren, wherein the practitioner holds a small doll with acupuncture points drawn upon it and taps specified points on the doll while thinking of the identified patient. Auricular acupuncture involves pinching part of the ear, inserting needles in the outside of the ear, or shining a laser pointer at parts of the external ear. Foot reflexology involves applying pressure to the soles of the foot. Again, the common element here is that disturbances such as anxiety are caused by disrupted energy flow, and these various modalities are all ways to restore a healthy balance to the body energy. Thus, energy therapies are said to work by holding your hand near specified centers of the patient's body, sticking it with needles, pressing on meridians, tapping them in specific sequences, warming them with fire, or shining laser pointers at them. Each approach has its own name, and they are similar in that they share a common theory of action and a lack of credible research support for effectiveness.

Psychologist Roger Callahan, the original inventor of TFT, began his career after graduating from the Syracuse University with a PhD in psychology, specializing in children with phobias and other anxiety disorders. For 30 years, he practiced some of the evidence-based therapies; however, when he found clients he was unable to help, he turned to novel unsupported treatments derived from a chiropractic technique of muscle testing and acupressure meridians (Callahan & Callahan, 2000). Rather than do systematic research on his methods, he took his tapping therapy, called Callahan Techniques at the time, to the popular media. Many of the shows he appeared on, such as those hosted by Leeza Gibbons and Regis Philbin, featured live treatment of children with phobias. Some of these can be viewed on YouTube, for example, an episode where he appeared with actress Betty White and treated several children (i.e., search for "Thought Field Therapy® Classics: The Leeza Show with Betty White"; aired October 12, 1996). In spite of critics warning about the demand characteristics (e.g., a person's expectation that they will be judged if they do not improve) of such television appearances, Callahan considered these appearances compelling evidence for the efficacy of his approach (Gaudiano & Herbert, 2000).

A more recent tapping therapy-related aid geared toward children is Tappy Bear, marketed by a proponent of Emotional Freedom Techniques (EFTs), an offshoot of TFT (Stock, 2015). Tappy Bear is a stuffed teddy bear with energy meridian points marked so the child can tap on the bear. Proponents also recommend that tapping on dolls can be useful for teaching EFT to children. Interestingly enough, years earlier, a randomized controlled study was conducted on EFT for fears (Waite & Holder, 2003) that assigned participants to receive regular EFT, EFT with sham treatment points, EFT tapping on a doll, and a no treatment group. Participants in the EFT, the sham group, and the doll group all had modest improvements in their subjective distress level that were statistically significantly better than the no treatment control group. The most logical explanation for this would be placebo or perhaps an element of exposure, as suggested by the authors. However, the results of this study lead the more enthusiastic proponents to explain these away by speculating that there could be benefits to tapping on the doll because there are meridian points in the finger tips. This is a classic example of what Lilienfeld, Lynn, and Lohr (2014) have noted as a hallmark indicator of pseudoscience, the use of ad hoc hypotheses to explain away failure or null results.

The research supporting such practices is typically quite weak. For example, Folkes (2002) treated children with TFT and conducted pretests and posttests of trauma symptoms. Thirty days after treatment, the clients reported reductions in symptoms. Such a study lacking proper controls fails to take into account the simple ameliorative effects of time alone, placebo influences, or the desire to please the therapist. A marginally better study was conducted by Church et al. (2012), who randomly assigned 16 male adolescents who had been exposed to abuse to either energy therapy or to no treatment. Thirty days later, the treated group had greater reductions in subjective anxiety and trauma symptoms than the untreated group. This type of design also did not control for placebo influences, the desire to please the therapists, or to demand characteristics of being in a study. Generally, fair tests compare an active treatment against a credible placebo treatment to truly determine the "real" effects of the active treatment. Comparing something against nothing will almost always show some positive effects of doing something against doing nothing. This is why in medication studies placebo pills that look identical to the experimental medicine are used. In psychotherapy research, equally plausible placebo or inert treatments must be used to ascertain the true effectiveness of newer (and older) treatments.

Pignotti (2005) did conduct a placebo-controlled randomized experiment evaluating real TFT voice technology (VT). Voice technology is the most advanced form of TFT that can cost $100,000 for training. The real TFT VT was compared to the fake version, wherein the tapping sequences were randomly assigned, as opposed to clients receiving tapped sequences as prescribed by the approved TFT methodology. Because clients in both groups reported similar dramatic improvements in their self-reported subjective distress levels, the results demonstrated that the precise procedures dictated by TFT theory were immaterial to the treatment's success, and that the results were most plausibly explained as a placebo treatment or elements of exposure that exist in these treatments. Similarly, it is now suggested that clinical trials of acupuncture compare "real" acupuncture, involving correct and precise needle insertion as dictated by acupuncture theory, against "fake" acupuncture, wherein needles are inserted at random positions, something acupuncture theory says will have no effect.

A recent systematic review of the evidence comparing the effectiveness of real acupuncture versus sham acupuncture concluded, "The evidence gathered was not sufficient to affirm the effectiveness of traditional acupuncture compared with sham acupuncture" (Lopes-Junior et al., 2016, p. 1). Similarly, with respect to TFT, EFT, and other tapping psychotherapies, McCaslin concluded, "The small successes seen in these therapies are potentially attributable to well-known cognitive and behavioral techniques that are included along with the energy manipulation. Psychologists and researchers should be wary of using such techniques, and make efforts to inform the public about the ill effects of therapies that advertise miraculous cures" (McCaslin, 2009, p. 249), a finding similar to that arrived at by Pignotti and Thyer (2009) and Koocher, McMann, and Stout (2014). If one takes a treatment known to be effective, say cognitive-behavioral therapy (CBT) and adds to it a placebo element such as tapping, needles, or foot poking, and compares the outcomes of CBT to CBT plus the placebo treatment, voila! One can claim that the "new" approach is as effective as the traditional therapy, and perhaps even a bit better due to the added placebo elements. It is not surprising that a systematic survey of mental health professionals found child and adolescent energy treatments such as acupuncture, Reiki, Qigong, energy field therapy, crystal healing, and tapping therapies to be seen as largely discredited (Koocher et al., 2015).

Neurofeedback Videogames. Biofeedback is a treatment that uses technology to help clients sense their body's reactions at levels not normally perceptible, in the hope that clients can learn to modulate these reactions. Biofeedback involves several different ways to assess bodily functioning (see Thyer et al., 1981, for more about biofeedback). Neurofeedback is a type of biofeedback that specifically measures brain activity. Scalp sensors can be used to measure brain wave patterns associated with relaxation and calmness versus arousal, a form of treatment called neurotherapy.

One neurofeedback videogame is called *MindLight,* and it is intended to reduce anxiety in youth. Here is how *MindLight* is described and some of its claims:

> *MindLight* incorporates several evidence-based strategies including relaxation and mindfulness techniques, attention bias modification methods, and neurofeedback mechanics that together produce an immersive game world through which children learn to manage and overcome anxiety symptoms ... *MindLight* is a video game aimed at children 8–12 years of age and is based on evidence-based principles of intervention with anxiety-disordered children and adults ... **The Science.** The game is an immersive training ground that uses evidence-based therapeutic practices including **neurofeedback mechanics** ... We believe that it is this in-game practice that canalizes new neural pathways and these new pathways may be the means by which playing *MindLight* forms resilient habits of mind that transfer to children's everyday lives. (The Play Nice Institute, n.d.; http://theplayniceinstitute.com)

Parents reading this description of *MindLight* could be understandably interested in purchasing this expensive system to treat their children and adolescents. The use of terms such as "evidence-based," "neurofeedback mechanics," "canalizes new neural pathways" all connote a strong science behind this device. A PsycINFO search on *MindLight* found one recent randomized controlled study of its use, using youth (ages 7–13 years) who were somewhat anxious. That is, they were not diagnosed with an anxiety disorder, but they scored high on a self-report anxiety scale. More than 60 children were randomly assigned to either or to another videogame control condition, a game not presumed to have antianxiety effects. Pre-treatment both groups scored similarly on measures of anxiety. After treatment, both groups showed similar improvements, thus *MindLight* was not shown to have any specific anti-anxiety effects, beyond factors such as the passage of time, placebo influences, or regression to the mean (Schoneveld et al., 2016). In other words, it does not live up to its therapeutic claims.

This is not the only test of *MindLight*. Tsui (2016) compared *MindLight* treatment with psychoeducational intervention in a randomized study. Again, both groups improved equally, likely for reasons similar to those of the Schoneveld et al. (2016) study, and again not supporting the specific anxiogenic effects of the expensive neurofeedback-based videogaming system. These negative results should not be surprising. Even if children are successful in using neurofeedback methods to modulate anxiety while connected to biofeedback devices in the clinic setting, or even at home, the transfer of such skills into everyday situations that evoke anxiety cannot be assumed. Overall, the generalizability of biofeedback-induced skills to provide strong and lasting improvements in mental disorders in everyday life has a very weak research base (Schoenberg & David, 2014; Simkin, Thatcher, & Lubar, 2014). Making exaggerated claims over the efficacy of biofeedback methods in the treatment of clinically anxious children, invoking science-like terminology, the use of parent testimonials on the biofeedback proponents' websites, and accepting as fact unproven mechanisms of action, all way ahead of the evidence curve, suggest the pseudoscientific nature of these therapies.

10.2 Research-Supported Approaches

In psychotherapy, the strongest evidence is not a parent's testimonial of how their child is said to have responded to a given treatment. It is not collection of anecdotes. It is not a study of a group of children assessed pre- and post-treatment. It is not a comparison of youth treated with the given treatment, and comparing their outcomes to other youth who did not get treated or received some other form of therapy. It is not, perhaps surprisingly, a large-scale, well-conducted randomized controlled trial (RCT) or experiment. Any individual RCT's findings, no matter how promising, need to be replicated by independent researchers lacking any conflicts of interest that may bias their evaluations. Rather, the strongest form of evidence consists of a systematic review of all the well-designed RCTs that evaluated the effects of a given treatment for youth with a specified disorder. Such systematic reviews are rare, and the evidence-informed practitioner must drill down into less-stringent research than systematic reviews, if need be.

One such study was reported by Chorpita et al. (2011), who found, "Review of the treatment outcome studies for childhood anxiety yielded 17 different treatment families with at least some level of empirical support ... The vast majority of these studies supported Cognitive Behavior Therapy (CBT) and its variants as well as exposure-based approaches" (p. 159). Seligman, Swedish, and Ollendick (2014) arrived at similar conclusions. A systematic review titled "Cognitive behavioural therapy for anxiety disorders in children and adolescents" by James et al. (2015) found "Cognitive behavioural therapy is an effective treatment for childhood and adolescent anxiety disorders" (p. 2) based on an appraisal of 41 RCTs involving 1,800 children. And more recently, Craske and Stein (2016) came to a similar conclusion: "Cognitive behavioural therapy (CBT) is the most empirically supported psychological treatment for youth and adult anxiety disorders" (p. 3052).

Thus, the evidence is good that CBT can be an effective treatment for children and youth who experience an anxiety disorder. But the evidence is not perfect, just the best available at present. The picture may change with time and the emergence of new studies. In the meantime, psychotherapists who embrace the evidence-based practice model will seriously discuss the use of CBT methods as a research-supported approach with their young clients and their caregivers.

10.3 Conclusion

It is difficult to prove that something works, especially in the field of psychotherapy, and particularly in attempting to help children. In science, most claims (e.g., "This treatment works!") are acknowledged to be provisional in nature, with such conclusions always being subject to revision as new data comes in. The history of health care services is littered with examples of treatments initially claimed to be effective, based on the existing research, only to be later determined to not work as well as initially asserted, or even to have harmful effects. In scientific skepticism, the burden of proof is on the person making the unusual claim. Before accepting the claim that "crystals alleviate anxiety," one should ask "Where is the evidence?" If there is none forthcoming or if it is scientifically weak, we can ignore the claim. But it is better to argue against pseudoscientific treatments, so as to help protect the public against honest-but-deluded therapists, and against the outright charlatans who know their treatment is bogus but who promote it as a means of acquiring income or professional accolades. Akin to the game of

Whack-A-Mole, new pseudoscientific therapies are constantly being promoted, as well as some very old ones, and it requires vigilance for the more evidence-based members of the professional to expose the lack of credible evidence and exaggerated claims associated with these treatments.

It is also difficult, but not as difficult, to make a strong claim that something does not work. Philosophically, this is akin to the problem of proving a negative. Like claiming black swans do not exist, to confidently assert that a given treatment does not work renders one liable to being proved incorrect, when positive examples emerge. We may be inclined to state that acupuncture meridian fields do not exist, but it is possible (albeit scarcely probable based on available evidence) that someday strong studies will demonstrate their existence. The honest scientific skeptic must remain open to such claims. Thus it is said that scientific skepticism is more akin to doubting claims, rather than denying their validity outright. Maybe, someday, a series of strong replicated experiments will show that homeopathic medicines can cure childhood anxiety states, or that thought field therapy has effects above and beyond placebo influences. If that happens, we will be delighted, happy that new scientific developments have given us useful tools to help anxious children. But in the meantime, constant vigilance is needed to discourage the promotion of pseudoscientific therapies said to help anxious youth. Acceptance, or even the tolerance, of such methods embedded within the existing structure of the mental health profession degrades the intellectual life of each discipline, erodes its credibility in the eyes of the public, and is a violation of professional ethical codes that require each member to promote high standards of practice. Failing to act is condoning fraud within one's field.

Works Cited in Sidebar

Ciochon, R. L. (1991). The ape that was. *Natural History*, *100*(11), 54.

Ciochon, R., Long, V. T., Larick, R., González, L., Grün, R., De Vos, J. … & Reagan, M. (1996). Dated co-occurrence of Homo erectus and Gigantopithecus from Tham Khuyen care, Vietnam. *Proceedings of the National Academy of Sciences*, *93*(7), 3016–3020.

Lozier, J. D., Aniello, P., & Hickerson, M. J. (2009). Predicting the distribution of Sasquatch in western North America: Anything goes with ecological niche modelling. *Journal of Biogeography*, *36*(9), 1623–1627.

References

American Psychiatric Association. (2013). *Diagnostic and statistical manual of mental disorders*. 5th edn. Washington, DC: Author.

Callahan, R. J. & Callahan, J. (2000). *Stop the nightmares of trauma*. Chapel Hill, NC: Professional Press.

Chorpita, B. F., Daleiden, E. L., Ebesutani. C., Young, J., Becker, K. D., Nakamura, B. J. … Starace, N. (2011) Evidence-based treatment for children and adolescents: An updated review of indicators of efficacy and effectiveness. *Clinical Psychology: Science and Practice*, *18*, 154–172.

Church, D., Pina, O., Reategui, C., & Brooks, A. (2012). Single-session of the intensity of traumatic memories in abused adolescents after EFT: A randomized controlled pilot study. *Truamatology*, *18*(3), 73–79.

Craske, M. G., & Stein, M. B. (2016). Anxiety. *Lancet*, *388*, 3048–3059.

Folkes, C. E. (2002). Thought field therapy and trauma recovery. *International Journal of Emergency Mental Health*, *4*(2), 99–104.

Gaudiano, B., & Herbert, J. (2000). Can we really tap our problems away? A critical analysis of Thought Field Therapy, *Skeptical Inquirer*, 24, July-August.

Hohman, M. (2014). Why acupuncture works for anxiety relief. Retrieved from www.everydayhealth.com

James, A. C., James, G., Cowdrey, F. A., Soler, A., & Choke, A. (2015). Cognitive behavioural therapy for anxiety disorders in children and adolescents. *Cochrane Database of Systematic Reviews*, Issue 2. Art. No.: CD004690. doi: 10.1002/14651858.CD004690.pub4

Koocher, G. P., McMann, M. R., & Stout, A. O. (2014). Controversial therapies for children. In C. A. Alfano & D. C. Beidel (eds.), *Comprehensive evidence-based interventions for children and adolescents* (pp. 31–41). New York: Wiley.

Koocher, G. P., McMann, M. R., Stout, A. O. & Norcross, J. C. (2015). Discredited assessment and treatment methods used with children and adolescents: A Delphi poll. *Journal of Clinical Child & Adolescent Psychology*, *44*, 722–729.

Lilienfeld, S. O., Lynn, S. J., & Lohr, J. M. (2014). Science and pseudoscience in clinical psychology: Initial thoughts, reflections, and considerations. In S. O. Lilienfeld, S. J. Lynn, & J. M. Lohr (eds.), *Science and pseudoscience in clinical psychology*. 2nd edn (pp. 1–16). New York: Guilford Press.

Lopes-Júnior, L. C., da Cruz, L. A. P., Leopoldo, V. C., de Campos, F. R., de Almeida, A. M., & Silveira, R. C. D. C. P. (2016). Effectiveness of traditional Chinese acupuncture versus sham acupuncture: A systematic review. *Revista Latino-Americana de Enfermagem*, *24*, Article ID e2762.

McCaslin, D. (2009). A review of efficacy claims in energy psychology. *Psychotherapy*, *46*, 249–256.

Mead, P. (n.d.). Thought field therapy for babies, children and teenagers. Retrieved from www.therapylifecentre.co.uk

National Health and Medical Research Council. (2015). Statement on homeopathy. Retrieved from www.nhmrc.gov.au

Native Remedies. (n.d.). AgoraFear Relief™: Homeopathic medicine for fear and nervousness prompted by new environments. Retrieved from www.nativeremedies.com

Natureal Mom. (2015). Crystals for kids & energy muse giveaway. Retrieved from www.naturealmom.com

Pignotti, M. (2005). Thought field therapy voice technology vs. random meridian point sequences: A single-blind controlled experiment. *The Scientific Review of Mental Health Practice, 4*(1), 72–81.

Pignotti, M., & Thyer, B. A. (2009). Some comments on *Energy psychology: A review of the evidence:* Premature conclusions based on incomplete evidence? *Psychotherapy, 46,* 257–261.

Ryan, K. (1996). Ten healing crystals for children. Retrieved from http://horoscopes.hypermart.net

Schoenberg, P. L., & David, A. S. (2014). Biofeedback for psychiatric disorders: A systematic review. *Applied Psychophysiology and Biofeedback, 39,* 109–135.

Schoneveld, E. A., Malmberg, M., Lichtwarck-Aschoff, A., Verheijen, G. P., Engles, R. C., & Granic, I. (2016). A neurofeedback video game (*MindLight*) to prevent anxiety in children: A randomized controlled trial. *Computers in Human Behavior, 63,* 321–333.

Seligman, L. D., Swidish, E. F., & Ollendick, T. H. (2014). Anxiety disorders in children. In C. A. Alfano & D. C. Beidel (eds.), *Comprehensive evidence based interventions for children and adolescents* (pp. 93–109). New York: Wiley.

Simkin, D. R., Thatcher, R. W., & Lubar, J. (2014). Quantitative EEG and neurofeedback in children and adolescents: Anxiety disorders, depressive disorders, comorbid addiction and attention-deficit/hyperactivity disorder, and brain injury. *Child and Adolescent Psychiatric Clinics of North America, 23,* 427–464

Stock, K. (2015). Using teddy bears for EFT tapping. Retrieved from www.eftuniverse.com/refinements-to-eft/using-teddy-bears-for-eft-tapping

The Play Nice Institute. (n.d.). Mindlight. Retrieved from http://theplayniceinstitute.com

Thyer, B. A. (2015). The DSM-5 definition of mental disorder: Critique and alternatives. In B. Probst (ed.), *Critical thinking in clinical assessment and diagnosis* (pp. 45–68). New York: Springer.

Thyer, B. A., Papsdorf, J. D., Himle, D., McCann, B. Caldwell, S., & Wickert, M. (1981). In-vivo distraction-coping training in the treatment of test anxiety. *Journal of Clinical Psychology, 37*, 754–764.

Tingle, S. (2013). Healing with crystals for kids. Retrieved from www.amazon .com/Healing-Crystals-Kids-Stephanie-Tingle/dp/1490933131/ref=sr_1_1? ie=UTF8&qid=1505506884&sr=8–1&keywords=Healing+with+crystals+ for+kids

Tsui, T. Y. L. (2016). *The efficacy of a novel videogame intervention (MindLight) in reducing children's anxiety.* Masters Thesis, Department of Psychology, Queens University, Kingston, Ontario, Canada. See https://qspace.library .queensu.ca/handle/1974/14821

Waite, W. L., & Holder, M. D. (2003). Assessment of the Emotional Freedom Technique: An alternative treatment for fear. *Scientific Review of Mental Health Practice, 2*, 2–26.

Yancey, V. F. (2003). The use of thought field therapy in educational settings. *Dissertation Abstracts International Section A: Humanities and Social Sciences, 63*(7-A), 2470.

11

Obsessions and Compulsions

Monica Pignotti and Bruce A. Thyer

Obsessive-compulsive disorder (OCD), which is more common than was once believed, is one of the most common mental disorders in children, said to have a prevalence occurring anytime during childhood of 2% to 3% (Helbing & Ficca, 2009). Approximately one-third to one-half of adults with OCD are said to have developed this condition during childhood, although relatively few children receive accurate diagnosis and treatment (American Psychiatric Association, 2013). Children and adolescents can present with a variety of symptoms, including "compulsive washing, checking, repeating, counting, ordering, hoarding, magical thinking or rituals involving other people as well as obsessions regarding contamination, aggressive thoughts, hoarding, somatic, religious, superstitious and sexual beliefs" (James, Farrell, & Zimmer-Gembeck, 2017, p. 9). OCD can be an extremely debilitating condition and individuals with OCD have been found to be ten times more likely to die from committing suicide than the general population (de la Cruz et al., 2016), making intervention as early as possible with effective interventions imperative.

The fifth edition of the *Diagnostic and Statistical Manual* (DSM-5), unlike earlier editions that grouped it with anxiety disorders, places OCD in its own category along with body dysmorphic disorder, hoarding disorder, and trichotillomania. Obsessions are unwanted recurrent and persistent thoughts, urges, and impulses that the person tries to ignore or suppress by performing an action known as a compulsion. Compulsions are repetitive behaviors the individual feels he or she must perform, imposing rigid rules. The purpose of these behaviors is to reduce anxiety and distress or prevent something they dread from occurring, although young children may not be aware of this purpose. Moreover, the obsessions and compulsions must take an hour or more a day, cause significant distress, or impair the person's ability to function in areas of their lives that are important to them. The obsessions and compulsions cannot be the result of a substance or be better explained by another mental disorder.

Practitioners (and caregivers of youth who meet the criteria for OCD) need to remain aware that these criteria are purely descriptive in nature. They do not explain anything. At present, no firm etiologies have been established for OCD, although numerous causative factors have been and are constantly being proposed and explored – neurological, genetic, cognitive, traumatic insult, learning experiences, infections, and so on.

> **Sidebar Box: Do superstitious rituals help cope with anxiety? by Stuart Vyse**
>
> If you were a school-aged child in England of the 1930s and you saw an ambulance go by, you would likely grab your collar and quickly recite:
>
> > Touch your collar
> > Touch your toes
> > Never go in one of those,
> > Touch your knee
> > Touch your chin
> > Never let the burglar in.
>
> The rhyme might vary depending upon your area of the country, and in some cases the ritual required that you maintain a grip on your collar until you had seen a dog or another four-legged animal (Opie & Opie, 1959). In England during that era, children spent more time outside than they do today, and there were lucky or unlucky omens associated with seeing nuns, trains, oil patches, people with wooden legs, and a variety of animals, including white horses, crows, ladybirds, and magpies.
>
> Many typically developing children show magical beliefs and rituals beginning at approximately age 2 and continuing throughout childhood (Evans et al., 2002). Often these rituals center on common early fears; although they appear similar in shape to the compulsive rituals of OCD, there is little understanding of the relationship, if any, between typical childhood rituals and the more pathological patterns of behavior shown in OCD (Evans et al., 1997). Indeed, early superstitious rituals are considered adaptive responses to anxiety, in contrast to the nonfunctional compulsions of OCD. Furthermore, many adults employ rituals to manage the stress of loss and to prepare for important performances (e.g., in sports and in the theater). There is now growing evidence that rituals can help adults manage anxiety,

which in turn can improve performance at a skilled activity (e.g., a timed math test; Brooks et al., 2016). Rituals are not magical incantations, but in both children and adults, performing a ritual can have psychological benefits. However, it is important to note that the ritual can be helpful even without any attached superstition (for a more detailed discussion, see Vyse, 2018).

Stuart Vyse, PhD, is a behavioral scientist and contributing editor for *Skeptical Inquirer* magazine. He is the author of the book *Believing in Magic: The Psychology of Superstition, updated ed* (2013).

11.1 Pseudoscience and Questionable Ideas

Because evidence-based practices are underutilized, this opens the door for pseudoscientific practices to proliferate, particularly for clients who may have tried an evidence-based approach and may not have had the proper preparation or had found it too uncomfortable to continue. While the practices described here are not meant to be an exhaustive list of such treatments, they are some examples that are widely promoted on the internet that we consider some of the most egregious offenders.

11.1.1 Energy Psychology and Energy Therapies

Energy psychology or energy therapies, more popularly known as tapping therapy, refer to a novel form of therapy whereby stimulation of specified acupressure points of the body is employed, usually by finger tapping while the person is focusing on an emotionally distressing situation or physical pain. The first energy therapy that employed tapping on acupressure points for psychological problems was thought field therapy (TFT; Callahan & Callahan, 2000) which was invented by psychologist Roger Callahan in the early 1980s, then known as Callahan Techniques. Soon thereafter, as Callahan promoted this tapping therapy in the media, offshoots began to proliferate, the most widespread one being emotional freedom technique (EFT) started by Gary Craig, an engineer who was a student of Callahan's. Although TFT began as a treatment for phobias, Callahan quickly expanded its uses to include trauma and a variety of other psychological issues including OCD. To date, no studies demonstrate the effectiveness of TFT, EFT, or any other tapping therapy for OCD, yet there have been numerous anecdotes by practitioners who employ this method on clients with OCD, including Callahan himself.

Callahan and other proponents of tapping therapies have claimed that these methods work equally well on adults and children; Callahan, as a psychologist, initially specialized in treating children, and many of his early television appearances involved treating children for phobias and sometimes even OCD on popular talk shows. An education-based website offers a course on EFT for parents of children who pull hair and pick skin, claiming parents will learn how to reduce their own stress regarding their children's skin picking or hair pulling as well as a tapping routine for the child to help reduce the urge to pick or pull (Paton & Kaylor, 2015). It also features Tappy Bear, a stuffed animal with meridian points that children can use to transfer their urge to pick or pull.

As is common in pseudoscientific practices, when a treatment fails to work or initial relief is temporary and does not hold up over time, ad hoc hypotheses are added to explain away failure (Lilienfeld, Lynn, & Lohr, 2014). In the case of TFT, Callahan claimed that the reason treatment results do not last is individual energy toxins (IET; Callahan & Callahan, 2000). An IET in TFT jargon is not necessarily a poison but can be any substance consumed or inhaled, including common foods. A chiropractic muscle-testing technique or a proprietary method conducted over the phone called voice technology identifies the IET. Once identified, the person is asked to abstain from that substance. Often these IETs can include commonly eaten foods such as wheat, dairy, soy, or corn, and eliminating these food groups can extremely limit the person's diet and lead even someone without OCD to obsess over what is in the food they eat. When someone is getting the TFT's telephone treatment, it is not uncommon for the person to be encouraged to call daily if they are having problems with their symptoms and check what substances they have consumed that are causing the symptoms. When treated initially with tapping, the person often experiences a reduction or elimination of their emotional distress, obsession, or compulsion, likely due to placebo effect, which often does not hold up over time. When the unwanted feelings return, the person is checked for toxins by Callahan's propriety assessment methods, trade secrets that have no scientific support.

For someone with OCD, the possibility of further reinforcing compulsions, especially checking compulsions when they are encouraged to check for toxins, is a possible harmful side effect. While in most instances for other conditions, tapping may be harmless and have some placebo effect, in the case of OCD, being encouraged to constantly check for toxins may actually be harmful. Additionally, repetitive actions could reinforce OCD symptoms, as some clients with OCD even have tapping rituals. One practitioner of EFT actually noted the potential for tapping to reinforce the chronic repetitive behaviors and thoughts that so many clients with OCD have and provided some suggested guidelines for attempting to minimize this possibility (Bressler, 2011). However, while it is good that Bressler is encouraging EFT practitioners to work only within their area of expertise, none of these methods has ever been tested in a properly conducted study, so even when licensed professionals knowledgeable about OCD are using it, whether it is effective in reducing this potential for harm is unknown.

Practitioners using EFT tapping do not usually check for toxins. Nevertheless, there is no evidence that this therapy is effective for any form of OCD. The way in which these therapies are promoted as being able to instantly eliminate problems, sometimes in minutes, is very attractive and may lead people to choose them over empirically supported therapies that have been shown through well-designed studies to work.

Some tapping therapy practitioners combine EFT with other questionable practices such as neurolinguistic programming (NLP) for OCD. For example, a practitioner of EFT and NLP, using typical pseudoscientific jargon about rewiring the brain, wrote up an anecdote about using his methods on a client with a compulsion to check her door lock, claimed that using his methods make exposure with response prevention (ERP) or medication unnecessary:

> By using FasterEFT to change those original records (whatever they may be) Pat will literally rewire the neocortex of her brain, so that the act of locking the door is no longer linked to danger or a threat to her life – her brain will therefore no longer be prompted to trigger the fight-freeze-or-flight response ... This means that Pat will not need to expose herself to the stress and trauma of ERP therapy or take medication; she will not need to try to resist the compulsion while feeling the anxiety; and she will experience a change in how she responds automatically. (Smith, 2016, paras. 32–34).

A Google search on TFT or EFT and OCD will reveal many similar articles promoting these methods and will provide no evidence for their efficacy other than testimonials and anecdotes. Some practitioners indicate that they combine EFT or TFT with some form of cognitive-behavioral therapy (CBT); nevertheless, there is no evidence that this in any way adds to the effectiveness of the therapy. Rosen and Davison (2003) used the analogy of a practitioner asking a client to wear a purple hat while doing a form of exposure therapy. A complex system of magnets could be placed within the hat and elaborate theories developed. However, since the therapy being conducted already had empirical support without the purple hat, all these complexities add nothing to the effectiveness of the treatment, other than perhaps to enhance placebo effect. The claims being made by proponents of tapping therapies are not much different from this mythical "purple hat" example.

11.1.2 Supplements and Dietary Changes

Supplements and dietary changes are popular forms of alternative treatments often making scientific-sounding claims with scant evidence to support them. St. John's Wort is one of the most popular remedies that, in addition to depression, is now beginning to be used for OCD. An internet search reveals many claims regarding this supplement for OCD. However, evidence does not support these claims and randomized controlled studies show no difference between St. John's Wort and placebo (Kobak et al., 2005). Some websites promoting St. John's Wort explain away null results saying that more research is needed to do longer follow-ups. However, no such research exists, so the claims of "promising" research appear to be premature. Inositol 5 HTP, fish oil/Omega 3, tryptophan, milk thistle, and N-Acetylcysteine (NAC) are also popularly promoted, with scant evidence to support their efficacy. Additionally, herbal and nutritional supplements are not without side effects and interactions if other medications are being taken; this would especially be the case when children are involved. One website does note that the doses need to be scaled down for children but does not say by how much. It is very risky to just guess, when children are involved.

Food allergies, also erroneously called "brain allergies," are also popular but unsupported factors believed to cause OCD. There appears to be no evidence other than anecdotal that this is the case. There are also claims that some foods will aggravate OCD, again with scant evidence. The Livestrong Foundation provides a list of foods to avoid if one has OCD, including processed foods. While this advice might make sense for some of these foods from the standpoint of healthy eating, they offer no scientific evidence that avoiding them will help OCD. Nevertheless, to sound scientific, they cite a study that involved depression and processed foods that had nothing to do with OCD. Other websites have testimonials from parents who changed their children's diet and their OCD supposedly disappeared. But testimony is akin to anecdote, and of little scientific standing. The problem with these testimonials is that we do not know whether the child had an actual diagnosis of OCD in the first place, or, if they did, if other factors could be responsible for the changes. Even though some children go on to develop chronic OCD in adulthood, other children with OCD may actually experience remission and become subsyndromal as time passes (James et al., 2017).

The unnecessary and non-empirically supported focus on food allergies as a cause of OCD could be particularly problematic when applied to children who suffer from the sudden onset of severe OCD symptoms, known as pediatric acute onset neuropsychiatric syndrome (PANS). Or, if OCD is preceded by a Group A streptococcal infection, the result has been called pediatric immune neuropsychiatric disorder associated with streptococcal infections (PANDAS; Toufexis et al., 2015). Children with PANS or PANDAS have been reported to have fears of food contamination and fears of choking, swallowing, or vomiting that can result in PANDAS anorexia, a condition where the child refuses to eat. If a parent or practitioner adds to this the belief that these symptoms are caused by food allergies and employs pseudoscientific testing for food allergies resulting in restrictions on the child's diet, that would likely reinforce the child's PANDAS anorexia, by adding a nocebo effect (negative suggestion) that food is an allergen or a toxin. Needless to say, this is the last thing a child with PANDAS needs.

11.1.3 Neurofeedback

Neurofeedback or EEG biofeedback is an intervention best known for treatment of attention-deficit/hyperactivity disorder (ADHD), where the person is hooked up to electrodes placed on specific sites on the skull corresponding to various brain sites and then plays a computer game where they earn rewards for increased brain wave activity at these specified sites. Since computer games are involved, this form of treatment has become popular with children. Currently, neurofeedback is used for a variety of conditions, even though evidence for many of these conditions, including OCD, is scant. Nevertheless, websites promoting neurofeedback claim it is the best treatment for OCD. They seem to be basing this on research showing OCD is related to specific areas of the brain. However, no randomized clinical trials actually test to see if this intervention helps with OCD. The only studies that have been conducted appear to be small, uncontrolled pilot studies (Surmeli &

Ertem, 2011). Once again, the promotions appeal to the fact that it is a painless treatment that is quick, easy, and comfortable for the client to engage in, in an attempt to make it more appealing than evidence-based approaches that can require a significant amount of work. The idea that people can gain control over the regions of their brains that are responsible for various conditions can be compelling and give the appearance of having a scientific basis. However, evidence is scant that neurofeedback accomplishes this, particularly for OCD.

11.1.4 Hypnosis and Past Life Regression

Hypnosis, particularly regressing a person to memories of past experiences, often used for trauma, is also used for OCD even though there is no evidence that this is effective. The celebrity Howie Mandel claims that he was successfully treated with hypnosis for his OCD, which involved fear of shaking people's hands (Singer, 2016). Some of the more exotic forms of hypnosis can involve past life regression, whereby the person is supposedly regressed to what they believe is a former lifetime. For example, one website states: "In Obsessive Compulsive Disorder, an individual is 'plagued' with thoughts, beliefs, and attitudes – usually originating from a traumatic death in a past life – that result [*sic*] in disempowering behaviors that seriously disrupt their present day life" (Heal Past Lives, n.d.). What follows is a lengthy list of various forms of OCD such as hoarding or "clean freaks" and what kind of trauma they suffered in a past life. It is claimed that those who are able to free themselves of their OCD through this process of past life regression will be free of it for the remainder of their "karmic cycle." No author is named for this article; it is listed as "channeled information."

Other forms of hypnotic regression may not involve past lives but are equally unsupported by any kind of scientific evidence that they are effective. One such approach, heart-centered hypnotherapy (HCH; Zimberoff, 2016) claims that it can cure OCD by regressing the person back to the trauma that caused the condition and connect with their inner child. The description claims the following:

> In HCH we help the client *to wash off the child* that was dirtied and, perhaps for the first time, begin to love this little girl or boy. We encourage the client to love the inner child the same way you would love and heal any child who was harmed or betrayed by their caregivers. When healed on the deep subconscious level where the original traumatizing event occurred, the person is able to stop the

OCD behavior because the triggering event is neutralized of its power. Without the original event's reservoir of fear and shame propelling it, the current triggering event has lost its commanding influence. (para. 6)

Some forms of hypnosis are aimed specifically at children and claim to help with a variety of conditions including OCD. Again, there appears to be the assumption that regression to some sort of trauma will cure whatever the problem is. For example, one practitioner of NLP and hypnosis employs a technique called talking puppet therapy whereby children are placed under hypnosis and encouraged to talk to a puppet about their problems (Knight, n.d.). The advantages to these approaches, he claims, are that they are drug free or can be used as complements to prescribed drugs. He makes no mention of the evidence-based non-drug interventions that do exist.

11.2 Research-Supported Approaches

The promotion and proliferation of pseudoscientific practices for OCD is especially troubling since well-researched, evidence-based practices for OCD have existed for quite some time (see Pignotti & Thyer, 2011, for a review of best practices). Since OCD can be so debilitating and have such an adverse impact on a person's life, it is vital that well-supported effective treatments are disseminated and made available and that the person with the disorder receives accurate information about what those arc. Currently, the intervention with the most support for OCD is therapist-assisted exposure therapy and response prevention, a type of behavior therapy (ERP or ETRP; Abramowitz, 1997; Fisher & Wells, 2005; Mantz & Abbott, 2017). Recent work also indicates the potential value of internet-guided ETRP for adolescents, which is less expensive but similarly effective (Lenhard et al., 2017). ERP treatments involve client exposure on a gradual basis to stimuli that trigger OCD symptoms and then having the client refrain from performing OCD rituals. Nevertheless, ERP is underutilized with only 50% of therapists who report cognitive-behavioral therapy as their primary orientation using ERP (Maltby & Tolin, 2005); among those who do not, that percentage would presumably be even lower. One of the main problems with ERP is that because this treatment can be difficult and uncomfortable, a minority of clients refuse treatment to begin with or drop out of treatment (Tolin & Maltby, 2008). However, readiness interventions involving motivational interviewing as an adjunct to ERP have been designed that have shown some promise in small clinical trials (Randall & McNeil, 2016). Additionally, education can be used with any family members who live with the individual who has OCD, so they can learn how to be helpful in carrying out homework assignments and not be overly accommodating or overly antagonistic (Renshaw, Steketee, & Chambless, 2005). Family involvement would be particularly relevant in the case of a child or adolescent living at home.

11.3 Conclusion

One might wonder what the appeal would be and why someone would choose an approach that had little scientific evidence over one that has solid evidence such as ERP for OCD. When it comes to OCD, a common theme in all these questionable approaches appears to be that they are painless or relaxing and certainly more pleasant than ERP. Nobody likes discomfort. We all would like to believe that there is an easy, comfortable way to cure whatever ails us. Additionally, grandiose claims are made, accompanied by jargon that sounds scientific to those who are not trained in the scientific method, which not only includes families seeking treatment for their child but also some mental health professionals not adequately trained in the scientific method. These claims can be very seductive. Which would you rather do? Have a relaxing hypnosis session, play a fun computer game, tap on your body while humming a tune, play with Tappy Bear, and talk to a puppet – or go through a course of ERP that requires exposure to what you fear and dread the most, that which evokes the most anxiety? Even if the exposure is gradual, there is no question which options would sound the most appealing to most people. However, ERP, as previously noted, has actually been shown to be efficacious through numerous randomized clinical trials and these other approaches have not. All of these more fun and relaxing approaches are unlikely to be helpful, beyond a temporary placebo effect, whereas with ERP, the person has a good chance to achieve clinically significant reduction or elimination of symptoms of OCD, even though the treatment is not easy.

What is the solution? First, mental health professionals need to be educated early, while they are still attending their university-based programs on not only the scientific method and evidence-based practice but also on distinguishing science from pseudoscience; then when they graduate and begin to practice, they will not fall for pseudoscientific marketing, which is directed not only to therapy consumers but also to practitioners. It is not easy to compete with the seductive claims being made on the internet, but those who teach in psychology, counseling, social work, and family therapy programs have to try harder and do a better job to educate mental health professionals as often and as early as we can, so they will graduate from their programs with a sound grounding in the scientific method, critical thinking, and inoculation from pseudoscientific practices.

Works Cited in Sidebar

Brooks, A. W., Schroeder, J., Risen, J. L., Gino, F., Galinsky, A. D., Norton, M. I., & Schweitzer, M. E. (2016). Don't stop believing: Rituals improve performance by decreasing anxiety. *Organizational Behavior and Human Decision Processes, 137,* 71–85.

Evans, D. W., Leckman, J. F., Carter, A., Reznick, J. S., Henshaw, D., King, R. A., & Pauls, D. (1997). Ritual, habit, and perfectionism: The prevalence and development of compulsive-like behavior in normal young children. *Child Development, 68*(1), 58–68.

Evans, D. W., Milanak, M. E., Medeiros, B., & Ross, J. L. (2002). Magical beliefs and rituals in young children. *Child Psychiatry and Human Development, 33*(1), 43–58.

Opie, I., & Opie, P. (1959). *The language and lore of school children.* Oxford: Oxford University Press.

Vyse, S. (2018). Do superstitious rituals work? *Skeptical Inquirer, 42*(2), 32–34.

References

Abramowitz, J. S. (1997). Effectiveness of psychological and pharmacological treatments for obsessive-compulsive disorder: A quantitative review. *Journal of Consulting and Clinical Psychology, 65,* 44–52.

American Psychiatric Association. (2013). *Diagnostic and statistical manual of mental disorders.* 5th edn. Washington, DC: Author.

Bressler, H. P. (2011) When is it safe to use EFT with OCD. Retrieved from www.eft-articles.com/eft-articles.taf?_function=articledetail&Article_ID=342

Callahan, R. J., & Callahan, J. (2000). *Stop the nightmares of trauma.* Chapel Hill, NC: Professional Press.

de la Cruz, L. F., Rydell, M., Runeson, B., Onofrio, B. M., Brander, G., Ruck, C. … & Mataix, D. (2016). Suicide in obsessive-compulsive disorder: A population-based study of 36788 Swedish patients. Molecular Psychiatry. Retrieved from www.nature.com/mp/journal/vaop/ncurrent/full/mp2016115a.html?foxtrotcallback=true

Fisher, P. L. & Wells, A. (2005). How effective are cognitive and behavioral treatments for obsessive-compulsive disorder: A clinical significance analysis. *Behavior Research and Therapy*, *43*(12), 1543–1558.

Heal Past Lives. (n.d.). Obsessive-compulsive disorder. Retrieved from www.healpastlives.com

Helbing M. L., & Ficca, M. (2009). Obsessive-compulsive disorder in school-age children. *Journal of School Nursing*, *25*, 15–26.

James, S. C., Farrell, L., & Zimmer-Gembeck, J. (2017). Description and prevalence of OCD in children and adolescents. In J. S. Abramowitz & B. L. McHaffey (eds.), *The Wiley handbook of obsessive compulsive disorders* (pp. 5–23). New York: Wiley.

Knight, G. (n.d.). Children & hypnosis. Retrieved from https://geoffrey-knight .com/hypnosis-articles/children-and-hypnosis.html

Kobak, K.A., Taylor, L. V., Bystritsky, A., Kohlenberg, C.J., Griest, J. H., Tucker, P. ... & Vapnik, T. (2005). St. John's wort versus placebo in obsessive-compulsive disorder: results from a double-blind study. *International Clinical Psychopharmacology*, *20*(6), 299–304.

Lenhard, F., Andersson, E., Mataix-Cols, D., Ruck, C., Vigerland, S., Hogstrom, J. ... & Serlachius, E. (2017). Therapist-guided, internet-delivered cognitive-behavioral therapy for adolescents with obsessive-compulsive disorder: A randomized controlled trial. *Journal of the American Academy of Child & Adolescent Psychiatry*, *56*, 10–19.

Lilienfeld, S. O., Lynn, S. J., & Lohr, J. M. (2014). Science and pseudoscience in clinical psychology: Initial thoughts, reflections, and considerations. In S. O. Lilienfeld, S. J. Lynn, & J. M. Lohr (eds.), *Science and pseudoscience in clinical psychology*. 2nd edn (pp. 1–16). New York: Guilford Press.

Maltby, N. & Tolin, D. F. (2005). A brief motivational intervention for treatment-refusing OCD patients. *Cognitive Behaviour Therapy*, *34*, 176–184.

Mantz, S. C., & Abott, M. J. (2017). Obsessive-compulsive disorder in paediatric and adult samples: Nature, treatment and cognitive processes. A review of the theoretical and empirical literature. *Behaviour Change*, *34*, 1–34.

Paton, S., & Kaylor, J. (2015). EFT for parents of children who pull hair & pick skin. Retrieved from www.udemy.com

Pignotti, M. & Thyer, B. A. (2009). Some Comments on "Energy Psychology: A Review of the Evidence": Premature Conclusions Based on Incomplete Evidence? *Psychotherapy Theory, Research, Training, Practice*, *46*, 257–261.

Pignotti, M., & Thyer, D. (2011). Guidelines for the treatment of obsessive compulsive disorder. *Best Practices in Mental Health*, *7*(2), 84–93.

Randall, C. & McNeil, D. W. (2017). Motivational interviewing as an adjunct to cognitive behavior therapy for anxiety disorders: A critical review of the literature. Cognitive and Behavioral Practice, *24*(3), 296–311.

Renshaw, K. D., Steketee, G., & Chambless, D. L. (2005). Involving family members in the treatment of OCD. *Cognitive Behaviour Therapy*, *34*, 164–175.

Rosen, G. M., & Davison, G. C. (2003). Psychology should list empirically supported principles of change (ESPs) and not credentialed trademarked therapies or other treatment packages. *Behavior Modification*, *27*, 300–312.

Singer, J. (2016). OCD and Hypnosis. Psych Central. Retrieved from https://psychcentral.com/lib/ocd-and-hypnosis/

Smith, R. (2016). OCD (obsessive compulsive disorder) and FasterEFT. Retrieved from https://fastereft.com/blog/ocd-obsessive-compulsive-disorder-fastereft/

Surmeli, T., & Ertem, A. (2011). Obsessive compulsive disorder and the efficacy of qEEG guided neurofeedback treatment: A case series. *Clinical EEG Neuroscience*, *42*, 195–201.

Tolin, D. F., & Maltby, N. (2007). Motivating treatment-refusing patients with obsessive-compulsive disorder. In H. Arkowitz, H. A. Westra, W. R. Miller, & S. Rollnick (eds.), *Motivational interviewing in the treatment of psychological problems* (pp. 85–108). New York: Guilford Press.

Toufexis, M. D., Hommer, R., Gerardi, D. M., Grant, P., Rothschild, L., D'Souza, P., & Murphy, T. K. (2015). Disordered eating and food restrictions in children with PANDAS/PANS. *Journal of Child and Adolescent Psychopharmacology*, *25*(1), 48–56. http://doi.org/10.1089/cap.2014.0063

Zimberoff, D. (2016) Treating OCD with hypnotherapy. Retrieved from http://web.wellness-institute.org/blog/treating-ocd-with-hypnotherapy

12

Trauma and Attachment

Jean Mercer

Evidence-based treatments for attachment problems focus on maladaptive behaviors of children toward familiar caregivers, especially failure to seek proximity to adults when threatened and readiness to go with strangers, and on the sense of caregivers that a child does not care about them or feel comforted by them. Diagnostic categories include reactive attachment disorder and disinhibited social engagement disorder (APA, 2013). Pseudoscientific treatments target a different series of behavior problems that resemble conduct disorders or callous-unemotional personality traits but are claimed to result from attachment difficulties; examples are cruelty to animals and other children, lying, theft, fascination with blood and gore, and unwillingness to show affection or make eye contact on the parent's terms. Pseudoscientific treatments may be concerned with continuing distress, anxiety, and irritability following known trauma exposure but may also target problems assumed to result from repressed or dissociated memories of trauma, including dissociative identity disorder, with "imaginary playmates" of early childhood sometimes considered as an aspect of dissociation.

Behaviors and disorders associated with trauma involve continuing distress following trauma exposure, including anxiety, flashbacks, and nightmares, as well as depression and irritability. These may be associated with attachment in the sense that when trauma has involved domestic violence, helping parent and child process memories of trauma together contributes to an improved relationship in which the child may seek protection and help from the parent when frightened. Diagnostic categories used in connection with evidence-based treatments include post-traumatic stress disorder (PTSD), acute stress disorder, and adjustment disorder.

12.1 Pseudoscience and Questionable Ideas

12.1.1 Diagnostic Controversies

Conventional practitioners are concerned with attachment difficulties that may place children in danger because of their willingness to go with strangers or may create a poor developmental trajectory for relationships between a child and caregivers or other children. However, conventional practitioners are aware of the research showing that attachment status in childhood is not of necessity associated with specific developmental outcomes, although disorganized attachment may be related to problematic development (Sroufe, 2005; see Woolgar & Scott, 2013, for cautions about overuse of attachment–related diagnoses). The term "reactive attachment disorder" in the past included both inhibited and disinhibited forms of problematic attachment behavior, but the *Diagnostic and Statistical Manual, 5th ed* (DSM-5) uses separate categories for reactive attachment disorder (RAD; difficulty in displaying typical attachment behavior toward caregivers) and disinhibited social engagement disorder (DSED; atypical social responsiveness to unfamiliar adults).

Pseudoscientific approaches to attachment problems attribute a broad range of serious mental health disturbances to attachment history under the names reactive attachment disorder (but not as defined in any edition of the DSM; see, e.g., Randolph, 2000) or simply "attachment disorder." These have included autism spectrum disorders, conduct disorders including serious violence throughout childhood, oppositional behavior, and a lack of "conscience" or empathy.

Conventional practitioners concerned with trauma reactions look at the traumatized child's continued suffering from remembered events and the extent to which stress reactions interfere with normative experiences and developmental progress. Pseudoscientific approaches to trauma assume that a traumatized child cannot consciously remember trauma or remembers it only in fragmented or somaticized ways, possibly because they dissociated the experience at the time it occurred and continue to dissociate. Disturbed or disturbing behaviors are attributed to the effects of ongoing repression or dissociation, as memories hidden in these ways are said to have powerful motivating influences for repetition of the trauma (e.g., an attack on another person) or other unwanted behaviors. Attachment and trauma have been linked pseudoscientifically by claims of "attachment-trauma" problems (Becker-Weidman, 2006) and by the idea that all adopted children are traumatized by separation from the birth mother, even in the absence of later mistreatment or misadventure (Verrier, 1993).

Developmental trauma disorder (DTD), a diagnostic category proposed for DSM-5 but not accepted (Rahim, 2014), was said by its proponents to result from repeated early experiences of trauma at the hands of, or in the context of, familiar caregivers (Cloitre et al., 2009). It was argued that children with these experiences often did not meet criteria for a diagnosis of PTSD (a diagnosis created for adults), and that in addition to PTSD-like symptoms they displayed disturbances in affect regulation, in attention and concentration, in self-image, in impulse control, and in aggression and risk taking. To receive the DTD diagnosis, a child would have to have experienced or witnessed multiple events of severe interpersonal violence and have had repeated changes of primary caregiver, repeated separations from the primary caregiver, or severe and persistent emotional abuse. Schmid, Petermann, and Fegert (2013) noted both pros and cons of the proposed diagnosis, pointing out that the assumed monocausal role of psychosocial factors in DTD has not been demonstrated by prospective studies, that DTD-like behaviors may cause traumatic events as well as being caused by them, that the description of symptoms is not age sensitive, and that false memories may be produced by aggressive exploration of possible trauma.

12.1.2 Assessment Practices

Well-validated observational protocols (Attachment Q-set; Vaughn & Waters, 1990; Strange Situation, Ainsworth et al., 1978) and screening instruments (Crittenden, Robson, & Tooby, 2015) for children's attachment characteristics were developed as research tools for populations, not as clinical assessments, and they do not yield diagnostic categories of any kind. Measures of disorganized attachment in young children have been developed and associated with developmental difficulties (Main & Solomon, 1990) but do not form a diagnostic category. Efforts to create assessments of RAD for school-age children have not been very successful. The use of the Adult Attachment Interview with adolescents has been criticized on developmental grounds (Warmuth & Cummings, 2015).

Pseudoscientific practices have included the use of the Randolph Attachment Disorder Questionnaire (RADQ; Randolph, 2000), a questionnaire to be filled out by an adult who knows the child well, together with a therapist. Randolph has stated that the RADQ does not assess RAD but instead measures a different problem "not yet" found in the DSM. Randolph attempted to validate the RADQ against her own diagnosis of the children, which she states that she can make accurately because children with attachment problems cannot crawl backward on command. RADQ scores have not been shown to correlate with other assessment instruments (Cappelletty, Brown, & Shumate, 2005).

The Child's Reaction to Traumatic Events Scale (CRTES; Jones, 2002) assesses memories of traumatic events in children younger than age 12 but is not likely to elicit memories of the very early experiences with caregivers that are said to cause DTD. Strand, Pasquale, and Sarmiento (2011), in a review of child and adolescent trauma measures, noted that few such measures have focused on children younger than age 6 or exclusively on adolescents.

12.1.3 Myths That Influence Treatment

Spiritual or Energy Explanations. Some pseudoscientific discussions of attachment and trauma posit nonmaterial factors such as demonic possession or interruption of energy flows (e.g., *qi*) as causes of emotional disturbance (Chen, 2000; Hammond & Hammond, 2010). These nonmaterial factors are not subject to scientific investigation, as they need not follow natural patterns of cause and effect or share natural mechanisms, so their inclusion helps to define some posited causes of emotional disturbance as pseudoscientific.

Neurophysiological Explanations. In pseudoscientific discussions of attachment and trauma concerns, beliefs in the power of statements about nervous system and neurotransmitter events may interfere with critical thinking. Important as these topics are in themselves, they act as myths when authors assume that neurophysiological information can take the place of empirical support of treatments. This is especially the case when conclusions about human beings are generalized without explanation from studies of a range of other species (notably, "modern attachment theory"; Schore & Schore, 2008; see Mercer, 2011). An occasional feature of the neurophysiological myth is the assumption that bilateral stimulation or movement, with activation of both brain hemispheres, has a special therapeutic value.

Beliefs about Attachment. Proponents of pseudoscientific mental health approaches reference various alternative beliefs about attachment for children, although much of their terminology is borrowed from established attachment frameworks (e.g., Bowlby, 1982). Alternative attachment theory asserts that emotional attachment of infant to mother occurs prenatally as a result of genetic similarity or of telepathic communication from mother to child and begins at the time of conception (see, e.g., publications of the Association for Pre- and Perinatal Psychology and

Health; www.apppah.org). This belief leads to the idea that adopted infants, even though they are separated from birth mothers months before attachment would ordinarily become apparent, will be filled with anger and grief at their loss and may sustain a psychological "primal wound" (Verrier, 1993) that will cause lasting sadness and depression, or alternatively, cruel and aggressive behavior as well as sexual promiscuity (Cline, 1992).

Sidebar Box: Does attachment parenting promote attachment? by Amy Tuteur

Attachment parenting is the dominant parenting ideology of early twenty-first-century America, yet it has no basis in science. It contains the word "attachment," yet its fundamental principle is at odds with attachment theory. It claims to recapitulate successful parenting in prehistory, yet prehistory was populated by multiple parenting cultures that changed over many centuries. Moreover, it ignores the fact that parenting in prehistory was remarkably *un*successful, plagued by extremely high levels of infant and child mortality. Simply put, it is a philosophical viewpoint masquerading as science.

Attachment parenting was created from whole cloth by William and Martha Sears, a pediatrician and nurse, respectively. The fundamental principle of attachment parenting, never clearly articulated, is that mother-infant attachment is problematic and uncertain, contingent on specific mothering behaviors including unmedicated childbirth, extended breastfeeding, and above all continuous physical proximity between mother and child (Sears & Sears, 1997). This is precisely opposite of the insights of Bowlby (Bretherton, 1992), Harlow (1958), and other founders of attachment theory. They discovered that attachment occurs spontaneously between caregivers and babies so long as the caregivers can be depended upon to reliably respond to the infants' most important physical and emotional needs. While, attachment theory tells us that children only need a "good enough" mother (Winnicott, 1971), attachment parenting insists that children need a perfectly giving, always available mother. Attachment parenting reflects a longing for the past – but it is a past that never existed.

Amy Tuteur, MD, is an obstetrician gynecologist. She is author of the book *Push Back: Guilt in the Age of Natural Parenting* (2016).

Dissociation and Repression. The claim that traumatic memories are repressed and inaccessible but continue to exercise a strong motivational influence has been discussed as the "trauma-memory argument" (Kihlstrom, 1996) and rejected on the ground that highly emotional events are likely to be remembered vividly rather than forgotten. Authors like van der Kolk (Cloitre et al., 2009) have put forward the idea that traumatic experiences may be responded to with dissociation and that reminders of the trauma also trigger dissociation leading to changes of behavior and awareness. This belief is also associated with the idea that traumatic memories are stored differently from ordinary episodic memory, with non-brain structures acting as encoders of traumatic events, and that "the body never lies" (Miller, 2006). Moreover, the concept of "catharsis," dissolution of lingering negative emotion by re-experiencing events, has been part of many alternative therapies, in spite of experimental evidence against such a process (Littrell, 2009).

Bodywork. Pseudoscientific theories of mental illness seem to have a special affinity for "bodywork" of various kinds, whether massage, physical restraint, dance therapy, or EMDR (see later). With respect to children, these forms of treatment may be presented as within the cognitive abilities of young children who are not capable of "talk therapies," or required when the initial problem occurred very early in development (McCullough, 2011).

Ritual Reenactment. Some pseudoscientific attachment and trauma treatments are based on the assumption that reenacting a normative infant experience with an older child or adult can replace early traumatic or inappropriate memories, recapitulating early development and thus negating the influence of the actual early experiences. It may be thought that physical reenactment, like feeding with a baby bottle or diapering, is needed (Thomas, 2000).

Disregarding Developmentally Appropriate Practice. Developmentally appropriate practice (DAP) is a cornerstone of early childhood education and of clinical interventions with children; it emphasizes the need to adjust communications and practices to a child's developmental level. Pseudoscientific approaches to attachment and trauma tend to ignore DAP and assume that full awareness, understanding, and memory go back to the time of conception and that prenatal events may be psychologically traumatic or may facilitate attachment. Children with poor attachment histories may alternatively be thought to have become "stuck" developmentally at the time of any trauma, even to the point where they may lack the capacity to associate cause and effect ("Find answers about . . .," 2017).

12.1.4 Pseudoscientific Treatments

The treatments described here are not only without a systematic evidence basis but in all cases are implausible either because of problems with internal logic or because of a lack of congruence with established information about child development.

Rebirthing. Rebirthing is a pseudoscientific treatment that involves an older child's ritual reenactment of the experience of birth. The goal is generally to cause an adopted child to become emotionally attached to the adoptive mother, a goal connected with the mistaken belief that attachment occurs prenatally. Rebirthing has been used together with holding therapy (see later) but should not be conflated with that approach. Although rebirthing's outcome has never been tested, its assumptions are not congruent with anything known about attachment. A child death during rebirthing has been documented (Mercer, Sarner, & Rosa, 2003).

Holding Therapy. Holding therapy is a broad term used to describe child mental health interventions that emphasize physical restraint of the child for therapeutic rather than for safety purposes. One of these methods, originally referred to as "rage reduction" therapy, employed physical restraints that ranged from an adult lying down on the supine child to having two or more adults hold the child lying down or on an adult's lap; the child was simultaneously poked and prodded uncomfortably, had their face grabbed by the adult to force eye contact, and was shouted at and accused of murderous wishes. Some weak studies have been claimed as evidence to support this treatment (Lester, 1997; Myeroff, Mertlich, & Gross, 1999), and other versions of the treatment have been suggested (Federici, 2005). The goal of these approaches is to produce child compliance, which they associate with attachment.

The terms "holding time," "prolonged parent-child embrace," and *Festhaltetherapie* are used to refer to some physical restraint methods. These methods have been associated with attachment problems, but their targets are autism and oppositional behavior as well. Holding time and the other related methods have the child held face to face with a parent, the therapist serving primarily as a coach. Young children may straddle the parent's lap and be held tightly against the adult's chest and neck, and older children lie supine with the parent prone on top of them, holding their arms tightly. This position is kept for an hour or more while the child cries and fights until exhausted and yielding. Parents are to do holding daily. A small number of weak supportive studies were published in the 1980s (Prekop, 1983) and one before-and-after study appeared more recently (Welch et al., 2006). Benz (2013) has described adverse psychological outcomes following these treatments.

Eye Movement Desensitization and Reprocessing (EMDR). EMDR is a technique suggested by Shapiro and various colleagues (e.g., Shapiro & Maxfield, 2002) for anxiety associated with memories of traumatic events. The client follows therapist instructions about rhythmic eye movements while rehearsing a distressing memory. EMDR has been used with children and adolescents, increasingly as children have been exposed to mass disasters. EMDR is based on the assumption that traumatic memories are stored in the body and uses eye movements as a form of "bodywork." Research on EMDR has characteristically used small numbers of participants in before-and-after designs, although there have been some randomized controlled trials (RCTs). Greyber, Dulmus, and Cristalli (2012) reviewed work on EMDR with adolescents and reported on five RCTs, all of which displayed methodological weaknesses such as the use of adequate control groups; these authors nevertheless concluded that the treatment had a positive outcome. Factors like patient engagement that are common to successful psychotherapies (Tschacher, Junghan, & Pfammatter, 2014), rather than specific techniques like EMDR, can be responsible for improved outcomes. Diehle et al. (2014) reported that EMDR and cognitive-behavioral therapy (CBT) were equally effective in a randomized study. In a review article, Higa-McMillan et al. (2016) recommended against generalizing from studies of EMDR with adults to probable outcomes for children and adolescents. However, Dorsey et al. (2017) considered EMDR for children's traumatic experiences to be "probably efficacious," while noting that the three EMDR studies reported in their review included CBT elements in two cases. Thus, the central eye movement component is akin to the hat in purple hat therapy (the previous chapter defines purple hat therapy).

One reason for the increasing use of EMDR with children and adolescents may be the relative ease of engaging young people with the process. As has been pointed out (Greenwald, 2009; Farkas et al., 2010), adolescents who have been maltreated are especially difficult to engage in therapy, because they are poorly motivated, see little benefit to treatment, and would prefer to avoid unpleasant memories. The ease of training and availability in crisis situations are also relevant (see Hasanovic et al., 2016). Material published by the EMDR Institute notes that there may be an increase in distress during the course of treatment, but this will be resolved (EMDR Institute, 2016).

Critical (or Traumatic) Incident Stress Debriefing (CISD). CISD is a method that draws an affected person's attention to a potentially traumatic experience soon after the event. The intention is to prevent potential posttraumatic symptoms from developing; this is thought to happen by preventing dissociation or "buried" memories from the experience. Some authors (e.g., Kirk & Madden, 2003) have recommended CISD for use with adolescents and warned against the dangers of delaying or omitting it. After examining 11 studies, Rose et al. (2002) concluded that CISD did not prevent posttraumatic stress symptoms and might actually result in a larger number of symptoms. A large randomized trial (Adler et al., 2008) with adults showed no significant advantage of CISD over two other conditions but showed no strong negative effects. In a meta-analysis of a small number of studies, Kramer and Landolt (2011) concluded that similar early interventions following a traumatic event might be helpful for children, while acknowledging that systematic research on this topic remains scarce.

Thought Field therapy (TFT). TFT is a treatment that attributes emotional problems to a disturbance of energy flow through and around the body. This disturbance is to be corrected by physical contact in the form of tapping on body meridians (imaginary lines); tapping may be done by a therapist or a client may be instructed by telephone where to tap and what patterns and tempo to use. A randomized controlled study of adult participants failed to support TFT (Pignotti, 2005). TFT for children has not been systematically investigated but has been used for children's trauma following genocide (Sakai, Connolly, & Oas, 2010). Dunnewold (2014) reported positive outcomes in some randomized controlled studies of TFT for adults but noted that the control groups used were problematic because they did not include placebo or active treatments. Nevertheless, proponents of TFT recommend the treatment for children ("Thought Field Therapy . . . ," 2016) and describe it as "highly effective" not only for posttraumatic symptoms but also for addictions, sleep problems, and grief. Like other belief systems based on posited energy flow, TFT is implausible in terms of current knowledge of nervous system functioning and is incongruent with evidence-based approaches to treating effects of trauma.

Somatosensory Treatments. "Bodywork" methods may range from gentle infant massage to the intense physical stimulation used by Wilhelm Reich in his attempts to break down "character armor" (Nelson, 1976). Currently, somatosensory methods tend to reference the idea that "the body keeps the score" (van der Kolk, 1994) by encoding traumatic events as muscle or visceral tension, which must be released to cure posttraumatic symptoms. The importance of bilateral stimulation is sometimes stressed (Perry & Szalavitz, 2006). Van der Kolk has recommended the bodywork practitioner Albert Pesso ("Training," 2012). The popular work of Alice Miller (2006) has been another source of this idea, which remains without systematic investigation. Children are also treated with Sensory Integration Therapy (SIT; Smith, Mruzek, & Mozingo, 2005) for autism spectrum disorder, attention-deficit/hyperactivity disorder, and specific learning disorders. SIT employs full-body movements and a "sensory diet" using deep pressure, weighted vests, and brushing of the skin. The specialized Wilbarger Protocol is intended to treat tactile defensiveness in autism spectrum disorder by brushing of the skin every two hours when the child is awake, but parents are warned not to brush the face, chest, or stomach, as this may cause adverse reactions such as vomiting ("The Wilbarger Protocol ...," 2015). Hyatt, Stephenson, and Carter (2009) reviewed work on SIT and concluded that it is ineffective.

12.2 Research-Supported Approaches

When young foster or adopted children show concerning behaviors related to attachment, such as a lack of preference for familiar caregivers or a willingness to go with strangers, one research-supported treatment is Attachment and Biobehavioral Catch-up (ABC; Dozier et al., 2009). RCTs have demonstrated long-term efficacy for this parent-child program, which focuses on increasing parents' sensitivity and responsiveness to children's hard-to-read attachment behaviors. Pseudoscientific views sometimes attribute antisocial, externalizing behaviors such as fire setting or cruelty to animals to difficulties of attachment. In a meta-analysis, Fossum et al. (2016) reported the effectiveness of cognitive-behavioral therapy for such disruptive behavior disorders, as did Battagliese et al. (2015). Parent-Child Interaction Therapy (PCIT; Eyberg et al., 2008) has received extensive research support and continues to be investigated with respect to maintenance of desired behavior and similar factors (Eyberg et al., 2014).

Various treatments are used for problems resulting from traumatic experiences. Dorsey et al. (2017) evaluated the evidence bases for CBT, EMDR, individual integrated therapy for complex trauma, group mind-body skills treatment, individual client-centered play therapy, individual mind-body skills treatment, individual psychoanalysis, and group crea-tive-expressive skills plus CBT. Dorsey and her colleagues gave the "well-established" rating to individual CBT with parent involvement, to individual CBT, and to group CBT.

Dorsey et al. rated group CBT with parent involvement and EMDR as "probably efficacious." However, it is notable that in discussing EMDR, the researchers commented on the need not only for larger studies but also for "studies that more clearly test the added benefit of EMDR-specific elements (i.e., bilateral sensory input)" (2017, p. 20), an impor-tant point because of the many general factors that EMDR shares with well-established treatments that do not include eye movement or other sensory components.

The remaining treatments evaluated by Dorsey et al., listed earlier in this section, were given lower ratings ranging from possibly efficacious, to experimental, to questionably efficacious. No adverse events or potential harms associated with any of the treatments were discussed.

Child-Parent Psychotherapy (CPP; Lieberman, Ghosh Ippen, & van Horn, 2006) is directed toward young children who witnessed domestic violence and their mothers who were involved in the violence. A rando-mized controlled trial resulted in decreased child behavior problems and lessened maternal distress. The ARC (attachment, self-regulation, and competency) treatment model has been reported as a promising treat-ment for young children with histories of trauma, in a pre/post study (Arvidson et al., 2011).

12.3 Conclusion

In spite of the existence of established evidence-based treatments for attachment and trauma disorders, and in spite of professionals' stated objections (e.g., Chaffin et al., 2006) to unconventional, implausible, non-evidence-based treatments, such treatments continue to be offered in the United States and elsewhere. Organizations of mental health profes-sionals are concerned about the continuing use of potentially harmful treatments for children (PHTCs; Mercer, 2017) but have been less than successful in fighting this. It is possible that treatments that target estab-lished disorders of child mental health or specific maladaptive behaviors have little appeal for some parents. Such parents may be more interested in changes in child behavior claimed by proponents of unconventional treatments, such as increased obedience, attentiveness, and affection toward parents. The parents may also be attracted by treatments that propose no need for change in parent behavior toward children ("not your fault") and by appeals to supernatural forces that may be familiar to those deeply involved in fundamentalist religious practices. Attribution of child behavior change to supernatural elements also implies the possibility of rapid and permanent "healing" of problems resulting from trauma or a poor attachment history, an appealing thought for parents.

The continuing use of pseudoscientific approaches to treatment of attachment and trauma-related disorders may be one more example of tendencies to ignore or deny scientific findings in the United States. Such rejections of rational thought in favor of positions without empirical support can be thought of, pessimistically, as aspects of the counter-Enlightenment posited by Isaiah Berlin (1973). If indeed a general anti-rationalist posture is responsible for pseudoscientific thinking about children's mental health, it is difficult to see how the public can be convinced of the need for evidence-based treatments.

Works Cited in Sidebar

Bretherton, I. (1992). The origins of attachment theory: John Bowlby and Mary Ainsworth. *Developmental Psychology*, *28*(5), 759–775.

Harlow, H. F. (1958). The nature of love. *American Psychologist*, *13*(12), 673–685.

Sears, W., & Sears, M. (1997). *The complete book of Christian parenting and child care: A medical and moral guide to raising happy healthy children*. Nashville: B&H Books.

Winnicott, D. W. (1971) *Playing and reality*. London: Tavistock.

References

Adler, A. B., Litz, B., Castro, C. A., Suvak, M., Thomas, J. L., Burrell, L. . . . & Bliese, P. D. (2008). A group randomized trial of critical incident stress debriefing provided to U.S. peacekeepers. *Journal of Traumatic Stress*, *21* (3), 253–263.

Ainsworth, M.D. S., Blehar, M. C., Waters, E., & Wall, S. (1978). *Patterns of attachment*. Hillsdale, NJ: Erlbaum.

American Psychiatric Association. (2013). *Diagnostic and statistical manual of mental disorders*. 5th edn. Washington, DC: American Psychiatric Association.

Arvidson, J., Kinniburgh, K., Howard, K., Spinazzolla, J., Strothers, H., Evans, M. . . . & Blaustein, M. E. (2011). Treatment of complex trauma in young children: Developmental and cultural considerations in application of the ARC intervention model. *Journal of Child and Adolescent Trauma, 4*, 34–51.

Battagliese, G., Caccetta, M., Luppino, O. I., Baglioni, C., Cardi, V., Mancini, F., & Buonanno, C. (2015). Cognitive-behavioral therapy for externalizing disorders: A meta-analysis of treatment effectiveness. *Behaviour Research and Therapy, 75*, 60–71.

Becker-Weidman, A. (2006). Treatment for children with trauma-attachment disorders: Dyadic Developmental Psychotherapy. *Child and Adolescent Social Work Journal, 23*(2), 147–171.

Benz, U. (2013). *Festhaltetherapien: Ein Plaedoyer gegen umstrittene Therapieverfahren.* Giessen: Psychosozial-Verlag.

Berlin, I. (1973). The counter-enlightenment. In P. Wiener (ed.), *Dictionary of the history of ideas* (pp. 100–112). New York: Scribner's.

Bowlby, J. (1982). *Attachment.* New York: Basic Books.

Cappelletty, G. G., Brown, M. M., & Shumate, S. E. (2005). Correlates of the Randolph Attachment Disorder Questionnaire in a sample of children in foster placement. *Child and Adolescent Social Work Journal, 22*(1), 71–84.

Chaffin, M., Hanson, R., Saunders, B. E., Nichols, T., Barnett, D., Zeanah, C. . . . & Miller-Perrin, C. (2006). Report of the APSAC Task Force on Attachment Therapy, Reactive Attachment Disorder, and Attachment Problems. *Child Maltreatment, 11*, 76–89.

Chen, K. (2000). Chinese qigong and qigong-associated mental disorders. British Medical Journal. Retrieved from www.bmj.com/2011/10/28/chinese-qigong-and-qigong-associated-mental-disorders

Cline, F. (1992). *Hope for high-risk and rage-filled children.* Evergreen, CO: EC Publications.

Cloitre, M., Stolbach, B. C., Herman, J. L., van der Kolk, B., Pynoos, R., Wang, J., & Petkova, E. (2009). A developmental approach to Complex PTSD: Childhood and adult cumulative trauma as predictors of system complexity. *Journal of Traumatic Stress, 22*(5), 399–408.

Crittenden, P., Robson, K., & Tooby, A. (2015). Validation of the School-Age Assessment of Attachment in a short-term longitudinal study. *Clinical Child Psychology and Psychiatry, 20*(3), 348–365.

Diehle, J., Opmeer, B. C., Boer, F., Mannarino, A. P., & Lindauer, R. J. (2014). Trauma-focused cognitive behavioral therapy or eye movement desensitization and reprocessing: What works in children with posttraumatic stress symptoms? A randomized controlled trial. *European Child and Adolescent Psychiatry, 26*, 227–236.

Dorsey, S., McLaughlin, K., Kerns, S., Harrison, J., Lambert, H., Briggs, E. . . . & Amaya, J. L. (2017). Evidence base update for psychosocial treatments for children and adolescents exposed to traumatic events. *Journal of Clinical Child and Adolescent Psychology, 46*(3), 303–330.

Dozier, M., Lindhiem, O., Lewis, E., Bick, J., Bernard, K., & Peloso, E. (2009). Effects of a foster parent training program on young children's attachment behaviors: Preliminary evidence from a randomized clinical trial. *Child and Adolescent Social Work, 26,* 321–332.

Dunnewold, A. L. (2014). Thought field therapy efficacy following large-scale traumatic events. *Current Research in Psychology, 5*(1), 34–39.

EMDR Institute. (2016). Frequent questions. Retrieved from www.emdr.com/ frequent-questions/

Eyberg, S. Boggs, S., & Jaccard, J. (2014). Does maintenance treatment matter? *Journal of Abnormal Child Psychology, 42,* 355–366.

Eyberg, S., Funderburk, B., Hembree-Kigin, T., McNeil, C., Querido, J., & Hood, K.K. (2008). Evidence-based psychosocial treatments for children and adolescents with disruptive behavior. *Journal of Clinical Child and Adolescent Psychology, 37,* 215–237.

Farkas, L., Cyr, M., Lebeau, T. M., & Lemay, J. (2010). Effectiveness of MASTR/ EMDR therapy for traumatized adolescents. *Journal of Child and Adolescent Trauma, 3,* 125–142.

Federici, R. S. (2005). *Help for the hopeless child.* Alexandria, VA: Author.

"Find answers about attachment issues." (2017). Retrieved from www.institute forattachment.ong[sic]/learn-about-attachment-disorder-common-questions

Fossum, S., Handegård, B. H., Adolfsen, F., Vis, S. A., & Wynn, R. (2016). A meta-analysis of long-term outpatient treatment effects for children and adolescents with conduct problems. *Journal of Child and Family Studies, 25*(1), 15–29.

Greenwald, R. (2009). *Treating problem behaviors.* New York: Routledge.

Greyber, L. R., Dulmus, C. N., & Cristalli, M. E. (2012). Eye movement desensitization reprocessing, posttraumatic stress disorder, and trauma: A review of randomized controlled trials with children and adolescents. *Child and Adolescent Social Work Journal, 29,* 409–425.

Hammond, F., & Hammond, I. (2010). *Pigs in the parlor: A practical guide to deliverance.* Kirkwood, MO: Impact Christian Books.

Hasanovic, M., Morris-Smith, J., Morgan, S., Oakley, S., & Sabanovic, S. (2016). EMDR trainings for Bosnia-Herzegovina mental health workers resulted with child training in Sarajevo for 75 EMDR psychotherapists aftermath the 1992–1995 war. *European Psychiatry, 33,* S277.

Higa-McMillan, C., Francis, S., Rith-Najarian, L., & Chorpita, B. (2016). Evidence base update: 50 years of research on treatment for child and adolescent anxiety. *Journal of Clinical Child and Adolescent Psychology*, *45*(2), 91–113.

Hyatt, K., Stephenson, J., & Carter, M. (2009). A review of three controversial educational practices: Perceptual motor programs, sensory integration, and tinted lenses. *Education and Treatment of Children*, *32*(2), 313–342.

Jones, R. T. (2002). *The Child's Reaction to Traumatic Events Scale (CRTES): A self-report traumatic stress measure*. Blacksburg: Virginia Polytechnic University.

Kihlstrom, J.F. (1996). The trauma-memory argument and Recovered Memory Therapy. In K. Pedzak & W.P. Banks (eds.), *The recovered/false memory debate* (pp. 297–311). San Diego: Academic.

Kirk, A. B., & Madden, L. L. (2003). Trauma related critical incident debriefing for adolescents. *Child and Adolescent Social Work Journal*, *20*(2), 123–134.

Kramer, D. N., & Landolt, M.A. (2011). Characteristics and efficacy of early psychological interventions in children and adolescents after single trauma: A meta-analysis. *European Journal of Psychotraumatology*, *2*, 7858

Lester, V. S. (1997). Behavior change as reported by caregivers of children receiving holding therapy. Retrieved from www.attach.org/lester.htm

Lieberman, A., Ghosh Ippen, C., & van Horn, P. (2006). Child-parent psychotherapy: 6-month follow-up of a randomized controlled trial. *Journal of the American Academy of Child and Adolescent Psychiatry*, *45*(8), 913–918.

Littrell, J. (2009). Expression of emotion: When it causes trauma and when it helps. *Journal of Evidence-Based Social Work*, *6*, 300–320.

Main, M., & Solomon, J. (1990). Procedures for identifying infants as disorganized/disoriented during the Ainsworth Strange Situation. In M. Greenberg, D. Cicchetti, & E.M. Cummings (eds.), *Attachment in the preschool years* (pp. 121–160). Chicago: University of Chicago Press.

McCullough, L. (2011). Bodywork, movement, and mental health. *Massage Bodywork*. Retrieved from www.massagetherapy.com/articles/index.php/article_id/2–27/Bodywork-Movement-and-Mental-Health

Mercer, J. (2011). Attachment theory and its vicissitudes: Toward an updated theory. *Theory and Psychology*, *21*, 25–45.

Mercer, J. (2017). Evidence of potentially harmful psychological treatments for children. *Child and Adolescent Social Work Journal*, *34*(2), 107–125.

Mercer, J., Sarner, L., & Rosa, L. (2003). *Attachment therapy on trial*. Westport, CT: Praeger.

Miller, A. (2006). *The body never lies*. New York: W. W. Norton.

Myeroff, R., Mertlich, G., & Gross, J. (1999). Comparative effectiveness of holding therapy with aggressive children. *Child Psychiatry & Human Development*, *29*(4), 303–313.

Nelson, A. (1976). Orgone (Reichian) therapy in tension headache. *American Journal of Psychotherapy*, *30*, 103–111.

Perry, B., & Szalavitz, M. (2006). *The boy who was raised as a dog*. New York: Basic Books.

Pignotti, M. (2005). Callahan fails to meet the burden of proof for Thought Field Therapy claims. *Journal of Clinical Psychology*, *61*(3), 251–255.

Prekop, J. (1983). Das Festhalten als Therapie bei Kindern mit Autismus-Syndrom. Anwendung der Therapie durch Festhalten nach Welch/ Tinbergen. Teil 1. *Fruehfoerderung Interdisziplinaer*, *2*(2), 54–64.

Rahim, M. (2014). Developmental trauma disorder: An attachment–based perspective. *Clinical Child Psychology and Psychiatry*, 19(4), 1–13.

Randolph, E. (2000). *Manual for the Randolph Attachment Disorder Questionnaire*. Evergreen, CO: The Attachment Center Press.

Rose, S., Bisson, J., Churchill, R., & Wessely, S. (2002). Psychological debriefing for preventing post traumatic stress disorder (PTSD). *Cochrane Database Systematic Reviews*, *2*, CD000560. Retrieved from www.ncbi.nlm.nih.gov/pubmed/12076399

Sakai, C. E., Connolly, S. M., & Oas, P. (2010). Treatment of PTSD in Rwandan child genocide survivors using thought field therapy. *International Journal of Emergency Mental Health*, *12*(1), 41–49. Retrieved from www.ncbi.nimh.gov/pubmed/20828089

Schmid, M., Peterman, F., & Fegert, J. M. (2013). Developmental trauma disorder: Pros and cons of including formal criteria in the psychiatric diagnostic systems. *BMC Psychiatry*, *13*(3), 1–12.

Schore, J. R., & Schore, A. N. (2008). Modern attachment theory: The central role of affect regulation in development and treatment. *Clinical Social Work Journal*, *36*, 9–20.

Shapiro, F., & Maxfield, L. (2002). Eye movement desensitization and reprocessing (EMDR): Information processing in the treatment of trauma. *Journal of Clinical Psychology*, *58*(8), 933–946.

Smith, T., Mruzek, D. W., & Mozingo, D. (2005). Sensory integration therapy. In J. W. Jacobson, R. M. Foxx, & J. A. Mulick (eds.), *Controversial therapies for developmental disabilities* (pp. 331–350). Mahwah, NJ: Erlbaum.

Sroufe, L. A. (2005). Attachment and development: A prospective, longitudinal study from birth to adulthood. *Attachment & Human Development*, *7*(4), 344–367.

Strand, V. C.,Pasquale, L. E., & Sarmiento, T. L. (2011). Child and adolescent trauma measures: A review. Retrieved from www.ncswtraumaed.org/wp-content/uploads/2011/07/Child-and-Adolescent-Trauma-Measures_A-Review_with-Measures.pdf

"The Wilbarger Protocol: Helping people sensitive to touch." (2015). Retrieved from www.nationalautismresources.com/wilbarger-protocol.html

Thomas, N. (2000). Parenting children with attachment disorders. In T. Levy (ed.), *Handbook of attachment interventions* (pp. 67–111). San Diego: Academic.

"Thought Field Therapy for babies, children, and teenagers." (2016). Retrieved from www.therapylifecentre.co.uk/tft-for-children/

"Training." (2012). Retrieved from www.pbsp.com/train/

Tschacher, W., Junghan, U. M., & Pfammatter, M. (2014). Towards a taxonomy of common factors in psychotherapy: Results of an expert survey. *Clinical Psychology and Psychotherapy, 21*, 82–96.

Van der Kolk, B. (1994). The body keeps the score: Memory and the evolving psychobiology of traumatic stress. *Harvard Review of Psychiatry, 1*(5), 253–265.

Vaughn, B. E., & Waters, E. (1990). Attachment behavior at home and in the laboratory: Q-sort observations and strange situation classifications of one-year-olds. *Child Development, 61*, 1965–1973.

Verrier, N. (1993). *The primal wound.* Lafayette, CA: Author.

Warmuth, K., & Cummings, E. M. (2015). Examining developmental fit of the Adult Attachment Interview in adolescence. *Developmental Review, 36*, 200–218.

Welch, M. G., Northrup, R. S., Welch-Horan, T. B., Ludwig, R. J., Austin, C. L., & Jacobson, J. S. (2006). Outcomes of Prolonged Parent-Child Embrace Therapy among 102 children with behavioral disorders. *Complementary Therapies in Clinical Practice, 12*(1), 3–12.

Woolgar, M., & Scott, S. (2013). The negative consequences of over-diagnosing attachment disorders in adopted children: The importance of comprehensive formulations. Clinical Child Psychology and Psychiatry. Retrieved from www.ncbi.nlm.nih.gov/pubmed/23575458

13

Feeding

Linda J. Cooper-Brown, Mary Louise E. Kerwin, and Keith E. Williams

Feeding problems in children are mostly mild, and usually transitory. In samples of young, largely typically developing children, the prevalence of feeding problems has ranged up to 25% (Benjasuwantep, Chaithirayanon, & Eiamudomkan, 2013), reflecting how common these problems are among children. Although many mild feeding problems are addressed by primary care providers or popular literature regarding food preparation and presentation (Finney, 1986), more severe feeding problems are often the focus of professional intervention. This chapter deals with these more severe feeding problems and discusses issues related to diagnosis and the most common approaches to treatment.

Infants and children with severe feeding problems are often at risk for malnutrition or nutritional deficiencies. The presentation of these feeding problems varies widely and includes (a) inappropriate mealtime behaviors (e.g., tantrums, throwing foods, spitting), (b) lack of self-feeding, (c) food selectivity by type or texture (e.g., eating only a few foods or eating only crunchy foods), (d) failing to advance texture from purees to table food, (e) food refusal, or (f) oral-motor skill deficits (e.g., problems chewing and/or swallowing) (Milnes & Piazza, 2013, Williams, Field, & Seiverling, 2010).

Severe feeding problems are typically the result of an interaction of multiple variables that include physical/medical, behavior/environment, and psychosocial difficulties. Physiological factors include anatomical abnormalities of the structures associated with eating, such as abnormalities of the oral cavity or poor coordination of the oral structures. These abnormalities result in deficits in sucking, chewing, and/or swallowing that can interfere with a child's ability, endurance, or motivation to eat. The infant or child may not be able to consume any nutrition by mouth or the deficits can lead to problems transitioning to the next steps such as from bottle to spoon or from purees to table foods. Chronic or acute conditions such as cardiorespiratory or gastrointestinal diseases, prematurity, food allergies, and metabolic dysfunction can also lead to feeding disorders. For example, children with gastroesophageal reflux often vomit frequently and experience pain with swallowing, and over time, the pain or discomfort resulting from the reflux becomes associated with the oral feedings. This can lead to avoidance behaviors such as turning away from food, batting at the spoon, spitting out the food, or tantrums in the presence of the utensils or food. A vicious cycle develops in which the child associates food and mealtimes with pain/discomfort and refuses to eat or contact food. Refusal to eat reduces the opportunities to practice eating (leading to further skill deficits) or to experience all of the positive social aspects of meals, which reduces further the likelihood the child will successfully eat when the medical/physical issues are resolved. Parents of children with feeding problems, especially those with comorbid chronic health conditions or developmental disabilities, may experience stress and anxiety surrounding feeding times. The actions taken by parents during meals may even lead to a worsening of existing feeding problems (Field, Garland, & Williams, 2003; Piazza et al., 2003; Sharp et al., 2011).

A child's feeding problem, regardless of origin, can result in inadvertent reinforcement of the negative mealtime feeding behaviors. Even if the original medical/biological variable is no longer occurring, these learned behaviors, such as the refusal to eat, are now associated with the meal or specific foods and are strengthened over time because of the consequences or reinforcement. Successful treatment involves not only addressing behaviors exhibited by the child but also the aspects of the environment maintaining these behaviors.

13.1 Pseudoscience and Questionable Ideas

13.1.1 Diagnosis as an Indicator of Who Warrants Clinical Attention

Feeding problems in children exist on a spectrum ranging from transient issues, largely without implications for growth and health, to severe, chronic issues associated with malnutrition or nutritional deficiencies. A major issue in the field is the lack of commonly used diagnoses or a diagnostic system differentiating feeding problems based upon their severity or need for clinical intervention. If one examines the titles of reviews of the feeding treatment literature over the years, the children are described as having "severe feeding problems" (Kerwin, 1999), "feeding disorders" (Linscheid, 2006), "feeding difficulties" (Davis et al., 2010), "food refusal" (Williams et al., 2010), and "feeding problems" (Lukens & Silverman, 2014).

Diagnostic problems in the area of childhood feeding problems have been long recognized (Kedesdy & Budd, 1998) but have not been adequately addressed. The *Diagnostic and Statistical Manual of Mental Disorders,* 4th ed, text revision (DSM-IV-TR) contained the diagnosis of feeding disorder of infancy and early childhood (American Psychiatric Association, 2000). Unfortunately, the diagnostic criteria for feeding disorder in the DSM-IV is not appropriate for most children referred to feeding programs. When applied to a sample of 234 children referred to a pediatric feeding program, only 12% of the children met the feeding disorder diagnostic criteria (Williams, Riegel, & Kerwin, 2009). Because feeding disorder of infancy and early childhood relied on the outdated criteria for failure to thrive, it excluded children who were not underweight, even if they were dependent upon tube feeds or oral supplements, eliminating most children referred for feeding treatment.

As a result, DSM-5 introduced a new diagnosis, avoidant/restrictive food intake disorder (ARFID). ARFID improves the clinical utility and provides a diagnosis for many children, as well as adolescents and adults, previously excluded from feeding or eating disorder diagnoses (Kreipe & Palomaki, 2012). When the ARFID diagnostic criteria were applied to a sample of 422 children referred to a pediatric feeding program, 63% of the sample met one of the criteria (Williams et al., 2015). While the ARFID diagnostic criteria do not share many of the shortcomings found in the DSM-IV's feeding disorder diagnostic criteria, it is not yet clear whether this diagnosis will become widely accepted by clinicians who treat children with feeding issues.

In contrast to eating disorders, most providers who treat children with feeding problems are not mental health providers. While most feeding programs employ psychologists or other mental health providers, these providers, like their non–mental health colleagues, often utilize the *International Classification of Disease,* 10th ed (ICD-10) diagnostic codes, rather than codes from the DSM. At this time, no commonly accepted term or diagnosis identifies children whose feeding problems warrant clinical treatment. Thus, while it is clear feeding problems exist on a spectrum, it is unclear where to make the division between children whose feeding problem will resolve without treatment and those with chronic feeding problems that will lead to adverse consequences.

13.1.2 Feeding Dynamics Approach

The most well-known, nonbehavioral approach for the treatment of feeding problems is Ellyn Satter's Feeding Dynamics approach, also called the Division of Responsibility or Trust Model (Satter, 1986a,

1990). This approach has been presented in several popular press books including *Child of Mine: Feeding with Love and Good Sense* (Satter, 2000) and *How to Get Your Child to Eat ... But Not Too Much* (Satter, 2012); theoretical articles (Satter, 1986a, 1986b); and on the website, *ellynsatterinstitute.org*. The Feeding Dynamics approach has been advocated widely in parenting magazines as well as other popular press outlets and has been endorsed by the Academy of Nutrition and Dietetics in the organization's position paper on nutrition guidance for healthy children age 2 to 11 (Ogata & Hayes, 2014).

In this model, feeding disorders of childhood are described as being "major distortions in eating, food regulation, or the food regulation based on and perpetuated by social and emotional factors" (Satter, 1986b, p. 358). In this approach, parent mealtime actions are described as a primary cause of feeding problems. For example, a proponent of the model says, "parents can be so insensitive to feeding cues that children do not get enough to eat, or so overbearing that children eat too much" (Satter, 1990, S181–189). The same proponent adds, "Sometimes the results are paradoxical: 'overfed' children fight back so vehemently that they undereat and grow poorly, whereas 'underfed' children put so much pressure on eating that they eat and gain too much weight" (Satter, 1990, S181–189). In the Feeding Dynamics approach, the caregiver is responsible for selecting foods to present at meals, selecting the location where food is offered, and when meals and snacks are offered. The children are responsible for what they will eat (from the foods offered) and how much they will eat (Eneli, Crum, & Tylka, 2008). In this mode, caregivers trust their children have the ability to self-regulate food intake. Sattler's approach advocates children be offered a range of foods, without restriction, on a schedule, and caregivers eat the same foods as their children to serve as models (Eneli et al., 2008).

The Feeding Dynamics approach states that any intervention that attempts to have the child eat a certain food or certain amount of food are contrary to this approach (Satter, 1995). A Feeding Dynamics website specifically lists the following interventions as being unnecessary and counterproductive: positive reinforcement (even in the form of praise), negative reinforcement (including withholding attention, presumably for inappropriate behavior), escape extinction, systematic approximation (including shaping, fading, or food chaining; Satter, 2016a). For example, the website suggests that positive reinforcement takes away a child's inborn desire to eat and their pride in mastery and escape extinction is *really* negative parenting that *really* undermines children's eating (Satter, 2016a).

There is simply no empirical evidence supporting these views on the effects of behavioral interventions on children's eating. Further, parents naturally use positive reinforcement when feeding their children, often in simple ways such as saying "yum" or commenting on the food while smiling. Parents also use successive approximation, again, often in simple ways by touching a taste of new food on the child's lip or pairing a preferred food with a novel food such as presenting a carrot dipped in ranch dressing. In other words, parents naturally shape their children's eating using all of these techniques.

Despite the claim that the Feeding Dynamics approach is "evidence-based, clinically-tested, and highly effective," no empirical evidence exists that demonstrates this approach has improved the feeding problems of any children. Instead, the literature examining the mealtime actions of parents and their typically developing children (e.g., Birch & Fisher, 1998) has been claimed as evidence supporting the Family Dynamics approach (Eneli et al., 2008). Because some results from this literature have been interpreted as evidence against current evidence-based practices, this chapter will dive deeper into parental pressure on eating and use of rewards for eating.

13.1.3 Undermining Evidence-Based Practices

Parental pressure on eating is one evidence-based practice that is critiqued by advocates of the Feeding Dynamics approach. In the popular media, parents are commonly exposed to messages that indicate parents should not pressure their child to eat in any way. For example, "pressure on children's eating always backfires" (Satter, 2016b) or "demanding that a child eat at least one bite of everything seems reasonable, but it's likely to backfire" (Parker-Pope, 2008). The research basis for these messages, however, is not conclusive.

The literature on pressure to eat has two major problems. One problem involves *causality* and the other is one of *measurement*. Much of this literature has erroneously concluded that a relationship between more pressure to eat and lower body weight means that parent behavior has caused the child's lower weight (for review, see Shloim et al., 2015). Unfortunately, these studies cannot determine whether the child's lower weight was the result of parent pressure or whether the child's weight spurred the parents to pressure the child to eat in an attempt to increase weight. Additional cross-sectional studies have revealed relationships between pressure to eat and both increased and decreased fruit and vegetable consumption (Bante et al., 2008; Wyse et al., 2011, respectively). Pressure to eat has also been associated with both increased and decreased intake of snack food (Brown et al., 2008; Sleddens et al., 2010, respectively). Again, it is not possible to determine whether parental behaviors were responsible for children's intake of fruits and vegetables or snack foods, or whether the children's eating behaviors, diet, or weight led the parents to use strategies that may be interpreted by some as applying pressure to eat. In two longitudinal studies, which attempt to address the methodological limitations of cross-sectional studies, parents adjusted their behavior to respond to their children's low intake or low weight (Spuijt-Metz et al., 2006; Webber et al., 2010); in a third longitudinal study, parental pressure to eat was not related to children's picky eating or weight status (Antoniou et al., 2016). These longitudinal studies with more methodological control suggest parental behavior does not cause eating problems. Instead, parents are reacting to poor eating and weight gain.

The pressure-to-eat literature is also problematic due to measurement issues. Pressure to eat is a nebulous construct that can be conceptualized from gentle encouragement to eat one's vegetables or taste new foods to forcing a child to clean their plate. Despite this broad continuum of parental behaviors, pressure to eat in the literature is often measured using the Pressure to Eat subscale from the Child Feeding Questionnaire (Birch et al., 2001). This subscale consists of the following four questions:

a. "My child should always eat all of the food on her plate."
b. "I have to be especially careful to make sure my child eats enough."
c. "If my child says 'I'm not hungry,' I try to get her to eat anyway."
d. "If I did not guide or regulate my child's eating, she would eat much less than she should."

Two of these questions involve having the child eat beyond the point of satiety (a & c), while the other two are more related to the parent ensuring adequate volume (b & d). This subscale, which arguably taps the extreme end of the continuum of parental behavior, has been associated with both weight status and lower vegetable consumption (Fisher et al., 2002). In contrast, however, when parental pressure is measured differently, it is positively related to vegetable consumption (Zeinstra et al., 2000). This last study measured pressure using the following three questions:

a. When you give your child vegetables, does he have to eat the whole portion?
b. Are you strict with your child concerning eating of vegetables?
c. Do you make your child eat vegetables when he does not want to?

Unlike the questions on the Pressure to Eat subscale (Birch et al., 2001), these questions are specific to vegetable intake and less related to overall intake.

How parental pressure is measured, therefore, affects the results and, in turn, the interpretation of these findings. Given the contradictory and ambiguous findings, there is no evidence that certain parent behaviors on the milder end of the continuum, such as providing prompts or encouragement to eat, will influence child eating behaviors in the same manner as other parent behaviors on the more extreme end of the continuum such as requiring the child to clean their plate or requiring the child to eat when not hungry. There is also no evidence that all parent behaviors broadly defined as pressure to eat will influence outcomes such as weight status or diet variety in the same way.

Use of rewards for eating is another evidence-based practice that is critiqued by advocates of the Feeding Dynamics approach. Because there is controversy between the claims of negative effects of rewards/incentives in the Feeding Dynamics approach and the use of positive reinforcement as a common component in behavioral interventions for feeding problems, we will briefly review some of the relevant literature on the use of rewards for eating. Four laboratory studies provide evidence that rewards adversely affect eating. When children were required to consume a specified amount of a target beverage or food to obtain access to a preferred activity or snack, children *reported* a decreased preference for the target beverage or food (Birch et al., 1982; Birch, Marlin, & Rotter, 1984; Mikula, 1989; Newman & Taylor, 1992). The purported negative effects of rewards shown in these four laboratory studies have been attributed to the over-justification effect in which the intrinsic motivation for an activity decreased when extrinsic motivation, in the form of tangible rewards, is introduced after engaging in the activity (such as eating a particular food; Hummel, 2014). Alternative explanations, however, are possible. In the two studies conducted by Birch and colleagues, the reward was contingent upon consuming a specific amount of a beverage; therefore, the observed reports of decreased preference for the beverage might be explained by satiation rather than over-justification.

In contrast to these limited laboratory studies, a large and growing literature has demonstrated the beneficial effects of reinforcement on eating behavior. Jane Wardle and Lucy Cooke have shown that children in both school and home settings evidence both increased intake and liking of novel and non-preferred vegetables after being rewarded for repeatedly tasting the vegetables (Cooke et al., 2011; Fildes et al., 2014;

Remington et al., 2012). Furthermore, tangible rewards (e.g., stickers) produced greater effects than praise alone, exposure to the vegetable only, or no intervention. In addition, two school-based programs, the Food Dudes (Horne et al., 2004) and the Kids' Choice Program (Hendy, Williams, & Camise, 2005; Hendy, Williams, & Camise, 2011) have demonstrated the success of token reward programs in increasing fruit and vegetable consumption in large groups of elementary school children. In one study, children demonstrated an increased preference for fruits and vegetables after the intervention, which is inconsistent with the over-justification effect (Hendy et al., 2005). In summary, these studies provide support for the use of positive reinforcement as a component of behavioral interventions in the treatment of feeding problems and do not provide support for any deleterious effects of rewards for eating.

While proponents of the Feeding Dynamics approach have argued against all forms of pressure to eat, including positive reinforcement, it is not clear these parent mealtime actions are always contraindicated, especially in the case of children with severe feeding problems. Further, no studies document the effectiveness of the Feeding Dynamics approach in the treatment of feeding problems, regardless of severity.

> **Sidebar Box: Should parents avoid feeding their children GMOs? by Natalie Newell**
>
> When people refer to "GMOs," they are usually referring to crops that are developed with genetic engineering (i.e., genetically modified organisms), which is a more precise type of plant breeding (GMO Answers, n.d.). Of course, most of our food has been modified over time through various breeding methods, but some parents may be hesitant to feed their children GMOs because of the "frankenfood" myths attached to genetic engineering. However, as Kavin Senapathy notes in the *Science Moms* documentary, "You can ask the question, 'how many people have gotten sick, died, gotten cancer, even gotten a cold or a cough as the result of eating GMOs?' And the answer is zero. There hasn't even been a sniffle associated with consuming an ingredient or product derived from a GMO" (Newell, 2017). The body of evidence gathered from studying genetically modified crops since their introduction three decades ago shows that genetically

modified products pose no greater health risk than their conventionally bred counterparts (Nicolia et al., 2014). Most food experts suggest that parents focus on encouraging their children to develop a healthy relationship with food, without spending unnecessary time and energy worrying about how the ingredients were bred.

Natalie Newell, MEd, is the director and producer of the *Science Moms* documentary, available for free on YouTube (search for "Science Moms: Full Film!").

13.1.4 Sequential Oral Sensory Approach

While not as well known as the Feeding Dynamics approach, the Sequential Oral Sensory (SOS) approach encompasses the areas of sensory, motor, behavioral, biological, nutrition, and environment in the treatment of feeding problems (Toomey & Ross, 2011). Like the behavioral approach to treatment, feeding problems are conceptualized as learned avoidance reactions developed from eating difficulties secondary to medical conditions, oral motor dysfunction, or another physical difficulty with eating. The SOS approach advocates teaching children to physically manage foods comfortably in several sequential steps: visual tolerance, smell, touch, taste, and eating (Toomey & Ross, 2011). In this approach, a therapist uses modeling, play, and praise to teach these steps. Since 1999, three unpublished studies have examined the efficacy of the SOS approach (Toomey & Ross, 2011). One study reported improved mealtime behaviors but did not report increased consumption of target foods (Creech, 2006). Another study reported the approach was successful in eliminating tube feeds in seven children and increasing diet variety in children not dependent upon tube feeds (Boyd, 2007). A third study reported that 19 of 30 children were weaned off tube feeds (Toomey, 2002). Although neither peer-reviewed research nor research by scientists not affiliated with the developer of this approach are currently available, a recent study compared the effectiveness of a modified version of the SOS approach and behavior intervention that included escape extinction and praise (Peterson, Piazza, & Volkert, 2016). This study did not find the modified version of the SOS approach to be effective in increasing acceptance of novel foods in three children with autism spectrum disorder. In summary, although the SOS approach is popular, there is little empirical evidence from well-controlled studies supporting this intervention.

13.2 Research-Supported Approaches

For the treatment of severe feeding problems, a large and growing body of evidence supports the use of behavioral interventions. A review of the treatment literature for severe feeding problems from 1970 to 1997 found only behavioral interventions met the methodological criteria to be considered effective interventions (Kerwin, 1999). A recent systematic review and meta-analysis of intensive multidisciplinary interventions for feeding disorders reported intensive treatment holds benefits for children with severe feeding problems and further that behavioral intervention was the central treatment element for increasing oral intake (Sharp et al., 2016). Other reviews found support for behavioral interventions in the treatment of food refusal (Williams, Field, & Seiverling, 2010) and food selectivity among children with autism spectrum disorders (Silbaugh et al., 2016). To date, more than 200 studies describing behavioral interventions for the treatment of severe feeding problems have been published in the peer-reviewed literature. While there is a need for improved measurement, more standardization of treatment approaches, and other methodological improvements (Sharp et al., 2016), the evidence supporting the use of behavioral interventions in the treatment of severe feeding problems is substantial.

Conditioned aversions to food and limited motivation to eat are prevalent among children with severe feeding problems. These broad issues have led to the widespread use of both positive and negative reinforcement strategies. Children dependent upon tube feeds may not understand the relation between hunger elimination and food consumption, even after tube feedings are discontinued. Until the child develops an internal motivation to eat, extrinsic motivation in the form of positive reinforcement can increase desired mealtime/eating behaviors. Interventions including positive reinforcement have been shown to increase bite acceptance, use of age-appropriate utensils, and variety of foods and liquids consumed, while also teaching the child food and meals can be pleasant experiences (e.g., Cooper et al., 1999; Patel et al., 2002; Riordan et al., 1984; Wilder, Normand, & Atwell, 2005).

Children who have learned to associate eating with discomfort may exhibit a range of inappropriate mealtime behaviors to avoid eating.

Behavioral interventions often include strategies to address negative reinforcement (escape or avoidance of particular foods, drinks, or the entire meal) by no longer permitting escape or avoidance (escape or avoidance extinction). Nonremoval of the spoon is one example of an escape extinction procedure and involves presenting a bite of food to the child and waiting until the bite is accepted (Hoch et al., 1994). As the child's refusal no longer leads to escape (the child learns to enjoy the food), acceptance of food increases.

To decrease response effort, numerous variations of stimulus-fading procedures have been incorporated into behavioral interventions. Researchers have blended preferred and non-preferred foods, systematically increased bite or drink size, and faded from a spoon to a cup (e.g., Groff et al., 2014; Groff et al., 2011; Kerwin et al., 1995; Mueller et al., 2004; Penrod, Gardella, & Fernand, 2012). Other research has addressed skill difficulties by altering food texture or adding liquid chasers to improve food movement in the mouth and improve chewing (Kadey et al., 2013; Vaz et al., 2012).

These are but a few examples of behavioral interventions used in the treatment of severe feeding problems. Feeding problems are not homogeneous and researchers have shown success with behavioral treatments that focus on the range of maintaining variables for these severe feeding problems.

13.3 Conclusion

Unfortunately, the treatment of severe feeding problems is a growing area of clinical concern. As premature infants survive at younger ages and more children survive chronic health issues, the number of children with severe feeding problems has continued to increase. Even though there is not a widely used diagnostic scheme for these severe feeding problems, an established and growing literature describes effective treatments for these problems. While the treatment of severe feeding problems is often a multidisciplinary endeavor, behavioral interventions provide the central treatment component. To date, there are more than 200 peer-reviewed studies describing the successful application of behavioral intervention for the treatment of feeding problems. In contrast, few peer-reviewed studies demonstrate the successful application of either the Feeding Dynamics approach or the SOS approach in the treatment of children with feeding problems. While either of these approaches may one day demonstrate utility with some children with feeding problems or certain types of feeding problems, neither approach is substantiated currently by empirical evidence.

Works Cited in Sidebar

GMO Answers. (n.d.). What is a GMO? Retrieved from https://gmoanswers.com

Newell, N. (Director & Producer). (2017). *Science Moms*. [Documentary]. United States: Independently produced.

Nicolia, A., Manzo, A., Veronesi, F., & Rosellini, D. (2014). An overview of the last 10 years of genetically engineered crop safety research. *Critical Reviews in Biotechnology, 34*(1), 77–88.

References

American Psychiatric Association. (2000). *Diagnostic and statistical manual of mental disorders* DSM-IV-TR fourth edition (text revision). Washington, DC: Author.

Antoniou, E. E., Roefs, A., Kremers, S. P. J., Jansen A., Gubbels J. S. … & Thijs C. (2016). Picky eating and child weight status development: A longitudinal study. *Journal of Human Nutrition and Dietetics, 29,* 298–307.

Bante, H., Elliott, M., Harrod, A. & Haire-Joshu, D., 2008. The use of inappropriate feeding practices by rural parents and their effect on preschoolers' fruit and vegetable preferences and intake. *Journal of Nutrition, Education, and Behavior, 40*(1), 28–33.

Benjasuwantep, B., Chaithirayanon, S., & Eiamudomkan, M. (2013). Feeding problems in healthy young children: Prevalence, related factors and feeding practices. *Pediatric Reports, 5*(2), 38.

Birch, L. L., Birch, D., Marlin, D. W., & Kramer, L. (1982). Effects of instrumental consumption on children's food preference. *Appetite, 3*(2), 125–134.

Birch, L. L., & Fisher, J. O. (1998). Development of eating behaviors among children and adolescents. *Pediatrics, 101*(Supplement 2), 539–549.

Birch, L. L., Fisher, J. O., Grimm-Thomas, K., Markey, C. N., Sawyer, R., & Johnson, S. L. (2001). Confirmatory factor analysis of the Child Feeding Questionnaire: A measure of parental attitudes, beliefs and practices about child feeding and obesity proneness. *Appetite, 36*(3), 201–210.

Birch, L. L., Marlin, D. W., & Rotter, J. (1984). Eating as the "means" activity in a contingency: Effects on young children's food preference. *Child Development,* 431–439.

Boyd, K. (2007). *The effectiveness of the Sequential Oral Sensory Approach group feeding program (Doctoral dissertation)*. ProQuest Dissertations & Theses database. Dissertation Abstraction International, B 69/01, p. 665.

Brown, K. A., Ogden, J., Vögele, C., & Gibson, E. L. (2008). The role of parental control practices in explaining children's diet and BMI. *Appetite*, *50*(2), 252–259.

Cooke, L. J., Chambers, L. C., Añez, E. V., & Wardle, J. (2011). Facilitating or undermining? The effect of reward on food acceptance. A narrative review. *Appetite*, *57*(2), 493–497.

Cooper, L. J., Wacker, D. P., Brown, K., McComas, J. J., Peck, S. M., Drew, J., Asmus, J., & Kayser, K. (1999). Use of concurrent operants paradigm to evaluate positive reinforcers during treatment of food refusal. *Behavior Modification*, *23*(1), 3–40.

Creech, E. (2006). *Behavioral changes across ten weeks of SOS Approach to Feeding Therapy*. Unpublished manuscript.

Davis, A. M., Bruce, A., Cocjin, J., Mousa, H., & Hyman, P. (2010). Empirically supported treatments for feeding difficulties in young children. *Current Gastroenterology Reports*, *12*(3), 189–194.

Eneli, I. U., Crum, P. A., & Tylka, T. L. (2008). The trust model: A different feeding paradigm for managing childhood obesity. *Obesity*, *16*(10), 2197–2204.

Field, D., Garland, M., & Williams, K. (2003). Correlates of specific childhood feeding problems. *Journal of Paediatric Child Health*, *39*, 299–304.

Fildes, A., van Jaarsveld, C. H., Wardle, J., & Cooke, L. (2014). Parent-administered exposure to increase children's vegetable acceptance: A randomized controlled trial. *Journal of the Academy of Nutrition and Dietetics*, *114*(6), 881–888.

Finney, J. W. (1986). Preventing common feeding problems in infants and young children. *Pediatric Clinics of North America*, *33*(4), 775–788.

Fisher, J. O., Mitchell, D. C., Smiciklas-Wright, H., & Birch, L. L. (2002). Parental influences on young girls' fruit and vegetable, micronutrient, and fat intakes. *Journal of the American Dietetic Association*, *102*(1), 58–64.

Groff, R. A., Piazza, C. C., Volkert, V. M., & Jostad, C. M. (2014). Syringe fading as treatment for feeding refusal. *Journal of Applied Behavior Analysis*, *47*(4), 834–839.

Groff, R. A., Piazza, C. C., Zeleny, J. R., & Dempsey, J. R. (2011). Spoon to cup fading as treatment for cup drinking in a child with intestinal failure. *Journal of Applied Behavior Analysis*, *44*(4), 949–954.

Hendy, H. M., Williams, K. E., & Camise, T. S. (2005). "Kids Choice" school lunch program increases children's fruit and vegetable acceptance. *Appetite*, *45*(3), 250–263.

Hendy, H. M., Williams, K. E., & Camise, T. S. (2011). Kid's Choice Program improves weight management behaviors and weight status in school children. *Appetite*, *56*(2), 484–494.

Hoch, T., Babbitt, R., Coe, D., Krell, D., & Hackbert, L. (1994). Contingency contacting: Combining positive reinforcement and escape extinction procedures to treat persistent food refusal. *Behavior Modification*, *18*, 106–128.

Horne, P. J., Tapper, K., Lowe, C. F., Hardman, C. A., Jackson, M. C., & Woolner, J. (2004). Increasing children's fruit and vegetable consumption: a peer-modelling and rewards-based intervention. *European Journal of Clinical Nutrition*, *58*(12), 1649–1660.

Hummel, J. (2014). Motivation: Origins of the extrinsic/intrinsic debate. *SOJ Psychology*, 1(1): 5. http://dx.doi. Page 2 of 5 org/10.15226/2374–6874/1/1/00104

Kedesdy, J. H., & Budd, K. S. (1998). *Childhood feeding disorders: Biobehavioral assessment and intervention*. Baltimore, MD: Paul H Brookes Publishing.

Kerwin, M. E. (1999). Empirically supported treatments in pediatric psychology: Severe feeding problems. *Journal of Pediatric Psychology*, *24*(3), 193–214.

Kerwin, M. L., Ahearn, W. H., Eicher, P.E., & Burd, D. (1995). The cost of eating: A behavioral economic analysis of food refusal. *Journal of Applied Behavior Analysis*, *28*, 245–260.

Kreipe, R. E., & Palomaki, A. (2012). Beyond picky eating: Avoidant/restrictive food intake disorder. *Current Psychiatry Reports*, *14*(4), 421–431.

Linscheid, T. R. (2006). Behavioral treatments for pediatric feeding disorders. *Behavior Modification*, *30*(1), 6–23.

Lukens, C. T., & Silverman, A. H. (2014). Systematic review of psychological interventions for pediatric feeding problems. *Journal of Pediatric Psychology*, *39*, 903–917.

Mikula, G. (1989). Influencing food preferences of children by 'if-then' type instructions. *European Journal of Social Psychology*, *19*(3), 225–241.

Milnes, S. M., & Piazza, C. C. (2013). Feeding disorders. *International Review of Research in Developmental Disabilities*, *44*, 143–166.

Mueller M. M., Piazza, C. C. Patel, M. R., Kelley, M. E., & Pruett, A. (2004). Increasing variety of foods consumed by blending nonpreferred foods into preferred foods. *Journal of Applied Behavior Analysis*, *37*(2), 159–170.

Newman, J., & Taylor, A. (1992). Effect of a means-end contingency on young children's food preferences. *Journal of Experimental Child Psychology*, *53*(2), 200–216.

Ogata, B. N., & Hayes, D. (2014). Position of the Academy of Nutrition and Dietetics: Nutrition guidance for healthy children ages 2 to 11 years. *Journal of the Academy of Nutrition and Dietetics*, *114*(8), 1257–1276.

Parker-Pope, T. (2008). 6 food mistakes parents make. Retrieved from www
.nytimes.com/2008/09/15/health/healthspecial2/15eat/

Patel, M. R., Piazza, C. C., Martinez, C. J., Volkert, V. M., & Santana, C. M.
An evaluation of two differential reinforcement procedures with escape
extinction to treat food refusal. *Journal of Applied Behavior Analysis, 35*
(4), 363–374.

Penrod, B., Gardella, L., & Fernand, J. (2012). An evaluation of a progressive
high-probability instructional sequence combined with low-probability
demand fading in the treatment of food selectivity. *Journal of Applied
Behavior Analysis, 45*(3), 527–537.

Piazza, C. C., Fisher, W. W., Brown, K. A., Shore, B. A., Patel, M. R., Katz, R. M.,
Sevin, … & Blakely-Smith, A. (2003). Functional analysis of inappropriate
mealtime behaviors. *Journal of Applied Behavior Analysis, 36*(2), 187–204.

Remington, A., Anez, E., Croker, H., Wardle, J., & Cooke, L. (2012). Increasing
food acceptance in the home setting: A randomized controlled trial of
parent-administered taste exposure with incentives. *The American
Journal of Clinical Nutrition, 95*(1), 72–77.

Riordan, M. M., Iwata, B. A., Finney, J. W., Wohl, M.K., & Stanley, A. E. (1984).
Behavioral assessment and treatment of chronic food refusal in handi-
capped children. *Journal of Applied Behavior Analysis, 17*, 327–341.

Satter, E. M. (1986a). The feeding relationship. *Journal of the American Dietetic
Association, 86*(3), 352–356.

Satter, E. M. (1986b). Childhood eating disorders. *Journal of the American
Dietetic Association, 86*(3), 357–361.

Satter, E. (1990). The feeding relationship: Problems and interventions.
The Journal of Pediatrics, 117(2), S181–S189.

Satter, E. (1995). Feeding dynamics: Helping children to eat well. *Journal of
Pediatric Health Care, 9*(4), 178–184.

Satter, E. (2000). *Child of mine: Feeding with love and good sense.* Chicago: Bull
Publishing Company.

Satter, E. (2012). *How to get your kid to eat: But not too much.* Chicago: Bull
Publishing Company.

Satter, E. (2016a). Intervening with Pediatric Feeding Disorders. Retrieved from
www.ellynsatterinstitute.org/htf/interveningwithfoodrefusal/

Satter, E. (2016b). Avoid pressure. Retrieved from http://ellynsatterinstitute.org/
htf/avoidpressure/

Sharp, W. G., Jaquess, D. L., Morton, J. S., & Herzinger, C. (2011). Pediatric
feeding disorders: A quantitative synthesis of treatment outcomes. *Clinical
Child and Family Psychology Review, 13*, 348–365.

Sharp, W. G., Volkert, V. M., Scahill, L., McCracken, C. E., & McElhanon, B.
(2016). A systematic review and meta-analysis of intensive

multidisciplinary intervention for pediatric feeding disorders: How standard is the standard of care? *The Journal of Pediatrics, 181*, 116–124.

Shloim, N., Edelson, L. R., Martin, N., & Hetherington, M. M. (2015). Parenting styles, feeding styles, feeding practices, and weight status in 4–12 year-old children: A systematic review of the literature. Frontiers in Psychology, *6*.

Silbaugh, B. C., Penrod, B., Whelan, C. M., Hernandez, D. A., Wingate, H. V., Falcomata, T. S., & Lang, R. (2016). A systematic synthesis of behavioral interventions for food selectivity of children with Autism Spectrum Disorders. *Review Journal of Autism and Developmental Disorders, 3*(4), 345–357.

Peterson, K. M., Piazza, C. C., & Volkert, V. M. (2016). A comparison of a modified sequential oral sensory approach to an applied behavior-analytic approach in the treatment of food selectivity in children with autism spectrum disorder. *Journal of Applied Behavior Analysis, 49*(3), 485–511.

Sleddens, E. F., Kremers, S. P., De Vries, N. K., & Thijs, C. (2010). Relationship between parental feeding styles and eating behaviours of Dutch children aged 6–7. *Appetite, 54*(1), 30–36.

Spruijt-Metz, D., Li, C., Cohen, E., Birch, L., & Goran, M. (2006). Longitudinal influence of mother's child-feeding practices on adiposity in children. *The Journal of Pediatrics, 148*(3), 314–320.

Toomey, K. (2002, March). *When children won't eat: Picky eaters and problem feeders*. Paper presented at the Society for Developmental and Behavioral Pediatrics Annual Conference, Chicago, IL.

Toomey, K. A., & Ross, E. S. (2011). SOS approach to feeding. *SIG 13 Perspectives on Swallowing and Swallowing Disorders (Dysphagia), 20* (3), 82–87.

Vaz, P. C., Piazza, C. C., Stewart, V., Volkert, V. M., Groff, R. A., & Patel, M. R. (2012). Using a chaser to decreasing packing in children with feeding disorders. *Journal of Applied Behavior Analysis, 45*(1), 97–105.

Webber, L., Cooke, L., Hill, C., & Wardle, J. (2010). Associations between children's appetitive traits and maternal feeding practices. *Journal of the American Dietetic Association, 110*(11), 1718–1722.

Wilder, D. A., Normand, M., & Atwell, J. (2005). Noncontingent reinforcement as treatment for food refusal and associated self-injury. *Journal of Applied Behavior Analysis, 38*, 549–553.

Williams, K. E., Field, D. G., & Seiverling, L. (2010). Food refusal in children: A review of the literature. *Research in Developmental Disabilities, 31*(3), 625–633.

Williams, K. E., Hendy, H. M., Field, D. G., Belousov, Y., Riegel, K., & Harclerode, W. (2015). Implications of Avoidant/Restrictive Food Intake

Disorder (ARFID) on children with feeding problems. *Children's Health Care*, *44*(4), 307–321.

Williams, K. E., Riegel, K., & Kerwin, M. L. (2009). Feeding disorder of infancy or early childhood: How often is it seen in feeding programs? *Children's Health Care*, *38*(2), 123–136.

Wyse, R., Campbell, E., Nathan, N., & Wolfenden, L. (2011). Associations between characteristics of the home food environment and fruit and vegetable intake in preschool children: A cross-sectional study. *BMC Public Health*, *11*(1), 1.

Zeinstra, G. G., Koelen, M. A., Kok, F. J., van der Laan, N., & de Graaf, C. (2010). Parental child-feeding strategies in relation to Dutch children's fruit and vegetable intake. *Public Health Nutrition*, *13*(6), 787–796.

14

Eating

Frances Bozsik, Brooke L. Bennett, Emily Stefano, Brooke L. Whisenhunt, and Danae L. Hudson

Eating disorders (EDs) are notoriously difficult to treat and continue to have the highest rates of mortality of any psychiatric condition (American Psychiatric Association, 2013). Therefore, it is understandable that treatment providers, researchers, and health professionals are eager to find effective treatments. The severity of the condition, diagnostic/assessment limitations, and difficulties surrounding treatment may lead providers to consider implementing treatments that have not yet undergone the rigor of scientific review. This chapter provides a brief summary of the symptoms of different eating disorders, an overview of the controversies surrounding the diagnosis and assessment of EDs in children and adolescents, and a review of treatments that are currently untested, ineffective, or even harmful.

EDs are characterized by disturbances in eating behavior that are typically driven by dissatisfaction with body weight and shape. The *Diagnostic and Statistical Manual of Mental Disorders,* 5th ed (DSM-5; American Psychiatric Association, 2013) recognizes three primary eating disorders: anorexia nervosa (AN), bulimia nervosa (BN), and binge eating disorder (BED).

AN is characterized by severe caloric restriction resulting in an extremely low body mass index (BMI) relative to an individual's age, sex, developmental state, and physical health. Among children and adolescents, this may be manifested as a failure to make expected weight gains (i.e., a BMI lower than the 5th percentile). Despite the individual being underweight, an intense fear of fatness or weight gain is also present. This fear may not be overtly endorsed by the individual but may be inferred when behaviors that interfere with weight gain (e.g., compulsive exercise) are present (Eddy, Murray, & LeGrange, 2015). Significant body image disturbance, overvaluation of weight and shape during self-evaluation, and a lack of recognition of the seriousness of low body weight are also key characteristics of AN.

BN is characterized by recurrent binge-purge cycles. Binge eating involves the consumption of an objectively large amount of food within a short period of time (i.e., two hours or less) accompanied by a sense of loss of control over eating. Following the binge episode, an attempt is made to "undo" the effects of calorie consumption through compensatory behaviors (e.g., self-induced vomiting, fasting). Weight often remains within the normal range due to inevitable calorie absorption during binge eating. Similar to AN, BN is characterized by an overemphasis on shape and weight during self-appraisal.

BED is also characterized by recurrent episodes of binge eating but does not include subsequent compensatory behaviors. During episodes of binge eating, the individual may experience any of the following: eating rapidly or until uncomfortably full, eating in the absence of hunger, eating alone out of embarrassment, or feeling disgusted following the eating episode. Although it may be present, fear of weight gain is not required for diagnosis.

14.1 Pseudoscience and Questionable Ideas

14.1.1 Diagnostic Controversies

Prior to the publication of DSM-5, an estimated 50%–60% of individuals with ED symptomology did not meet criteria for an ED despite problematic and dangerous eating-related behavior (Peebles et al., 2010). This problem led to a broadening of the criteria for diagnoses of AN and BN in DSM-5. For example, in DSM-4-TR, the criteria for AN required loss of menstruation and a specific amount of weight loss that are no longer present in DSM-5. "Other specified feeding or eating disorder" (OSFED) and "Unspecified feeding or eating disorder" (UFED) became "catchall" categories intended to include individuals who do not meet criteria for an ED but have symptoms serious enough to warrant a diagnosis. Due to these changes percentage of individuals presenting with ED symptoms who were diagnosed with OSFED and UFED was reduced by 17% while diagnoses of AN increased by 12% (Mancuso et al., 2015). However, 29% of patients continued to receive an OSFED diagnosis suggesting that broadening the criteria did not entirely solve the problem.

The primary concern with the OSFED diagnosis is treatment related. First, because the category encompasses vastly different eating behaviors, it is difficult for treatment providers to identify the most effective treatment for their patients (Lock, 2010a). Treatment manuals tend to focus on specific disorders rather than elaborating on effective, generalizable treatment components, which makes it difficult for providers to find evidence-based treatment options for OSFED. Additionally, patients with a diagnosis of OSFED have the potential to be denied access to treatment by their insurance companies as OSFED is often misperceived as less severe than other eating disorders (Peebles et al., 2010). Similarly, patients and their parents can misinterpret their symptoms as not dangerous because they did not meet criteria for a "full eating disorder." These misperceptions persist despite research showing that 60% of patients with an eating disorder not otherwise specified (DSM-IV-TR terminology for OSFED) diagnosis qualified for hospitalization based on the medical severity of their condition (Peebles et al., 2010).

14.1.2 Questionable Assessment Practices

ED assessments can be challenging for several reasons. Due to the nature of EDs, the disorder may be purposely hidden or denied by the individual. Gender may also influence symptom presentation (e.g., males are less likely to endorse preoccupation with shape and weight control; Walcott, Pratt, & Patel, 2003). One of the primary difficulties relates to the assessment of weight status. While currently used as a primary marker of severity in adult ED populations, the assessment of BMI in children and adolescents should be more nuanced. Due to their developmental stage and the associated growth that occurs within this time frame, BMI changes rapidly in this group compared to adults (Freedman & Sherry, 2009). While a stable BMI cutoff is based on height and weight for adults (i.e., 18.5), interpretation of BMI in children cannot be made without accounting for age and sex (CDC, 2015). This consideration is particularly important for adolescent females who have less body fat than older females, so a lower BMI can have more serious health implications. Ultimately, BMI values should be adjusted for the age, sex, and ethnicity of the individual (Stice & Bohon, 2013).

14.1.3 Myths That Influence Treatment

The successful treatment of EDs first requires accurate identification of those individuals in need of treatment. Misperceptions regarding who develops eating disorders or how they develop can hinder this process.

Only White, Affluent Females Living in Developed Countries Develop Eating Disorders. Recognized by Austin (2011), one myth that potentially impacts treatment access is that only females who are White, affluent, and living in developed countries develop eating disorders. EDs are far more ubiquitous than this myth suggests. In a US adolescent sample, similar prevalence rates of ED symptoms have been found across Black, American Indian, Asian/Pacific Islander, and White females (Austin et al., 2008). Among US males, findings suggest a greater prevalence of disordered eating behavior within other racial/ethnic groups compared to White males (Austin et al., 2008). Further, while it is true that EDs are more prevalent among females, maladaptive weight control behavior (e.g., purging, diet product use) increased among adolescent males from 1995 to 2005 (Chao et al., 2008). Despite similar prevalence rates of AN, BN, and BED among women in the United States, non-Latina Whites are the most likely to seek treatment for an ED (Marques et al., 2011) – a factor that may be partially responsible for perpetuating the myth that White individuals are affected by EDs at a higher rate than non-White individuals.

Although recent findings suggest Western countries have the highest prevalence rate of eating disorders (Makino, Tsuboi, & Dennerstein, 2004; Qian et al., 2013), the existence of EDs in non-Western countries has been documented since the 1970s (Hoek, 2006; Makino et al., 2004). Differences in prevalence estimates may be due to actual differences in the number of ED cases but may also be influenced by differences in data collection procedures (e.g., use of convenience samples, assessment of EDs without standardized clinical interviews; Makino et al., 2004; Qian et al., 2013).

Several studies have also examined the relationship between high socioeconomic status (SES), EDs, and weight control behaviors. An equivocal relationship has been found, suggesting that disordered eating does not disproportionately occur among those of elevated SES (Hay, Girosi, & Mond, 2015; Striegel-Moore et al., 2003; Wardle & Griffith, 2001). Taken together, this information cautions against selectively screening White, affluent females for eating disorders.

Parents Are the Primary Cause of Eating Disorder Development. Bulik (2014) articulated the myth that the family is to blame for the development of an ED. This belief was first suggested in the late nineteenth century when Gull (1874) advised that the family should be separated from a child with AN for fear they inhibit the re-feeding process. More recently, Minuchin, Rosman, and Baker (1978) suggested that an "anorectic family" fosters the development of AN through maladaptive familial patterns such as enmeshment, fostering family loyalty and dependence over autonomy, and so on. The etiology of EDs is extremely complex and multifaceted; while some family dynamics may put the child at higher risk for developing disordered eating (e.g., parental ED pathology, critical weight-related comments), no definitive parenting style or familial pattern has been identified as a primary cause of ED development (LeGrange et al., 2010; Mazzeo & Bulik, 2009).

This myth has particular relevance to the treatment of children and adolescents with eating disorders for two reasons. First, children and adolescents are often reliant on guardians for treatment (e.g., consent, transportation, payment). If parents are afraid of receiving blame for their child's ED, they may be hesitant to seek treatment for their child. Second, family-based treatment (FBT) has been established as one of the most efficacious treatments for EDs within this age group (Lock, 2015). FBT asserts that parent and family participation is integral and essential, rather than problematic, for successful treatment and recovery. While parenting styles and modeling behaviors that are obstructive to the adolescent's recovery (e.g., compulsive exercise, preoccupation with weight and appearance) need to be addressed through the course of treatment, an improved family environment can be achieved without placing blame on parents (Mazzeo & Bulik, 2009).

Patients Choose to Have an Eating Disorder. The myth that some patients have chosen to have an eating disorder also threatens treatment success. This belief stems from the fact that those with EDs are often ambivalent about treatment and change (Waller, 2012). This ambivalence is most commonly associated with AN (Vitousek, Watson, & Wilson, 1998), but it is also seen in BN and BED (Hepworth & Paxton, 2007). Despite the devastating psychological and physical consequences of EDs, patients place extreme value on their weight and shape, making it difficult to embrace treatment goals and recovery. However, the occurrence of ambivalence does not indicate that the individual has autonomously chosen to have an eating disorder. Current evidence-based treatment approaches employ techniques for addressing indecision about recovery (Geller, Williams, & Srikameswaran, 2001; Vitousek et al., 1998).

Sidebar Box: Is it possible for breatharians to live without food or water? by Joe Nickell

Some mystics claim to practice inedia – that is, to suspend all eating and, sometimes, even drinking. But are inedics genuine, or do they deceive – either themselves or others? In 1980, a cult founded by one Wiley Brooks raised just such questions; he espoused not only giving up eating meat but eventually living off nothing but light and air!

Since ancient times, extreme fasting has taken a variety of cultural forms. For example, visionaries (like Jesus in Matthew 4: 1–11) went into the wilderness to fast, hoping to thereby experience holy revelations. And in the early Christian era, mostly male hermits subsisted on bread and water to contemplate the world's end.

During the thirteenth and fourteenth centuries, a religious fasting fad attracted women like the future Saint Catherine of Sienna (1347–1380). She imagined demonic torture, exhibited stigmata, and experienced visions – which the author of *Holy Anorexia* attributed to "an eating/vomiting pattern typical of acute anorexia." Being vainglorious, he says, Catherine "starved herself to death." A very late example of this type was Therese Neumann (1898–1962), whom suspicious church authorities monitored. Tests of her urine revealed that after fasting she had, secretly, resumed intake of food and drink.

The nineteenth century tended to see inedics more as prodigies than holy persons and included sideshow artists styled "Living Skeletons." Finally, first described scientifically in 1868, came those recognized as having anorexia, whose refusal of food stemmed from emotional conflict.

As to Wiley Brooks – who espoused reverting from carnivorism to vegetarianism, then fruitarianism, liquidarianism, and finally to breatharianism – his followers' faith was badly shaken when Brooks was discovered making nighttime forays to buy junk food.

Joe Nickell, PhD, is a paranormal investigator and senior research fellow for the Committee for Skeptical Inquiry (CSI). Among many other books, he is author of *The Science of Ghosts* (2012).

14.1.4 Implausible Treatments

Implausible treatments are those treatments that have not been empirically examined and that are not derived from a science-based theory. Therefore, all treatments that fall in this category should only be used with utmost caution.

Due to the overemphasis on body shape and weight within the EDs, various experiential treatments have been created with the hope of moving the emphasis from the body's appearance to its function. One such therapy is dance or movement therapy. Currently, existing research on dance therapy for EDs relies on case studies or anecdotes (Evan, 1991; Krantz, 1999), with a notable lack of empirical evidence regarding its efficacy. Another experiential treatment proposed for treating EDs is yoga. A relatively new phenomenon, yoga for EDs has begun appearing in the literature. Although preliminary research may appear promising (Carei et al., 2010; McIver, O'Halloran, & McGartland, 2009), results conflict with existing research that suggests group treatment for patients with EDs may cause more harm than good (Colton & Pistrang, 2004). Additionally, treatment studies on the use of yoga are limited in number, and most studies have weaknesses in their designs (e.g., observational design, no control groups, or small sample sizes). Therefore, additional research is needed before experiential treatments can be considered efficacious in the treatment of EDs.

Similar problems exist for other newly proposed treatments for EDs such as meditation or mindfulness-based treatment and acceptance and commitment therapy (ACT). Mindfulness-based treatments typically involve training in meditation for the purpose of targeting core issues such as making conscious food choices, developing an awareness of hunger and satiety cues, and responding to emotions (Kristeller & Wolever, 2011). ACT is a cognitive-behavioral treatment that targets the unwillingness to accept negative thoughts, feelings, and emotions. Although preliminary results appear promising for symptom alleviation through mindfulness-based treatments (Manlick, Cochran, & Koon, 2013; Wanden-Berghe, Sanz-Valero, & Wanden-Berghe, 2011) and ACT (Heffner et al., 2002), the existing research is primarily exploratory, the quality of the research varies greatly, and sample sizes are generally small. There is a clear need for randomized controlled trials of these treatments.

14.1.5 Ineffective Treatments

While a growing body of literature is examining effective psychological treatments for adolescent EDs, ineffective treatments are scarcely reviewed (Gowers & Bryant-Waugh, 2004; Keel & Haedt, 2008; Lock, 2010b). The lack of available information about treatments that *do not* work may result in practitioners' inadvertent use of treatments that exacerbate, rather than alleviate, ED symptoms and psychological impairment (Hoagwood et al., 2001). Owing in part to the dearth of literature focused on child and adolescent ED treatment, previous reviews have instead extrapolated from the adult literature (Keel & Haedt, 2008; van den Heuvel & Jordaan, 2014).

In the treatment of AN, no medication has been approved by the US Food and Drug Administration (FDA). Further, pharmacotherapy has generally been shown to be ineffective in treating AN symptoms (Flament, Bissada, & Spettigue, 2012; Herpertz et al., 2011; van den Heuvel & Jordaan, 2014). Medications have been prescribed to address amenorrhea resulting from AN (i.e., contraceptives and hormone replacement therapy). However, they are not recommended, because they do not effectively treat adolescent AN (Flament et al., 2012; Hay et al., 2014). Additionally, hormonal supplementation does not improve other medical consequences of AN, such as bone density or nutritional status (Rosen, 2010), and research has not investigated its impact on symptoms such as fixation on weight and shape. Psychiatrists or primary care physicians may occasionally prescribe medication to target comorbid anxiety and depression among patients with AN (Rosen, 2010). Although there is evidence for the effectiveness of selective serotonin reuptake inhibitors (SSRIs) for depression (Cujipers et al., 2013), evidence suggests that they may not be effective in severely malnourished patients (Flament et al., 2012; Rosen, 2010).

Regarding psychological treatments, therapist-led and self-guided cognitive-behavioral therapy (CBT) for BED has been shown to reduce binge eating in adults but has not been shown to be effective in promoting weight loss for patients who are overweight or who have obesity (Grilo & Masheb, 2005). This is of importance because those who present for treatment for BED often do so with the goal of losing weight (Herpertz et al., 2011). Equine-related treatment has also been used to treat EDs. This form of treatment includes both equine-assisted psychotherapy and therapeutic horseback riding. Touted as an experiential approach that helps patients become more aware of changes in mood, there is evidence that this treatment is no better than the passage of time (Anestis et al., 2014).

14.1.6 Potentially Harmful Treatments

This section focuses on treatment approaches and "self-help" strategies for children and adolescents with eating disorders that may have unintended harmful effects for the patient.

Online Self-Help. A subset of individuals with EDs report visiting pro-eating disorder (pro-ED) websites for support, validation, and motivation to lose weight (Rouleau & vonRanson, 2011; Wilson et al., 2006). These websites typically include content supporting harmful eating behavior (e.g., purging methods, tips for concealing symptoms), "inspiring" images of thin people (i.e., "thinspiration"), and forums for communicating with other individuals with eating disorders. Pro-ED sites have been shown to promote disordered eating behavior (Wilson et al., 2006) and competition among visitors (Rouleau & vonRanson, 2011). In fact, regular use of these sites is associated with greater ED severity (Custers & van den Bulck, 2009).

Considered to be an antidote to pro-ED websites, "pro-recovery" sites also exist. These sites are meant to offer anonymous online support and empower those attempting to recover from an ED. Research has suggested that pro-ED website viewers often simultaneously seek out pro-recovery websites (Harper, Sperry, & Thompson, 2008). While some individuals who visit pro-recovery sites report an interest in learning about others' experiences, finding support, and exchanging information (Aardoom et al., 2014), use of these sites may also result in harmful consequences. Keski-Rahkonen and Tozzi (2005) found that pro-recovery sites were reportedly helpful in the initial stages of recovery but became potential treatment barriers in that participants found a continued "focus on food" and competition among those in the forum to be unhelpful during the final stages of recovery.

Medication. Given the well-known range of side effects that can accompany the use of medication, investigation of the use of pharmacotherapy for the treatment of EDs should continue with caution. Most notably, patients with an ED are especially at risk of developing metabolic syndrome and insulin resistance (Rosen, 2010). Some other significant side effects associated with specific medications include thyroid stimulation (olanzapine combined with SSRIs or risperdone), arrhythmias (tricyclic antidepressants), hepatoxicity (naltrexone), increased risk of seizures (buproprion), and cognitive problems (topiramate) among others (van den Heuvel & Jordaan, 2014). Interactions between medications and associated physical symptoms of an ED can also render an otherwise beneficial medication harmful. This is particularly true for any medication that has an impact on the cardiovascular system, as this system can be compromised in those with AN or BN (Powers & Cloak, 2012).

Unlike AN, there is evidence that select methods of pharmacotherapy may be effective in treating BN and BED. Specifically, fluoxetine coupled with therapy has been found to be effective in treating children and adolescents with BN (van den Heuvel & Jordaan, 2014). However, while fluoxetine has been approved for the treatment of BN in children and adolescents, it also carries a risk of increased suicidality (van den Heuvel & Jordaan, 2014). Further, topiramate has been found effective in the treatment of BN and BED. However, it is recommended only when alternate treatment options have been ineffective, as it is associated with a number of adverse side effects and is contraindicated for those at a low weight (APA, 2006).

Specific Treatments. A survey of practitioners found that clinicians reported using several non-empirically supported or harmful treatment approaches, such as hypnotherapy and recovered memory therapy (von Ranson & Robinson, 2006). Recovered memory therapy (RMT) is a therapeutic approach that calls upon the clinician to assist the client in recovering memories that have been repressed or hidden from consciousness. The targeted repressed memories tend to be traumatic in nature, often consisting of forgotten childhood sexual abuse. The treatment goal is accomplished through the use of techniques such as guided imagery, body work, sedation, and flashback analysis (Stocks, 1998). One of the major harmful aspects of this therapeutic approach is the risk of generating false memories. Guided imagery lends itself quite well to the fabrication of memories, even if this is not initially intended (Loftus & Pickrell, 1995). Additionally, "recoveries" of lost memories of abuse have resulted in hugely deleterious effects on the family system and high-profile lawsuits (Pope & Hudson, 1996). RMT has been used to target EDs, in part because of a belief that childhood abuse has a causal role in the development of BN (Pope & Hudson, 1996). While this may be the case for some with EDs (Smolak & Murnen, 2001), this therapy does not directly address ED symptoms, and its relevance to the treatment of eating disorder symptoms is worthy of further scrutiny.

Hypnotherapy has been used to treat EDs within the context of harmful therapy approaches like RMT as well as within evidence-based treatments, including CBT. Hypnotherapy heavily relies upon relaxation training, imagery, and therapist suggestion. Establishing the efficacy of this approach has been elusive due to poorly designed studies (Barabasz, 2007;

Vanderlinden & Vandereycken, 1988) and widely differing treatment approaches (Jamieson, 2007). While this technique is not associated with the severe adverse effects resulting from other RMT techniques, one should still consider the potential harm that could occur during its administration. Individuals with EDs tend to be highly suggestible, adapting to the suggestions of others more than their counterparts without EDs (Bachner-Melman et al., 2016). While hypnotherapy might be particularly effective with a highly suggestible individual, the clinician may have unintended power in influencing the individual's behavior or memory, resulting in harmful consequences.

Other Considerations. Finally, there are circumstances under which otherwise beneficial treatments could be considered harmful. First, outpatient therapy should not be considered as the primary treatment option if an individual has a BMI below 15.0 or is otherwise medically unstable (Fairburn & Cooper, 2014). Dietary or nutritional counseling interventions are considered ineffective, and potentially detrimental, as sole treatments of AN (Hay et al., 2014; Lock, 2010b; NICE, 2004). Additionally, concurrent substance abuse or depression that would otherwise interfere with treatment may need to be addressed prior to ED treatment (Fairburn & Cooper, 2014; NICE, 2004), as comorbid disorders have the potential to nullify the effects of an otherwise successful treatment course.

Similar to the effect that pro-ED websites can have on those with EDs, inpatient and day treatment programs should be considered carefully. Due to the cohabitation and group therapy typically involved in these programs, they can unintentionally create a competitive environment involving ED symptom severity and become a forum for learning new maladaptive weight control behaviors (Colton & Pistrang, 2004). Lastly, certain treatments that are otherwise indicated for individuals with an ED might be contraindicated for other co-occurring diagnoses. For example, bright light therapy has been shown to be effective in decreasing AN and BN symptoms in adolescents (Krystaet al., 2012) but may harm an individual with co-occurring bipolar disorder or ocular problems (Golden et al., 2005). It is important that clinicians consider the individuality of each patient while creating a treatment plan.

14.2 Research-Supported Approaches

It is difficult to make strong conclusions about the most efficacious evidence-based treatments for adolescent EDs due to the limited availability of high-quality, controlled treatment studies (Couturier, Kimber,

& Szatmari, 2013; Keel & Haedt, 2008). However, the body of literature is currently growing (Lock, 2015), and existing evidence points to several established treatment approaches.

Recent meta-analyses have identified FBT as the first-line treatment for adolescent AN (Couturier et al., 2013; Lock, 2015; Lock & Le Grange, 2015). FBT is based on the notion that the adolescent is best understood through their relationship with immediate family members. Consequently, treatment should focus on the family unit as a whole (Lock, 2011; Lock & Le Grange, 2015). The child's ability to function at an appropriate developmental level is seen as diminished as a result of the ED, and parents are encouraged to assert temporary control over the child's eating until the severity of the ED has decreased (Lock, 2011; Lock & Le Grange, 2015). Initial treatment sessions focus on weight restoration and family dynamics within the context of the eating disorder. After weight has stabilized and ED symptoms have decreased, control over the patient's eating slowly transitions from the parents to the patient, and family issues unrelated to the ED are addressed.

There is support for CBT as an effective treatment for adolescent BN and BED, though more research is needed (Dalle Grave et al., 2015; Hay, 2013; Lock, 2015; Wilfley, Kolko, & Kass, 2011). Outpatient CBT for eating disorders typically occurs over the course of six months and includes 15–20 sessions (Fairburn, 2008; Waller et al., 2007). CBT focuses on identifying, monitoring, and changing the cognitive and behavioral processes that maintain the patient's eating disorder pathology. Early treatment emphasizes in-session weighing, self-monitoring, meal planning, and psychoeducation, with the primary goals of weight restoration or stabilization. Later stages of treatment focus on more complex maintenance factors and mechanisms including overvaluation of weight and shape, low self-esteem, perfectionism, interpersonal functioning, and mood dysregulation.

14.3 Conclusion

The identification and/or treatment of EDs in adolescents and children can be difficult or nuanced in comparison to adults. Assessment and treatment of EDs can be hampered further by existing myths and stereotypes in popular culture about who can have an eating disorder or what caused the condition. Once an adolescent has been properly identified as having an eating disorder, additional barriers to recovery may come in the form of ineffective, implausible, or harmful treatment practices. Furthermore, a number of recently developed treatments have not yet been tested with scientific rigor. It is important to note that, in general, treatment of EDs in children and adolescents has not been studied to the same degree as that of adults (Wilson, Grilo, & Vitousek, 2007). Future research may one day demonstrate that some treatments (e.g., yoga, ACT) are more effective with this group than the literature currently suggests.

The number of children and adolescents with identified eating disorders is growing (Wilksch, 2014), suggesting a strong need for effective ED treatments. Family-based therapy and cognitive-behavioral therapy are two evidence-based treatments that have demonstrated success in treating a variety of eating disorders. However, additional research is needed to fill in the gaps and enhance the effectiveness of existing treatments. This research is crucial as successful ED treatment during childhood and adolescence can offset costs associated with EDs in adulthood (e.g., stunted physical development, health consequences, reduced intimacy, disruptions or delays in life plans).

Work Cited in Sidebar

Nickell, J. (2017). Mystery of Mollie Fancher, the 'Fasting girl,' and others who lived without eating. *Skeptical Inquirer*, *41*(6), 18–21.

References

Aardoom, J. J., Dingemans, A. E., Boogaard, L. H., & Van Furth, E. F. (2014). Internet and patient empowerment in individuals with symptoms of an eating disorder: A cross-sectional investigation of a pro-recovery focused e-community. *Eating Behaviors*, *15*(3), 350–356.

American Psychiatric Association. (2006). Practice guidelines for the treatment of patients with eating disorders (3rd edn). Retrieved from http://psychia tryonline.org/pb/assets/raw/sitewide/practice_guidelines/guidelines/eating disorders.pdf

American Psychiatric Association. (2013). Feeding and eating disorders. In *Diagnostic and statistical manual of mental disorders*. 5th edn. Arlington, VA: American Psychiatric Publishing.

Anestis, M. D., Anestis, J. C., Zawilinski, L. L., Hopkins, T. A., & Lilienfeld, S. O. (2014). Equine-related treatments for mental disorders lack empirical support: A systematic review of empirical investigations. *Journal of Clinical Psychology*, *70*(12), 1115–1132.

Austin, S. B. (2011). The blind spot in the drive for childhood obesity prevention: Bringing eating disorders prevention into focus as a public health priority. *American Journal of Public Health, 101*(6), e1–e4.

Austin, S. B., Ziyadeh, N. J., Forman, S., Prokop, L. A., Keliher, A., & Jacobs, D. (2008). Screening high school students for eating disorders: Results of a national initiative. *Preventing Chronic Disease, 5*(4), 1–10.

Bachner-Melman, R., Lev-Ari, L., Levin, R., & Lichtenberg, P. (2016). Think yourself thin: Concern for appropriateness mediates the link between hypnotizability and disordered eating. *International Journal of Clinical and Experimental Hypnosis, 64*(2), 225–238.

Barabasz, M. (2007). Efficacy of hypnotherapy in the treatment of eating disorders. *International Journal of Clinical and Experimental Hypnosis, 55*(3), 318–335.

Bulik, C. (2014, February). *Eating disorders essentials: Replacing myths with realities.* Presentation at the meeting of NIMH Alliance for Research Progress, Rockville, MD.

Carei, T. R., Fyfe-Johnson, A. L., Breuner, C. C., & Brown, M. A. (2010). Randomized controlled clinical trial of yoga in the treatment of eating disorders. *Journal of Adolescent Health, 46*(4), 346–351.

Centers for Disease Control and Prevention. (2015). About child and teen BMI. Retrieved from www.cdc.gov/healthyweight/assessing/bmi/childrens_bmi/about_childrens_bmi.html

Chao, Y. M., Pisetsky, E. M., Dierker, L. C., Dohm, F. A., Rosselli, F., May, A. M., & Striegel-Moore, R. H. (2008). Ethnic differences in weight control practices among U.S. adolescents from 1995 to 2005. *International Journal of Eating Disorders, 41*(2), 124–133.

Colton, A., & Pistrang, N. (2004). Adolescents' experiences of inpatient treatment for anorexia nervosa. *European Eating Disorders Review, 12*(5), 307–316.

Couturier, J., Kimber, M., & Szatmari, P. (2013). Efficacy of family-based treatment for adolescents with eating disorders: A systemic review and meta-analysis. *International Journal of Eating Disorders, 46*(1), 3–11.

Cujipers, P., Sijbrandij, M., Koole, S. L., Andersson, G., Beekman, A. T., & Reynolds, C. F. (2013). The efficacy of psychotherapy and pharmacotherapy in treating depressive and anxiety disorders: A meta-analysis of direct comparisons. *World Psychiatry, 12*(2), 137–148.

Custers, K., & van den Bulck, J. (2009). Viewership of pro-anorexia websites in seventh, ninth and eleventh graders. *European Eating Disorders Review, 17*(3), 214–219.

Dalle Grave, R., Calugi, S., Sartirana, M., & Fairburn, C. G. (2015). Transdiagnostic cognitive behaviour therapy for adolescents with an eating disorder who are not underweight. *Behaviour Research and Therapy, 73*, 79–82.

Eddy, K. T., Murray, B. B., & Le Grange, D. (2015). Eating and feeding disorders. In M. K. Dulcan (ed.), *Dulcan's textbook of child and adolescent psychiatry* (pp. 435–460). Arlington, VA: American Psychiatric Publications.

Evan, B. (1991). The fog, the moon, the sun, and a pathway to dance/movement therapy. In R. Benov (ed.), *Collected works by and about Blanche Evan* (pp. 152–154). San Francisco, CA: Blanche Evan Dance Foundation.

Fairburn, C. G. (2008). *Cognitive behavior therapy and eating disorders*. New York: Guilford Press.

Fairburn, C. G., & Cooper, Z. (2014). Eating disorders: A transdiagnostic protocol. In D. H. Barlow (ed.), *Clinical handbook of psychological disorders: A step-by-step treatment manual* (pp. 670–702). New York: Guilford Press.

Flament, M. F., Bissada, H., & Spettigue, W. (2012). Evidence-based pharmacotherapy of eating disorders. *International Journal of Neuropsychopharmacology*, *15*(2), 189–207.

Freedman, D. S., & Sherry, B. (2009). The validity of BMI as an indicator of body fatness and risk among children. *Pediatrics*, *124*(Supplement 1), S23–S34.

Geller, J., Williams, K. D., & Srikameswaran, S. (2001). Clinician stance in the treatment of chronic eating disorders. *European Eating Disorders Review*, *9*(6), 365–373.

Golden, R. N., Gaynes, B. N., Ekstrom, R. D., Hamer, R. M., Jacobsen, F. M., Suppes, T. . . . & Nemeroff, C. B. (2005). The efficacy of light therapy in the treatment of mood disorders: A review and meta-analysis of the evidence. *American Journal of Psychiatry*, *162*(4), 656–662.

Gowers, S., & Bryant-Waugh, R. (2004). Management of child and adolescent eating disorders: The current evidence base and future directions. *Journal of Child Psychology and Psychiatry*, *45*(1), 63–83.

Grilo, C. M., & Masheb, R. M. (2005). A randomized controlled comparison of guided self-help cognitive behavioral therapy and behavioral weight loss for binge eating disorder. *Behaviour Research and Therapy*, *43*(11), 1509–1525.

Gull, W. W. (1874). Anorexia nervosa (apepsia hysterica, anorexia hysterica). *Transactions of the Clinical Society of London*, *7*, 22–28.

Harper, K., Sperry, S., & Thompson, J. K. (2008). Viewership of pro-eating disorder websites: Association with body image and eating disturbances. *International Journal of Eating Disorders*, *41*(1), 92–95.

Hay, P. (2013). A systemic review of evidence for psychological treatments in eating disorders: 2005–2012. *International Journal of Eating Disorders*, *46*(5), 462–469.

Hay, P., Chinn, D., Forbes, D., Madden, S., Newton, R., Sugenor, L. . . . & Ward, W. (2014). Royal Australian and New Zealand College of Psychiatrists clinical practice guidelines for the treatment of eating disorders. *Australian and New Zealand Journal of Psychiatry*, *48*(11), 977–1008.

Hay, P., Girosi, F., & Mond, J. (2015). Prevalence and sociodemographic correlates of DSM-5 eating disorders in the Australian population. *Journal of Eating Disorders*, *3*(19), 1–7.

Heffner, M., Sperry, J., Eifert, G. H., & Detweiler, M. (2002). Acceptance and commitment therapy in the treatment of an adolescent female with anorexia nervosa: A case example. *Cognitive and Behavioral Practice*, *9*(3), 232–236.

Hepworth, N., & Paxton, S. J. (2007). Pathways to help-seeking in bulimia nervosa and binge eating problems: A concept mapping approach. *International Journal of Eating Disorders*, *40*(6), 493–504.

Herpertz, S., Hagenah, U., Vocks, S., von Wietersheim, J., Cuntz, U., & Zeeck, A. (2011). The diagnosis and treatment of eating disorders. *Deutsches Arzteblatt International*, *108*(40), 678–685.

Hoagwood, K., Burns, B. J., Kiser, L., Ringeisen, H., & Schoenwald, S. K. (2001). Evidence-based practice in child and adolescent mental health services. *Psychiatric Services*, *52*(9), 1179–1189.

Hoek, H. W. (2006). Incidence, prevalence and mortality of anorexia nervosa and other eating disorders. *Current Opinion in Psychiatry*, *19*(4), 389–394.

Jamieson, G. A. (2007). *Hypnosis and conscious states: The cognitive neuroscience perspective*. New York: Oxford University Press.

Keel, P. K., & Haedt, A. (2008). Evidence-based psychosocial treatments for eating problems and eating disorders. *Journal of Clinical Child & Adolescent Psychology*, *37*(1), 39–61.

Keski-Rahkonen, A., & Tozzi, F. (2005). The process of recovery in eating disorder sufferers' own words: An Internet-based study. *International Journal of Eating Disorders*, *37*(Supplement1), S80–S86.

Krantz, A. M. (1999). Growing into her body: Dance/movement therapy for women with eating disorders. *American Journal of Dance Therapy*, *21*(2), 81–103.

Kristeller, J. L., & Wolever, R. Q. (2011). Mindfulness-based eating awareness training for treating binge eating disorder: The conceptual foundation. *Eating Disorders*, *19*(1), 49–61.

Krysta, K., Krzystanek, M., Janas-Kozik, M., & Krupka-Matuszczyk, I. (2012). Bright light therapy in the treatment of childhood and adolescence depression, antepartum depression, and eating disorders. *Journal of Neural Transmission*, *119*(10), 1167–1172.

LeGrange, D., Lock, J., Loeb, K., & Nicholls, D. (2010). Academy for eating disorders position paper: The role of the family in eating disorders. *International Journal of Eating Disorders*, *43*(1), 1–5.

Lock, J. (2010a). Controversies and questions in current evaluation, treatment, and research related to child and adolescent eating disorders. In W. S. Agras (ed.), *The Oxford handbook of eating disorders* (pp. 51–72). New York: Oxford University Press.

Lock, J. (2010b). Treatment of adolescent eating disorders: Progress and challenges. *Minerva Psichiatrica, 51*(3), 207–216.

Lock, J. (2011). Evaluation of family treatment models for eating disorders. *Current Opinion in Psychiatry, 24*(4), 274–279.

Lock, J. (2015). An update on evidence-based psychosocial treatments for eating disorders in children and adolescents. *Journal of Clinical Child & Adolescent Psychology, 44*(5), 707–721.

Lock, J., & Le Grange, D. (2015). *Treatment manual for anorexia nervosa: A family-based approach*. New York: Guilford Press.

Loftus, E. F., & Pickrell, J. E. (1995). The formation of false memories. *Psychiatric Annals, 25*(12), 720–725.

Makino, M., Tsuboi, K., & Dennerstein, L. (2004). Prevalence of eating disorders: A comparison of Western and non-Western countries. *Medscape General Medicine, 6*(3), 49.

Mancuso, S. G., Newton, J. R., Bosanac, P., Rossell, S. L., Nesci, J. B., & Castle, D. J. (2015). Classification of eating disorders: Comparison of relative prevalence rates using DSM-IV and DSM-5 criteria. *The British Journal of Psychiatry, 206*(6), 519–520.

Manlick, C. F., Cochran, S. V., & Koon, J. (2013). Acceptance and commitment therapy for eating disorders: Rationale and literature review. *Journal of Contemporary Psychotherapy, 43*(2), 115–122.

Marques, L., Alegria, M., Becker, A. E., Chen, C. N., Fang, A., Chosak, A., & Diniz, J. B. (2011). Comparative prevalence, correlates of impairment, and service utilization for eating disorders across US ethnic groups: Implications for reducing ethnic disparities in health care access for eating disorders. *International Journal of Eating Disorders, 44*(5), 412–420.

Mazzeo, S. E., & Bulik, C. M. (2009). Environmental and genetic risk factors for eating disorders: What the clinician needs to know. *Child and Adolescent Psychiatric Clinics of North America, 18*(1), 67–82.

McIver, S., O'Halloran, P., & McGartland, M. (2009). Yoga as a treatment for binge eating disorder: A preliminary study. *Complementary Therapies in Medicine, 17*(4), 196–202.

Minuchin, S., Rosman, B. L., & Baker, L. (1978). *Psychosomatic families: Anorexia nervosa in context*. Cambridge, MA: Harvard University Press.

National Institute for Clinical Excellence. (2004). Eating disorders: Core interventions in the treatment and management of AN, BN and related eating disorders. Retrieved from www.nice.org.uk/nicemedia/ pdf/CG9FullGuideline.pdf

Peebles, R., Hardy, K. K., Wilson, J. L., & Lock, J. D. (2010). Are diagnostic criteria for eating disorders markers of medical severity? *Pediatrics, 125* (5), e1193–e1201.

Pope, H. G., & Hudson, J. I. (1996). "Recovered memory" therapy for eating disorders: Implications of the Ramona verdict. *International Journal of Eating Disorders, 19*(2), 139–145.

Powers, P. S., & Cloak, N. L. (2012). Psychopharmacologic treatment of obesity and eating disorders in children and adolescents. *Child and Adolescent Psychiatric Clinics of North America, 21*(4), 831–859.

Qian, J., Hu, Q., Wan, Y., Li, T., Wu, M., Ren, Z., & Yu, D. (2013). Prevalence of eating disorders in the general population: A systematic review. *Shanghai Archives of Psychiatry, 25*(4), 212–223.

Rosen, D. S. (2010). Identification and management of eating disorders in children and adolescents. *Pediatrics, 126*(6), 1240–1253.

Rouleau, C. R., & von Ranson, K. M. (2011). Potential risks of pro-eating disorder websites. *Clinical Psychology Review, 31*(4), 525–531.

Smolak, L., & Murnen, S. K. (2001). Gender and eating problems. In R. H. Striegel-Moore & L. Smolak (eds.), *Eating disorders: Innovative directions in research and practice* (pp. 91–110). Washington, DC: American Psychological Association.

Stice, E., & Bohon, C. (2013). Eating disorders. In T. P. Beauchaine & S. P. Hinshaw (eds.), *Child and adolescent psychopathology* (pp. 715–738). Hoboken, NJ: John Wiley & Sons.

Stocks, J. T. (1998). Recovered memory therapy: A dubious practice technique. *Social Work, 43*(5), 423–436.

Striegel-Moore, R. H., Dohm, F. A., Kraemer, H. C., Taylor, C. B., Daniels, S., Crawford, P. B., & Schreiber, G. B. (2003). Eating disorders in White and Black women. *American Journal of Psychiatry, 160*(7), 1326–1331.

van den Heuvel, L. L., & Jordaan, G. P. (2014). The psychopharmacological management of eating disorders in children and adolescents. *Journal of Child and Adolescent Mental Health, 26*(2), 125–137.

Vanderlinden, J., & Vandereycken, W. (1988). The use of hypnotherapy in the treatment of eating disorders. *International Journal of Eating Disorders 7* (5), 673–679.

Vitousek, K., Watson, S., & Wilson, G. T. (1998). Enhancing motivation for change in treatment-resistant eating disorders. *Clinical Psychology Review, 18*(4), 391–420.

von Ranson, K. M., & Robinson, K. E. (2006). Who is providing what type of psychotherapy to eating disorder clients? A survey. *International Journal of Eating Disorders, 39*(1), 27–34.

Walcott, D. D., Pratt, H. D., & Patel, D. R. (2003). Adolescents and eating disorders: Gender, racial, ethnic, sociocultural, and socioeconomic issues. *Journal of Adolescent Research, 18*(3), 223–243.

Waller, G. (2012). The myths of motivation: Time for a fresh look at some received wisdom in the eating disorders? *International Journal of Eating Disorders, 45*(1), 1–16.

Waller, G., Cordery, H., Corstorphine, E., Hinrichsen, H., Lawson, R., Mountford, V., & Russell, K. (2007). *Cognitive behavioral therapy for eating disorders: A comprehensive treatment guide.* Cambridge: Cambridge University Press.

Wanden-Berghe, R. G., Sanz-Valero, J., & Wanden-Berghe, C. (2011). The application of mindfulness to eating disorders treatment: A systematic review. *Eating Disorders, 19*(1), 34–48.

Wardle, J., & Griffith, J. (2001). Socioeconomic status and weight control practices in British adults. *Journal of Epidemiology and Community Health, 55*(3), 185–190.

Wilfley, D. E., Kolko, R. P., & Kass, A. E. (2011). Cognitive-behavioral therapy for weight management and eating disorders in children and adolescents. *Child and Adolescent Psychiatric Clinics of North America, 20*(2), 271–285.

Wilksch, S. M. (2014). Where did universal eating disorder prevention go? *Eating Disorders, 22*, 184–192.

Wilson, G. T., Grillo, M., & Vitousek, K. M. (2007). Psychological treatment of eating disorders. *American Psychologist, 62*(3), 199–216.

Wilson, J. L., Peebles, R., Hardy, K. K., & Litt, I. F. (2006). Surfing for thinness: A pilot study of pro–eating disorder web site usage in adolescents with eating disorders. *Pediatrics, 118*(6), e1635–e1643.

15

Toileting

Michael I. Axelrod and Joseph P. Deegan

Historically speaking, toilet training, perhaps more than any other developmental task, has been plagued by pseudoscientific assertions. For example, Freud cautioned parents about training their children too early suggesting infant trauma resulting from negative toilet training experiences was a source of psychological defects in adulthood. While toilet training has been the recipient of many pseudoscientific claims, elimination disorders, such as bedwetting, have been met with perhaps even more nonscientific interpretations leading to outlandish and, in some cases, dangerous treatment approaches. This chapter addresses pseudoscientific conceptualizations, explanations, and recommendations for toilet training and the two most common child and adolescent elimination disorders, nocturnal enuresis (i.e., bedwetting) and encopresis (i.e., fecal soiling).

Though it is less often looked back upon with the same sentimental nostalgia as a child's first words or steps, successful toileting is a notable developmental milestone for both parents and children. Toilet training is generally defined as the mastering of skills necessary for independent urination and defecation in a manner consistent with social conventions (Kiddoo et al., 2006). Day and nighttime bladder and bowel control are markers of successful toilet training. Children who can engage in the independent task of toileting, from initially recognizing the physiological urges through washing hands when done, are said to be fully toilet trained. In the United States and many European countries, toilet training typically begins between 21 and 36 months of age (see Choby & Shefaa, 2008). As for successful toilet training, between 40% and 60% of all children achieve daytime bladder and bowel control by about 36 months of age (Blum, Taubman, & Nemeth, 2004). Of note, the general sequence for obtaining daytime and nighttime bladder and bowel control has differed across studies.

Failure to successfully achieve nighttime bladder control results in nocturnal enuresis (NE), defined as repeated voiding at night, accidental or on purpose, into clothing or the bed, at least twice a week for three consecutive months, in children older than age 5 (APA, 2013). The *Diagnostic and Statistical Manual of Mental Disorders,* 5th ed (DSM-5; APA, 2013) identifies two courses: primary and secondary. Primary enuresis includes children who have never achieved bladder control, while secondary enuresis develops after urinary continence has been established and typically emerges between ages 5 and 8. The spontaneous remission rate is between 5% and 10% per year (APA, 2013), suggesting some children achieve nighttime continence without ever receiving treatment.

NE is one of the most frequent and persistent childhood problems presented in primary care medicine. Prevalence data indicate that as many as 33% of five-year-old children meet criteria for NE, and approximately 25% of six-year-old boys and 15% of six-year-old girls wet the bed nightly or almost nightly (Byrd et al., 1996; Friman, 2008a). NE can continue into adolescence. At age 12, 8% of boys and 4% of girls still meet the diagnostic criteria for NE, and between 1% and 3% of adolescents still wet the bed (see Axelrod et al., 2014; Friman, 2008a).

Encopresis describes those individuals who have difficulty with control of the bowel. According to the DSM-5, encopresis involves the repeated passage of feces, voluntary or involuntary, in inappropriate places (e.g., clothing) at least once a month over at least three consecutive months for children with a chronological age of at least 4 years. While there are two primary courses of encopresis, retentive and nonretentive, the overwhelming majority (90%–95%) of those diagnosed have the retentive type (Friman, 2008b). The hallmark of retentive encopresis is a history of functional constipation. If left untreated, functional constipation may lead to fecal impaction (a condition in which the colon is so full of stool that peristalsis is inhibited) and eventually incontinence (referred to as retentive encopresis, or RE; Christopherson & Friman, 2010). The second course, nonretentive encopresis, involves encopresis either without a history of constipation or after having previously achieved fecal continence (APA, 2013).

Parents of children with encopresis often believe their child's condition is rare. The fact that encopresis is mentioned in the popular press only infrequently may contribute to this misconception (Christopherson & Mortweet 2001). However, encopresis is not an uncommon childhood problem. It is estimated that 4% of 4-year-old and 1.6% of 11- to 12-year-old children meet criteria for encopresis, with boys being three to six times more likely to present with the condition (Abi-Hanna & Lake, 1998; Christopherson & Friman, 2010; van der Wal, Benninga, &

Hirasing, 2005). Encopresis and constipation make up as many as 3% to 5% of primary care pediatric and 30% of pediatric gastroenterology referrals (Culbert & Banez, 2007; Loening-Baucke, 1993). Encopresis is especially problematic as it is far less likely than NE to remit with age, with as many as 64% of children continuing to experience symptoms into adolescence (Staiano et al., 1994; Sutphen et al., 1995).

15.1 Pseudoscience and Questionable Ideas

15.1.1 Toilet Training

Freud's Stages. Most pseudoscientific accounts of toilet training are rooted in Freud's stages of psychosocial development. The theory posits that children move through psychosexual stages associated with pleasure areas of the body (i.e., oral, anal, genital) and that virtually all aspects of personality are influenced by one's success or failure navigating related developmental challenges (Kalat, 2013). Accordingly, an individual becomes fixated or stuck at a stage when their development within that stage is impeded or disturbed. Freud's theory was taken to suggest that a toddler's experience with toilet training would profoundly impact his or her personality and the later development of psychological disorders (Hunt, 1979). For example, Anna Freud noted that harsh and regimented toilet training would require the toddler to use certain defense mechanisms (e.g., repression, aggression against self) that later manifested into symptoms consistent with obsessive-compulsive disorder (e.g., aversion to dirty hands, extremes in regularity and uniformity, repetitive behavior; Young-Bruehl, 2008). In sum, Freudian theory suggests problems with toilet training or any other early developmental task serve as a foundation for psychopathology.

Training's Influence on Personality. Freud's theory has helped promote the notion that one's personality is shaped, in part, by their toilet training experiences. This perspective suggests abnormal personalities are associated with unusual toilet training practices (e.g., early or overly harsh toilet training). Relating toilet training experiences to later adult personality characteristics has been used to justify discrimination and prejudice. For example, anthropologist Geoffrey Gorer, claiming to aid the allied war effort against Japan, suggested Japanese mothers' hasty attempts to toilet train infants were responsible for "the overwhelming brutality and sadism of the Japanese at war" (Gorer, 1943, quoted in Barnouw, 1963, p. 121). According to Gorer, repressed rage in the Japanese people resulted from early and strict cleanliness training associated with toileting habits (Barnouw, 1963). At approximately the same time, American anthropologist Weston Le Barre also implicated harsh toilet training experiences for why Japanese people were "the most compulsive in the world" (Barnouw, 1963, p. 122); Ruth Benedict, another American anthropologist, suggested the Japanese propensity toward cleanliness and predictability was a result of negative toilet training experiences (Harris, 2001). These theories were never supported by empirical research. In fact, research conducted after the war found Japanese children were rarely exposed to unusually harsh toilet training practices (see Harris, 2001).

Ineffective Practices. Freud's theory has also influenced parenting experts to recommend ineffective toilet training approaches. The famous pediatrician Dr. Benjamin Spock, in the 1940s, suggested a passive approach to toilet training, believing independent toileting would develop naturally (Ritblatt et al., 2003). He specifically stated, "the healthy child wants to master new skills, prefers to be clean, wants to wear grown-up clothes, likes to please and co-operate with his mother most of the time" (Spock & Bergen, 1964, p. 116). Spock's recommendation coincided with widespread use of washing machines and disposable undergarments, making this approach more sensible (Seim, 1989). Two decades later, Dr. T. Berry Brazelton, another well-known pediatrician, advised parents to follow their child's lead in determining when to begin toilet training (Ritblatt et al., 2003).

Many parents adopted Spock's and Brazelton's perspectives and, perhaps related, the mean age at which children are fully toilet trained has risen dramatically since the 1940s. Research indicates parental decision making regarding when to initiate toilet training is associated with delays in toilet training (Blum et al., 2004). That is, children who achieve independence later have parents who initiate the toilet training process later. Consequently, parental decisions to delay toileting training impact when children successfully achieve this developmental milestone. Parental beliefs about child readiness indicators (e.g., adequate motor skills to pull down/up pants), ineffective toilet training practices (e.g., inconsistency), and inappropriate responses to accidents (e.g., harsh punishment) are also associated with delays in successful toilet training (Ritblatt et al., 2003). Finally, extended use of disposable diapers may promote urinary incontinence and delay successful toilet training (Simon & Thompson, 2006).

Most interesting among these factors is the widespread use of non-evidence-based toilet training strategies including those that emphasize letting the child determine the training parameters (e.g., when to begin). Beginning toilet training too early or late or using ineffective toilet training methods might come at a cost to children and their parents. Stress in the family, parent-child conflict, stool withholding and dysfunctional voiding are potential consequences of failed toilet training (Lang, 2008; Ritblatt et al., 2003).

15.1.2 Nocturnal Enuresis

Psychodynamic Case Formulation. Like toilet training, most pseudoscientific conceptualizations of NE are rooted in a psychodynamic perspective, which proposes NE is a symptom of some underlying emotional disturbance rooted in abnormal psychosexual development (see Mishne, 1993). For example, psychodynamic formulations suggest NE is a form of displaced aggression against parents, suppressed masturbation, or regression to a safe and secure developmental period (i.e., infancy; Fenichel, 1945; Winnicott, 1953). Psychodynamic theorists have also characterized NE as a conflict between mother and child resulting in the child demanding their mother's love by "weeping through the bladder" (Imhof, 1956, cited by Butler, 1987, p. 29). Finally, Sperling (1965) suggested NE was a symptom of a disturbed personality. Specifically, she noted that children with NE were unable to endure instinctual and emotional distress, required immediate release of this distress, and demanded immediate gratification. According to Sperling (1965), NE was "the vehicle through which this discharge and gratification are achieved" (p. 28).

Developmental, Psychiatric, and Psychosomatic Themes. Interpretations of NE from developmental, psychiatric, and psychosomatic theories have also offered pseudoscientific conceptualizations. MacKeith (1972) suggested stress during a sensitive developmental period when bladder control emerges might lead to bedwetting. Stressful events during early childhood might include poor parent-child attachment and anxieties resulting from separation. Psychosomatic theory posits that elevated levels of anxiety affect bladder function and urinary continence. Werry (1967), observing anxiety may irritate the bladder, proposed that chronic anxiety could disturb the establishment of nighttime bladder control. Finally, a psychiatric framework for NE, borrowing from a psychodynamic position, suggests a relationship between urinary incontinence and emotional disturbances. Several authors have suggested NE is character-istic of significant psychopathology, including delinquency and social withdrawal (see Michaels & Steinberg, 1953; Sperling, 1965).

Psychodynamic Treatment. Questionable practices in treating NE often stem from psychodynamic conceptualizations. For example, psy-choanalysis works to reverse the suppressions, repressions, and dis-placements associated with bedwetting to achieve self-understanding and promote changes within the personality. An emphasis is also placed on the mother-child relationship, which is a source of the NE within a psychodynamic framework (Mishne, 1993). Finally, Sperling (1965) recommended treatment focus on teaching the child to con-trol their impulses and feelings (e.g., anxiety, resentment, sadness) without "discharging them immediately through urination, whether it be into the toilet or into the bed" (p. 29). Regarding treatment targets, psychodynamic approaches focus on these underlying causes of incontinence and strengthening the personality structure rather than symptom removal (i.e., bedwetting). Research on psychother-apy in general to treat NE has found it to be no more effective than no treatment (see Brown et al., 2008; Christopherson & Mortweet, 2001).

Chiropractic Manipulation, Hypnosis, and Acupuncture. Complementary and alternative medicine has proposed numerous interventions for NE. Chiropractic treatment, usually involving the correction of vertebral subluxations that are said to cause nerve interference and bedwetting, is widely espoused by the field as a proven cure (Ernst & Harkness, 2001). However, empirical evidence fails to support the claim that chiropractic care is an effective treatment. Ernst and Harkness (2001), in their review of the literature, described how those studies using rigorous methodologies found spinal manipulation fails to demonstrate clini-cally relevant reductions in bedwetting frequency. Hypnosis and acu-puncture have also been touted as effective treatments for NE. Hypnotism, characterized by intense concentration, extreme relaxa-tion, and high suggestibility, has been used to treat NE for many years (see Glazener, Evens, & Cheuk, 2005). Acupuncture, widely used in China as a treatment for NE, relies on suppression of spinal and supraspinal reflexes associated with bladder contraction via piercing specific body areas with fine needles (Zheng-tao Lv et al., 2015). However, neither of these treatments has been rigorously evaluated using sound experimental methods, and evidence for their effectiveness in treating NE is quite limited.

Diet. Diet and nutrition have also been implicated as causes of bladder irritability and urinary incontinence. For example, beverages containing caffeine have been shown to have a diuretic effect (Riesenhuber et al., 2006). Other findings suggest possible etiological associations between bladder activity and nutrients such as potassium, protein, and vitamin D. However, these findings have not been confirmed experimentally, and possible mechanisms to account for these associations require further study (Dallosso et al., 2004). Regarding specific dietary recommendations, most of the findings are anecdotal, and well-controlled empirical studies examining diet as a treatment for NE are sparse.

15.1.3 Encopresis

Psychodynamic Conceptualization. Encopresis has a history that is well rooted in the psychodynamic literature. For instance, psychodynamic theorists once largely held the opinion that complications during toilet training would create psychosexual tensions and inner conflict that seeded maladaptive personality characteristics (S. Freud, 1905/2000). The more specific etiologies proposed by these theorists are manifold; some early authors suggested a relationship between soiling and aggression, anal sexuality, jealousy, and punishment of parents (Morichaw-Beauchant, 1922). Fenichel (1945) and others described the origination of encopresis to be masturbatory, while another commonly espoused notion was that encopresis was the result of unresolved oedipal conflicts (A. Freud, 1963).

Psychogenic Etiology. As behaviorism increased in popularity throughout the twentieth century, it quickly began to take hold as a more appropriate lens with which to view encopresis. However, encopresis as having psychogenic causation was an idea already established; as a result, psychopathology has been linked to encopresis (Friman & Jones, 1998). Specifically, emotional and behavior problems and psychological variables (e.g., anxiety, defiance, poor parent-child relationship) have traditionally been implicated as causes of encopresis (Friman, 2008b). Finally, many believe encopresis to be an indicator of sexual abuse (Campbell, Cox, & Borowitz, 2009). However, there is no well-controlled research documenting such a relationship (Mellon, Whiteside, & Friedrich, 2006).

Talk Therapy. Talk therapy can be effective for other psychological problems, but, to date, no well-controlled studies have documented its effectiveness as the primary treatment for encopresis (Christopherson & Mortweet, 2001). Though it may be appropriate to consider psychotherapeutic treatment if other problems are interfering with the standard treatment approach (e.g., anxiety), there is a paucity of research demonstrating consistent behavioral problems in encopretic populations or supporting talk therapy as an efficacious first-line treatment (Christopherson & Friman, 2010). Moreover, failure to treat a child's constipation and fecal impaction, which is more likely when talk therapy is used by itself, may result in serious medical complications (e.g., bowel perforation, toxic megacolon).

Punishment. The terms "lazy," "purposeful," and "defiant" are often used to describe children with encopresis (Christopherson & Wassom, 2013). Although there is little evidence for its effectiveness, it should not be surprising, given these descriptors, that punishment is an often used practice (Christopherson & Mortweet, 2001). However, the extant literature indicates punishing incontinence may be contraindicated, as attempting to punish a behavior that is out of a child's volitional control is likely to have a negative effect. Specifically, the use of punishment is frequently associated with negative emotional reactions, avoidance of the punisher, and aggression, and aversive consequences are more likely to discourage, rather than encourage, a path toward continence (Robson & Leung, 1991). Further, in extreme cases, parents' unrealistic expectations paired with aversive treatment methodologies may even lead to child abuse (Krugman, 1985; Schmitt, 1987).

Pain Medications and Antidiarrheal Agents. Certain pharmacological interventions, namely pain medications and antidiarrheal agents, have a long-standing history, not just as pseudoscientific treatments for encopresis but also as treatments that may exacerbate already agonizing symptoms. Additionally, these approaches to treatment are especially notable in their need to be dispelled by the scientific literature because of their intuitive appeal. It fits logically that the child with extreme gastrointestinal discomfort be provided pain relief, which traditionally comes in the form of medication. However, many pain medications (and some anticonvulsants) actually relax the intestine, potentially worsening future constipation in lieu of immediate pain relief (Friman, 2008b).

In the case of antidiarrheal agents, it is first important to mention that the child who is having daily bowel movements but is not actually expelling all the waste matter from the rectum can gradually accumulate fecal matter in the colon to the point of impaction. So, simply because the child appears to be having bowel movements of some sort does not mean that they are not constipated. For instance, it is not uncommon for a child with encopresis to have frequent, small, pebbly stools or liquid feces that resembles diarrhea. Given this seemingly overactive bowel, it is not hard to imagine why antidiarrheal agents might be a parent's logical next step (see Christopherson & Mortweet, 2001). However, using such antidiarrheal agents might actually promote encopretic symptomology. The term "paradoxical diarrhea" has been coined to describe the seepage of feces around hard stool in the colon and rectum that the child has been unable to pass (Christopherson & Mortweet, 2001). The child may be presenting with seemingly uncontrollable diarrhea because his or her fecal impaction has risen to a level where liquid is the only way the colonic system can effectively expel feces. So, treating such fecal impaction with antidiarrheal agents is not likely to produce the intended effect of independent continence long term. Taken together, encopresis appears to primarily be an organic dysfunction of the bowel, and a survey of the available literature suggests that those interventions most likely to be successful are those that treat it as such.

Sidebar Box: Does self-acupressure work for constipation? by Harriet Hall

Constipation is a common complaint, affecting somewhere between 1% and 30% of children. It can sometimes be due to underlying diseases, but it is usually "functional," meaning the child is healthy but has difficulty defecating. Sometimes the stool is hard and difficult to pass, and sometimes a child is simply unwilling to defecate because of a previous painful bowel movement or other psychological factors. Functional constipation is usually treated with dietary changes, laxatives, and behavioral intervention.

A less conventional treatment is perineal acupressure, where the area between the scrotum or vagina and the anus is massaged. A randomized controlled study in adults in 2014 (Abbott et al., 2015) found that self-acupressure was effective for constipation, improving both bowel function and quality of life. Applying finger pressure to the perineum in intermittent pulses is supposed to break up the hard stool in the rectum, making it easier to pass. For females, using a finger in the vagina would probably work even better but might not be as readily accepted. This type of pressure is essentially a noninvasive method of disimpaction that has nothing to do with acupressure.

Acupressure purportedly uses the Ren 1 acupoint, an imaginary point on the perineum that is said to nourish "kidney yin," remediating an imbalance of energy in the kidney. Sticking needles in that spot is used in traditional acupuncture to treat everything from constipation and hemorrhoids to loss of consciousness, asphyxiation from drowning, and manic psychosis! Acupressure is a variant of acupuncture, a prescientific treatment system based on myths. Acupuncture has been extensively studied and found to be a theatrical placebo (Colquhoun & Novella, 2013).

So perineal "acupressure" stripped of the Oriental mumbo-jumbo is simply perineal massage or perhaps it would be better to call it transperineal fecal disimpaction. The study has not been replicated and the treatment has not been studied in children. Might it help? Possibly, since we know manual disimpaction (using a gloved finger in the rectum to break up the stool and scoop it out) is effective. But what if there is no hard stool in the rectum? In that case, the potential benefit seems much less likely. However, for adults, there is not an apparent downside to trying self-acupressure (or perineal massage); it is unlikely to cause any harm. For small children, it would be harder to justify. Having an adult massage a child's perineum for constipation has not been studied. Moreover, due to the connotations of touching that area, the acupressure option is more complicated. For more information about self-acupressure, see Hall (2014).

Harriet Hall, MD, is a retired family physician, co-editor of the Science Based Medicine blog, and co-author of the book *Women Aren't Supposed to Fly: The Memoirs of a Female Flight Surgeon* (2008).

15.2 Research-Supported Approaches

15.2.1 Toilet Training

Bladder and bowel control requires children to have prerequisite readiness skills, and most experts recommend these readiness skills be present prior to initiating toilet training (Choby & Shefaa, 2008). Readiness skills generally fall into the following categories: behavioral (child follows instructions and accepts parental decisions), cognitive (child understands urges are followed by trips to the bathroom), language (child uses words to indicate a need to urinate or defecate), and physical (child recognizes urges and has adequate motor skills to pull pants up and down). While the literature is clear that the presence of readiness skills is critical to successful toilet training, the lack of empirical research comparing different toilet training approaches complicates the landscape. What is currently known from the research is that methods employing positive reinforcement for successful toileting episodes are most effective (see Kiddoo et al., 2006). Specifically, successful toileting episodes are rewarded with positive parental attention and/or tangible items (e.g., stickers, candy, screen time). In addition to the use of positive reinforcement to increase the child's use of the toilet during elimination, many toilet training protocols call for the parent to instruct the child to sit briefly on the toilet multiple times across the day (e.g., 2–3 min on the toilet every 15 min or when the child is likely to urinate or have a bowel movement).

15.2.2 Nocturnal Enuresis

It is likely multiple etiologies play a role in NE, although combinations of causal variables might differ from child to child. The most common causal factors in the literature are genetics (i.e., family history), maturational delays (e.g., bone growth, build, secondary sex characteristics), and slowness to arouse (Fergusson, Horwood, & Sannon, 1986; von Gontard, Heron, & Joinson, 2011; Yeung, Diao, & Sreedhar, 2008). In addition, there are many possible pathophysiological explanations for NE such as urinary tract infections and diabetes (Friman, 2008a). Children with NE do not appear to be any different psychologically than their peers (Erdogen et al., 2008; Friman et al., 1998). Any relationship between enuresis and psychopathology might be associated with unique subject characteristics (i.e., older age, admission to specialized pediatric clinic; see Baeyens et al., 2005).

The urine alarm, a moisture sensitive device alerting the sleeping child they have urinated, is considered the most effective treatment for NE (Mellon & McGrath, 2000; Shepard, Poler, & Grabman, 2016). Moreover, the urine alarm has yielded the most successful long-term outcomes when compared to other treatments (Ahmed et al., 2013; Kiddoo, 2012). Finally, pairing the urine alarm with positive reinforcement for dry nights has been found to be effective for children who failed to achieve nighttime continence with the use of the alarm by itself (Axelrod et al., 2014). Pharmacological interventions (e.g., desmopressin, imipramine) are often physicians' first pass at treatment (Invie & Axelrod, 2011). However, research on the short- and long-term effectiveness of these medications for NE is mixed. Friman (2008a) recommended desmopressin be employed only as an adjunct should the urine alarm and positive reinforcement fail to produce positive outcomes, or if an immediate treatment response is needed.

15.2.3 Encopresis

In the overwhelming majority of cases (90%–95%), encopresis results from functional constipation. Chronic constipation typically results in fecal impaction (i.e., solid and immobile fecal matter), packing the colon and rectum tightly where the normal pushing action of the colon is insufficient to pass the stool (Christopherson & Friman, 2010). Children experiencing painful bowel movements because of fecal impaction are likely to avoid future bowel movements leading to stool toileting refusal (Friman, 2008a). Consequently, more stool accumulates in the colon and rectum, becoming even more dry and hard, and more difficult to pass. Described as learned-based resistance, this recurrent cycle makes the child more likely to avoid having bowel movements (Friman, 2008a). Children with constipation and fecal impaction may develop abnormal stretching and enlargement of muscles and nerves in the rectal area, which reduces the urge to have bowel movements, possibly weakens the internal sphincter, and affects the child's ability to voluntarily direct the external sphincter during defecation (Friman & Jones, 1998).

Like NE, empirical research fails to support a causal relationship between psychopathology and encopresis. In fact, the literature suggests that behavior problems might be more of a consequence, rather than a cause, of encopresis (Christopherson & Purvis, 2001). Large-scale analyses of norming populations across multiple standardized child-behavior rating scales have shown no systematic differences between children with encopresis and other children of the same age and gender (see Friman et al., 1988; Gabel et al., 1986; Loening-Baucke, Cruikshank, & Savage, 1987).

Regarding treatment, research has consistently identified medical intervention involving disimpaction of the colon and laxative therapy to increase and maintain bowel regularity plus behavioral interventions (e.g., teaching appropriate defecation dynamics, scheduling frequent and brief toilet sits, utilizing a reward system for successful toileting episodes) to be the most effective treatment (see Shepard et al., 2016). Laxative therapy alone is not likely to be enough to remedy encopresis. Short- and long-term improvement rates are higher for children receiving comprehensive treatment involving both medical and behavioral interventions (see Axelrod, Tornehl, & Fontanini-Axelrod, 2015). Moreover, behavioral interventions appear to reduce the duration children are on laxatives because of their constipation (see Axelrod et al., 2016). Several authors also recommend education and demystification of encopresis and cleanliness training (e.g., taking off soiled clothing, cleaning soiled skin, laundering soiled clothing) to encourage independence and add effort to fecal accidents without punishing the child's behavior (see Axelrod, Tornehl, & Fontanini-Axelrod, 2016).

15.3 Conclusion

Unsubstantiated assertions regarding toilet training and elimination disorders have been highlighted in this chapter. Toilet training, an important developmental milestone, and the two most common elimination disorders, NE and encopresis, have been besieged with pseudoscientific conceptualizations resulting in procedures and treatments that are ineffective and potentially harmful. Understanding readiness signs before toilet training, recognizing the role relevant physiology plays in the etiology of elimination disorders, and knowing the research on effective and ineffective intervention approaches should help parents and practitioners in conceptualizing the problems from an evidence-based perspective and support positive outcomes for children.

Works Cited in Sidebar

Abbott, R., Ayres, I., Hui, E., & Hui, K. K. (2015). Effect of perineal self-acupressure on constipation: A randomized controlled trial. *Journal of General Internal Medicine, 30*(4), 434–439.

Colquhoun, D., & Novella, S. P. (2013). Acupuncture is theatrical placebo. *Anesthesia & Analgesia, 116*(6), 1360–1363.

Hall, H. (2014). Study of "acupressure" for constipation. Retrieved from https://sciencebasedmedicine.org

References

Abi-Hanna, A., & Lake, A. M. (1998). Constipation and encopresis in childhood. *Pediatrics in Review, 19*, 23–31.

Ahmed, A. A., Amin, M. M., Ali, M. M., & Shalaby, E. A. (2013). Efficacy of an enuresis alarm, desmopressin, and combination therapy in the treatment of Saudi children with primary monosymptomatic nocturnal enuresis. *Korean Journal of Urology, 54*, 783–790.

American Psychiatric Association. (2013). *Diagnostic and statistical manual of mental disorders* 5th edn. Washington, DC: Author.

Axelrod, M. I., Tornehl, C., & Fontanini-Axelrod, A. (2014). Enhanced response using a multicomponent urine alarm treatment for nocturnal enuresis. *Journal for Specialists in Pediatric Nursing, 19,* 172–183.

Axelrod, M. I., Tornehl, M., & Fontanini-Axelrod, A. (2015). A review of encopresis for the school psychologist: Treatment considerations. *WSPA Sentinel, 14,* 22–24.

Axelrod, M. I., Tornehl, M., & Fontanini-Axelrod, A. (2016). Co-occurring autism and intellectual disability: A treatment for encopresis using a behavioral intervention plus laxative across settings. *Clinical Practice in Pediatric Psychology, 4,* 1–10.

Baeyens, D., Roeyers, H., Vande Walle, J., & Hoebeke, P. (2005). Behavioral problems and attention-deficit hyperactivity disorder in children with enuresis: A literature review. *European Journal of Paediatrics, 164,* 665–672.

Barnouw, V. (1963). *Culture and personality.* Homewood, IL: Dorsey Press.

Blum, N. J., Taubman, B., & Nemeth, N. (2004). Why is toilet training occurring at older ages? A study of factors associated with later training. *The Journal of Pediatrics,* 145, 107–111.

Butler, R. J. (1987). *Nocturnal enuresis: Psychological perspectives.* Bristol, UK: Wright.

Brown, R. T., Antonuccio, D., DuPaul, G. J., Fristad, M. A., King, C. A., Leslie, L. K. … & McCormick, G. (2008). *Childhood mental health disorders: Evidence base and contextual factors for psychosocial, psychopharmacological, and combined interventions.* Washington, DC: American Psychological Association.

Byrd, R. S., Weitzman, M., Lanphear, N. E., & Auinger, P. (1996). Bed-wetting in U.S. children: Epidemiology and related behavior problems. *Pediatrics, 98,* 414–419.

Campbell, L. K., Cox, D. J., & Borowitz, S. M. (2009). Elimination disorders: Enuresis and encopresis. In M. C. Roberts & R. G. Steele (eds.), *Handbook of pediatric psychology.* 4th edn (pp. 481–490). New York: Guilford Press.

Choby, B., & Shefaa, G. (2008, November). Toilet training. *American Family Physician, 78*(9), 1059–1064.

Christopherson, E. R., & Friman, P. C. (2010). *Elimination disorders in children and adolescents.* Cambridge, MA: Hogrefe Publishing.

Christopheron, E. R. & Mortweet, S. L. (2001) *Treatments that work with children: Empirically supported strategies for managing childhood problems.* Washington, DC: American Psychological Association.

Christopherson, E. R., & Purvis, P. C. (2001). Toileting problems in children. In C. E. Walker & M. C. Roberts (eds.), *Handbook of clinical child psychology*. 3rd edn (pp. 453–469). New York: Wiley.

Christopherson, E. R., & Wassom, M. (2013, Fall). Managing encopresis in the pediatric setting. *American Academy of Pediatrics: Section on Developmental and Behavioral Pediatrics Newsletter*. Retrieved from https://static1.squarespace.com/static/54e0cb17e4b033d521c72764/t/551bee f6e4b0e383d17166ac/1427894006898/ManagingEncopresisF2013.pdf

Culbert, T. P., & Banez, G. A. (2007). Integrative approaches to childhood constipation and encopresis. *Pediatric Clinics of North America, 54,* 927–947.

Dallosso, H. M., McGrother, C. W., Matthews, R. J., & Donaldson, M. K. (2004). Nutrient composition of the diet and the development of overactive bladder: A longitudinal study in women. *Neurourology and Urodynamics, 23,* 204–210.

Erdogen, A., Akkurt, II., Boettjer, N. K., Yurtseven, E., Can, G., & Kiran, S. (2008). Prevalence and behavioral correlates of enuresis in young children. *Journal of Paediatrics and Child Health, 44,* 297–301.

Ernst, E., & Harkness, E. (2001). Spinal manipulation: A systematic review of sham-controlled, double-blind, randomized clinical trials. *Journal of Pain and Symptom Management, 22,* 879–889.

Fenichel, O. (1945). *The psychoanalytic theory of neurosis*. New York: Norton.

Fergusson, D. M., Horwood, L. J., & Sannon, F. T. (1986). Factors related to the age of attainment of nocturnal bladder control: An 8-year longitudinal study. *Pediatrics, 78,* 884–890.

Freud, A. (1963). The concept of developmental lines. *Psychoanalytic Study of the Child, 18,* 245–265.

Freud, S. (2000). Three essays on the theory of sexuality (rev. edn). New York: Basic Books. (Original work published 1905)

Friman, P. C. (2008a). Evidence-based therapies for enuresis and encopresis. In R. G. Steele, T. D., Elkin, & M. C. Roberts (eds.), *Handbook of evidence-based therapies for children and adolescents: Bridging science and practice* (pp. 311–333). New York: Springer.

Friman, P. C. (2008b). Encopresis and enuresis. In M. Hersen & D. Reitman (eds.), *Handbook of psychological assessment, case conceptualization, and treatment*, vol. 2: *Children and adolescents* (pp. 589–621). Hoboken, NJ: Wiley.

Friman, P.C., Handwerk, M.L., Swearer, S.M., McGinnis, J.C., & Warzak, W.J. (1998). Do children with primary nocturnal enuresis have clinically signifi cant behavior problems? *Archives of Pediatric and Adolescent Medicine, 152,* 537-539.

Friman, P. C., & Jones, K. M. (1998). Elimination disorders in children. In T. S. Watson & F. M. Gresham (eds.), *Handbook of child behavior therapy* (pp. 239–260). New York: Plenum Press.

Friman, P. C., Mathews, J. R., Finney, J. W., Christopherson, E. R., & Leibowitz, M. (1988). Do children with encopresis have clinically significant behavior problems? *Pediatrics, 82*, 407–409.

Gabel, S., Hegedus, A. M., Wald, A., Chandra, R., & Chaponis, D. (1986). Prevalence of behavior problems and mental health utilization among encopretic children. *Journal of Developmental and Behavioral Pediatrics, 7*, 293–297.

Glazener, C. M., Evans, J. H., & Cheuk, D. K. (2005, April). Complementary and miscellaneous interventions for nocturnal enuresis in children. *Cochrane Database of Systematic Reviews*. doi:10.1002/14651858.CD005230

Harris, M. (2001). *The rise of anthropological theory: A history of theories of culture* (updated edn). Walnut Creek, CA: AltaMira Press.

Hunt, J. M. (1979). Psychological development: Early experience. *Annual Review of Psychology, 30*, 103–143.

Invie, B., & Axelrod, M. I. (2011). School psychologist as parent health resource: A review of nocturnal enuresis. *WSPA Sentinel, 11*, 22–24.

Kalat, J. W. (2013). *Introduction to psychology*. 10th edn. Belmont, CA: Wadsworth.

Kiddoo, D. A. (2012). Nocturnal enuresis. *Canadian Medical Association Journal, 184*, 908–911.

Kiddoo, D., Klassen, T. P., Lang, M. E., Friesen, C., Russell, K., Spooner, C., & Vandermeer, B. (2006). The effectiveness of different methods of toilet training for bowel and bladder control. *Evidence Report/Technical Assessment No. 147*. Prepared by the University of Alberta Evidence-based Practice Center, under contract number 290-02-0023.

Krugman, R. D. (1985). Fatal child abuse: Analysis of 24 cases. *Pediatrician, 12* (1), 68–72.

Lang, M. E. (2008). Among healthy children, what toilet-training strategy is most effective and prevents fewer adverse events (stool withholding and dysfunctional voiding)? Part B (Clinical commentary). *Paediatrics & Child Health, 13*, 203–204.

Launing-Baucke, V. (1993). Chronic constipation in children. *Gastroenterology, 105*, 1557–1564.

Loening-Baucke, V. A., Cruikshank, B., & Savage, C. (1987). Defecation dynamics and behavior profiles in encopretic children. *Pediatrics, 80*, 672–679.

MacKeith, R. C. (1972). Is maturation delay a frequent factor in the origins of primary nocturnal enuresis? *Developmental Medicine and Child Neurology, 14*, 217–223.

Mellon, M. M., & McGrath, M. L. (2000). Empirically supported treatments in pediatric psychology: Nocturnal enuresis. *Journal of Pediatric Psychology*, *25*, 193–214.

Mellon, M. W., Whiteside, S. P., & Friedrich, W. N. (2006). The relevance of fecal soiling as an indicator of child sexual abuse: A preliminary analysis. *Developmental and Behavioral Pediatrics*, *27*, 25–32.

Michaels, J. J., & Steinberg, A. (1953). Persistent enuresis and juvenile delinquency. *British Journal of Delinquency*, *3*, 114–123.

Mishne, J. M. (1993). Primary nocturnal enuresis: A psychodynamic clinical perspective. *Child and Adolescent Social Work Journal*, *10*, 469–495.

Morichaw-Beauchant, R. (1922). False incontinence in children. *Paris Medical*, *12*, 83.

Robson, W., & Leung, A. (1991). Advising parents on toilet training. *American Family Physician*, *44*(4), 1263–1266

Riesenhuber, A., Boehm, M., Posch, M., & Aufrict, C. (2006). Diuretic potential of energy drinks. *Amino Acids*, *31*, 81–83.

Ritblatt, S. N., Obegi, A. D., Hammons, B. S., Ganger, T. A., & Ganger, B. C. (2003). Parents' and child care professionals' toilet training attitudes and perspectives: A comparative analysis. *Journal of Research in Childhood Education*, *17*, 133–146.

Schimtt, B. D. (1987). Seven deadly sins of childhood: Advising parents about difficult developmental phases. *Child Abuse & Neglect*, *11*(3), 421–432.

Seim, H. C. (1989). Toilet training in first children. *Journal of Family Practice*, *29*, 633–636.

Shepard, J. A., Poler, J. E., & Grabman, J. H. (2016). Evidence-based psychosocial treatments for pediatric elimination disorders. *Journal of Clinical Child & Adolescent Psychology*. Advance online publication. http://dx .doi.org/10.1080/15374416.2016.1247356

Simon, J. L., & Thompson, R. H. (2006). The effects of undergarment type on urinary continence of toddlers. *Journal of Applied Behavior Analysis*, *39*, 363–368.

Sperling, M. (1965). Dynamic considerations and treatment of enuresis. *Journal of the American Academy of Child Psychiatry*, *4*, 19–31.

Spock, B., & Bergen, M. (1964). Parents' fear of conflict in toilet training. *Pediatrics*, *34*, 112–116.

Staiano, A., Andreotti, M. R., Greco, L., Basile, P., & Auricchio, S. (1994). Long-term follow-up of children with chronic idiopathic constipation. *Digestive Diseases and Sciences*, *39*, 561–564.

Sutphen, J. L., Borowitz, S. M., Hutchinson, R. L., & Cox, D. J. (1995). Long-term follow-up of medically treated childhood constipation. *Clinical Pediatrics*, *34*, 576–580.

van der Wal, M. F., Benninga, M. A., & Hirasing, R. A. (2005). The prevalence of encopresis in a multicultural population. *Journal of Pediatric Gastroenterology and Nutrition, 40*, 345–348.

von Gontard, A., Heron, J., & Joinson, C. (2011). Family history of nocturnal enuresis and urinary incontinence. *Journal of Urology, 185*, 2303–2307.

Werry, J. S. (1967). Enuresis – a psychosomatic entity? *Canadian Medical Association Journal, 97*, 319–327.

Winnicott, D. W. (1953). Transitional objects and transitional phenomena. *International Journal of Psychoanalysis, 34*, 89–97.

Yeung, C. K., Diao, M., & Sreedhar, B. (2008). Cortical arousal in children with severe enuresis. *New England Journal of Medicine, 358*, 2414–2415.

Young-Bruehl, E. (2008). *Anna Freud: A biography*. 2nd edn. New Haven, CT: Yale University Press.

Zheng-tao, L., Song, W., Wu, J., Yang, J., Wang, T., Wu, C. … & Gao, F. (2015, January). Efficacy of acupuncture in children with nocturnal enuresis: A systematic review and meta-analysis of randomized controlled trials. *Evidence-Based Complementary and Alternative Medicine*. doi:10.1155/2015/320701

16

Sleep

Stephanie Jackson and Sarah Morsbach Honaker

Throughout time, sleep has remained somewhat of an enigma. Sleep medicine is a relatively young specialty as medical disciplines go, and its practice was widely regarded as "experimental" until 1975. Despite the tremendous advances that have been made since Alfred Loomis identified the distinctive brain waves of non-REM sleep in 1937 (Shepard et al., 2005), science still has a great deal to learn about the complex physiology and pathology related to slumber. A degree of mystery surrounds the act of sleeping, and this fact lends itself well to propagating ideas, beliefs, and practices that are rooted in pseudoscience.

Insomnia is the most common sleep-related complaint in patients of all ages. It accounted for 5.5 million adult outpatient physician visits in 2010 (Ford et al., 2014) and impacts up to 30% of children and 3%–12% of adolescents, with higher prevalence rates in those with neurodevelopmental disorders, psychiatric conditions, or other chronic illnesses. Insomnia is defined as a persistent problem with falling asleep, staying asleep, remaining asleep long enough, and/or achieving quality sleep. This problem must occur despite adequate opportunity (differentiating insomnia from sleep deprivation) and adequate circumstances for sleep (i.e., sleeping environment is safe, quiet, and otherwise conducive to sleep). The problem must also lead to some daytime consequence (e.g., fatigue, impairment; Fricke-Oerkermann, 2007; ICSD-3, 2014).

Pseudoscientific attempts at curing insomnia have been described since antiquity. For example, ancient Egyptians are said to have written the name of an insomnia spirit on a laurel leaf to be placed under their mattress or pillow (Amulets for Health and Healing, n.d.). During the Middle Ages, drinking the gallbladder contents from a castrated boar was a go-to method for inducing sleep. Sea slug entrails were used in Japan and fried lettuce in France (Rodriguez McRobbie, 2009). Marijuana and alcohol have been used for hundreds of years, and opium from poppies is probably the oldest sleep medication known, used by both ancient Greeks and Egyptians (Kirsch, 2011). Warm milk, elderberry blossoms, iris, chamomile, hops, valerian, and catnip represent some of the less illicit therapeutic options, and settlers in early American colonies would eat raw onion to aid sleep (Carter, 1999; Wing, 2001).

The treatment goal when addressing insomnia is achieving an adequate total amount of restful sleep overnight, and age is the primary determinant of the amount of sleep the brain requires: A newborn infant typically needs 14–17 hours of sleep per 24-hour period, and toddlers generally require 11–14 hours. Preschool and school-age children require 10–13 and 9–12 hours of sleep per night, respectively, and adolescents require 8–10 hours of sleep (Paruthi et al., 2016). Most adults function well with 7–9 hours of sleep per night. When counseling parents of pediatric patients with sleep problems, one major factor is ensuring that expectations are appropriate for the child's age. Reassurance would be the only treatment indicated for a 10-year-old child who is "only" sleeping 10 hours per night, for instance – provided there is no daytime dysfunction.

16.1 Pseudoscience and Questionable Ideas

16.1.1 Diagnostic and Assessment Controversies

Before discussing the controversies, it will be helpful to briefly review a number of indices that are important for insomnia assessment and treatment (Carney et al., 2012). Sleep onset latency (SOL) is an estimate of the number of minutes from bedtime to sleep onset, with a SOL of greater than 30 minutes suggestive of a sleep onset difficulty. Wake after sleep onset (WASO) is a measure of the number of minutes awake after sleep onset and before the final awakening, calculated by summing the number of minutes awake at each awakening. Like SOL, a WASO of longer than 30 minutes is typically considered problematic. An important indicator of insomnia severity is sleep efficiency, which is calculated by dividing the total time asleep by the total time in bed. For example, an individual who goes to bed at 9 p.m., falls asleep at 10 p.m., is awake one hour during the night, wakes at 6 a.m., and gets out of bed at 7 a.m. would have a sleep efficiency of 70% (7 hours asleep/10 hours in bed). A sleep efficiency of 85% or less typically warrants intervention. These indices can be assessed using subjective (e.g., sleep diary) or objective (e.g., actigraphy, sleep study) measures of sleep. Actigraphy provides an objective estimate of sleep-wake patterns, measured via an accelerometer worn for an extended period of time (i.e., 1–2 weeks), and it has strong validation in pediatric populations (Meltzer et al., 2012). The sleep diary, a retrospective daily report of a child's sleep pattern, is also considered a useful clinical tool in the assessment and treatment of pediatric insomnia (Honaker & Meltzer, 2014).

Sleep Studies for Insomnia. Many patients and practitioners believe incorrectly that an overnight sleep study (polysomnogram) is a necessary and helpful tool when diagnosing insomnia. Polysomnography is indicated when there is concern for sleep-disordered breathing (e.g., sleep apnea, hypoventilation, sleep-related hypoxemia), parasomnia (e.g., sleepwalking, night terrors, REM-sleep behavior disorder), sleep-related movement disorder (e.g., periodic limb movements), nocturnal seizures, and narcolepsy or other causes of excessive daytime sleepiness. Of note, when evaluating narcolepsy or excessive daytime sleepiness, a mean sleep latency test (MSLT) is required in addition to overnight polysomnography. If the primary complaint is an inability to initiate or maintain sleep, an overnight sleep study is generally not useful and is not indicated unless the sleep disturbance is accompanied by symptoms suggestive of one of the previously mentioned conditions (Aurora et al., 2012). While polysomnography does yield indices that are often used to assess insomnia, such as SOL, WASO, and sleep efficiency, these indices often do not reflect "typical" sleep patterns, as the individual is sleeping in a novel environment. Additionally, a sleep study represents a single night of sleep, whereas an insomnia diagnosis requires a longer duration of symptoms.

Commercial Trackers. Commercial pedometer devices with sleep-tracking ability have risen in popularity in recent years. Several small studies have been done to assess the reliability of these trackers in identifying sleep problems. Meltzer et al. (2015) compared the FitBit Ultra to polysomnography in young people ages 3–17. In both the "normal" and "sensitive" modes, there were discrepancies in measurement of total sleep time, the amount of wake time during the night, and sleep efficiency. While in "normal" mode, total sleep time was overestimated by 41 minutes, and sleep efficiency by 8%. In "sensitive" mode, total sleep time was *under*estimated by more than 1.5 hours and sleep efficiency by 21%. Similar findings were observed when comparing the FitBit Ultra to two brands of medical-grade actigraphs (Meltzer et al., 2015). The SenseWear Pro3 Arbmand™ was compared to actigraphy and polysomnography in 20 adolescents (Roane et al., 2015). This device measures multiple variables to distinguish wakefulness from sleep, and there were no significant differences between the armband and polysomnography for any of the sleep parameters assessed. There were differences, however, in wake-after-sleep-onset time and sleep onset latency when the armband was compared to the actigraph. In other studies comparing commercial trackers (i.e., FitBit and Jawbone) with polysomnography, total sleep time and sleep efficiency were overestimated and wake time after sleep onset was underestimated (Evenson, Goto, & Furberg, 2015). In summary, commercially available sleep trackers are of limited value due to inaccuracy, and information from these devices should be interpreted cautiously.

16.1.2 Myths That Influence Treatment

Insomnia as Just a Symptom of Something Else. One common misconception is that insomnia is usually secondary to a psychiatric or pain condition, and once that condition is treated, the insomnia will resolve. This can lead to a delay in instituting proper treatment, which can result in poor outcomes for the patient. Sleep deprivation, which is present to varying degrees in 10%–40% of high school students, impairs emotional regulation, and an increase in suicidality is associated with the presence of sleep problems (Clarke & Harvey, 2012). The relationship between mood disorders and insomnia is complex, and insomnia has been shown to be a risk factor for recurrence of depressive episodes and possibly also an independent marker of eventual suicidal behavior in patients with depression (Bernert & Joiner, 2007). Breslau et al. (1996) found that young adults with insomnia, when compared to those without sleep complaints, were 16 times more likely to have major depression, 7 times more likely to have generalized anxiety disorder, and twice as likely to have drug or alcohol dependence in their lifetime, regardless of gender. When sleep disturbance was eliminated from the list of criteria used to diagnose major depression, a strong association was still seen: depression was present in 22% of patients reporting insomnia and in 37% of those reporting both hypersomnia and insomnia.

Studies examining depression treatment outcomes further highlight the complex relationship between insomnia and mood disorders. In adults, residual insomnia symptoms were present in almost half of those who responded to an antidepressant therapy for depression (Nierenberg et al., 1999). There is mounting evidence that combining depression treatment with treatment for insomnia significantly improves the efficacy of antidepressant therapy. A higher number of adolescent patients recovered from their depression when a youth-adapted cognitive-behavioral therapy for insomnia (CBT-I) program was incorporated into their treatment, and this recovery was more rapid than that experienced by those who did not receive specific insomnia-focused treatment (Clarke et al., 2015). When antidepressant medication (escitalopram) was partnered with a brief, symptom-focused CBT-I, remission rates were nearly twice as high as those in patients receiving escitalopram plus control therapy (Manber, 2008). In another study involving 166 adolescents with depressive disorder, 70% of the participants with ongoing depression or incomplete remission during the post-treatment analysis had persistent sleep disturbance, compared with only 2.6% of those who were in full remission (Manglick et al., 2013). Even gradual sleep extension with improved sleep hygiene (e.g., sleeping on a more regular schedule) has been shown to produce a decrease in depressive symptoms in adolescents with chronic sleep reduction (Dewald-Kaufmann, Oort, & Meijer, 2013). While young children with depression who were treated with fluoxetine had an opposite effect, Emslie and colleagues (2012) found that adolescents were less responsive to the selective serotonin reuptake inhibitor (SSRI) when substantial insomnia was present. (Emslie et al., 2012). Insomnia is inarguably linked to mood disorders but should be considered a separate treatable condition. Addressing sleep concerns while psychiatric therapy is underway and is recommended for optimal management. Emerging evidence suggests a similarly complex relationship between insomnia and pain conditions in pediatric populations, with pain predicting worse sleep, impaired sleep predicting higher next-day pain, and insomnia as a common residual symptom after addressing pain (Valrie et al., 2013).

Bed-Sharing. A fair amount of controversy has surrounded the issue of bed-sharing with young children. While the benefits of close parental contact are not generally disputed, there can be significant safety issues when infants (and particularly newborns) share a sleeping surface with another person. A 2012 meta-analysis published in the *Journal of Pediatrics* examined all major studies addressing the risk of sudden infant death syndrome (SIDS) and bed-sharing over a more than 20-year period. Every study included in that analysis found an increased risk of SIDS in infants who shared beds with their caregivers, particularly with parents who smoke. In babies younger than 3 months of age, the risk of SIDS was 10 times higher (Vennemann et al., 2012). For maximum safety, the American Academy of Pediatrics recommends that infants be placed on their backs on a firm sleeping surface. There is no disadvantage to using special crib mattresses that purport to reduce the chance of rebreathing carbon dioxide (as long as these mattresses meet safety standards); however, these will not reduce the risk of SIDS if infants are placed in the prone position. "Bedside sleepers," which attach to the side of the parental bed, may be a safe alternative, but there is not yet evidence that any variety of in-bed sleepers reduce the risk of SIDS or suffocation ("SIDS and other sleep-related infant deaths," 2016).

Ideas about bed-sharing vary by culture and type of household. It is suggested that between 40% and 80% of children in the United States co-sleep with their parents at some time (Ramos, 2003), and the prevalence of bed-sharing in China is >71% at 23 months, ~38% at age 5–6 years, and ~17% in early adolescents (Jiang, 2016). In Switzerland, 44% of toddlers and school-aged children share the bed with their parent at least once per week (Jenni, 2005). One important factor to take into consideration is whether or not the bed-sharing is reactive or intentional. Parents who choose to bed-share based on cultural or ideological reasons report fewer sleep complaints than those who bed-share in an attempt to alleviate their child's sleep problem (Ramos, 2003). In a study of more than 1,450 Chinese adolescents, children who shared the bed with their parents had a later bedtime and wake time than those who slept independently, but there was no difference in sleep duration. Bedtime resistance, sleep anxiety, and poor sleep quality were more frequent in the bed-sharers, as was daytime sleepiness. It is unclear if this latter finding was related to poorer quality of sleep in the bed-sharers, particularly since other studies have failed to show similar findings (Jiang, 2016). It is also unclear to what degree reactive bed-sharing may have played a role. In an 18-year longitudinal study of 205 Euro-American families in California, bed-sharing was not associated with sleep disturbance, sexual pathology, or any other problems, but it also did not confer any noticeable benefits (Blanchard & Vermilya, 2007; Okami, Weisner, & Olmstead, 2002). In sum, there is little evidence that bed-sharing between older children and their caregivers is problematic. Thus, decision making around bed-sharing with children older than 1 year of age is best considered a personal family decision based on individual beliefs and preferences.

Crib Bumpers. Crib bumpers were originally designed to prevent infants from getting their heads or limbs stuck in between the crib slats. However, since changes in safety regulation around the size of crib slats, these devices are no longer necessary. Further, bumper pads have been implicated as a contributory factor in several infant deaths (Scheers, Woodard, & Thach, 2016; Thach, Rutherford, & Harris, 2007). As a result, the American Academy of Pediatrics now recommends not using these devices in infant cribs (American Academy of Pediatrics, 2016; Lemons, 2003). Unfortunately, popular culture has been slow to follow, and these devices can still be readily purchased at many major baby retailers.

Commercial Devices to Prevent SIDS. In an effort to prevent SIDS, parents may be tempted to purchase devices that are marketed as SIDS monitors. These devices purportedly monitor infant breathing or heart rate and are designed to alarm for apnea (pauses in breathing) or bradycardia (slowing heart rate). However, there is no evidence to suggest that any of these devices reduce the risk of SIDS (American Academy of Pediatrics, 2016). Similar to crib bumpers, these devices are still readily available for purchase by parents.

Undermining Extinction-Based Interventions. Very young children with difficulty sleeping often exhibit symptoms of what was formerly known as behavioral insomnia of childhood. This condition can involve limit-setting issues and/or sleep onset association disorder, and infants and children affected by this tend to require parental presence to initiate and maintain sleep. Behavioral sleep intervention encompasses a variety of approaches used by parents to encourage an infant to fall asleep independently and self-soothe following night wakings, including unmodified extinction (sometimes referred to as "cry it out") and modified extinction approaches such as the Ferber method (Ferber, 2006; Morgenthaler et al., 2006). These approaches are highly efficacious in reducing infant and toddler night wakings, with support from multiple randomized controlled trials (Mindell et al., 2006). These approaches, which often involve infant crying, are controversial, and there are several misconceptions regarding this type of treatment that deserve clarification. Sleep-training programs have mixed evidence in children younger than 6 months of age (Crichton & Symon, 2016; Douglas & Hill, 2013; Kempler et al., 2016). Prior to that time, circadian rhythm functioning may not be fully developed, preventing the brain's ability to sleep through the night. Additionally, children younger than 6 months may still need to eat during the night, and some (though not all) behavioral sleep intervention approaches limit parental intervention throughout the night. Prior to 6 months, many providers instead advocate measures geared toward preventing maladaptive behaviors and encouraging self-soothing at bedtime (France & Blampied, 1999; Owens, France, & Wiggs, 1999).

Another common misperception is that behavioral sleep approaches involving crying are harmful for infants and may cause emotional or attachment difficulties. Critics of behavioral sleep intervention often cite studies describing long-term negative outcomes associated with crying in infants who suffer chronic neglect; however, we are not aware of any studies showing adverse infant outcomes associated with behavioral sleep intervention. In contrast, several scientific studies have found a lack of adverse outcomes in either the short term or up to five years later. In one randomized controlled trial, both graduated extinction and bedtime fading were found to improve sleep in infants aged 6–16 months, and neither technique was associated with elevated infant stress (as evidenced by cortisol level), emotional/behavioral problems, or impaired parent-infant attachment (Gradisar, 2016). Price and colleagues (2012) examined child and infant outcomes five years after behavioral sleep intervention and did not find any long-term effects, either positive or adverse. In sum, the evidence to date shows clear benefits to behavioral sleep intervention, and no adverse outcomes.

Sidebar Box: Do aliens abduct people while they are sleeping? by W. Blake Smith

Since the alleged alien abduction case of Betty and Barney Hill in September 1961, stories of people being abducted by aliens have become quite popular and have developed some very specific patterns. These stories often involve frightening accounts of people waking to find they are paralyzed and surrounded by entities they perceive as extraterrestrials. Movies like *Close Encounters of the Third Kind* and books like Whitley Strieber's *Communion* have provided a template for what these alleged alien abductions look like.

The good news is that there is no credible evidence that anyone is actually being taken by aliens to be experimented on. But that does not mean the people reporting it are lying. Several interesting psychological effects may be going on in these cases. First, for the sincere experiencer, the sensation of being paralyzed and sensing creatures, monsters, or evil intelligences is quite common and can be explained by a sleep condition called *sleep paralysis* (Blackmoore, 1998). When you have normal sleep, your body becomes paralyzed during your dream state, which is helpful to prevent you from acting out your dreams. But in sleep paralysis, something gets out of sync and your mind wakes up, yet your body is still paralyzed. People often report a heavy pressure on their chest and the inability to move – but it usually passes fairly quickly.

It is a frightening experience, but it is not dangerous, supernatural, paranormal, or extraterrestrial (Sagan, 1996).

The other effect going on in many alien abduction stories happens when therapists hypnotize victims and try to help them "recover" their memories. Such recovered memories are extremely unreliable, and it is possible that the hypnotist may be actually helping create *false memories*. Investigations have shown that the people performing these memory recovery sessions are likely helping to create or enhance the victim's memory with untrustworthy narratives that fit their interest in alien abductions (Clancy, 2009).

Modern physics and astronomy suggest that it is extremely unlikely that any aliens are actually visiting the Earth and conducting experiments, but for the sufferer of sleep paralysis or the victim of false memories, it could be very difficult to shake the belief that something very unusual has happened.

W. Blake Smith is the producer and co-host of *MonsterTalk*, a science show about monsters and official podcast of *Skeptic* magazine.

16.1.3 Alternative Treatment Approaches with Little to No Research Support

Weighted Blankets. Weighted blankets have been increasingly used to aid sleep, particularly in children with autism spectrum disorder and other developmental disorders. It has been postulated that the sensory input these blankets provide leads to decreased stress and a lower level of arousal, thus promoting better sleep; however, their therapeutic efficacy has yet to be substantiated (Creasey & Finlay, 2013). In a multicenter study involving 67 children aged 5–16 with autism spectrum disorder and chronic sleep disturbance, there was no significant difference between sleep onset latency, sleep efficiency, wake time after sleep onset, or total sleep time when weighted blankets were compared to control blankets (Gringras et al., 2014). Despite the lack of evidence supporting their objective value in improving children's sleep, weighted blankets are preferred by some children and caregivers. Improper use reportedly led to the death of one Canadian child (AETMIS Summary, 2009), and parents should thus be counseled regarding proper use, the presence of any contraindications, and the likelihood that the use of weighted blankets may not lead to any noticeable benefit.

Specialty Mattresses. The ideal sleeping space/mattress should certainly be comfortable, but whether or not the type of mattress has any impact on one's quality of sleep is debatable. One small study involving adult married couples did not reveal any differences in actigraphic sleep measures, self-reported sleep, or daytime symptoms when specially designed pressure-relief mattresses were compared to conventional mattresses (Mccall, Boggs, & Letton, 2012). There is at least one randomized crossover trial underway examining the effect of a novel Sound-To-Sleep mattress technology in children with autism and sleep difficulties (Frazier et al., 2017); however, data in this area is limited for children with insomnia, and this is a topic that may warrant further investigation.

Essential Oils and Aromatherapy. Essential oils are widely used to promote sleep, and several studies have investigated their effectiveness – many of which rely on self-report of sleep parameters. Self-reported sleep-quality measures should be interpreted cautiously, however, as these may not always reflect true sleep habits as accurately as more objective methods. In adults who underwent polysomnography, self-reported sleep times were overestimated (Silva et al., 2007), and comparisons of self-report with actigraphy have produced mixed results. Self-reports of average nightly sleep duration differed by 1.9 hours when compared to actigraphy in male adolescents (Guedes et al., 2016); in young adults with mental health problems, habitual sleep duration was *under*estimated by 30 minutes if they reported insomnia and *over*estimated by 1 hour in those without insomnia (Biddle et al., 2015).

Perhaps the most extensively studied oil is lavender, and weak evidence indicates that it may improve sleep. Lillehei et al. (2015) found that lavender combined with sleep hygiene, compared with sleep hygiene alone, led to improvements in *self-reported* sleep quality but not sleep quantity in college students with perceived sleep issues. Lavender was found to reduce crying and stress in newborn infants, with decreased cortisol levels found in both mothers and babies in one small study (Field et al., 2008); however, the mothers involved were noted to touch their infants more when the oil was used, a potential confounding factor. Several other small studies have shown weakly positive results with lavender use (e.g., Lewith, Godfrey, & Prescott, 2005). Inconsistent results, confounding factors, and incomplete knowledge of the exact mechanisms involved warrant caution before investing in aromatherapy.

16.2 Research-Supported Approaches

While many treatment approaches have limited or mixed effectiveness for pediatric insomnia, a wealth of evidence supports the efficacy of cognitive and behavioral approaches (Meltzer & Mindell, 2014). As noted earlier, extinction approaches are efficacious in infants and toddlers (Mindell et al., 2006). In older children and adolescents, a variety of packaged treatment interventions, including cognitive-behavioral therapy for insomnia, have demonstrated efficacy (Moore, 2012). Specific treatment components include sleep scheduling, conditioning sleepiness, stimulus control, effective parental limit-setting, addressing fears and worries, arousal reduction, and cognitive strategies to address maladaptive thoughts or beliefs about sleep (Puncochar & Honaker, 2018).

16.3 Conclusion

As sleep disruption is associated with multiple adverse outcomes and impacts a variety of comorbid conditions, timely and effective treatment of insomnia is imperative. Providing the best care for insomnia includes not only an understanding of evidence-based approaches but also a recognition of ineffective treatments as well as those with mixed efficacy. The consequences of utilizing treatment approaches without demonstrated efficacy range from mild (e.g., investing money in aromatherapy) to severe (e.g., child injury or death associated with an unsafe sleep environment). Another potential consequence is that the pursuit of an ineffective method can prevent or delay the implementation of a method with known efficacy. There is also variability in the extent to which pseudoscientific approaches have been studied in clinical trials; it is certainly possible that approaches that are not evidence-based to date could later have demonstrated efficacy once we develop a better understanding of the target users. Further, technological improvements in devices, such as commercial sleep trackers, could ultimately lead to better performance in sleep measurement. However, parents, individuals, and providers must make decisions based on the information that is available today and thus should pursue research-supported approaches to improve sleep.

Works Cited in Sidebar

Blackmore, S. (1998). Abduction by aliens or sleep paralysis? *Skeptical Inquirer*, *22*(3), 23–28.

Clancy, S. A. (2009). *Abducted: How people come to believe they were kidnapped by aliens*. Cambridge, MA: Harvard University Press.

Sagan, C. (1996). *The demon haunted world: Science as a candle in the dark*. New York: Random House.

References

AETMIS. Summary: Weighted blankets and vests: Safety, efficacy and issues related to their use in different intervention settings. 2009. Retrieved from www.inesss.qc.ca/fileadmin/doc/ AETMIS/Rapports/ServicesSociaux/ 2010_04_res_en.pdf

American Academy of Pediatrics. (2016). SIDS and other sleep-related infant deaths: Updated 2016 recommendations for a safe infant sleeping environment. *Pediatrics*, e20162938.

Amulets for Health and Healing. (n.d.). Retrieved from https://faculty .georgetown.edu/jod/apuleius/renberg/MEDICALAMULETS.HTML

Aurora, R. N., Lamm, C. I., Zak, R. S., Kristo, D. A., Bista, S. R., Rowley, J. A., & Casey, K. R. (2012). Practice parameters for the non-respiratory indications for polysomnography and multiple sleep latency testing for children. *Sleep*, *35*(11), 1467–1473. http://doi.org/10.5665/sleep.2190

Bernert, R. A., & Joiner, T. E. (2007). Sleep disturbances and suicide risk: A review of the literature. *Neuropsychiatric Disease and Treatment*, *3*(6), 735–743.

Biddle, D. J., Robillard, R., Hermens, D. F., Hickie, I. B., & Glozier, N. (2015). Accuracy of self-reported sleep parameters compared with actigraphy in young people with mental ill-health. *Sleep Health*, *1*(3), 214–220. doi:10.1016/j.sleh.2015.07.006

Blanchard, D. S., & Vermilya, H. L. (2007). Bedsharing: Toward a more holistic approach in research and practice. *Holistic Nursing Practice*, *21*(1), 19–25. doi:10.1097/00004650-200701000-00005

Breslau, N., Roth, T., Rosenthal, L., & Andreski, P. (1996). Sleep disturbance and psychiatric disorders: A longitudinal epidemiological study of young adults. *Biological Psychiatry*, *39*(6), 411–418. doi:10.1016/0006-3223(95) 00188-3

Carney, C. E., Buysse, D. J., Ancoli-Israel, S., Edinger, J. D., Krystal, A. D., Lichstein, K. L., & Morin, C. M. (2012). The consensus sleep diary: Standardizing prospective sleep self-monitoring. *Sleep*, *35*(2), 287–302. http://doi.org/10.5665/sleep.1642

Carter, A. J. (1999). Dwale: An anaesthetic from old England. *British Medical Journal, 319*(7225), 1623–1626.

Clarke, G., & Harvey, A. G. (2012). The complex role of sleep in adolescent depression. *Child and Adolescent Psychiatric Clinics of North America, 21* (2), 385–400. doi:10.1016/j.chc.2012.01.006

Clarke, G., Mcglinchey, E. L., Hein, K., Gullion, C. M., Dickerson, J. F., Leo, M. C., & Harvey, A. G. (2015). Cognitive-behavioral treatment of insomnia and depression in adolescents: A pilot randomized trial. *Behaviour Research and Therapy, 69,* 111–118. doi:10.1016/j.brat.2015.04.009

Creasey, N., & Finlay, F. (2013). Question 2: Do weighted blankets improve sleep in children with an autistic spectrum disorder? *Archives of Disease in Childhood, 98*(11), 919–920. doi:10.1136/archdischild-2013-305011

Crichton, G. E., & Symon, B. (2016). Behavioral management of sleep problems in infants under 6 months – what works? *Journal of Developmental & Behavioral Pediatrics, 37*(2), 164–171.

Dewald-Kaufmann, J., Oort, F., & Meijer, A. (2013). The effects of sleep extension and sleep hygiene advice on sleep and depressive symptoms in adolescents: A randomized controlled trial. *Journal of Child Psychology and Psychiatry, 55*(3), 273–283. doi:10.1111/jcpp.12157

Douglas, P. S., & Hill, P. S. (2013). Behavioral sleep interventions in the first six months of life do not improve outcomes for mothers or infants: A systematic review. *Journal of Developmental & Behavioral Pediatrics, 34*(7), 497–507.

Emslie, G. J., Kennard, B. D., Mayes, T. L., Nakonezny, P. A., Zhu, L., Tao, R. … & Croarkin, P. (2012). Insomnia moderates outcome of serotonin-selective reuptake inhibitor treatment in depressed youth. *Journal of Child and Adolescent Psychopharmacology, 22*(1), 21–28. doi:10.1089/cap.2011.0096

Evenson, K. R., Goto, M. M., & Furberg, R. D. (2015). Systematic review of the validity and reliability of consumer-wearable activity trackers. *The International Journal of Behavioral Nutrition and Physical Activity, 12,* 159. http://doi.org/10.1186/s12966-015-0314-1

Ferber R. (2006). *Solving your child's sleep problems: New, revised, and expanded edition*. New York: Fireside.

Field, T., Field, T., Cullen, C., Largie, S., Diego, M., Schanberg, S., & Kuhn, C. (2008). Lavender bath oil reduces stress and crying and enhances sleep in very young infants. *Early Human Development, 84*(6), 399–401. doi:10.1016/j.earlhumdev.2007.10.008

Ford, E. S., Wheaton, A. G., Cunningham, T. J., Giles, W. H., Chapman, D. P., & Croft, J. B. (2014). Trends in outpatient visits for insomnia, sleep apnea, and prescriptions for sleep medications among US adults: Findings from the National Ambulatory Medical Care Survey 1999–2010. *Sleep, 37*(8), 1283–1293. http://doi.org/10.5665/sleep.3914

France, K. G., & Blampied, N. M. (1999). Infant sleep disturbance: Description of a problem behaviour process. *Sleep Medicine Reviews 3*(4): 265–280.

Frazier, T. W., Krishna, J., Klingemier, E., Beukemann, M., Nawabit, R., & Ibrahim, S. (2017). A randomized, crossover trial of a novel sound-to-sleep mattress technology in children with autism and sleep difficulties. *Journal of Clinical Sleep Medicine, 13*(1), 95–104. doi:10.5664/jcsm.6398

Fricke-Oerkermann, L., Plück, J., Schredl, M., Heinz, K., Mitschke, A., Wiater, A., & Lehmkuhl, G. (2007). Prevalence and course of sleep problems in childhood. *Sleep, 30*(10), 1371–1377.

Gradisar, M., Jackson, K., Spurrier, N. J., Gibson, J., Whitham, J., Williams, A. S. … & Kennaway, D. J. (2016). Behavioral interventions for infant sleep problems: A randomized controlled trial. *Pediatrics, 137*(6). doi:10.1542/peds.2015-1486

Gringras, P., Green, D., Wright, B., Rush, C., Sparrowhawk, M., Pratt, K. … & Wiggs, L. (2014). Weighted blankets and sleep in autistic children – a randomized controlled trial. *Pediatrics, 134*(2), 298–306. doi:10.1542/peds.2013-4285

Guedes, L. G., Abreu, G. D., Rodrigues, D. F., Teixeira, L. R., Luiz, R. R., & Bloch, K. V. (2016). Comparison between self-reported sleep duration and actigraphy among adolescents: Gender differences. *Revista Brasileira de Epidemiologia, 19*(2), 339–347. doi:10.1590/1980-5497201600020011

Honaker, S. M., & Meltzer, L. J. (2014). Bedtime problems and night wakings in young children: An update of the evidence. Paediatric Respiratory Reviews. http://doi.org/10.1016/j.prrv.2014.04.011

International Classification of Sleep Disorders. (2014). S.l.: American Academy of Sleep Medicine.

Jenni, O. G. (2005). A longitudinal study of bed sharing and sleep problems among Swiss children in the first 10 years of life. *Pediatrics, 115*(1), 233–240. doi:10.1542/peds.2004-0815e

Jiang, Y., Chen, W., Spruyt, K., Sun, W., Wang, Y., Li, S. … & Jiang, F. (2016). Bed-sharing and related factors in early adolescents. *Sleep Medicine, 17*, 75–80. doi:10.1016/j.sleep.2015.08.022

Kempler, L., Sharpe, L., Miller, C. B., & Bartlett, D. J. (2016). Do psychosocial sleep interventions improve infant sleep or maternal mood in the postnatal period? A systematic review and meta-analysis of randomised controlled trials. *Sleep Medicine Reviews, 29*, 15–22. http://doi.org/10.1016/j.smrv.2015.08.002

Kirsch, D. B. (2011). There and back again. *Chest, 139*(4), 939–946. doi:10.1378/chest.10-1235

Lemons, J. A. (2003). Apnea, sudden infant death syndrome, and home monitoring. *Pediatrics, 111*(4 Pt 1), 914–917. Retrieved from http://www.ncbi.nlm.nih.gov/pubmed/12671135

Lewith, G. T., Godfrey, A. D., & Prescott, P. (2005). A single-blinded, randomized pilot study evaluating the aroma of Lavandula augustifolia as a treatment for mild insomnia. *The Journal of Alternative and Complementary Medicine, 11*(4), 631–637. doi:10.1089/acm.2005.11.631

Lillehei, A. S., Halcón, L. L., Savik, K., & Reis, R. (2015). Effect of inhaled lavender and sleep hygiene on self-reported sleep issues: A randomized controlled trial. *The Journal of Alternative and Complementary Medicine, 21*(7), 430–438. doi:10.1089/acm.2014.0327

Manber, R., Edinger, J. D., Gress, J. L., San Pedro-Salcedo, M. G., Kuo, T. F., & Kalista, T. (2008). Cognitive behavioral therapy for insomnia enhances depression outcome in patients with comorbid major depressive disorder and insomnia. *Sleep, 31*(4), 489–495.

Manglick, M., Rajaratnam, S. M., Taffe, J., Tonge, B., & Melvin, G. (2013). Persistent sleep disturbance is associated with treatment response in adolescents with depression. *Australian & New Zealand Journal of Psychiatry, 47*(6), 556–563. doi:10.1177/0004867413481630

Mccall, W. V., Boggs, N., & Letton, A. (2012). Changes in sleep and wake in response to different sleeping surfaces: A pilot study. *Applied Ergonomics, 43*(2), 386–391. doi:10.1016/j.apergo.2011.06.012

Meltzer, L. J., Hiruma, L. S., Avis, K., Montgomery-Downs, H., & Valentin, J. (2015). Comparison of a commercial accelerometer with polysomnography and actigraphy in children and adolescents. *Sleep, 38*(8) 1323–1330. doi:10.5665/sleep.4918

Meltzer, L. J., & Mindell, J. A. (2014). Systematic review and meta-analysis of behavioral interventions for pediatric insomnia. *Journal of Pediatric Psychology, 39*(8), 932–948. http://doi.org/10.1093/jpepsy/jsu041

Meltzer, L. J., Montgomery-Downs, H. E., Insana, S. P., & Walsh, C. M. (2012). Use of actigraphy for assessment in pediatric sleep research. *Sleep Medicine Reviews, 16*(5), 463–475. http://doi.org/10.1016/j.smrv.2011.10.002

Mindell, J. A., Kuhn, B., Lewin, D. S., Meltzer, L. J., & Sadeh, A. (2006). Behavioral treatment of bedtime problems and night wakings in infants and young children. *Sleep, 29*(10), 1263–1276. Retrieved from www.ncbi.nlm.nih.gov/entrez/query.fcgi?cmd=Retrieve&db=PubMed&dopt=Citation&list_uids=17068979

Moore, M. (2012). Behavioral sleep problems in children and adolescents. *Journal of Clinical Psychology in Medical Settings, 19*(1), 77–83. http://doi.org/10.1007/s10880-011-9282-z

Morgenthaler, T. I., Owens, J., Alessi, C., Boehlecke, B., Brown, T. M., Coleman, J. ... Swick, T. J. (2006) Practice parameters for behavioral treatment of bedtime problems and night wakings in infants and young children. *SLEEP*, *29*(10), 1277–1281.

Nierenberg, A. A., Keefe, B. R., Leslie, V. C., Alpert, J. E., Pava, J. A., Worthington, J. J. . . . & Fava, M. (1999). Residual symptoms in depressed patients who respond acutely to fluoxetine. *Journal of Clinical Psychiatry*, *60*(4), 221–225. http://doi.org/10.4088/JCP.v60n0403

Okami, P., Weisner, T., & Olmstead, R. (2002). Outcome correlates of parent-child bedsharing: An eighteen-year longitudinal study. *Journal of Developmental & Behavioral Pediatrics*, *23*(4), 244–253. doi:10.1097/00004703-200208000-00009

Owens, L. J., France, K. G., & Wiggs, L. (1999). REVIEW ARTICLE: Behavioural and cognitive-behavioural interventions for sleep disorders in infants and children: A review. *Sleep Medicine Reviews*, *3*(4), 281–302. doi:10.1053/smrv.1999.0082

Paruthi, S., Brooks, L. J., D'ambrosio, C., Hall, W. A., Kotagal, S., Lloyd, R. M. . . . & Wise, M. S. (2016). Recommended amount of sleep for pediatric populations: A consensus statement of the American Academy of Sleep Medicine. *Journal of Clinical Sleep Medicine*, *12*(6), 785–786. doi:10.5664/jcsm.5866

Price, A. M., Wake, M., Ukoumunne, O. C., & Hiscock, H. (2012). Five-year follow-up of harms and benefits of behavioral infant sleep intervention: Randomized trial. *Pediatrics*, *130*(4), 643–651. http://doi.org/10.1542/peds.2011-3467

Punocochar, B. D., & Honaker, S. M. (2018). Sleep. In S. Hupp (ed.), *Child and adolescent psychotherapy: Components of evidence-based treatments for youth and their parents*. Cambridge: Cambridge University Press.

Ramos, K. (2003). Intentional versus reactive cosleeping. *Sleep Research Online*, *5*(4), 141–147.

Roane, B. M., Van Reen, E., Hart, C. N., Wing, R., & Carskadon, M. A. (2015). Estimating sleep from multisensory armband measurements: Validity and reliability in teens. *Journal of Sleep Research*, *24*, 714–721. doi:10.1111/jsr.12317

Rodriguez McRobbie, L. (2009, March 20). Fried lettuce, slug entrails and other insomnia cures. Retrieved from http://mentalfloss.com/article/21307/fried-lettuce-slug-entrails-and-other-insomnia-cures

Scheers, N., Woodard, D. W., & Thach, B. T. (2016). Crib bumpers continue to cause infant deaths: A need for a new preventive approach. *Journal of Pediatrics*, *169*, 93–97e1. http://doi.org/10.1016/j.jpeds.2015.10.050

Shepard, J. W., Buysse, D. J., Chesson, A. L., Dement, W. C., Goldberg, R., Guilleminault, C. . . . & White, D. P. (2005). History of the development of sleep medicine in the United States. *Journal of Clinical Sleep Medicine*, *1*(1), 61–82.

SIDS and other sleep-related infant deaths: Updated 2016 recommendations for a safe infant sleeping environment. (2016). *Pediatrics, 138*(5). doi:10.1542/peds.2016-2938

Silva, G. E., Goodwin, J. L., Sherrill, D. L., Arnold, J. L., Bootzin, R. R., Smith, T. ... & Quan, S. F. (2007). Relationship between reported and measured sleep times: The Sleep Heart Health Study (SHHS). *Journal of Clinical Sleep Medicine, 3*(6), 622–630.

Thach, B. T., Rutherford, G. W., & Harris, K. (2007). Deaths and injuries Attributed to infant crib bumper pads. *Journal of Pediatrics, 151*(3). http://doi.org/10.1016/j.jpeds.2007.04.028

Valrie, C. R., Bromberg, M. H., Palermo, T., & Schanberg, L. E. (2013). A systematic review of sleep in pediatric pain populations. *Journal of Developmental and Behavioral Pediatrics, 34*(2), 120–128. http://doi.org/10.1097/DBP.0b013e31827d5848

Vennemann, M. M., Hense, H., Bajanowski, T., Blair, P. S., Complojer, C., Moon, R. Y., & Kiechl-Kohlendorfer, U. (2012). Bed sharing and the risk of sudden infant death syndrome: Can we resolve the debate? *The Journal of Pediatrics, 160*(1). doi:10.1016/j.jpeds.2011.06.052

Wing, Y. (2001). Herbal treatment of insomnia. *Hong Kong Medical Journal, 7,* 392–402.

17

Disruptive Behavior and Conduct

*Jeremy Jewell, Madison Schoen, Sydney Thompson,
Emily Fischer, and Sarah Conoyer*

Disruptive behavior disorders such as oppositional defiant disorder
(ODD) and conduct disorder (CD) are currently some of the most
prevalent disorders in childhood and adolescence. One study concluded
that the 12-month prevalence of ODD was 8.3%, while the 12-month
prevalence of CD was 5.4% (Kessler et al., 2012). Symptoms of ODD
include frequent defiance of authority, arguing, and displays of anger
(American Psychiatric Association, 2013). Youth diagnosed with ODD
often have difficulty getting along with peers and adults and typically
exhibit significant behavior problems in both the classroom and at home.
CD tends to be a more severe disorder and symptoms include aggression
toward others, theft or destruction of property, and the serious violation
of rules. Symptoms of CD can vary widely regarding their focus on harm
to self or others. For example, some symptoms that include rule breaking
(e.g., truancy) do not directly harm others, while other symptoms (e.g.,
being physically cruel) reflect a danger to others. Additionally, the
severity of CD symptoms varies widely with some symptoms being less
severe (e.g., staying out at night beyond curfew) compared to other more
severe symptoms (e.g., using a weapon in a fight). Both ODD and CD
appear to be more prevalent in males than females, and the average age
of onset in CD is typically later than that of ODD (APA, 2013).

Juvenile delinquency is also highly relevant to these disorders. While
ODD and CD are psychiatric diagnoses, juvenile delinquency is best
defined as the state a youth enters when he or she commits a crime, is
arrested, and becomes court involved. Data regarding total crimes from
the Office of Juvenile Justice and Delinquency Prevention indicates that
there were 2,751 arrests of minors aged 10 to 17 per 100,000 minors in the
year 2015 (OJJDP, 2017). Additionally, this data shows that arrests of
males were more than double those of females. A study using self-report
data from the National Longitudinal Survey of Youth found that the
cumulative arrest rate by age 18 was between approximately 16% and
27% (Brame et al., 2012). Of course many youth may be arrested once

and then are deterred from committing crimes in the future, while first arrest for some other youth may predict a lifetime characterized by criminal involvement and incarcerations.

> **Sidebar Box: Is lying always a sign of psychological problems? by Robert S. Feldman**
>
> American society certainly seeks to promote honesty. Consider national icons like George Washington, who is recalled as never telling a lie, or Abe Lincoln, whose nickname is Honest Abe. More recently, consider the negative reaction to modern-day presidents when they get caught lying. Our concerns about the act of lying go even further: persistent lying is seen as symptomatic of a considerable number of psychological disorders, including oppositional defiant disorder (i.e., falsely blaming others) and conduct disorder (i.e., lies for own benefit).
>
> Yet if we look at decades of psychological research, the realities about lying and deception are quite different. In fact, lying is not only ubiquitous, but studies also suggest that lying is actually a social skill that promotes effective interaction with others. Consider evidence from a study that I conducted with children and early adolescents. In it, my colleagues and I found that as children grew into adolescents, they became more effective liars – that is, it was harder to detect deception in children as they got older, a finding that has been confirmed by a considerable body of research. But what was particularly intriguing was that the greater the deception skills of adolescents, the better were their social skills, as judged by their teachers and parents. In other words, the most socially skilled adolescents were also the ones who were most effective liars (Feldman, 2010; Lavoie et al., 2017; Talwar & Lee, 2008).
>
> Although one extreme interpretation of this finding is that lying somehow makes you popular, that seems unlikely. More probable is that socially competent adolescents may understand better the value of providing supportive but not necessarily accurate information ("you did a great job on that class presentation"), or they know when to withhold information that is unwelcome to others, potentially because it is hurtful ("you seem to be putting on weight").
>
> Coupled with findings that lying is frequent in everyday life (on average, lies occur at a rate of around three lies in ten minutes

during interactions between those who are meeting for the first time; Feldman, Forrest, & Happ, 2002), these results suggest that lies per se are not a good indicant of psychological disorder. Indeed, one could argue the opposite: that lying, at least in moderation, is a sign of psychological health.

Robert S. Feldman, PhD, is Senior Advisor to the Chancellor and Professor of Psychological and Brain Sciences at the University of Massachusetts Amherst. He is author of the book *The Liar in Your Life: The Way to Truthful Relationships* (2010).

17.1 Pseudoscience and Questionable Ideas

17.1.1 Harmful Therapeutic Practices

Scared Straight and Similar Programs. The Scared Straight program, as well as other similar programs, seeks to expose delinquent or at-risk youth to adult prisoners who are currently incarcerated to supposedly allow these youth to hear and see for themselves the consequences of their actions if they continue to pursue a criminal path. Scared Straight programs were first introduced to the public in a 1978 documentary of the same name (Shapiro, 1978). This original film documented an intervention program held by the "Lifers" at a New Jersey prison. In this original film, which won the Best Documentary Academy Award in 1979, these adult prisoners are shown berating, intimidating, and verbally threatening a group of at-risk teens. In the decades since this original production, Scared Straight programs have cropped up across the nation. Relatedly, this original documentary has evolved into a hit television series titled *Beyond Scared Straight* (Shapiro, 2011). To help the reader understand the nature of these programs, it is helpful to examine a diatribe in *Beyond Scared Straight* where an adult inmate screams the following at an at-risk youth:

You think you're a tough motherf***** right? I'll stick my foot so far up you're a** you'll be able to taste my shoelaces ... I like mother****** like you, you're pretty to me, man ... I'll be all up in you're a** boy. I'll sell (you) to somebody ... you're gonna be somebodies b****. (Season 4, episode 6, *Beyond Scared Straight*)

While this rage-filled monologue is certainly offensive and distasteful to most, the aims of this program are intuitive to many as well. Specifically, many parents of delinquent youth, court personnel, and police may believe that giving these youth a "taste of what's to come" will discourage them from future crime. But while the program itself appears to be simple, straightforward, and intuitive, results of nine high-quality research studies on the effectiveness of Scared Straight programs are shocking themselves. Specifically, a 2005 review by Petrosino and colleagues found that participants in these programs were on average 1.6 to 1.7 times more likely to criminally reoffend compared to a control group (Petrosino, Turpin-Petrosino, & Buehler, 2005). Another more recent review of these programs was conducted by Petrosino as a follow-up to the original 2005 review. This follow-up review found that no new randomized trials have been conducted on Scared Straight or similar programs and again concluded that these programs were harmful to the youth (Petrosino et al, 2013). Because of the strong evidence regarding the harmfulness of this type of program, the Coalition for Juvenile Justice and the National Council of Juvenile and Family Court Judges have condemned the *Beyond Scared Straight* program as ineffective and misleading (Hupp & Jewell, 2015). Additionally, in a 2011 editorial, Laurie O. Robinson (assistant attorney general for the federal Office of Justice Programs) and Jeff Slowikowski (acting administrator of the federal Office of Juvenile Justice and Delinquency Prevention) wrote, "Scared Straight is not only ineffective but is potentially harmful. And it may run counter to the law" (Robinson & Slowikowski, 2011). Specifically, these programs likely violate the Juvenile Justice and Delinquency Prevention Act of 1974 that prohibits any minor from having "sight or sound" contact with the general adult inmate population. In short, while Scared Straight programs may be popularly appealing and intuitive, there seems no doubt that they actually *increase* rather than decrease criminality in offenders.

Catharsis and Primal Scream Therapy. The idea of catharsis was first described by Aristotle who believed that viewing dramatic plays evoked strong emotions in the audience and provided a beneficial emotional cleansing (Halliwell, 1987). Thousands of years later, Sigmund Freud took Aristotle's idea further, developing what has been known as the hydraulic theory of emotion. The premise of this theory is that emotions are like a physical fluid that if constrained can damage a human being but if released or "vented" can prevent damage to one's psychological self. The phrase "don't bottle up your anger" comes directly from this theory and can be found throughout the media for the past several decades. The therapy technique that is the result of this theory is the cathartic expression of emotion, anger more specifically as it relates to the topic of this chapter.

One of the most notorious of these therapies is Primal Scream Therapy, which swept the nation in the 1970s. This therapy was created by Arthur Janov as a way to cure various types of mental illness. The tenet of the therapy is that painful childhood events cause existing mental illness, and the primary means of therapy involves accessing the unconscious and extracting the emotions and physical feelings of painful memories to the surface by literally screaming and thrashing on the floor (Janov, 1970). Janov's book, *Primal Scream* (1970), was read and promoted by Mick Jagger and John Lennon, who both went through the treatment and praised its effectiveness (Kaufmann, 1974). In fact, John Lennon's first solo album called *Plastic Ono Band* was highly influenced by his experience with Primal Scream Therapy (Hall, 2012). However, while this therapy gained a great deal of attention in the popular press, researchers agree that no scientific studies published have established the efficacy of the treatment (Lohr et al., 2007). Some researchers question the premise of the therapy itself. For example, Beyerstein (2001) notes that the therapy is founded on the idea that individuals are processing emotions that they were unable to feel in their childhood due to the immaturity of their brains. Beyerstein adds, however, that "our understanding of neural development makes such claims extremely unlikely" (Beyerstein, 2001, p. 77). Another study using a panel of 101 expert mental health professionals polled their familiarity with various treatments and their opinion regarding their credibility. The study found that 94% of the sample were familiar with Primal Scream Therapy, and their ratings showed it to be "certainly discredited" (Norcross, Koocher, & Garofalo, 2006).

While Primal Scream Therapy has been promoted as a therapy for many types of mental illness, general catharsis techniques have been promoted as a way to alleviate anger as well. For example, ideas like thinking of someone who angers you while punching a pillow have been promoted in self-help books such as *Facing the Fire: Experiencing and Expressing Anger Appropriately* (Lee, 1993) as well as by other mental health professionals (Bushman, Baumeister, & Stack, 1999). However, cathartic techniques meant to decrease anger have actually been shown to be ineffective or even increase anger in a number of experimental studies. For example, in a relatively large study of undergraduate college students, Bushman (2002) experimentally evoked anger and then gave the participants different instructions to cope with this anger. Bushman found that participants who were told to punch a punching bag while thinking of what had made them angry were afterward more angry and more aggressive in comparison to participants in the control group who were told to just sit quietly after becoming angered. In the words of the author, "The results from the present research show that venting to reduce anger is like using gasoline to put out a fire – it only feeds the flame" (Bushman, 2002, p. 729). Cathartic techniques were also found to be either ineffective or harmful in a review of studies that examined these techniques with the authors stating, "A review of pertinent research leads to the recommendation that catharsis be abandoned as a therapeutic tool" (Lewis & Bucher, 1992, p. 385). Overall, these cathartic techniques appear to be harmful instead of helpful.

17.1.2 Other Unsupported Approaches

Boot Camps. Boot camps, also known as correctional boot camps or shock incarceration, are correctional treatment settings that are styled after military basic training experiences. They often require participants to dress in uniform, occur in an isolated environment, emphasize physical activity as a therapeutic treatment, and provide interaction with supervising treatment providers in a similar manner to that of a military superior. Boot camps first originated in 1983 in Georgia and Oklahoma, and they expanded throughout the United States in the 1980s and 1990s, (McKenzie, Wilson, & Kider, 2001). Therapeutic elements and treatments that may be provided to juveniles in boot camps vary widely. For example, while some boot camps offer very limited therapeutic treatment, others may offer substance abuse treatment, different psychotherapies, and aftercare to support reentry into the community. Given the relative few characteristics that seem to define boot camps, as well as the high amount of variability in treatment components, research into the effectiveness of boot camps is difficult to interpret.

One of the first systematic meta-analyses examining the effects of boot camps on participant recidivism was conducted by McKenzie et al. (2001). These authors identified 29 existing studies on the effectiveness of boot camps and 44 unique samples that compared boot camp participants to comparison groups. The authors concluded that boot camp participants were equally likely to reoffend compared to comparison groups. More specifically, these authors found that boot camp participants had lower recidivism rates than comparison groups in nine studies but higher recidivism rates than comparison groups in eight studies, with the remaining samples showing no difference between the two groups. The authors also went on to examine whether particular program characteristics could predict a greater impact on recidivism in boot camp participants, and they found that no program characteristics of juvenile boot camps impacted program effectiveness. The inability of boot camps to impact participant recidivism has been reaffirmed in two more recent reviews as well (Mead & Steiner 2010; Wilson, McKenzie, & Mitchell 2008).

Animal-Assisted Therapy (AAT). Researchers have been interested in the effects animals have on humans as early as Sigmund Freud, who believed that dogs could help his patients relax during sessions (McKenzie, 2012). The popularity of using animals in therapy grew in the 1960s when Boris Levinson, a child psychologist, released his book titled *Pet-Oriented Child Psychotherapy*, in which he discussed the benefits a pet can have on therapy clients (Kruger & Serpell, 2006). Animal-Assisted Therapy (AAT) has been most commonly used with dogs, horses, and dolphins, while less commonly used with cats, rabbits, birds, guinea pigs, and even cows.

As AAT has continued to become more prevalent, its effectiveness has come into question. When reviewing the literature on the value of AAT, the overall quality of the research literature is poor. For example, a recent review on equine-assisted therapy found that many of the existing studies on the topic did not utilize a control group and none of the studies used random assignment (Anestis et al., 2014). Another recent review listed common flaws in AAT studies, which included a lack of standardized treatment manuals, among many others (Herzog, 2014). Another important consideration regarding AAT is whether this therapy produces long-term psychological symptom change as opposed to short-term mood change such as pleasure due to the novelty of the situation (Lilienfeld & Arkowitz, 2008). These issues are important in evaluating the effectiveness and clinical value of AAT (for a review of one type of AAT, see Marino & Lilienfeld, 2007).

While a poll suggests that animal programs are available to incarcerated juveniles or adults in 38 states in the United States (Furst, 2006), there is a surprising lack of research on the topic of AAT for juvenile delinquency. In fact, a review of the current literature did not produce a single high-quality study that used AAT for juvenile delinquency or for youth with conduct disorder with a sample of sufficient statistical size, employing random assignment and utilizing a control group. The most relevant study found was by Jasperson (2013), who compared the effectiveness of adding a therapy dog to a psychoeducation treatment group for adult female inmates. Results of the study indicated that the addition of the therapy dog did not increase the effectiveness of the treatment program (Jasperson, 2013). Thus, little scientifically valid data currently reflects the value of AAT.

17.1.3 Undermining Components of Research-Supported Approaches

Undermining Rewards. Over the years, many people have expressed concerns around whether or not rewards actually motivate children to improve or engage in activities. This debate commenced in the 1970s with a surge of experiments investigating the impact of external rewards on intrinsic motivation with various populations ranging from preschool children to college students (Deci, 1971; Greene, Sternberg, & Lepper, 1976; Lepper et al. 1973). To the present day, multiple experiments have investigated whether or not rewards have any impact on intrinsic motivation to actually complete a preferred task. The majority of these studies include the claim that rewards are the cause of a decline in intrinsic motivation; however, as noted by Holmes (2016) many of these experiments contain nonsignificant results or lack true control groups. Holmes also noted that despite the fact that these studies do not adequately support this idea, there has still been little research to support or deny these claims and the early flawed studies are often still cited to perpetuate the notion that rewards are ineffective.

In the area of education, rewards are described as "systems for reinforcement" and considered evidence-based strategies for teachers to employ given the right context and functional analysis of behavior. Furthermore, a What Works Clearinghouse practice guide on reducing problem behavior in elementary schools recommends programs that incorporate teaching appropriate behaviors and then rewarding students when those behaviors are exhibited (Epstein et al., 2008). Such a strategy is providing tangible rewards when first teaching a new behavior or skill to assist in providing external feedback to increase the appropriate behavior. For example, Positive Behavioral Intervention Supports (PBIS) systems emphasize the use of tangible tokens or reinforcement. However, the goal is that as students become more fluent in behaviors, these tangible rewards are not as necessary as students begin to rely more on environmental or self-managed feedback (Sugai & Simonsen, 2012). In addition, PBIS systems provide rewards as a form of social acknowledgement (Warren et al., 2006). At times this may be in the form of a privilege, such as adolescents having the opportunity to park in the faculty parking lot for a week.

Overall, rewards are commonly used in evidence-based approaches to changing behavior. Undermining rewards discourages the use of an evidence-based approach.

Undermining Praise. Praising children has often been controversial in nature, with critics fearing that praise will spoil children or make them feel that they are entitled. For example, Raeburn (2012) wrote an article titled "Why It's a Bad Idea to Praise Children," arguing that praise is an ineffective form of control. However, research suggests that spontaneous praise given by parents at home when children were between 14 and 38 months significantly predicted several traits in children by age 7 or 8. These traits include a preference for challenging tasks, the attribution of success and failure to effort, and the willingness to generate strategies for improvement. This research shows that parental praise can endow children with the confidence and tools for success later in life (Gunderson et al., 2013).

Another study compared the effects of labeled and unlabeled praise and time-out on preschool children's ability to correctly participate in a choice-discrimination task. The children were divided into a labeled group and an unlabeled group. Children in the labeled praise group received labeled praise for making the right decision and labeled time-outs for making the wrong decision. Children in the unlabeled group received general praise for making the correct decision, and were put in time-out for making the incorrect decision. Researchers found the children who received labeled praise and labeled time-outs were significantly more likely to make the right choice when compared to the children who received unlabeled praise and unlabeled time-outs (Bernhardt, Fredricks, & Forbachs, 1978).

Moreover, praise is typically a primary component to evidence-based approaches for treating behavior problems in children (Garland, 2018). Thus, Raeburn's (2012) suggestion that "any praise – 'is a bad thing,'" really misses the mark.

Undermining Time-Out. Time-out is a discipline strategy that removes children from opportunities to earn positive reinforcement for a certain period of time (Kostewicz, 2010). Many educators and even parents use time-out as a discipline approach. Some of their reasons for using time-out include increases in compliance and decreases in disruptive and oppositional behaviors (Morawaska & Sanders, 2011). However, like rewards and praise, some people describe time-out as being ineffective.

For example, Rosemond (2012, p. 202) said, "time-out is not a generally effective consequence, especially with highly defiant children" (see Hupp & Jewell, 2015, for further discussion of undermining time-out).

Research, on the other hand, shows that time-out is indeed effective at helping to change behavior. For example, one study reviewed the potential effects time-out can have on a child's behavior in the home setting (Morawaska & Sanders, 2011). This study showed that the implementation of time-out, as part of a behavior management plan, reduced behaviors such as aggression and noncompliance. Another study focused on the effects of time-out in the classroom setting (Fabiano et al., 2004). Compared to the control group, results showed that time-out conditions were better at reducing aggression, destruction of property, and noncompliance. Another study focused on the potential effect of verbal instructions to go to time-out (Donaldson et al., 2013). With six preschool-aged male participants, results showed that time-out was effective in reducing disruptive behaviors, such as tantrums, and increasing compliant behaviors.

Many other studies contribute to the notion that time-out is a primary component to evidence-based approaches (Garland, 2018). Thus, suggesting that time-out is too weak to be effective neglects a large research base.

17.2 Research-Supported Approaches

While ODD, CD, and juvenile delinquency are all prevalent and incur significant financial and human costs to society, several treatments have been shown to be effective. These treatments can be implemented in an out-of-home placement, can include behavioral parent training while the youth remains in the home, or can be delivered individually to the youth to increase their emotional coping and social skills. Evidence-based treatments (EBTs) that can be implemented in out-of-home placements include Multidimensional Treatment Foster Care (MTFC), which consists of multiple components that include behavioral parent training for foster parents, skills training for the youth, school-based behavioral interventions, and more. Studies have shown that MTFC is effective at reducing recidivism using a variety of measures (Chamberlain, Leve, & DeGarmo, 2007; Chamberlain & Reid, 1998). If the youth remains in the home, behavioral parent training programs such as the Positive Parenting Program (Triple P; Prinz et al., 2009) or Functional Family Therapy (Sexton & Turner, 2010) can be effective. Other approaches and treatments delivered solely to the youth include Aggression

Replacement Training (ART), which teaches youth to cope with anger and build prosocial skills. ART has been found to increase social skills and moral reasoning and decrease problem behavior in participants (Gundersen & Svartdal, 2006). Another similar program, the Relaxation Skills Violence Prevention (RSVP) that teaches relaxation skills such as deep breathing and guided imagery was found to decrease stress and anger and increase coping in detained youth (Jewell & Elliff, 2013). Finally, some approaches that allow the youth to rejoin their broader community have been found to be effective as well. For example, Community Based Mentoring seeks to connect at-risk youth to prosocial adults in their community to provide positive role models and build relationships with others. An evaluation of a Community Based Mentoring program found that alcohol and drug initiation, truancy, parent relationships, peer relationships, and a number of personality variables were all positively impacted by participation in the program compared to a waitlist control group (Tierney, Grossman, & Resch, 2000). See Garland (2018) for components of EBTs.

17.3 Conclusion

While ODD and CD continue to be two of the most prevalent psychiatric disorders diagnosed in youth, pseudoscientific treatments as well as commonly used treatments lacking empirical support continue to be frequently employed. Perhaps more disturbingly, some of these treatments are not only ineffective but actually cause significant harm to those they are intended to treat. For example, Scared Straight and similar programs have consistently been shown to increase participants' likelihood of reoffending. Similarly, therapeutic techniques that involve catharsis, or the venting of one's anger, have been experimentally shown to actually increase rather than decrease anger. Military-style boot camps are also frequently employed both locally and at the state level to rehabilitate court-involved youth. However, decades of research have also shown that these interventions in general do not have any effect on participants. Additionally, other treatments such as AAT, while popular, have had little to no well-designed research conducted on their effectiveness. Given that all therapy, and especially AAT, requires significant investments in both time and money, future research regarding the effectiveness of these relatively untested therapies is critically needed. On the other hand, numerous options for treatments have gained significant empirical support. These EBTs can be employed in a number of contexts including out-of-home placement, in the home with the entire family, and within an individual therapy context. Further research that continues to differentiate between treatments that are effective and ineffective is still needed.

Works Cited in Sidebar

Feldman, R. S. (2010). *The liar in your life: The way to truthful relationships*. New York: Twelve/Hachette.

Feldman, R. S., Forrest, J. A., & Happ, B. H. (2002). Self-presentation and verbal deception: Do self-presenters lie more? *Basic and Applied Social Psychology, 24(2)*, 163–170.

Lavoie, J., Yachison, S., Crossman, A., & Talwar, V. (2017). Polite, instrumental, and dual liars: Relation to children's developing social skills and cognitive ability. *International Journal of Behavioral Development, 41(2)*, 257–264.

Talwar, V., & Lee, K. (2008). Little liars: Origins of verbal deception in children. In S. Itakura & K. Fujita (eds.), *Origins of the social mind: Evolutionary and developmental views* (pp. 157–178). New York: Springer.

References

American Psychiatric Association. (2013). *Diagnostic and statistical manual of mental disorders (DSM-5®)*. Arlington, VA: American Psychiatric Association Publishers.

Anestis, M. D., Anestis, J. C., Zawilinski, L. L., Hopkins, T. A., & Lilienfeld, S. O. (2014). Equine-related treatments for mental disorders lack empirical support: A systematic review of empirical investigations. *Journal of Clinical Psychology, 70(12)*, 1115–1132.

Bernhardt, A. J., Fredericks, S., & Frobach, G. B. (1978). Comparison of effects of labeled and unlabeled praise and time-out upon children's discrimination learning. *Psychological Reports, 42(3)*, 771–776.

Beyerstein, B. L. (2001). Fringe psychotherapies: The public at risk. *The Scientific Review of Alternative Medicine, 5(2)*, 70–79.

Brame, R., Turner, M. G., Paternoster, R., & Bushway, S. D. (2012). Cumulative prevalence of arrest from ages 8 to 23 in a national sample. *Pediatrics, 129(1)*, 21–27.

Bushman, B. J. (2002). Does venting anger feed or extinguish the flame? Catharsis, rumination, distraction, anger, and aggressive responding. *Personality and Social Psychology Bulletin, 28(6)*, 724–731.

Bushman, B. J., Baumeister, R. F., & Stack, A. D. (1999). Catharsis, aggression, and persuasive influence: Self-fulfilling or self-defeating prophecies? *Journal of Personality and Social Psychology, 76*(3), 367.

Chamberlain, P., Leve, L. D., & DeGarmo, D. S. (2007). Multidimensional treatment foster care for girls in the juvenile justice system: 2-year follow-up of a randomized clinical trial. *Journal of Consulting and Clinical Psychology, 75*(1), 187.

Chamberlain, P., & Reid, J. B. (1998). Comparison of two community alternatives to incarceration for chronic juvenile offenders. *Journal of Consulting and Clinical Psychology, 66*(4), 624.

Deci, E. L. (1971). Effects of externally mediated rewards on intrinsic motivation. *Journal of* Personality *and Social Psychology, 18*(1), 105.

Donaldson, J. M., Vollmer, T. R., Yakich, T. M., & Van Camp, C. (2013). Effects of a reduced time-out interval on compliance with the time-out instruction. *Journal of Applied Behavior Analysis, 46*, 369–378. doi: 10.1002/jaba.40

Epstein, M., Atkins, M., Cullinan, D., Kutash, K., & Weaver, R. (2008). Reducing behavior problems in the elementary school classroom: A practice guide (NCEE #2008–012). Washington, DC: National Center for Education Evaluation and Regional Assistance, Institute of Education Sciences, U. S. Department of Education. Retrieved from http://ies.ed.gov/ncee/wwc/publications/practiceguides

Fabiano, G. A., Pelham, W. E., Manos, M. J., Gnagy, E. M., Chronis, A. M., Onyango, A. N. ... & Swain, S. (2004). An evaluation of three time-out procedures for children with attention/deficit hyperactivity disorder. *Behavior Therapy, 35*, 449–469. doi: 10.1016/S0005-7894(04)80027-3

Furst, G. (2006). Prison-based animal programs: A national survey. *The Prison Journal, 86*(4), 407–430.

Garland, A. (2018). Disruptive behavior and conduct. In S. Hupp (ed.), *Child and adolescent psychotherapy: Evidence-based treatment components for youth and their parents*. Cambridge: Cambridge University Press.

Greene, D., Sternberg, B., & Lepper, M. R. (1976). Overjustification in a token economy. *Journal of Personality and Social Psychology, 34*(6), 1219.

Gunderson, E. A., Gripshover, S. J., Romero, C., Dweck, C. S., Goldin-Meadow, S., & Levine, S. C. (2013). Parent praise to 1-to-3 year olds predicts children's motivational frameworks 5 years later. *Child Development, 84*(5), 1526–1541.

Gundersen, K., & Svartdal, F. (2006). Aggression replacement training in Norway: Outcome evaluation of 11 Norwegian student projects. *Scandinavian Journal of Educational Research, 50*(1), 63–81.

Hall, R. (2012, February 20). *Primal scream: The trauma behind John Lennon's brilliant Plastic Ono Band*. Retrieved from www.gibson.com/News-Lifestyle/Features/en-us/john-lennon-0220-2012.aspx

Halliwell, S. (ed.). (1987). *The Poetics of Aristotle:* Translation *and commentary*. Chapel Hill: University of North CarolinaPress.

Herzog, H. (2014). Does animal-assisted therapy really work? *Psychology Today*. Retrieved from www.psychologytoday.com/blog/animals-and-us/201411/does-animal-assisted-therapy-really-work

Holmes, J. D. (2016). *Great myths of education and learning*. Hoboken, NJ: John Wiley & Sons. doi: 10.1002/9781118760499.ch5

Hupp, S., & Jewell, J. (2015). *Great myths of child development*. Hoboken, NJ: John Wiley & Sons.

Janov, A. (1970). *The primal scream*. Crystal Lake, IL: Delta Publishing.

Jasperson, R. A. (2013). An animal-assisted therapy intervention with female inmates. *Anthrozoös, 26*(1), 135–145.

Jewell, J. D., & Elliff, S. J. (2013). An investigation of the effectiveness of the Relaxation Skills Violence Prevention (RSVP) program with juvenile detainees. *Criminal* Justice *and* Behavior, *40*(2), 203–213.

Kaufmann, W. (1974). An anatomy of the primal revolution. *Journal of Humanistic Psychology, 14*(4), 49–62.

Kessler, R. C., Avenevoli, S., Costello, E. J., Georgiades, K., Green, J. G., Gruber, M. J. … & Sampson, N. A. (2012). Prevalence, persistence, and sociodemographic correlates of DSM-IV disorders in the National Comorbidity Survey Replication Adolescent Supplement. *Archives of General Psychiatry, 69*(4), 372–380.

Kostewicz, D. E. (2010). A review of time-out ribbons. *Behavior Analysis: Research and Practice, 11*, 95–104. doi: 10.1037/h0100693

Kruger, K. A., & Serpell, J. A. (2006). Animal-assisted interventions in mental health: Definitions and theoretical foundations. In A. H. Fine (ed.), *Handbook on animal-assisted therapy: Theoretical foundations and guidelines for practice* (pp. 21–38). Cambridge, MA: Academic Press.

Lee, J. (1993). *Facing the fire: Experiencing and expressing anger appropriately*. New York: Bantam.

Lepper, M. R., Greene, D., & Nisbett, R. E. (1973). Undermining children's intrinsic interest with extrinsic reward: A test of the "overjustification" hypothesis. *Journal of Personality and social Psychology, 28*(1), 129.

Lewis, W. A., & Bucher, A. M. (1992). Anger, catharsis, the reformulated frustration-aggression hypothesis, and health consequences. *Psychotherapy: Theory, Research, Practice, Training, 29*(3), 385.

Lilienfeld, S., & Arkowitz, H. (2008). Is animal assisted therapy really the cat's meow? *Scientific American*. Retrieved from www.scientificamerican.com/article/is-animal-assisted therapy/

Lohr, J. M., Olatunji, B O., Baumeister, R. F., & Bashman, B. J. (2007). The psychology of anger venting and empirically supported alternatives that do no harm. *Scientific Review of Mental Health Practice, 5*(1), 53–64.

MacKenzie, D. L., Wilson, D. B., & Kider, S. B. (2001). Effects of correctional boot camps on offending. *The Annals of the American Academy of Political and Social Science, 578*(1), 126–143.

Marino, L., & Lilienfeld, S. O. (2007). Dolphin-assisted therapy: More flawed data and more flawed conclusions. *Anthrozoös, 20*(3), 239–249.

McKenzie, S. (2012). Roll over Freud: Rise of animal therapy. Retrieved from www.cnn.com/2012/11/30/sport/equine-horse-therapy-mental-health/index.html

Meade, B., & Steiner, B. (2010). The total effects of boot camps that house juveniles: A systematic review of the evidence. *Journal of Criminal Justice, 38*(5), 841–853.

Morawaska, A., & Sanders, M. (2011). Parental use of time out revisited: A useful or harmful parenting strategy? *Journal of Child and Family Studies, 20*, 1–8. doi: 10.1007/s10826-010-9371-x

Nimer, J., & Lundahl, B. (2007). Animal-assisted therapy: A meta-analysis. *Anthrozoös, 20*(3), 225–238.

Norcross, J. C., Koocher, G. P., & Garofalo, A. (2006). Discredited psychological treatments and tests: A Delphi poll. *Professional Psychology: Research and Practice, 37*(5), 515–522.

OJJDP statistical briefing book (2017, March 27). Retrieved from, www.ojjdp.gov/ojstatbb/crime/JAR_Display.asp?ID=qa05200

Petrosino, A., Turpin-Petrosino, C., & Buehler, J. (2005). Scared Straight and other juvenile awareness programs for preventing juvenile delinquency. *The Scientific Review of Mental Health Practice, 4(1)*, 48–54.

Petrosino, A., Turpin-Petrosino, C., Hollis-Peel, M. E., & Lavenberg, J. G. (2013). "Scared Straight" and other juvenile awareness programs for preventing juvenile delinquency. *Cochrane Database of Systematic Reviews, 4.* doi: 10.1002/14651858.CD002796.pub2

Prinz, R. J., Sanders, M. R., Shapiro, C. J., Whitaker, D. J., & Lutzker, J. R. (2009). Population-Based Prevention of Child Maltreatment: The U.S. Triple P System Population Trial. *Prevention Science, 10*, 1–12.

Raeburn, P. (2012). Why it's a bad idea to praise children. Retrieved from www.psychologytoday.com

Robinson, L., & Slowikowski, J. (2011, January 31). Scary – and ineffective. Retrieved from http://articles.baltimoresun.com/2011–01-31/news/bs-ed-scared-straight-20110131_1_straight-type-programs-straight-program-youths

Rosemond, J. (2012). Parent-*babble: How parents can recover from fifty years of bad expert advice.* Kansas City, MO: Andrews McMeel Publishing, LLC.

Sexton, T. L., & Turner, C. W. 2010. The effectiveness of functional family therapy for youth with behavioral problems in a community practice setting. *Journal of Family Psychology, 24(3)*, 339–348.

Shapiro, A. (Producer). (2011). *Beyond Scared Straight* [Television series]. A&E TV.

Shapiro, A. (Producer). (1978). *Scared Straight!* [Documentary]. New Video Group.

Sugai, G., & Simonsen, B. (2012). Positive behavioral interventions and supports: History, defining features, and misconceptions. Center for PBIS & Center for Positive Behavioral Interventions and Supports. Retrieved from www.pbis.org/

Tierney, J. P., Grossman, J., & Resch, N. L. (2000). *Making a* difference: *An* impact study *of Big Brothers/Big Sisters*. Philadelphia, PA: Public/Private Ventures.

Warren, J. S., Bohanon-Edmonson, H. M., Turnbull, A. P., Sailor, W., Wickham, D., Griggs, P., & Beech, S. E. (2006). School-wide positive behavior support: Addressing behavior problems that impede student learning. *Educational Psychology Review, 18*(2), 187–198.

Wilson, D. B., Mackenzie, D. L., & Mitchel, F. N. (2008). Effects of correctional boot camps on offending. *Campbell Collaboration Reviews*. Retrieved from www.campbellcollaboration.org/library/effects-of-correctional-boot-camps-on-offending

18

Substance Use

Mariann Suarez

Substance abuse disorder (SUD), as defined by the *Diagnostic and Statistical Manual of Mental Disorders* – 5th ed (DSM-5), refers to a condition in which a person displays a recurrent and maladaptive pattern of substance use within a 12-month period, leading to clinically significant impairment or distress, as manifested by 2 of 11 symptom-specific criteria, categorized into four major groupings: impaired control, social impairment, risky use, and pharmacology, along with a diagnostic clinical rating based on a subclassification continuum of symptoms (American Psychiatric Association, 2013). SUD typifies a long-standing international health care crisis including national costs to the US population approximating $700 billion yearly (National Institute on Drug Abuse [NIDA], 2012). A lack of empirical attention to best practices for youth with SUD fuels this crisis. For example, while 10 million youth *each year* qualify for an SUD evaluation, only 1 million will be identified for such services. A large portion will concurrently present with comorbid psychiatric disorders, and a subset will further evidence risk of homicide and mortality (NIDA, 2012). Despite these startling statistics, evidence-based diagnostic and clinical practices for youth with SUD remain the exception, rather than the standard (Lilienfeld et al., 2007; Naar & Suarez, 2011). Instead, ineffective practices pervade the core contexts where young people spend most of their developmental years. Practitioners choosing to blindly accept and utilize ineffective practices risk professional ethical violations and may cause harm (Lilienfeld et al., 2015; Naar & Suarez, 2011).

18.1 Pseudoscience and Questionable Ideas

18.1.1 Diagnostic Controversies

Early Views. Philosophical controversies about SUD permeate history, and criteria specific to youth remain overlooked. Highlighted by White

(2014), categorical labels for persons deemed to overuse substances emerged during the fifth century B.C., when Herodotus first coined the term "drunkenness," branding it as a "body and soul sickness." Aristotle further shaped the paradigms and diagnostic controversies present in modern-day twentieth-century practices, proposing one of the first distinctions between functional and organic etiologies for persons with a proclivity to use substances. Concurrent with these centurial philosophical debates, the expansion of illicit substances, such as opioids and cocaine, and of novelty substances, such as coffee, tea, and tobacco, garnered international attention. However, the developmentally sensitive diagnostic needs of youth remained stagnantly absent (Naar & Suarez, 2011).

For instance, during the seventeenth to eighteenth centuries, the disease model of addiction gained popularity, dominating diagnostic theories for adults, with little consideration paid to youth (Satel & Lilienfeld, 2014). Specifically, the addiction model hypothesizes SUD as a chronic disease stemming from an organic brain defect that prevents people of volitional choice in their actions. Debate surrounding the addiction model continues to predominate twenty-first-century diagnostic practices, despite the large evidentiary base refuting solely organic explanations – particularly for youth. For example, it was not until the latest DSM revision of SUDs when the symptom classification of addiction was removed as a diagnostic category (American Psychiatric Association, 2013).

Yet the addiction label endures in present-day clinical vernacular, utilized by national research organizations, such as the US Department of Health and Human Services (HHS; HHS, 2016). While philosophically derived terms may befit the diagnostic practices for adults with SUD, the lack of empirical support for a diagnostically evidence-based, organic-only explanation for youth with SUDs remains sparse (Kaminer & Winters, 2015).

Questionable Utility of the DSM-5 for Youth. Application of DSM-5 diagnostic criteria to youth bears a plethora of criticisms, due to a lack of empirical research tailored to their specific diagnostic and emerging developmental needs (Arnett, 2015; Kaminer & Winters, 2015). Practices shown to benefit adults with SUD continue to flow into the best practice literature for youth (Miller & Rollick, 2012; Naar & Suarez, 2011); however, the same cannot be said for similar sophistication in diagnostic practice (Kaminer & Winters, 2015).

The discrepancy poses an ethical problem for practitioners seeking to uphold the Hippocratic Oath when utilizing DSM-5's primarily adult-based categorical classification system with youth, as contextual, developmental, and functional assessment practices are oft void (Coghill & Sonuga-Barke, 2012; Naar & Suarez, 2011). Given the clinical importance of diagnostic practices as the springboard guiding treatment, upholding the ethical principle to "do no harm" becomes even more disconcertingly controversial when the actual empirical utility of the DSM-5 for youth with SUD is analyzed. Described later, Kaminer and Winters (2015) present a strong rationale of the questionable utility for the four broad symptom-based terminologies (i.e., tolerance, withdrawal, hazardous use, and craving) utilized in the DSM-5 for youth with SUD.

Tolerance to substances can vary depending on a person's chronological age (i.e., younger youth may have lower tolerances when first experimenting with substances, as compared to older youth evidencing more seasoned substance use patterns). The potential risk for identifying a false-positive diagnosis based on nondevelopmentally sensitive diagnostic criteria creates a potential risk for younger aged youth engaging in normative substance experimentation. In contrast, older youth with more seasoned substance use patterns may be underdiagnosed and pose a risk of receiving a false negative diagnosis.

Withdrawal symptoms are not typically a diagnostic focus for youth with SUDs – the nomenclature of time impedes it. Specifically, the criteria require evidence of intensive and consistent substance use over time. However, due to their age, the majority of youth cannot meet this diagnostic threshold. Overall criteria require intensive and consistent behaviors of substance use and the associated deleterious symptom presentations better befit SUD symptoms in adults.

Hazardous substance use patterns and *craving symptoms* also appear less relevant for youth, as their emerging developmental processes may hinder an appropriate fit with the adult-based diagnostic systems. Hazardous diagnostic symptoms may reflect normative developmental behavior for youth who are situationally experimenting with risk-taking behaviors, yet they do not present with the spectrum of other SUD diagnostic criteria. In parallel, cravings require a person to experience notable physiological and psychological malaise. The accuracy in subjective reports of these symptoms for youth has not yet been empirically evaluated.

The lack of developmentally sensitive SUD diagnostic criteria highlights potential risks of harm to youth. Some young people may erroneously meet diagnostic criteria – risking overdiagnosis; on the other hand, youth with an actual need may be misidentified and underdiagnosed or overlooked (Kaminer & Winters, 2015).

18.1.2 Problematic Prevention Efforts

Attitudinal Change and Public Awareness Campaigns. Despite a lack of scientific support, numerous health care initiatives gravitate to the myth that offering unsolicited education and advice to persons who are ambivalent about change magically changes their behavior (Miller & Rollnick, 2012; Naar & Suarez, 2011). For example, the predominance of public health and school-related programs promoting these attitude-changing methods typically report outcomes based on self-reported change in attitudes and knowledge, rather than actual objective changes in behavior (Stockings et al., 2016). Furthermore, the lack of evidential credibility for attitudinal change and public awareness campaigns to effect *any* behavioral change in youth SUD becomes even more concerning when studies continue to commonly exclude youth at higher risk for other comorbid issues (Degrnardt et al., 2016). Similarly, public awareness and mass media campaigns, endorsing a disease-only model of addiction and offering only generalized education about abstinence (e.g., the 1980s "Just Say No" campaign) may actually increase, rather than reduce, illicit drug use in young populations (Hornik et al., 2008). Given these results, organizations choosing to spend limited financial resources may have as good as, or possibly even better a chance in funding services tailored to treatment that actually help young people make changes, as compared to attitudinal or public awareness campaigns (Naar & Suarez, 2011).

Drug Abuse Resistance Education (DARE). Subject to decades of controversy, DARE exemplifies one of the most well-known, ineffective in-school drug prevention programs (Lilienfeld et al., 2007). Akin to other controversial areas in the SUD field, the DARE program evolved and has made a global impact on treatments deemed to work by both the lay public and professionals. A review of the iterations of this theoretically derived program developed in 1983 is summarized next. At best, the present-day DARE program is supported by only weak evidence (Arkowitz & Lilienfeld, 2017), and it is still not ready for national implementation (Caputi & McLellan, 2017).

The original DARE program involved uniformed police officers teaching children (grades 5 and 6) in the school setting about the risks of drug use and social skills deemed to help resist peer pressure. These attempts did not pan out, with many evaluative studies indicating DARE helped to shift attitudes about substance use, but not any actual change in SUD behaviors (Ringwalt et al., 1994; Rosenbaum & Hanson, 1998). For example, despite the lack of empirical support for influencing change in behavior, DARE continued to receive robust funding from the national government (e.g., the 1994 Safe and Drug-Free Schools and Communities Act), corporations (e.g., Warner Bros.), and private foundations (e.g., American Express Philanthropic Program). Subsequently, the implementation and notoriety of the program became widespread, with 80% of schools in the United States and more than 52 countries utilizing the program by 2001 (Weiss et al., 2005).

Despite the widespread use of DARE, studies discounting the program during the 1990s emerged and governmental funding began to dwindle. Concurrently, research on the utility of evidence-based practices in SUD began to blossom (Gandhi et al., 2007). Null findings indicated the DARE program had little to no effectiveness in preventing drug use for students of any age. Shockingly, some evidence showed participation in DARE might actually lead to increased drug use (Rosenbaum & Hanson, 1998). Concurrent with the surprising results that DARE could potentially cause harm to youth, federal regulations and practice guidelines for organizations to receive funding for prevention-based programs changed (Petrosino, 2003).

In 1998, the US Department of Education implemented new policies via the Safe and Drug Free Schools legislation, requiring school-based drug and violence programs seeking federal grant money to provide documentation of research-based effectiveness; DARE failed to meet these requirements (Petrosino, 2003). As a result, by 2001 the Department of Education excluded DARE from its SAMHSA National Registry of Evidence-based Programs and Practices Programs (NREPP), as it did not meet the criteria for being either an "exemplary" or "promising" program. Federal grant monies were significantly reduced (Weiss et al., 2017).

Interestingly, a large-scale evaluation by Weiss et al. (2005) reported that at the time of the new legislation, many school districts believed they had to switch to a program on the NREPP's list yet were not actually forced to drop DARE. The new federal regulations also provided options and time extensions (i.e., up to 2 years), for school districts to choose programs with research effectiveness. However, the authors found no school districts that chose to follow up with these choices (Weiss et al., 2017).

Although governmental support for DARE to school districts was slashed, the program quickly rebounded, receiving a $13.7 million grant in 2001 from The Robert Wood Johnson Foundation to develop and test a new version of the DARE – Taking Charge of Your Life (TCYL; The Robert Wood Johnson Foundation, 2009). Consequently, funding remained available for DARE to be implemented in schools. The eight-year pilot study (2001–2009) sought to evaluate the effectiveness of enhancing students' skills to act on their desire to not use substances. Akin to the paucity of evidence for the original DARE, the TCYL DARE was never evaluated in a national randomized control trial, and evaluation results remained dismal (Sloboda et al., 2009). Subsequently, after this 8-year national trial, evaluations indicated that youth without a history of substance use did not evidence any specific gains in outcomes after participation in TCYL, and funding was terminated.

In 2009, DARE again renewed itself, adopting the preexisting Keepin' it REAL (KiR) program, previously designated by SAMHSA's NREPP as a research-supported program in 2006 (SAMHSA, 2006). Developed by researchers at Pennsylvania State and Arizona Universities, KiR focuses on encouraging middle school students to refuse, explain, avoid, and leave situations where substances are used. While controversy exists about the minimal standards required by NREPP to achieve designation as an effective prevention program (i.e., number and quality of studies; Caputi & McLellan, 2017), KiR achieved such status based only on four systematic reviews (Ghandi et al., 2007), and it later gained notable accolades being classified as a model program by the National Dropout Prevention Network in 2009, as well as promising by the Department of Justice in 2012 (Lyman, 2016).

The controversies surrounding NREPP's criteria to achieve status on its list of research-supported programs are beyond the scope of this chapter (see Miller, 2012); however, the questionable leniency afforded to organizations choosing to adopt and make changes to such programs without providing evidence is relevant to the perpetuation of DARE (Singh et al., 2011). In their comprehensive review, Caputi and McLellan (2017) spotlight the main loopholes any organization can use to attain designated status on the list, without recourse for not providing any evidence for modifications to the program. That is, when DARE adopted and adapted the KiR program, it finally achieved NREPP status without having to provide any evidence for alterations (e.g., having police officers implement KiR instead of teachers). Subsequently, national funding could again be allotted to schools implementing the updated program. Paralleling prior iterations of DARE, prevention practices with potential risk to youth were again nationally offered to vulnerable populations (Caputi & McLellan, 2017).

In short, the most promising evidence for the DARE version of KiR is weak due to a lack of both empirical review and evidence of the many adaptations implemented to a range of youth populations. At best, extensive caution is warranted to schools choosing to utilize this third iteration of the DARE program due to its clearly questionable utility for national implementation. Overall, while DARE served as a staple in schools for several decades, the program has been identified as an approach that probably causes harm (Lilienfeld, 2007), as well as a Possibly Discredited Treatment via a Delphi Poll of 138 national experts (Koocher et al., 2014).

> **Sidebar Box: Are specialized goggles effective at preventing impaired driving? by Miranda Meeker and LeAnna Kehl**
>
> Specialized goggles that replicate the effects of alcohol (e.g., Fatal Vision® goggles) are used in demonstrations in the United States and internationally in schools and on college campuses to simulate feelings of intoxication among their users. The goggles sufficiently impair a user's ability to see by altering their perceptual field. The individuals chosen to wear the goggles are often asked to participate in a variety of sobriety tasks, sports, games, or simulated driving (Innocorp, ltd., n.d.a). The goggles tend to create a feeling of being unbalanced, making these tasks difficult. In addition to the various tasks, students often watch testimonials from the families of victims of impaired driving accidents.
>
> Although these specialized goggles were commonly used before any well-designed research had been conducted to study their effectiveness, the goggles have been described to be an evidence-based educational product that could be used to teach the potential consequences of misusing and abusing alcohol (Innocorp, ltd., n.d.b). Specialized goggles are often used as a preventative measure to demonstrate the impaired ability to drive. Although many people believe that these goggles are an effective preventative tool, no studies provide sufficient evidence that this tool actually reduces impaired driving.

One randomized control study provided evidence that individuals wearing the goggles did initially become less accepting of impaired driving immediately after using the goggles when compared to a control group. Yet, the individuals watching the demonstration did not report a similar change in their attitudes toward impaired driving (Jewell, Hupp, & Luttrell, 2004). Additionally, when attitude changes were examined four weeks after the demonstration, this change was not upheld (Jewell & Hupp, 2005). Also, when students were asked about their self-reported behavior, rather than their attitudes alone, the individuals in the goggles group did not report engaging in less risky driving behavior than the control group. Overall, very little evidence indicates that specialized goggles like these are effective at preventing impaired driving behavior.

Miranda Meeker, BS, and LeAnna Kehl, BA, are both graduate students in the Clinical Child and School Psychology master's program at Southern Illinois University Edwardsville.

18.2 Problematic Treatments

18.2.1 Twelve-Step and Mutual Aid Groups.

Self-help interventions, often labeled under the umbrella term of 12-step or mutual aid groups, have received mixed reviews when applied to youth (Dishion et al., 1999; Foxcroft & Tsertsvadze, 2012). Notably, many original tenets of the 12-step program, Alcoholics Anonymous (AA), founded by Bill Wilson in 1939 (Alcoholics Anonymous, 1953), have been modified, aggrandized, and scaffolded in attempts to better fit supposed modern-day societal mores (Miller & Kurtz, 1994). For example, these authors point out how many 12-step or mutual aid groups incorporate ineffective practices, such as confrontation, endorsement of the disease model of addiction, labeling of persons with SUD as being in "denial," and adopting an antiscientific stance. Yet in its original form, AA did not support a disease etiology of SUD and encouraged members to seek involvement in research and other helpful treatment formats (Miller & Kurtz, 1994). The original AA instead emphasized a humanistic acceptance of the person within a safe environment, rather than taking the popularized confrontational stance characteristic of more recent 12-step and mutual aid groups (Miller & Kurtz, 1994).

Although the efficacy of 12-step and mutual aid groups for youth with SUD is sorely lacking, it is important to recognize that the AA model was not originally intended for empirical evaluation, nor purported to be an ecologically valid resource for young people (MacKillop & Gray, 2015). The foundational essence has, in some ways, also been hijacked by its nonempirical integration into generic 12-step substance treatments and groups predominantly tailored to adults, not youth (Miller & Rollnick, 2012). For example, when young people are referred to groups predominantly composed of adults, they typically will be the minority. The average age of AA and Narcotics Anonymous (NA) members is 47 and 43, respectively; only 2% of members are younger than age 21 (Sussman, 2010). The main empirical concern for youth's participation in groups created for adults centers on the increased risk of their prematurely learning a more sophisticated repertoire from adults with more seasoned adult SUD behaviors. For example, coercion dynamics and deviancy-training methods (e.g., reinforcement of antisocial behaviors via group discussions) indicate youth with ambivalence to attend treatment may find a more intrinsically rewarding internal motivation to learn novel antisocial behaviors, rather than focus on benefits potentially gained from program participation when placed in an age-inappropriate group (Dishion & Snyder, 2016).

Evaluations of the utility of 12-step groups when paired with evidence-based practices for youth are emerging. Sussman (2010) reviewed 19 studies of a mix of youth with a spectrum of substance preferences involved in AA and NA groups. Peer groups tailored to an overall 12-step model reportedly showed promise in reducing drug use; however, large attrition rates and lack of long-term outcomes make interpretation of findings difficult, as the actual degree of benefit remains unknown. As a mainstream SUD treatment staple widely available and free, there appears to be some promising utility to these approaches as a natural community resource, especially when integrated with more well-established treatments. For example, one recent study by Kelly et al. (2016) evaluated a 12-step treatment that also integrated elements of motivational enhancement and cognitive-behavioral therapy (see the Research-Supported Approaches section). Results demonstrated greater adherence to abstinence behaviors.

Overall, as posited by MacKillop and Gray (2015) in their review of 12-step and other variations of self-help programs for adults with SUD, there are promising components, such as there being free and accessible community resources with an appreciable foundation based on humanism and acceptance, gaining research merit when paired with evidence-based approaches. However, the lack of specific empirical support and lack of developmentally sensitive focus on the needs of youth are sparse. As such, efforts to "keep the baby" but "throw out the bathwater" may best suit practitioners, including such mutual aid supports into their treatment with youth (MacKillop & Gray, 2015).

The Johnson Model. In the 1960s, Vernon Johnson (1986) coined the term "Intervention." Interventions typically involve an orchestrated attempt by one or more persons (usually family and friends) to have the person of interest seek professional help when they experience a traumatic event, crisis, SUD, or other serious problem. While there are several types of interventions, the Johnson Model holds the gold standard status as the premiere exemplar of a potentially harmful treatment (Lilienfeld, 2007).

Johnson Interventions focus on creating a confrontation by a group of supporters to help the person of interest see the consequences of their addiction (Association of Intervention Specialists, 2016). Confrontation methods are deemed to precipitate a crisis in the person's life that is not threatening, damaging, nor fatal, and coercive tactics are used to urge the person to enter treatment and prevent further consequences of his or her supposed disease. Evaluations of the Johnson Intervention evidenced poor, and potentially harmful, outcomes (Lilienfeld, 2007). For example, relapse rates for substance abuse are higher than any other method of referral to outpatient substance abuse treatment.

Moreover, ethical and civil liberty violations may occur when methods to capture or confine the targeted person involve physical force. These coercive actions may actually be illegal, as they deprive a person of liberty without the due process of law. Practitioners choosing to violate the Hippocratic Oath by employing such ineffective techniques when other evidence-based treatments are available are concerning (Lilienfeld et al., 2015). The evidence is clear – Johnson Interventions bear a significant potential for harm.

18.3 Research-Supported Approaches

A few approaches clearly stand out for youth with SUD. Evidence-based approaches show consistently strong efficacy and positive outcomes for young people with SUD and their families to functionally maximize their human potential (Naar & Suarez, 2011).

Behavioral and cognitively oriented approaches predominate the literature in the effectiveness of preventative efforts and treatments for youth with SUD (Bobek et al., 2018; Hogue et al., 2018). The main tenets of these evidence-based interventions include the use of specific skills-training protocols in areas best suited to a young person's own "approach versus avoidance responses" when faced with a choice to use substances. For example, evidence-based approaches focus on teaching skills shown to help a young person respond in a healthier manner by using protocols focusing on problem solving, coping skills, social skills, and acceptance-based practices, as well as maintenance and goal-planning skills, within a developmentally sensitive therapeutic and ecological informed context. These treatments include contingency management approaches, Multidimensional Family Therapy, Multisystemic Therapy, the Adolescent Community Reinforcement Approach, and Functional Family Therapy (Stoner, 2016). Other third-wave behavioral approaches (Hayes, 2004) for adults with SUD, such as Acceptance and Commitment Therapy and Dialectical Behavior Therapy, may also show promise for youth with SUD.

18.4 Conclusion

Driven by centuries of philosophical debate, SUDs remain in the forefront of public controversy (i.e., 2016's Surgeon General's Report on Alcohol, Drugs and Health; HHS, 2016). Despite the historical attention, the biopsychosocial and developmental needs specific to youth with SUD have been ignored. Underscoring this neglect, practitioners seeking to uphold the Hippocratic Oath and implement evidence-based practices are often faced with ethical quagmires due to the multitude of problematic prevention and treatment options. In contrast, behavioral and cognitive approaches offer clear evidence of utility for young people with SUD.

Works Cited in Sidebar

Innocorp, ltd. (n.d.a). Fatal Vision® Roadster – Pedal Kart (only). Retrieved from https://fatalvision.com
Innocorp, ltd. (n.d.b). Fatal Vision® Community Event Pack. Retrieved from https://fatalvision.com

Jewell, J., & Hupp, S. D. (2005). Examining the effects of fatal vision goggles on changing attitudes and behaviors related to drinking and driving. *Journal of Primary Prevention*, *26*(6), 553–565.

Jewell, J., Hupp, S., & Luttrell, G. (2004). The effectiveness of fatal vision goggles: Disentangling experiential versus onlooker effects. *Journal of Alcohol and Drug Education*, *48*(3), 63–84.

References

Alcoholics Anonymous. (1953). *Twelve steps and twelve traditions*. New York: A.A. World Services.

American Psychiatric Association. (2013). *Diagnostic and statistical manual of mental disorders*. 5th edn. Arlington, VA: Author.

Arkowitz, H., & Lilienfeld, S.O. (2017). *Facts and fictions in mental health*. The Atrium, UK: Wiley Blackwell.

Arnett, J. (2015). *Emerging adulthood: The winding road from the late teens through the twenties*. 2nd edn. New York: Oxford University Press.

Association of Intervention Specialists. (2016 March). "What is the Johnson Model?" Retrieved from www.associationofinterventionspecialists.org

Bobek, M., Piazza, N., John, T., Fischer, J., & Hogue, A. (2018). Substance use. In S. Hupp (ed.), *Child and adolescent psychotherapy: Components of Evidence-based treatment for youth and their parents*. Cambridge: Cambridge University Press.

Caputi, T., & McLellan, T. (2017). Truth and D.A.R.E.: Is D.A.R.E.'s new Keepin' it REAL curriculum suitable for American nationwide implementation? *Drugs: Education, Prevention and Policy*, *24*, 49–57.

Coghill, D. & Sonuga-Barke, E. (2012). Annual Research Review: Categories versus dimensions in the classification and conceptualisation of child and adolescent mental disorders – implications of recent empirical study. *Journal of Child Psychology and Psychiatry*, *53*, 469–489.

Degenhardt, L., Stockings, E., Patton, G., Hall, W., & Lynskey, M. (2016). The increasing global health priority of substance use in young people. *The Lancet Psychiatry 3*(3), 251–264.

DeJong, W. (1987). A short-term evaluation of Project D.A.R.E. (Drug Abuse Resistance Education): Preliminary indications of effectiveness. *Journal of Drug Education*, *17*, 279–294.

Dishion, T. J., McCord, J., & Poulin, F. (1999). When interventions harm: Peer groups and problem behavior. *American Psychologist*, *54*(9), 755–764.

Dishion, T. J., & Snyder, J. J. (2016). Coercion dynamics: Past, present, and future. In T. J. Dishion & J. J. Snyder (eds.), *The Oxford handbook of coercive relationship dynamics*. New York: Oxford University Press.

Foxcroft, D. R., & Tsertsvadze, A. (2012). Cochrane Review: Universal school-based prevention programs for alcohol misuse in young people. *Evidenced-Based Child Health*, 7, 450–575.

Gandhi, A. G., Murphy-Graham, E., Petrosino, A., Chrismer, S. S., & Weiss, C. H. (2007). The devil is in the details: Examining the evidence for "proven" school-based drug abuse prevention programs. *Evaluation Review*, *31*(1), 43–74.

Hayes, S. C. (2004). Acceptance and commitment therapy, relational frame theory, and the third wave of behavioral and cognitive therapies. *Behavior Therapy*, *35*(4), 639–665.

Hogue, A., Henderson, C. E., Becker, S. J., & Knight, D. K. (2018). Evidence base on outpatient behavioral treatments for adolescent substance use, 2014–2017. Outcomes, treatment delivery, and promising horizons. *Journal of Clinical Child and Adolescent Psychology*, *47*(4), 499–526.

Hornik, R., Jacobson, L., Orwin, R., Piesse, A., & Kalton, G. (2008). Effects of the national youth anti-drug media campaign on youths. *American Journal of Public Health*, *98*(12), 2229–2236.

Johnson, V. E. (1986). *Intervention: How to help someone who doesn't want help: A step-by-step guide for families and friends of chemically dependent persons*. Center City, MN: Hazelden.

Kaminer, Y. & Winters, K. (2015). DSM-5 criteria for youth substance disorders: Lost in translation? *Journal of the American Academy of Child & Adolescent Psychiatry*, *54*(5), 350–351.

Kelly, J., Yeterian, J., Cristello, J., Kaminer, Y., Kahler, C., & Timko, C. (2016). Developing and testing twelve-step facilitation for adolescents with substance use disorder: Manual development and preliminary outcomes. *Substance Abuse*, *10*, 55–64.

Koocher, G., McMann, M. Stout, A., & Norcross, J. (2014). Discredited assessment and treatment methods used with children and adolescents: A Delphi poll. *Journal of Clinical Child & Adolescent Psychology*, *44*(5), 722–729.

Lilienfeld, S. O. (2007). Psychological treatments that cause harm. *Perspectives on Psychological Science*, *2*(1), 53–70.

Lilienfeld, S. O., Lynn, S. J., & Lohr, J. M. (2015). Science and pseudoscience in clinical psychology. In S. O. Lilienfeld, S. J. Lynn, & J. M. Lohr (eds.), *Science and pseudoscience in clinical psychology*. 2nd edn. New York: Guilford Publications, Inc.

Lyman, M. D. (2016). *Drugs in society: Causes, concepts, and control*. 7th edn. London & New York: Routledge.

MacKillop, J., & Gray, J. (2015). Controversial treatments for alcohol use disorders. In S. O. Lilienfeld, S. J. Lynn, & J. M. Lohr (eds.), *Science and pseudoscience in clinical psychology*. 2nd ed. New York: Guilford Publications, Inc.

Miller, W. R., & Kurtz, E. (1994). Models of alcoholism used in treatment: Contrasting A.A. and other perspectives with which it is often confused. *Journal of Studies on Alcohol*, 55(2), 159–166.

Miller, W. R., & Rollnick, S. R. (2012). *Motivational interviewing: Helping people change*. 3rd edn. New York: Guilford Publications, Inc.

Naar, S., & Suarez, M. (2011). *Motivational Interviewing with adolescents and young adults*. New York: Guilford Publications, Inc.

National Institute on Drug Abuse. (2012, December). Principles of drug addiction treatment: A research-based guide. 3rd edn. Retrieved from www.drugabuse.gov/publications/principles-drug-addiction-treatment-research-based-guide-third-edition

Petrosino, A. (2003). Standards for evidence and evidence for standards: The case of school-aged drug prevention. *Annals of the American Academy of Political and Social Science*, 587, 180–207.

Ringwalt, C., Greene, J., Ernett, S., Iachan, R. Clayton, R., & Leukefeld, C. (1994). *Past and future direction of the D.A.R.E. Program: An evaluation review*. Research Triangle Park, NC: Research Triangle Institute.

Rosenbaum, D., & Hanson, G. (1998). Assessing the effects of school-based drug education: A 6-year multilevel analysis of project D.A.R.E. *Journal of Research in Crime and Delinquency*, 35(4), 381–412.

Satel, S., & Lilienfeld, S. O. (2014). Addiction and the brain-disease fallacy. *Frontiers in Psychiatry*, 4, 141.

Stockings, E., Hall, W., Lynskey, M., Marley, K., Reavley, N., Strang, J. ... & Degenhardt, L. (2016). Prevention, early intervention, harm reduction, and treatment of substance use in young people. *The Lancet Psychiatry*, 3 (3), 280–296.

Singh, R., Jimerson, S., Renshaw, T., Saeki, R., Hart, S., Earhart, J., & Stewart, K. A. (2011). Summary and synthesis of contemporary empirical evidence regarding the effects of the drug abuse resistance education program (D.A.R.E.). *Contemporary School Psychology*, 15, 93.

Sloboda, Z., Stephens, R., Stephens, P., Grey, S., Teasdale, B., Hawthorne, R. ... & Marquette, J. (2009). The adolescent substance abuse prevention study: A randomized field trial of a universal substance abuse prevention program. *Drug and Alcohol Dependence*, 102, 1–10.

Stoner, S. A. (2016, March). Treating youth substance use: Evidence based practices and their clinical significance: Alcohol and Drug Institute, University of Washington. Retrieved from http://adai.uw.edu/pubs/pdf/2016youthsubstusebrief.pdf

Substance Abuse and Mental Health Services Administration. (2006). *Keepin' It Real*. Retrieved from www.nrepp.samhsa.gov

Sussman, S. (1). A review of Alcohoics Anonymous/Narcotics Anonymous program for teens. *Evaluation & the Health Professions, 33*(1), 26–55. http://doi.org/10.1177/016327870936186

The Robert Wood Johnson Foundation. (2009, January). Funded: "Taking Charge of Your Life" curriculum longitudinal study findings released. Retrieved from www.rwjf.org/en/about-rwjf/newsroom-content/2009/03/the-robert-wood-johnson- funded-take-charge-of-your-li.html

US Department of Education. (1998). *Safe and drug-free schools program: Notice of final principles of effectiveness.* Washington, DC: Author.

US Department of Health and Human Services (HHS). (2016 November). *Office of the Surgeon General, facing addiction in America: The Surgeon General's Report on Alcohol, Drugs and Health.* Washington, DC: Author.

Weiss, C., Murphy-Graham, E., & Birkeland, S. (2005). An alternate route to policy influence: How evaluations affect D.A.R.E. *American Journal of Evaluation, 26*, 12–30.

Weiss, C., Murphy-Graham, E., Petrosino, A., & Gandhi, A. (2017). The fairy godmother-and her warts. *American Journal of Evaluation, 29*(1), 29–47.

White, W. (2014). Slaying the dragon: The history of addiction treatment and recovery in America. 2nd edn. Bloomington, IL: Chestnut Health Systems/Lighthouse Institute.

19

Skepticism and Psychotherapy

Stephen Hupp and Kathleen Dyer

The mind is a terrible thing – there are so many ways that our minds can be deceived. Many of us have been tricked into believing that aliens land in our cornfields, that Sasquatches run through our forests, that ghosts haunt our homes, or even that demons possess our souls. Even worse, there are so many ways that our mind can fool itself. Sensory illusions, logical fallacies, and cognitive biases constantly deceive us. It's nearly impossible to avoid myths, misperceptions, and other mistakes. Even when we devise studies to test our hypotheses, we are deceived by spurious correlations, uncontrolled confounds, and other design flaws that impede our goal of revealing some truth. Sometimes our minds even make us wonder if any "truth" can ever really be known.

On the other hand, the mind is also a wonderful thing. Our mind has the ability to be skeptical, an ability that helps us protect against trickery by others and the biases that influence our own perceptions. If the occasion calls, we'll need this ability, skeptical thinking, to save us from an alien invasion, from a stray asteroid, or from ourselves.

Reading through these chapters, it's really exhausting to thinking about how much time, money, and effort are spent using therapy practices that are questionable, ineffective, or even harmful. And this book covers just one part of the bigger problem. One of the limitations of this book is that it has focused largely on symptoms of diagnoses covered in the *Diagnostic and Statistical Manual of Mental Disorders* – 5th ed (DSM-5; American Psychiatric Association, 2013). It's a fair criticism of this book to say that there are many other areas covered in psychotherapy that are not directly tied to a disorder. To chip away at this limitation, the first Sidebar Box in this chapter describes one of the most egregious forms of pseudoscience that was not covered earlier – conversion therapy.

Another fair criticism of this book could be the term *pseudoscience* itself. It's human nature to place concepts into categories, and this book largely emphasizes two categories – pseudoscience in psychotherapy (i.e., demonstrably ineffective approaches) and science in psychotherapy (i.e., evidence-based approaches). The reality is that there is a lot of gray area between pseudoscience and science, often referred to as the "demarcation" problem (Pigliucci, 2014). Where should we demarcate the line between pseudoscience and science? The extreme examples are easy, but what about the middle ground? Surely treatment components are emerging now that have little to no research support. If a therapist uses these components, are they practicing pseudoscience? Are they using science? Upon what does the answer depend on? We need to leave room for emerging techniques without calling something pseudoscience too quickly. You may have noticed this book often hedges by using the phrase "questionable ideas," and that was done to leave the door open for some of these approaches to develop a research base. Interested readers should also check out Strosahl's (2018) article entitled "Some Reflections on the Stormy Marriage of Science, Would-Be Science, and 'Pseudoscience.'" But please don't stop there! In response to that article, Lilienfeld and Gaudiano (2018) made a convincing case for why and when the term "pseudoscience" is warranted. In short, there are some exciting debates in our field when it come to pseudoscience.

Despite these critiques of this book, it is our hope that we have reached one primary goal – for readers to embrace scientific skepticism, especially when it comes to psychotherapy with youth. In particular, if therapists embrace scientific skepticism, then they will be less likely to use ineffective and harmful approaches.

> **Sidebar Box: What is gay conversion therapy? by Sheldon W. Helms**
>
> More than ever before, members of the LGBT community enjoy a level of inclusion that would have seemed unattainable only a generation ago. Although much work still needs to be done, progress has been made in marriage equality and open military service, as well as in employment and housing rights for LGBT citizens.
>
> Unfortunately, forces are still at work in our society that spread outmoded and unsupported ideas about sexual minorities. One of them goes under the moniker "Gay Conversion Therapy," a collection of ineffective techniques purporting to convert people from gay to straight (or, in the case of people who are transsexual, to "solidify" their birth sex as the one they express and experience). These techniques have a long and sordid history (Vider & Byers, 2015), and one would think that we would be rid of them in the twenty-first century. Sadly, that is not the case.

In modern history, this phenomenon began as a quasi-religious movement that mostly involved "praying the gay away" and took place inside churches and synagogues. The now defunct Exodus International was one of the first to make those messages public in the 1970s and 1980s, promising to cure millions of people willing to live according to their principles. Michael Bussee, one of the founders of Exodus who has since left the organization, said in a interview that he never saw a single person change their sexual orientation through these methods (Gonzales, 2010). He did, however, see people becoming less and less interested in sex. But, of course, abstinence from sex is not the same thing as changing from gay to straight.

Even some psychologists and psychiatrists have jumped on this bandwagon, often using (or misapplying) outdated ideas by Freud, Jung, and Adler to justify their positions. A few of these therapists use aversion therapy (Scot, 2017), sometimes involving substances to induce vomiting, and others electric shocks, meant to associate unpleasant and painful experiences with same-sex images. In addition to being cruel, these techniques have not had the desired effect.

The truth is, we do not yet know what causes sexual orientation. But a majority of the research strongly suggests two things: (a) sexual orientation is varied throughout the animal kingdom, with homosexuality and bisexuality being harmless variants found in hundreds of species, and (b) sexual orientation is not vulnerable to change efforts by quasi-religious or pseudoscientific means.

Fortunately, the American Psychological Association's (2009) resolution statement makes their position clear:

> The American Psychological Association advises parents, guardians, young people, and their families to avoid sexual orientation change efforts that portray homosexuality as a mental illness or developmental disorder and to seek psychotherapy, social support and educational services that provide accurate information on sexual orientation and sexuality, increase family and school support, and reduce rejection of sexual minority youth.

Sheldon W. Helms, MA, is a professor of psychology at Ohlone College. He is also host of the ShelShocked podcast.

19.1 Scientific Skepticism

Scientific skepticism, broadly speaking, is a movement that promotes the use of science and critical thinking to evaluate claims about the world. It is concerned with differentiating pseudoscience from science, with the goal of protecting the public from both fraud and misunderstanding. Scientific skepticism is largely distinct from religious skepticism and veers away from religious issues (unless they are presented as a form of science).

Scientific skepticism is also not part of one particular academic or scientific discipline; rather, it is a movement of laypeople who, together with scientists, value science as a source of guidance. The term "skeptic" is often used to identify proponents of scientific skepticism. It means more than simply being hard to convince. The term reflects a key feature of scientific investigation, the requirement that evidence be presented publically and be subject to both critique and revision. Scientists are trained to look for biases and flaws in evidence to identify weaknesses in a body of knowledge; all of this is done to expand knowledge. Skeptics seek to apply these principles by practicing critical thinking in everyday life.

The movement of scientific skepticism originally focused on debunking the claims of the paranormal, such as extrasensory perception, alien abduction, and Bigfoot. As the movement has grown, it has targeted pseudosciences that affect broader swathes of the public such as health care frauds. This movement has plenty of room for scientists who study child development and practitioners who provide care to children. In fact, as the chapters in this book demonstrate, pseudoscience is widespread in child-focused discipline, as everywhere else.

19.2 Skeptical Organizations, Conferences, and Other Resources

While skepticism has existed throughout most of human history, the organized movement is very young. The Committee for the Scientific Investigation of Claims of the Paranormal (CSICOP) was founded in 1976. It still exists today as the Committee for Skeptical Inquiry (CSI) and is a cornerstone of the contemporary skeptical movement. CSI hosts a meeting for scientific skeptics called CSICon, and it publishes one of the premier skeptical publications for skeptics – *Skeptical Inquirer*. Another prominent organization, the Skeptics Society, was formed in

1992 and publishes the other flagship publication for the skeptical movement – *Skeptic Magazine*.

The James Randi Educational Foundation (JREF), founded in 1996, has also made important contributions to skepticism. For many years, the JREF hosted one of the most important skeptical conferences called The Amaz!ng Meeting (TAM). It also sponsors the Million Dollar Challenge, whereby anyone claiming a paranormal ability can earn a million dollar prize simply for demonstrating the ability under controlled conditions. The claimant and a panel of scientific skeptics together develop a scientifically sound protocol that both parties agree will detect the ability if it exists, and the JREF implements that test. To date, no one has been able to claim the prize, though many have tried.

All of these organizations have overlapping memberships. Their publications and conferences draw from similar speaker lists, prominently featuring scientists and science educators, such as Carl Sagan in years past, and more recently Neil deGrasse Tyson and Bill Nye, the Science Guy. The conferences also include other experts in the art of deception – performers of magic and illusion such as James Randi, Penn and Teller, and Michael Carbonado. In recent years, television personalities such as Adam Conover (*Adam Ruins Everything*) and Timothy Caulfield (*A User's Guide to Cheating Death*) have attended skepticism conferences.

Similar conferences and organizations can be found locally across the United States. For example, the Northeast Conference on Science and Skepticism (NECSS) is co-hosted by the New York City Skeptics and the New England Skeptical Society. There are also many international conferences and organizations such as the Question, Explore, Discover (QED) conference in England, a joint effort by the Merseyside Skeptic Society and the Greater Manchester Skeptic Society. A growing list of other countries has also started to host skeptical conferences.

Podcasting is a large part of the skeptical movement. The most popular skeptical podcast is *The Skeptics' Guide to the Universe*. Other notable skeptical podcasts include *The Prism Podcast, Skepticality, Inquiring Minds*, and *MonsterTalk*. A few television shows promote a skeptical mind-set including *MythBusters, Adam Ruins Everything, Reanimated History, A User's Guide to Cheating Death*, and *Bullshit*. Additionally, *The Carbonaro Effect* is a fun way to watch unsuspecting people experiencing magic right in front of their eyes in public places. Many of them appear to be more likely to believe in the magical occurrences than they are to believe that they are currently being taped as part of a hidden camera magic television show.

All of these organizations and resources have affiliated websites with plenty of useful information, and a few key general interest books for every skeptic's bookshelf include the following:

- *The Demon Haunted World: Science as a Candle in the Dark* (Sagan, 1995)
- *Flim-Flam! Psychics, ESP, Unicorns, and Other Delusions* (Randi, 1987)
- *Why People Believe Weird Things: Pseudoscience, Superstition, and Other Confusions of Our Time* (Shermer, 2010)
- *The Skeptics' Guide to the Universe: How to Know What's Really Real in a World Increasingly Full of Fake* (Novella et al., 2018).

19.3 Skepticism in Psychology

Disagreeing with Freud's claims about psychology, John B. Watson was an early skeptic in psychology who helped move the discipline in a scientific direction. Similarly, B. F. Skinner carried the scientific psychology torch with his research and books such as *Science and Human Behavior* (1953). These days, people with expertise in psychology are prominently featured in skeptical organizations and resources. As mentioned in the first chapter of this book, Ray Hyman is a professor emeritus of psychology and a founder of the modern skeptical movement. Psychology Professor Richard Wiseman is one of the three Research Fellows on the staff of the Committee for Skeptical Inquiry (CSI); other psychology professors represented on the CSI Executive Council include James E. Alcock, Scott O. Lilienfeld, and Elizabeth Loftus. In fact, nearly 20% of the CSI Fellows come from the field of psychology, including Thomas Gilovich, Steven Pinker, Carol Tavris, and Stuart Vyse.

When it comes to psychotherapy, the Society of Clinical Psychology (Division 12 of the American Psychological Association) has continued to emphasize evidence-based practices for years. A website by this society shares information about evidence-based treatments (EBTs) and also points out some treatments that are controversial (www.div12 .ort/psychologcial-treatments). Additionally, the Association of Behavioral and Cognitive Therapies (ABCT) has always emphasized a scientific focus. In 2018, ABCT's flagship journal, *the Behavior Therapist* (available for free through www.abct.org), published a special issue called "Pseudoscience in Mental Health Treatment." The special issue includes 11 excellent articles (some of which were written by contributors to this book) that identified challenges and potential solutions related to pseudoscience in psychology (see Codd, 2018, for an introduction). For a while, the ABCT conference included a special interest group related to pseudoscience, but that special interest group has not continued in recent years. Please, somebody start it back up! Finally, a few fantastic books related to skeptical psychology follow:

- *How We Know What Isn't So: The Fallibility of Human Reason in Everyday Life* (Gilovich, 1991)
- *50 Great Myths of Popular Psychology: Shattering Widespread Misperceptions about Human Behavior* (Lilienfeld et al., 2010)
- *Thinking, Fast and Slow* (Kahneman, 2011)
- *Alternative Psychotherapies: Evaluating Unconventional Mental Health Treatments* (Mercer, 2014)
- *Science and Pseudoscience in Clinical Psychology*, 2nd ed (Lilienfeld, Lynn, & Lohr, 2015)
- *Mistakes Were Made (But Not By Me): Why We Justify Foolish Beliefs, Bad Decisions, and Hurtful Acts* (Tavris & Aronson, 2015)

19.4 Skepticism in Child and Adolescent Development

Child development, as a scientific discipline, was founded by G. Stanley Hall, the first person to earn a doctoral degree in psychology in the United States. Hall also founded the American Psychological Association, serving as its first president and was also the founder and leader of the so-called child study movement, the precursor to the child development discipline, in the very late 1800s. Hall used empirical methods to explore children's knowledge. The scientific study of children was controversial at the time, being opposed both by some educators who resented the implied criticism that schools were ineffective and by others who asserted that it was morally wrong to objectify children by scientific study. But the movement grew, and began to influence teaching as well as parent education and clinical psychology. Hall was its undisputed leader during the formative years of the discipline (Davidson & Benjamin, 1987).

Hall was also one of the founders of the American Society for Psychical Research in 1884, an organization devoted to scientifically studying parapsychology. He was skeptically minded and believed that the methods of science could be used to empirically investigate paranormal claims. When it became clear that the organization was not satisfied with honest scientific answers to such claims, he resigned from the society in protest and remained an outspoken critic of parapsychology (Pickren, 2010). In other words, the person considered the father of the discipline of child development endorsed and practiced scientific skepticism.

The discipline of child development has confronted pseudoscience in the guise of some silly things that exploit consumers, such as the Mozart Effect, the debunked notion that fetuses or children will be smarter if they are exposed to Mozart's music. Unfortunately, the child development discipline currently faces pseudoscience that threatens the health and well being of many families. That is, the anti-vaccination movement promotes the conspiracy theory that routine childhood vaccinations cause autism spectrum disorder, and this movement is likely responsible for a reduction in vaccination rates, prompting a resurgence of previously controlled infections (e.g., measles). The rejection of false memories is another pseudoscience needing the science of child development to confront. Child care workers have been incarcerated due to the debunked notion that children cannot possibly have false memories of abuse implanted through suggestion.

Much of the work of the Society of Clinical Child and Adolescent Psychology (Division 53 of the American Psychological Association) has emphasized evidence-based practices in child psychology. Its website (www .effectivechildrentherapy.org) includes information about EBTs and identifies several ineffective treatments. During the writing of this book, and with prompting from discussion on the division's listserv, the website added facilitated communication as a treatment that has been "Tested and Does Not Work." In fact, it has recently added several other treatments into this category. It is hoped that this book will help them identify a few more!

Jean Mercer's Childmyths blog covers many topics related to skepticism in child development. Similarly, the *Science Moms* documentary is available for free on YouTube (search "Science Moms: Full Film!"). A few books related to skepticism in child development follow:

- *Great Myths of Child Development* (Hupp & Jewell, 2015)
- *Great Myths of Adolescence* (Jewell et al., 2019)
- *Thinking Critically About Child Development*, 4th ed (Mercer, Hupp, & Jewell, forthcoming, 2020)

19.5 Conclusion

There's so much pseudoscience in the world, making scientific skepticism sorely needed. We hope that, like the other chapters in this book, this last chapter has pointed you toward many other places you can learn about scientific skepticism and critical thinking related to psychotherapy for youth. So many more resources are out there than we could have included, so enjoy the journey in discovering more. Of course, you may also want to learn more about what treatment approaches actually do work for youth. If so, then a great starting point is the companion book *Child and Adolescent Psychotherapy: Components of Evidence-Based Treatments for Youth and Their Parents* (Hupp, 2018). On a final note, it's also worth considering how we can teach youth about skepticism. To that end, the final Sidebar Box herein discusses skepticism in the context of education for youth.

> **Sidebar Box: Should children be taught about pseudoscience? by Henry Hupp**
>
> The importance of pseudoscience has fallen between the cracks for many educators in American schools. If more teachers incorporated critical thinking about pseudoscience into lectures and discussions, students would be able to better prepare themselves for a future of differentiating what is truth and what is fiction. In his address to congressional representatives about quackery, James Randi (1999) explained, "a properly educated and informed public would know about this, and protective laws would not be required. Again, education is the key." In this excerpt from his speech, Randi was speaking about how the government needs to intervene on pseudoscientific practices plaguing the United States. More education about pseudoscience would help people be able to defend themselves from misinformation.
>
> To fully educate the American people, the schooling system is one critical place students can learn about skepticism at an early age so they can continue to use critical thinking throughout adulthood. What people learn when they are young can shape their beliefs as adults. The main takeaway is that what youth learn matters, and everyone deserves the opportunity to be taught critical thinking about pseudoscience at school. For more about teaching skepticism to youth, see Lilienfeld (2017).
>
> **Henry Hupp** attends Edwardsville High School. He conducted a Science Fair project on energy necklaces and the placebo effect.

Works Cited in Sidebars

American Psychological Association (2009). Resolution on appropriate affirmative responses to sexual orientation distress and change efforts. Retrieved from www.apa.org

Gonzales, D. (2010). Exodus co-founder: I never saw one of our members become heterosexual. Video retrieve from www.youtube.com.

Lilienfeld, S. O. (2017). Teaching skepticism: How early can we begin? *Skeptical Inquirer, 41*(5), 30–31.

Randi, J. (1999). James Randi on quackery and the need for science education. Retrieved from www.skeptic.com

Scot, J. (2017). Shock the gay away: Secrets of early gay aversion therapy revealed. Retrieved from www.huffingtonpost.com

Vider, S., & Byers, D. S. (2015). A half-century of conflict over attempts to "cure" gay people. Retrieved from www.time.com

References

American Psychiatric Association (2013). *Diagnostic and statistical manual of mental disorders*. 5th edn. Arlington, VA: Author.

Codd, T. R. (2018). Pseudoscience in mental health: What remedies are available? *The Behavior Therapist, 41*(1), 1–3.

Davidson, E. S.,& Benjamin, L. T. (1987). A history of the child study movement in America. In J.A . Glover & R. R. Ronning (eds.), *Historical foundations of education psychology*. New York: Plenum Press

Gilovich, T. (1991). *How we know what isn't so*. New York: Free Press.

Hupp, S. (2018). *Child & adolescent psychotherapy: Components of evidence-based treatment for youth and their parents*. Cambridge: Cambridge University Press.

Hupp, S., & Jewell, J. (2015). *Great myths of child development*. Malden, MA: Wiley.

Jewell, J. D, Prinstein, M., Axelrod, M. I., & Hupp, S. (2019). *Great myths of adolescence*. Malden, MA: Wiley.

Kahneman, D. (2011). *Thinking, fast and slow*. New York: Farrar, Straus, & Giroux.

Lilienfeld, S. O., & Gaudiano, B. A. (2018). Pseudoscience in behavior therapy: Concurrences, confusions, and clarifications – Response to Strosahl. *The Behavior Therapist, 41*(6), 273–280.

Lilienfeld, S. O., Lynn, S. J., & Lohr, J. M. (2015). *Science and pseudoscience in clinical psychology*. New York: The Guilford Press.

Lilienfeld, S. O., Lynn, S. J., Ruscio, J., & Beyerstein, B. L. (2010). *50 great myths of popular psychology: Shattering widespread misconceptions about human behavior*. New York: John Wiley & Sons.

Mercer, J. (2014). *Alternative psychotherapies: Evaluating unconventional mental health treatments.* New York: Rowman & Littlefield.

Mercer, J., Hupp, S., & Jewell, J. (forthcoming, 2020). *Thinking critically about child development: Examining myths & misunderstandings.* 4th edn. Washington, DC: Sage.

Novella, S., & Novella, B., Santa Maria, C., Novella, J., & Bernstein, E. (2018). *The skeptics' guide to the universe: How to know what's really real in a world increasingly full of fake.* New York: Grand Central Publishing.

Pickren, W., & Rutherford, A. (2010). *A history of modern psychology in context.* Hoboken, NJ: Wiley.

Pigliucci, M. (2014). Demarcation and pseudoscience. *Skeptical Inquirer, 38*(1). Retrieved from www.csicop.org

Randi, J. (1987). *Flim-flam!: Psychics, ESP, unicorns and other delusions.* Buffalo, NY: Prometheus Books.

Sagan, C. (1995). *The demon-haunted world: Science as a candle in the dark.* New York: Random House.

Shermer, M. (2010). *Why people believe weird things: Pseudoscience, superstition, and other confusions of our time.* New York: St. Martin's Griffin.

Skinner, B. F. (1953). *Science and human behavior.* New York: Free Press.

Strosahl, K. (2018). Some reflections on the stormy marriage of science, would-be science, and "pseudoscience." *The Behavior Therapist, 41*(5), 237–247.

Tavris, C., & Aronson, E. (2015). *Mistakes were made (but not by me): Why we justify foolish beliefs, bad decisions, and hurtful acts.* Boston: Mariner Books.

Index

Acceptance and Commitment Therapy (ACT), 106, 212
actigraphy, 244, 252
active control groups, 60
acupuncture, 89, 230
acute stress disorder, 172
adaptive functioning, defined, 14
adjustment disorder, 172
adolescents
  depression, 127
  developmental changes, 10
  introduction to, 9–11
  lying behavior, 261–262
  parents and, 10–11
  skepticism and development, 297–298
Adult Attachment Interview (AAI), 174
adult depression, 126–127
adverse childhood experiences (ACEs), 9
age-specific manifestations of depression, 128
aggression and psychosis link, 98
Aggression Replacement Training (ART), 269
AgoraFear Relief homeopathy, 145–146
Agoraphobia, 141
Alcock, James E., 296
alcohol and insomnia, 243–244
Alcoholics Anonymous (AA), 283–285
alien abductions while sleeping, 250–251
alternative treatments for depression, 132
amenorrhea, 213
American Academy of Pediatrics, 20, 247
American Psychiatric Association, 66
American Psychological Association, 1, 3, 293
ancient Chinese medicine, 148
anger increase with cathartic techniques, 264–265
Animal Assisted Therapy (AAT), 266–267, 270
anorexia nervosa (AN), 206–207, 209–210, 213
anti-diarrheal agents for toilet training, 232–233
antidepressant medication, 21
antiepileptic medication, 21
antipsychotic medication, 21
antiscience *vs.* pseudoscience, 2
Anxetin homeopathy, 145
anxiety
  autism spectrum disorder and, 28
  fear of monsters, 141–142
  implausible treatments, 145–153
  introduction to, 140–141
  questionable ideas and pseudoscience, 143–153
  research supported approaches, 153–154
  sleep deprivation, 246
  summary of, 154–155
  superstitious rituals, 160–161
anxiolytic medication, 21
Applied Behavior Analysis (ABA), 24
applied behavior analysis (ABA), 39
aromatherapy for insomnia, 252
assessments, 130–132, 174–175, 244–246. *See also* questionable assessment practices
Association of Behavioral and Cognitive Therapies (ABCT), 296
Attachment, Self-Regulation, and Competency (ARC) treatment, 182
Attachment and Biobehavioral Catch-up (ABC), 181
attachment parenting, 6
attention deficit hyperactivity disorder (ADHD)
  autism spectrum disorder and, 28
  brain balancing, 57
  brain training, 54–56
  criticism as invalid disorder, 51–53
  depression and, 130
  dietary interventions, 54
  introduction to, 50

medication use alone, 58
over prescription of medication for, 113
questionable assessments, 18
questionable ideas and pseudoscience,
    51–58
research supported approaches, 59
summary of, 59–60
vision therapy, 71
working memory deficits, 72
attitudinal change programs for substance
    use, 279
auditory integration therapy, 34
auricular acupuncture, 149
Autism Diagnostic Interview-Revised
    (ADI-R), 31
Autism Diagnostic Observation Schedule
    (ADOS), 31
Autism Research institute (ARI), 37
autism spectrum disorder (ASD)
    cold mothers and, 29
    diagnosis of, 52
    implausible treatments, 31–35
    ineffective treatments, 35–36
    introduction to, 28–29
    mistaken causes of, 29–30
    potentially harmful treatments, 36–39
    questionable assessment practices, 30–31
    research supported approaches, 39–40
    summary of, 40
    vaccines, 29–30
    weighted blankets for insomnia, 251–252
availability heuristic, 31
Avoidant/Restrictive Food Intake Disorder
    (ARFID), 191

Barkley, Russell, 51
base intentional interaction, 35
base-rate neglect, 112
bashing evidence-based approaches, 4
Beck, Aaron, 126–127
bed-sharing, 247–248
bedwetting. *See* Nocturnal Enuresis
Behavior Assessment System for Children-
    Third Edition (BASC-3), 130
behavior interventions/therapy
    feeding problems, 191–193, 198

insomnia, 249–250
Intellectual Disabilities, 24
substance use disorder, 286
tic disorders, 85–86
Behavior Therapist, 296
behavioral optometry. *See* vision therapies
Benedict, Ruth, 228
Beyond Scared Straight program, 262–263
Bigfoot fears, 141–142
binge eating disorder (BED), 206–207,
    209–210, 215
biofeedback, 88, 152–153
biological models of tic disorders, 82
Bipolar Spectrum Disorder (BPSD)
    diagnostic controversies, 111–113
    ineffective treatments, 113–115
    introduction to, 110–111
    naturopathic medicine, 115–116
    questionable ideas and pseudoscience,
        111–115
    research supported approaches, 116–117
    summary of, 117–118
blind faith, 16
blinded raters, 60
bodily fluids imbalance and psychosis, 103
body mass index (BMI), 206
bogus expertise/interventions, 3, 16
boot camps for disruptive behavior
    disorders, 265–266, 270
brain balancing and ADHD, 57
Brain Gym International (BGI), 69–70
brain injuries, 20
brain training and ADHD, 54–56
bran imaging studies, 67
Brazelton, T. Berry, 228
breatharians, 211
Brooks, Wiley, 211
bulimia nervosa (BN), 206–207,
    209–210, 215
Bunge, Mario, 2
Bussee, Michael, 293

Callahan, Roger, 149, 161–162
CAM approaches. *See* complementary and
    alternative medicine (CAM)
    approaches

cannabis use, 100
casein-free diets, 32–33
catharsis for disruptive behavior disorders, 263–265
Centers for Disease Control and Prevention (CDC), 30
central nervous system stimulants, 87
character armor, 181
chelation therapy, 37
Child Feeding Questionnaire, 194
Child-Parent Psychotherapy (CPP), 182
childhood depression, 125, 126–127, 128–129
children/child development
    changes to, 10
    introduction to, 9–11
    parents and, 10–11
    psychosis and, 98
    teaching about pseudoscience, 299
Children's Depression Inventory-Second Edition (CDI-2);, 130
child's reaction to traumatic events scale (CRTES), 175
chiropractic therapy/treatments, 34–35, 87, 162
Coalition for Juvenile Justice, 263
Cognitive-Behavior Therapy (CBT)
    anxiety, 151, 154
    depression, 134–135
    eating disorders, 217
    obsessive compulsive disorder, 163–164
    psychosis, 106
    trauma and attachment, 181–182
cognitive behavioral therapy for insomnia (CBT-I), 247
cognitive bias and autism, 31
cognitive debiasing strategies, 116
cognitive distortion hypothesis, 112
cognitive symptoms of psychosis, 96
cognitive therapy for substance use disorder, 286
commercial sleep trackers, 245–246
Committee for Skeptical Inquiry (CSI), 294–295, 296
Committee for the Scientific Investigation of Claims of the Paranormal (CSICOP), 294

Complementary and Alternative Medicine (CAM)
    autism spectrum disorder, 31–32
    Bipolar Spectrum Disorder, 115–116
    Intellectual Disabilities, 19–20
    tic disorders, 89
Comprehensive Behavioral Intervention for Tics (CBIT), 82, 90
Comprehensive System, 131
conceptual controversies in tic disorders, 81–82
conduct disorders (CD), 260–261, 269
confirmatory bias, 31
Conners Comprehensive Behavior Rating System (Conners), 130
convulsive therapies, 104
Cooke, Lucy, 195
corpus collosum, 67
craniosacral therapy (CST), 22–23
cravings in substance use, 278
creative symbols, 35
crib bumpers for infants, 248–249
Critical (or traumatic) incident stress debriefing (CISD), 180
critical thinking about psychology, 1–2
crystal healing, 147, 154
cultural beliefs, 16–17
curriculum-based measurement (CBM), 75

dance therapy, 212
deep brain stimulation (DBS), 90
Defeat Autism Now (DAN!), 37
Delphi poll, 132
Demon-Haunted World: Science as a Candle in the Dark (Sagan), 5
dental appliances and tics, 89–90
dependent variables, 60
depression
    adolescent depression, 127
    adult depression, 126–127
    age-specific manifestations, 128
    alternative treatments, 132
    childhood depression, 125, 126–127, 128–129
    depressive equivalent, 126
    diagnosis of, 52

diagnostic issues and controversies, 125–130

herbal treatments, 134

introduction to, 124–125

projective measures for assessment, 130–132

psychoanalytic dream interpretation, 133

questionable ideas and pseudoscience, 125–132

research supported approaches, 134–135

selective serotonin reuptake inhibitors for, 213

sleep deprivation, 246, 247

subtypes, 128

summary of, 135

desirable difficulty in learning, 68

Developmental, Individual Differences, Relationship-based model (DIR/ Floortime), 35

developmental theories in toilet training, 229–230

Developmental Trauma Disorder (DTD), 174

Diagnostic and Statistical Manual of Mental Disorders (DSM-5)

  anxiety, 140, 145

  Avoidant/Restrictive Food Intake Disorder, 191

  Bipolar Spectrum Disorder, 110

  depression, 124

  eating disorders, 206–207

  feeding problems, 191

  Nocturnal Enuresis, 226

  obsessive compulsive disorder, 159

  psychosis, 96–97

  substance use disorder, 276, 277–278

  tic disorders, 80, 83

diagnostic controversies

  defined, 4

  depression, 125–130

  eating disorders, 207–208

  insomnia, 244–246

  questionable ideas and pseudoscience, 143–145

  substance use disorder, 276–279

  trauma and attachment, 173–174

diathesis-stress model of psychotic disorders, 101

diets/dietary supplements

  attention deficit hyperactivity disorder, 54

  autism spectrum disorder, 32

  casein-free diets, 32–33

  intellectual disabilities and, 19

  obsessive compulsive disorder, 164–165

  tic disorders, 86–87

  toilet training, 231

dimethylglycine (DMG), 32

Direct Instruction, 24

Disease Model of Addiction, 277

Disinhibited Social Engagement Disorder, 172, 173

disorganization symptoms of psychosis, 96

disorganized attachment, 173

disruptive behavior disorders

  catharsis and primal scream therapy, 263–265

  introduction to, 260–261

  lying behavior, 261–262

  questionable ideas and pseudoscience, 262–269

  research supported approaches, 269–270

  Scared Straight program, 6, 262–263, 270

  summary of, 270–271

Disruptive Mood Dysregulation Disorder (DMDD), 125, 128, 129, 130

Dissociative Identity Disorder (DID), 99–100

Division 53 of the American Psychological Association. *See* Society for Clinical Child and Adolescent Psychology

DMPS (2,3-dimercaptopropane-1-sulfonate), 37

DMSA (2,3-dimercaptosuccinic acid), 37

Dolphin-Assisted Therapy (DAT), 37–39

dopamine and tic disorders, 87

Down Syndrome (DS), 16

Drug Abuse Resistance Education (DARE), 279–282

drug use/abuse, 98–99, 100–101, 246. *See also* substance use disorder

drunkenness, 277

dyslexia, 71
dyspraxia, 71
dysthymia. *See* Persistent Depressive
    Disorder

eating disorders (EDs)
    breatharians, 211
    diagnostic controversies, 207–208
    eating disorders, 207–216
    energy psychology/energy therapies,
        161–164
    feeding problems in children, 190–198
    implausible treatments, 212
    ineffective treatments, 213
    introduction to, 206–207
    learning, 67–74
    myths influencing treatment, 208–210
    obsessive-compulsive disorder, 161–167
    potentially harmful treatments, 214–216
    psychosis, 97–104
    questionable assessment practices, 208
    questionable ideas and pseudoscience,
        207–216
    research supported approaches, 216–217
    summary of, 217–218
    tic disorders, 81–84, 86–89
    trauma and attachment, 173–181
echolocation healing effects, 38
educational kinesiology, 69–71
Emotional Freedom Technique (EFT), 150,
    161–162, 163–164, 168
emotional thinking, 35
Encopresis, 231–233, 236–237
energy psychology/energy therapies,
    161–164
energy treatments, 148–152
epilepsy, 67
essential oils for insomnia, 252
evidence-based practices (EBPs), 193–196
evidence-based treatments (EBTs)
    anxiety, 144
    bashing of, 4
    importance of, 296
    introduction to, 1, 2, 3
    in learning, 74
    rewards for behavior reinforcement, 267

tic disorders, 87, 89
Exner, John, 131
exorcism, 102
exorcism practices, 16
expectancy effects for ADHD, 56
experimental treatments, 116–117
exploited expertise, 3
Exposure Therapy and Response
    Prevention, 167–168
extra-terrestrial beings, 5
eye movement desensitization and
    reprocessing (EMDR), 179–180,
    181–182

facilitated communication (FC), 36–37
*Facing the Fire: Experiencing and
    Expressing Anger Appropriately*
    (Lee), 264
false memories, 251
false research support, 3
family-based treatment (FBT), 210, 217
family therapy and psychosis, 106
far transfer improvements, 73
FasterEFT, 163
Fatal Vision goggles, 282–283
fear of monsters, 141–142
Federal Trade Commission (FTC), 54
Feeding Dynamics approach, 191–193, 195
feeding problems in children
    diagnosis of, 190–191
    evidence-based practices, critique of,
        193–196
    Feeding Dynamics approach,
        191–193, 195
    genetically modified organisms and,
        196–197
    introduction to, 189–190
    questionable ideas and pseudoscience,
        190–198
    research supported approaches, 198–199
    Sequential Oral Sensory (SOS)
        Approach, 197–198
    summary of, 199–200
Festhaltetherapie, 178
finger tapping therapy, 161
fish oil supplements, 164

FitBit Ultra, 245–246
food allergies, 164–165
Food Dudes program, 196
food dyes and ADHD, 53
foot reflexology, 149
Freud, Anna, 227
Freud, Sigmund, 133, 225, 227–228,
   263–264, 266
Functional Family Therapy, 269

gallbladder contents and insomnia, 243
gay conversion therapy, 292–293
gene expression, 15
General Anxiety Disorder, 141
genetically modified organisms (GMOs),
   196–197
genetics and psychosis, 101–102
Gigantopithecus fears, 142
Gilovich, Thomas, 296
gluten-free diets, 32–33
Gorer, Geoffrey, 227–228
Greater Manchester Skeptic
   Society, 295
Guerrilla Skepticism on Wikipedia
   (GSoW) project, 6

habit reversal training (HRT), 82, 90
hallucinogens, 100
healing with crystals, 147
Heart-Centered Hypnotherapy (HCH),
   166–167
herbal treatments for depression, 134
Hippocratic Oath, 278, 285
holding therapy, 178–179
Holding Time, 178
homeopathy, 105, 145–146
Hyman, Ray, 296
hyperactivity and sugar, 6
hyperbaric oxygen therapy (HBOT), 35–36
hyperkinesis, 51
hypersomnia, 246
hypnosis/hypnotherapy
   eating disorders, 215–216
   obsessive-compulsive disorder, 166–167
   tic disorders, 87–88
   toilet training, 230

illusory correlation, 31
implausible treatments
   anxiety, 145–153
   autism spectrum disorder, 31–35
   eating disorders, 212
   Intellectual Disabilities, 19–20
   introduction to, 4
   tic disorders, 86–89
individual energy toxins (IET), 162
Individuals with Disabilities Education Act
   (IDEA), 18
ineffective treatments
   autism spectrum disorder, 35–36
   eating disorders, 213
   Intellectual Disabilities, 19–20
   toilet training, 228–229
inflated research support, 3
Inositol 5 HTP, 164
insight oriented therapies, 143
insomnia
   approaches with no research support,
     251–253
   bed-sharing, 247–248
   commercial sleep trackers, 245–246
   diagnostic and assessment controversies,
     244–246
   introduction to, 243–244
   myths that influence treatment, 246–250
   questionable ideas and pseudoscience,
     244–253
   research supported approaches, 253
   sleep studies, 245
   summary of, 253
Institute for Applied Human Potential, 20
Institutes for the Achievement of Human
   Potential, 20
insulin coma therapy (ICT), 103–104
Intellectual Disabilities
   autism spectrum disorder and, 28
   blind faith, 16
   craniosacral therapy, 22–23
   diets/dietary programs, 19
   implausible/ineffective treatments, 19–20
   introduction to, 14–15
   miracle cures, 17
   myths influencing treatments, 15–18

Intellectual Disabilities (cont.)
  neural organization techniques, 20
  potentially harmful treatments, 20–22
  psychotropic medication, 21–22
  questionable assessment practices, 18–19
  research supported approaches to, 23–24
  summary of, 24
  as uneducable and unfit, 17–18
*International Classification of Disease-
    Tenth Edition* (ICD-10) diagnostic
    codes, 191
Interpersonal psychotherapy (IPT),
    134–135
Irlen Syndrome. *See* Scotopic Sensitivity
    Syndrome

Jagger, Mick, 264
James Randi Educational Foundation
    (JREF), 295
Janov, Arthur, 264
Johnson Model of intervention, 285
Journal of Pediatrics, 247
juvenile delinquency, 260, 269
Juvenile Justice and Delinquency
    Prevention Act (1974), 263

Keepin' it REAL (KiR) program, 281, 282
Kids' Choice Program, 196

Le Barre, Weston, 228
learning
  educational kinesiology, 69–71
  introduction to, 66–67
  left *vs.* right brain, 67–68
  pseudoscience and questionable ideas,
    67–74
  research supported approaches, 74–75
  summary of, 75–76
  teaching children based on learning
    styles, 68–69
  vision therapies, 71–72
  working memory training, 72–74
learning styles, 68–69
left-brain learning, 67–68
Lennon, John, 264
Levinson, Boris, 266

Lilienfeld, Scott O., 296
lithium treatment, 117
Livestrong Foundation, 164
lobotomy, 104
Loftus, Elizabeth, 296
longitudinal studies on feeding
    disorders, 194
lying behavior, 261–262

magical thinking, 114
magnesium, 32
Magnetic Field Deficiency Syndrome, 19
magnetic field therapy, 19
Major Depressive Disorder (MDD),
    124–125, 128, 129
maladaptive behaviors, 182
maladaptive weight control behaviors, 216
malaria-induced convulsions, 104
Mandel, Howie, 166
marijuana and insomnia, 243–244
massage therapy, 34–35, 89
Massed Trial Training, 24
mean sleep latency test (MSLT), 245
Meares-Irlen Syndrome. *See* Scotopic
    Sensitivity Syndrome
medical interventions/therapy
  ancient Chinese medicine, 148
  anorexia nervosa, 213, 214–215
  deep brain stimulation, 90
  tic disorders, 85
  toilet training, 232–233
medication
  antidepressant medication, 21
  antiepileptic medication, 21
  antipsychotic medication, 21
  anxiolytic medication, 21
  attention deficit hyperactivity
    disorder, 58
  Intellectual Disabilities, 21–22
  lithium treatment, 117
meditation and tic disorders, 89
mental disorders, 83–84
Merseyside Skeptic Society, 295
milk thistle, 164
mindfulness-based therapy, 106, 212
Mindlight, 152

minimal brain dysfunction, 51
miracle cures, 17
misleading research support, 3
mixed cerebral dominance, 70
mood regulation, 35
motivational enhancement therapy, 284
motivational interviewing, 286
motor tics, 84
movement therapy, 212
moxibustion, 149
Multidimensional Treatment Foster Care
    (MTFC), 269
music cognition, 67
music therapy, 34
mutual aid groups, 283–285
myths influencing treatment, 4, 15–18
    blind faith, 16
    defined, 4
    eating disorders, 208–210
    insomnia, 246–250
    miracle cures, 17
    overview of, 15–18
    religious beliefs, 16–17
    trauma and attachment, 175–178
    uneducable/unfit children myth, 17–18

N-Acetylcysteine (NAC), 164
Narcotics Anonymous (NA), 284
National Center for Complementary and
    Integrative Health (NCCIH), 31
National Council of Juvenile and Family
    Court Judges, 263
National Dropout Prevention Network, 281
National Health and Medical Research
    Council (NHMRC), 105, 146
National Longitudinal Survey of
    Youth, 260
National Registry of Evidence-based
    Programs and Practices Programs
    (NREPP), 280, 281
naturopathic doctors (ND)/medicine,
    115–116
"near transfer" of abilities, 56
negative symptoms of psychosis, 96
Neumann, Therese, 211
neural organization techniques, 20

Neurocognitive Disorder, 143
neurodevelopmental disorders, 83
neurofeedback, 152–153, 165–166
Neurolinguistic Programming (NLP),
    163, 167
neurological repatterning, 69
neuromythologies, 67
neuroscience, 66–67
neurotic traits, 83
New England Skeptical Society, 295
New York City Skeptics, 295
no research support, 3
Nocturnal Enuresis (NE), 225–226,
    229–231, 235–236
non-REM sleep, 243
nonretentive encopresis, 226
Northeast Conference on Science and
    Skepticism (NECSS), 295
nutritional interventions for tic
    disorders, 86

obsessive-compulsive disorder (OCD)
    hypnosis and past-life regression,
        166–167
    introduction to, 159–160
    as neurodevelopmental disorder, 83
    neurofeedback, 165–166
    questionable ideas and pseudoscience,
        161–167
    research supported approaches, 167–168
    summary of, 168–169
    superstitious rituals for anxiety, 160–161
    supplements and dietary changes, 164–165
Office of Juvenile Justice and Delinquency
    Prevention (OJJDP), 260
omega 3 fatty acids, 32
online self-help, 214
oppositional defiant disorder (ODD),
    260–261, 269
oral reading fluency, 75
orgone therapist, 10
other specified feeding or eating disorder
    (OSFED), 208
overconfidence bias, 31
overly broad focus, 4
oxytocin hormone, 33

panic attacks, 149
Panic Disorder, 141
Parent-Child Interaction Therapy
    (PCIT), 181
parents/parenting
  attachment parenting, 6
  child development, 10–11
  poor parenting and psychosis, 100
  Positive Parenting Program, 269
  pseudoscience and, 10–11
  psychosis from poor parenting, 100
  report measures of ADHD, 18
past-life regression, 166–167
pediatric acute onset neuropsychiatric
    syndrome (PANS), 165
pediatric bipolar disorder (PBD), 110, 111
pediatric immune neuropsychiatric
    disorder associated with streptococcal
    infections (PANDAS), 165
peer reviewed journals, 2, 71
perceptual-motor training, 69, 70. *See also*
    educational kinesiology
Persistent Depressive Disorder
    (Dysthymia), 124
persistent motor/vocal tic disorder, 80
personality shaping and toilet training,
    227–228
Pet-Oriented Child Psychotherapy
    (Levinson), 266
phenylketonuria, 32
physical factors in feeding problems,
    189–190
Pinker, Steven, 296
placebo effect, 59, 72
plausibility concept, 7–9
podcasts for skeptics, 295–296
Polarity Therapy, 148
polysomnography, 245
Positive Behavioral Intervention Supports
    (PBIS) systems, 267
Positive Parenting Program, 269
positive symptoms of psychosis, 96
possible efficacious treatments, 116–117
posttraumatic stress syndrome (PTSD),
    149, 172, 174
potentially harmful treatments (PHTs)

autism spectrum disorder, 36–39
  eating disorders, 214–216
  Intellectual Disabilities, 20–22
  overview of, 9–10
  pseudoscience and, 9–10
potentially harmful treatments for children
    (PHTCs), 9, 182
praising for behavior reinforcement, 268
premonitory urges (PUs), 80
pressure to eat, 194
Primal Scream (Janov), 264
primal scream therapy, 263–265
pro-ED websites, 214–215
probably efficacious treatments, 116–117
problem solving, 35
problematic development, 173
projective measures for assessment, 130–132
Prolonged Parent-Child Embrace, 178
pseudoscience. *See also* questionable ideas
    and pseudoscience
  children and adolescents, 9–11
  defined, 3–4
  learning, 67–74
  plausibility concept, 7–9
  potential harmfulness, 9–10
  questionable ideas and, 2–4
  skepticism, 5–6, 7
  summary of, 11
  teaching children about, 299
  tic disorders, 81–84, 86–89
psychiatric theories in toilet training,
    229–230
psychoanalytic dream interpretation, 133
psychodynamic treatment for
    depression, 132
psychodynamic treatment for toilet
    training, 229, 230, 231
psychogenic etiology of toilet training, 231
psychology and skepticism, 296–297
psychomotor patterning, 20
psychosis
  danger of youth with, 98–99
  diagnosing children, 98
  drug use/abuse, 100–101
  historically ineffective treatments, 103–104
  imbalance of body fluids, 103

inconsistent diagnostic criteria, 97–98
introduction to, 96–97
poor parenting and, 100
questionable ideas and pseudoscience, 97–104
research supported approaches, 105–106
spiritual etiology and treatment, 102
split personalities myth, 99–100
substance use/abuse, 98–99, 100–101
summary, 106–107
symptoms of, 96
youth feelings about, 102
psychosomatic theories in toilet training, 229–230
psychotherapy for Bipolar Spectrum Disorder, 113
psychotropic medication, 21–22
puberty, 10
public awareness campaigns for substance use, 279
punishment in toilet training, 232
purple hat component, 4

Qi energy force, 148
quantum energy, 148
Question, Explore, Discover (QED) conference, 295
questionable assessment practices
attention deficit hyperactivity disorder, 18
autism spectrum disorder, 30–31
eating disorders, 208
Intellectual Disabilities, 18–19
introduction to, 4
trauma and attachment, 174–175
questionable ideas and pseudoscience, 2–4
anxiety, 143–153
attention deficit hyperactivity disorder, 51–58
Bipolar Spectrum Disorder, 111–115
depression, 125–132
diagnostic controversies, 143–145
disruptive behavior disorders, 262–269
insomnia, 244–253
substance use disorder, 276–285
toilet training, 227–233

"rage reduction" therapy, 178
Randi, James, 299
Randolph Attachment Disorder Questionnaire (RADQ), 174–175
randomized control trials (RCTs), 55
anxiety, 153
Bipolar Spectrum Disorder, 114
EMDR and, 179
insulin coma therapy, 103
lacking in brain training, 55
lacking in neurofeedback studies, 165
Rapid Prompting Method (RPM), 37
Reactive Attachment Disorder, 172, 173
rebirthing, 178
recovered memory treatment (RMT), 215
Reich, Wilhelm, 10, 181
Reiki, 148
relational-based interventions, 35
Relaxation Skills Violence Prevention (RSVP), 270
religious beliefs, 16–17
representativeness heuristic, 31
research supported approaches
anxiety, 153–154
attention deficit hyperactivity disorder, 59
autism spectrum disorder, 39–40
Bipolar Spectrum Disorder, 116–117
depression, 134–135
disruptive behavior disorders, 269–270
eating disorders, 216–217
feeding problems in children, 198–199
insomnia, 253
in learning, 74–75
obsessive-compulsive disorder, 167–168
psychosis, 105–106
substance use disorder, 285–286
tic disorders, 90
toilet training, 234–237
trauma and attachment, 181–182
retentive encopresis, 226
rewards for behavior reinforcement, 267–268
Reynolds Adolescent Depression Scale-Second Edition (RADS-2), 130
right-brain learning, 67–68

Rimland, Bernard, 37

risky, unrealistic, difficult, or expensive
 (RUDE), 114

Robert Wood Johnson Foundation, 281

Rorschach Inkblot Test, 131

rule-breaking conduct, 260

safe, easy, cheap, and sensible (SECS), 114

Sagan, Carl, 5

Saint Catherine of Sienna, 211

Satter, Ellyn, 191–193

Scared Straight program, 6, 262–263, 270

schizophrenia, 97–98, 99–100, 105

schizophrenigenic mother, 100

School-based Response to Intervention
 (RtI) systems, 74–75

science communication, 6

Science Moms documentary, 196

scientific skepticism, 294

Scotopic Sensitivity Syndrome (SSS), 72

second generation antipsychotics
 (SGA), 117

Selective Mutism, 140

selective serotonin reuptake inhibitors
 (SSRIs), 213, 247

self-acupressure for toilet training, 233–234

self-esteem and behavioral therapy, 85

self-hypnosis, 88

Senapathy, Kevin, 196

sense of self, 35

SenseWear Pro3 Arbmand, 245

sensory integration therapy, 33–34, 89

Separation Anxiety Disorder, 140

Sequential Oral Sensory (SOS) Approach,
 197–198

severe mood dysregulation
 (SMD), 129

sexual abuse, 36, 231

shared attention, 35

shock therapy, 104

SIDS monitors, 249

skepticism
 in child and adolescent development,
  297–298
 introduction to, 5–6, 7
 organizations and conferences, 294–296

in psychology, 296–297
 psychotherapy and, 291–292
 scientific skepticism, 294
 summary of, 298–299

Skeptics Society, 294

Skinner, J.B., 296

Sleep Apnea, 143

sleep deprivation, 243, 246

sleep diary, 245

sleep onset latency (SOL), 244–245

sleep paralysis, 250–251

Social Anxiety Disorder, 140

Society for Clinical Child and Adolescent
 Psychology, 1

Society of Clinical Psychology, 296

socioeconomic status (SES), 209

somatosensory treatments, 181

specialty mattresses for insomnia, 252

specific learning disorder (SLD), 66, 75

Specific Phobias, 140, 143–144

spiritual healing, 89, 102

split personalities myth, 99–100

Spock, Benjamin, 228

St. John's Wort herb, 164

Stages of Psychosocial Development,
 227–228

substance use disorder (SUD)
 diagnostic controversies, 276–279
 Drug Abuse Resistance Education,
  279–282
 Fatal Vision goggles, 282–283
 introduction to, 276
 problematic prevention efforts, 279–282
 problematic treatments, 283–285
 questionable ideas and pseudoscience,
  276–285
 research supported approaches, 285–286
 summary of, 286

sudden infant death syndrome (SIDS),
 247, 249

sugar consumption and ADHD, 54

superstitious rituals for anxiety, 160–161

supplements. *See* diets/dietary
 supplements

swearing, as symptom of tic disorders, 84

Systematic Instruction, 24

Taking Charge of Your Life (TCYL), 281
talk therapy, 231–232
Talking Puppet Therapy, 167
Tappy Bear, 150, 161–162, 168
Tavris, Carol, 296
TFT Voice Technology, 151
Therapeutic Touch, 148
Thought Field Therapy (TFT), 148, 155,
    161, 162, 180
tic disorders
  biofeedback training, 88
  CAM approaches, 89
  chiropractic therapy/treatments, 87
  classification as mental disorders,
    83–84
  comorbid symptoms and, 84
  conceptual controversies, 81–82
  dental appliances and, 89–90
  diagnostic controversies, 83–84
  hypnosis/relaxation training, 87–88
  introduction to, 80–81
  motor *vs.* vocal tics, 84
  myths and behavioral treatments,
    85–86
  myths and medical treatments, 85
  nutritional and dietary supplements, 86
  pseudoscience and questionable ideas,
    81–84
  questionable and implausible treatments,
    86–89
  research supported approaches, 90
  summary of, 91
  swearing, as symptom, 84
time-outs for behavior reinforcement,
    268–269
tinted lenses in vision therapy, 72
toilet training
  Encopresis, 231–233, 236–237
  ineffective practices, 228–229
  introduction to, 225–227
  Nocturnal Enuresis, 225–226, 229–231,
    235–236
  questionable ideas and pseudoscience,
    227–233
  research supported approaches,
    234–237

self-acupressure for, 233–234
summary of, 237
tolerance to substance use, 278
Tong Ren therapy, 149
Tourette, Georges Gilles de la, 81–82, 84
Tourette Association of America, 82
Tourette's disorder, 80, 84
trauma and attachment
  diagnostic controversies, 173–174
  introduction to, 172
  myths influencing treatment, 175–178
  questionable assessment practices,
    174–175
  questionable ideas and pseudoscience,
    173–181
  research supported approaches,
    181–182
  summary of, 182–183
trepanning, 102
Trobriand islanders, 113
tryptophan, 164
12 step programs, 283–285
two-way communication, 35

uneducable/unfit children myth, 17–18
unspecified feeding or eating disorder'
    (UFED), 207
U.S. Department of Education, 280
U.S. Department of Health and Human
    Services (HHS), 277
U.S. Food and Drug Administration,
    19, 213

vaccines and autism spectrum disorder,
    29–30
vision therapies, 71–72
vitamin B6, 32
vocal tics, 84
Voice Technology, 162
Vyse, Stuart, 296

wake after sleep onset (WASO),
    244–245
Wakefield, Andrew, 29–30
Wardle, Jane, 195
Watson, John B., 296

weighted blankets for insomnia, 251–252
well-established treatments, 116–117
Wilson, Bill, 283
Wiseman, Richard, 296
witchcraft, 16

withdrawal from substance use, 278
working memory training, 72–74

yoga therapy, 212
youth with psychosis, 98–99

Printed by Integrated Books International,
United States of America